To the memory
of my grandmother
Mary Antoinette Tunstall
from whom I first heard
the story of the Ridges

CHEROKEE TRAGEDY

THE CIVILIZATION OF THE AMERICAN INDIAN SERIES

CHEROKEE TRAGEDY

The Ridge Family and the Decimation of a People

Second Edition, Revised

by

Thurman Wilkins

UNIVERSITY OF OKLAHOMA PRESS : NORMAN

Other books by Thurman Wilkins

Clarence King: A Biography (New York, 1958)
Thomas Moran: Artist of the Mountains (Norman, 1966)

Library of Congress Cataloging-in-Publication Data

Wilkins, Thurman.
  Cherokee tragedy.

  (The Civilization of the American Indian series; v. 169)
  Bibliography: p. 381.
  Includes index.
  1. Ridge, Major, ca. 1771–1839. 2. Cherokee Indians—Biography. 3.
Cherokee Indians—Government relations. 4. Cherokee removal, 1838. 5.
Cherokee Indians—History. I. Title. II. Series.
E99.C5W57 1986   973'.0497   85–20260
ISBN 0–8061–1966–7 (cloth)
ISBN 0–8061–2188–2 (pbk.)

The paper in this book meets the guidelines for permanence and durability of the Committee on Production Guidelines for Book Longevity of the Council on Library Resources, Inc. ∞

6   7   8   9   10   11   12   13   14   15   16   17   18   19   20

CONTENTS

ILLUSTRATIONS

MAPS

PREFACE TO THE SECOND EDITION

W HEN General Winfield Scott was ordered to command the rounding up of the Cherokees in 1838, he remarked that they were the most interesting Indians in America. Indeed, to many Americans of that time they were more fascinating than any other tribe, and they were perceived to have made the most substantial progress toward "civilization" of any tribe north of Mexico. In a short time they had developed schools and churches in response to missionary work among them. They created a Cherokee syllabary by which they became literate in only a few years. They established a newspaper, the *Cherokee Phoenix*, printed in Cherokee and English. They instituted libraries as well as literary and temperance societies and adopted written laws, including a constitution that provided for a republican form of government modeled upon that of the United States. They even had plans for a museum and a national academy.

But in 1830, at the instigation of President Jackson, Congress passed a law to remove all eastern Indians beyond the Mississippi. Georgia, in violation of several treaties guaranteeing Indian sovereignty, quickly extended state jurisdiction over Cherokee lands within her chartered limits. Forthwith Cherokee civilization was in woeful jeopardy. Soon a minority faction known as the Ridge or Treaty party declared that Cherokee civilization could be salvaged, along with the people themselves, only if they would migrate to the West. This book recounts the lives of two leaders of that party, Major Ridge and his son John, with considerable attention paid to a close relative, Elias Boudinot.

The scope of their story necessarily coincides with a broad swath of Cherokee history. It is told from a variety of sources: letters, diaries, memoirs, reminiscences, and other personal papers; federal and state archives; congressional documents; missionary reports and correspondence; contemporary newspapers and periodicals; and, in significant respects, the work of scholars. The research was begun over two decades ago, and a Guggenheim fellowship gave me an unobstructed year in which to complete the groundwork, but the writing was delayed while I completed a book on Thomas Moran, the American landscape painter. The first edition of *Cherokee Tragedy* was published in the summer of 1970, and now that fifteen years have passed, the time has come for a revised edition, which eliminates some excess details, corrects a few factual errors, reconsiders certain points of development, and takes advantage of the findings of recent scholarship.

In the course of work on both editions I have contracted large and varied obligations. First, I would like to express again my gratitude for the help received from the John Simon Guggenheim Memorial Foundation. I wish also to acknowledge the aid and encouragement of many individuals—in particular the late Major General Lee B. Washbourne (a descendant of Major Ridge), Caroline Hinkley, A. M. Gibson, John S. Ezell, Jack Haley, the late E. E. Dale, the late Muriel Wright, Leslie Teets, Ruella Looney, John R. Lovett, John A. Mahey, Dean Krakel, Paul Rossi, Martin Wenger, Sarah Hirsch, Marie Keene, Guy Logsdon, Sherrod East, G. N. Scaboo, Jane F. Smith, Carmelita Ryan, Evans Walker, Elmer Parker, Sarah Jackson, Robert Kvasnicka, Michael Pilgrim, James Walker, John H. Martin, Albert Blair, Margaret Blaker, Herman J. Viola, and Ruth Butler.

I would like to acknowledge further help from Lulie Barnes, T. L. Ballenger, John O. Larson, the late Leslie Bliss, Herbert C. Schulz, Haydee Noya, Eugene P. Sheehy, the late Roland Baughman, Charles E. Mixer, Kenneth Lohf, Mary Lou Lucy, Helen Givens, Edward T. James, Carolyn Jakeman, Jennie Rathbun, Lewis Leary, the late Mary Bryan, Archibald Hanna, Mary G. Jewitt, Elizabeth F. Johnson, Willard Mercer, Edward T. Malone, J. Roy McGinty, John W. Bonner, Clemens de Baillou, Helen Hutzler and her son John, Emily Marsh, Edward A. Shaw, Mary E. Stith, Hubbard Ballou, Fred Duncan, James Abajian, William G. McLoughlin, Kevin Feeney, Susan Hall, and Linda Sack. Indulgence is begged in the case of names that may have been inadvertently omitted.

The collections of numerous libraries and manuscript depositories have served me well in my researches, and I wish to acknowledge specifically my debts to the following institutions: the Columbia

University Library, my principal research base; the Queens College Library; the New York Public Library; the National Archives; the Library of Congress; the National Anthropological Archives of the Smithsonian Institution; the University of Oklahoma Library; the Oklahoma Historical Society; the Gilcrease Institute of American History and Art; the University of Tulsa Library; the library of the Northeastern Oklahoma State University; the Kansas State Historical Society; the University of Kansas Library; the University of Texas Library; the Newberry Library; the Houghton Library; the Yale University Library; Old Salem and the Moravian Archives at Winston-Salem, North Carolina; and the Moravian Archives at Bethlehem, Pennsylvania.

Other depositories I wish to thank are the University of North Carolina Library; the Georgia Department of Archives and History; the Georgia Department of Natural Resources; the University of Georgia Library; the Rome, Georgia, Public Library; the Cornwall, Connecticut, Free Library; the Princeton University Library; the Henry E. Huntington Library; the Bancroft Library; the Oregon State Library; the Bandon, Oregon, Public Library; the American Philosophical Society; the Presbyterian Historical Society; the Pennsylvania Historical Society; the New-York Historical Society; the Museum of the American Indian, Heye Foundation; the American Museum of Natural History; and the Arkansas Historical Commission.

Without doubt my greatest debt is still to my former wife, Sophie Wilkins, not merely for her translation of Moravian Missionary papers from a difficult German dialect in a difficult German script, but also for her steady support and encouragement, without which the first edition of this book might never have been completed. I also wish to acknowledge the kind and meticulous consideration I received from Cecil Scott, Richard Marek, and Alick Bartholomew, my editors at the Macmillan Company, publisher of the first edition. I am equally indebted to John N. Drayton and Sarah Morrison, my editors at the University of Oklahoma Press.

T.W.

Bandon, Oregon

Indeed I tremble for my country when I reflect that God is just. — THOMAS JEFFERSON

Cherokee blood, if not destroyed, will win its courses in beings of fair complexions, who will read that their ancestors became civilized under the frowns of misfortune, & the causes of their enemies. — JOHN RIDGE

CHEROKEE TRAGEDY

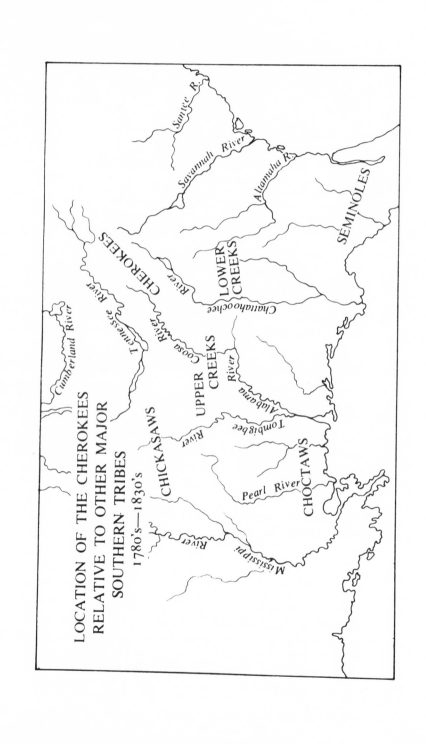

LOCATION OF THE CHEROKEES
RELATIVE TO OTHER MAJOR
SOUTHERN TRIBES
1780's—1830's

CHEROKEES

CHICKASAWS

UPPER CREEKS

LOWER CREEKS

CHOCTAWS

SEMINOLES

Cumberland River

Tennessee River

Coosa River

Santee R.

Savannah River

Altamaha R.

Chattahoochee River

Alabama River

Tombigbee River

Pearl River

Mississippi River

1 • BORDER WARRIOR

I F there was a crime in the Treaty of 1835, it was more YOUR crime than OURS." So ran the first complete sentence on a yellowed sheet of stationery, frayed at the edges, the first of two fragmentary pages from a memorandum to the Congress of the United States. The words were written in a neat, compact hand by an educated Cherokee of that faction widely known as the Treaty party of the Cherokee Nation, so named because its members supported the Treaty of New Echota. Signed by candlelight and hearth glow near midnight on December 29, 1835, in a crowded house at the old Cherokee capital, it had soon set in motion a mournful train of events that would carry most of that nation to a new home in Indian territory beyond the Mississippi and even beyond the young state of Arkansas.

The tattered sheets bearing their self-justification were salvaged with the papers of a distinguished Cherokee family—the one whose branches bore the names of Ridge, Boudinot, and Watie—from a farm house in northeastern Oklahoma a century after the treaty had been signed. "We were all opposed to selling our country east," the faded words continued,

but by State laws, you (meaning your countrymen) abolished our government, annihilated our laws, suppressed our authorities, took away our lands, and turned us out of our houses, denied us the rights of men, made us outcasts and outlaws in our own land, plunging us at the same time into an abyss of moral degradation which was hurling our people to swift destruction. It was in this state of things, when all Cherokee laws were abolished, when we had no longer a government or a country, that the Ridges & Boudinot with their compatriots stepped forward to snatch their people from ruin, secure payments for property which they no longer possessed, and lead them to a country in the West

3

abounding in the gifts of nature where the Cherokee power might be re-established and the Cherokee name perpetuated throughout all time. They were full-blooded Cherokees,* who loved their countrymen more than they loved their country or their own lives. They knew the danger they had incurred . . . ; but they were willing to die if the sacrifice were necessary to save their people. The whole three were murdered in a single day without trial or arrest.[1]

. . . All on one brilliant Saturday morning in late June, 1839—one dragged from his bed at daybreak to receive twenty-six stabs from knives; another lured forth on an errand of mercy, only to be knifed from behind, then hacked with a tomahawk; and the third ambushed and shot from his horse at the edge of a lonely highway just as the horse lowered its head for a drink from the stream that swirled across the sandstone ford.

The murders, called lawful executions by the faction that had secretly ordered them, came in the aftermath of a political struggle crowned with disaster for the Cherokee Indians: the forced exodus from their ancestral homelands in southern Appalachia and their journey west over a route so marked with new-dug graves that it was ever afterwards known as the Trail of Tears. Often told, usually from the point of view of the executioners, the Ross faction (just as the account of Richard III of England, in Shakespeare's play and elsewhere, was permanently slanted by those who had destroyed him), the story of the Cherokee removal calls for a reevaluation in a time like ours, when the problems of a minority people surrounded by an overwhelming and hostile majority are everywhere apparent.

It is idle to ask whether the Cherokee Nation in the 1830s could have closed ranks and prevailed against the white settlers and their state. The fact is that the outside pressures had split the Cherokees apart; they were divided and ready to be conquered. To review what happened to them, and how and why it happened, is nevertheless illuminating. Immediately the question of leadership becomes the focus of interest, then as now.

Outstanding among the Cherokee leaders of that day were Major Ridge and his son, John Ridge, men of uncommon intellect and forcefulness, as Sam Houston advised his colleagues in Congress.

*Although the Ridges, Boudinot, and Stand Watie all had some amount of white blood, they customarily styled themselves "full-blooded Cherokees."

Major Ridge. A lithograph published by Thomas L. McKenney and James Hall in The Indian Tribes of North America, *from an 1834 painting probably by Charles Bird King.* Smithsonian Institution, National Anthropological Archives, Neg. No. 45113B.

"These Indians are not inferior to white men," he insisted. "John Ridge was not inferior in point of genius to John Randolph. His father, in point of native intellect, was not inferior to any man."[2]

The Ridges had long since been on the side of progress. They were among the first Cherokees to adopt the manners and customs of the whites. Major Ridge, called Kah-nung-da-tla-geh in Cherokee,* erected a house after the European style in the Indian country, cleared land for a small plantation, dressed like a white man of his status, and educated his children at white schools in Georgia, Tennessee, North Carolina, and Connecticut. His grandson, John Rollin Ridge, who often wrote under the sobriquet of Yellow Bird — a translation of his Indian name — seeking to redeem his grandfather's memory from oblivion, further wrote: "His son, John Ridge, and his nephew, Elias Boudinot, followed the path of this aged pioneer of Cherokee civilization, and their names are upon record as the foremost among those who labored to redeem their people from the savage state. They organized the party of civilization."[3]

It would have been more accurate to describe Major Ridge as merely one — and not the first — of those early Cherokees who had adopted the ways of white men. However, the impact of The Ridge's example upon his tribesmen would be hard to overrate. Until his final stand on western emigration toppled him from a pinnacle of esteem, the Cherokees had held him as a hero, a farsighted torchbearer, the apostle of tribal salvation through enlightenment. Yet The Ridge had begun life as one "accustomed to war and hunting, and to the habits and modes of thought of the Indian warrior," as noted by Thomas L. McKenney, first U.S. commissioner of Indian affairs, and Judge James Hall, who go on to describe The Ridge's "abandoning those habits, and by deliberate choice adopting the customs of civilized men, and persevering in them unchangeably through life."[4]

The exact year of The Ridge's birth is not certain — perhaps 1770, more likely 1771.[5] His birthplace was the scattered town of

---

*This book uses for Major Ridge's name the spelling employed by his son John Ridge, as printed in McKenney and Hall's *Indian Tribes of North America.* John Rollin Ridge, the major's grandson, spelled the name Ka-nun-da-cla-ga. John P. Brown, in *Old Frontiers,* spelled it Ganun-da-le-gi. There are in addition several other variant spellings. Because of his lack of Cherokee, the writer makes no attempt to account for the various spellings and presumably the various pronunciations, but assumes that some of them result from the fact that Cherokee occurred in three distinct dialects.

Hiwassee, at Savannah Ford on the Hiwassee River, a cold, clear torrent that brawled from a cleft in the Appalachian Mountains. The settlement was in what is now Polk County, Tennessee. Outside the village spread fields of corn, beans, pumpkins, sweet potatoes, and tobacco, while beyond rippled a prairie of waving grass. The grass sheltered countless strawberry plants, and when the berries were ripe, the ground seemed carpeted in crimson. The plain was bordered by forests of oak, maple, pine, sourwood, and hickory trees. Peaches and wild apples abounded, along with several kinds of plums, and at either end of the straggling settlement the forest walls closed down against the river, vine-draped and flowery as another Eden.[6] "The scenery affords a fine combination of the grand and beautiful," wrote McKenney and Hall, as though to account for The Ridge's oratorical powers, "and those who imagine that the germs of poetry and eloquence may be planted in the young mind by the habitual contemplation of bold and attractive landscape, would readily select this as a spot calculated to be richly fraught with such benign influences."[7]

It was then the custom for a Cherokee to assume more than one name during his lifetime. When small, The Ridge was called Nung-noh-hut-tar-hee, or "he who slays the enemy in the path," usually rendered in English as The Pathkiller. He had three older brothers, all of whom died young, so he was the eldest child to reach maturity. A younger brother, who in time took the name Oo-watie, or The Ancient One, would never achieve the distinction of The Ridge, but he was destined to outlive his brother. There was also a sister, as well as another brother, who died young.[8]

Their mother was a half-blood woman of the Deer clan; her father, a Scots frontiersman whose name and history seem to have escaped the record. Her husband, The Ridge's father, was noted for his prowess as a hunter, and among the Cherokees the hunter was honored next to the warrior; but his name remains in doubt. Perhaps it was Oganstota, or perhaps Dutsi (pronounced Duchee), or even Tar-chee,[9] the last two being variations of one another. Perhaps The Ridge's father used each name at a different period of his life, a not unlikely possibility. He was never famous in council, but in 1775 he joined a war party sent by the chief Old Hop "down the Tennessee against the French Indians of the Illinois-Wabash region."[10] In that foray he took a scalp on the Kaskaskia River.[11]

It would become a family tradition to claim descent "from a long line of Cherokee chiefs and warriors."[12] But no genealogy can be constructed with any degree of certainty. One descendant, as well as the Cherokee scholar Emmet Starr, relates one or the other parent of The Ridge to the high chief Attakullakulla, or The Little Carpenter, so called for his skill at "joining" a treaty. A small man physically, Attakullakulla was large in mind, the Solon of the Cherokees. While still a youth, known as Ookoonaka, or The White Owl, he had gone with Sir Alexander Cuming to London, where His Majesty King George II had received him along with six other Cherokees. "He was marked," according to Felix Walker, his contemporary, "with two large scars on each cheek; his ears were cut and banded with silver, hanging nearly down to his shoulder, in the notion of the Indians a mode of distinction";[13] and as the years passed, he matured into the wisest chief of all. Sometimes it is said that Dutsi was his son; sometimes, his grandson.[14] At any rate, if the Ridge family is truly descended from The Little Carpenter, the connection relates it to such leaders as Old Hop, Dragging Canoe, Nancy Ward, Doublehead, and Old Tassel, as well as Sequoyah, who achieved fame as the inventor of the Cherokee syllabary.[15]

When The Ridge was small, the Cherokees had no method of writing, and preservation of their history depended on the memories of the conjurors, the Adawehis, who had learned the tribal traditions word for word as they had come down from ancient times. On solemn feast days, especially those for the Green Corn, when Cherokees gathered at the seven-sided town house in every village, the conjurors rehearsed the stories of tribal origin and migration. Wearing leggings of white deerskin and fanning themselves with large bird wings, they spoke in a dialect different from common Cherokee, some words so archaic that no one could tell their meaning any longer. Few then doubted the claim of the Adawehis that the Great Smokies had been modeled long before the Ani-Yunwiyah, the Real People, had arrived in their coves and valleys. There had been a time when the earth was soft and wet and very flat, and the Great Buzzard, the father of all subsequent buzzards, had flown across the wet land until his wings grew weary. His wings were so tired on reaching the Cherokee country that they began to droop and strike the mud, and wherever a wing struck, it gouged a valley, and wherever it flapped upward, it raised a mountain. That was how the Great Smokies had been formed, the conjurors said.[16]

They also told of the wanderings of the Ani-Yunwiyah in ancient times before they came to the mountains formed by the Great Buzzard's wings. The Real People had once lived in a distant country—

no one knew how far away—but it became so crowded that the Real People had to separate from all the others there and search for a new home. Long wandering brought them to a mountainous land of snow and ice, too cold for a good life. At a council the conjurors of that ancient time proclaimed that a warmer climate could be found in a place beyond the mountains "because it lay nearer the sone setting," and so the Real People built snowshoes and crossed the mountains, but instead of reaching a warmer home, they came to a land of arctic night, so cold that many people died. And they moved again, and the sun came up, and they reached a country where the Real People could survive. There they lived for a long, long time—how long, no one could later remember. They prospered and increased until the land became so overcrowded that the Real People had to separate once more and seek a new home. In their further migration they came to a wide river, which they crossed on a bridge made by weaving vines together—mostly giant grapevines. At last they settled down near Otter Peaks, where they lived for many generations and skirmished with their grandfathers, the Delawares. Finally the Real People drifted farther south and west, into the coves and hollows of the Great Smokies.[17]

Sometimes the conjurors told of wars with the Iroquois, from whom the Real People had parted long before, and of warfare with the Shawnees to the south, before the Real People could drive the Shawnees north. And once while holding a council with the latter, the chief of the Real People had remained silent for three whole days, as if weighing whether to make peace. On the fourth day he told his warriors to meet the Shawnee delegation with tokens of friendship. A great dance followed, belts of wampum were exchanged, and on the seventh day the Shawnee chief declared: "I shall go now and tell my people of the success of my mission." Then he added: "From the seashore, strange sounds have struck my ear! I shall go and learn their meaning. In thirteen moons I shall come and inform my brother of the meaning." And in thirteen moons he kept his promise and brought word of strange men who had come from the ocean—Unakas with light hair and pale skins.[18]

The conjurors not only told of their forefathers' day; they also brought their stories down to recent times. They even foretold the outcome of the current struggle between the Cherokees and the Unakas.

"Our elder brother," they said, meaning the white man, "has become our neighbor."

He is now near to us, and already occupies our ancient habitations. . . . But this is as our forefathers told us. . . . They said, "Our feet are turned toward the West—they are never to turn around. Now mark what our forefathers told us. Your elder brother will settle around you—he will encroach upon your lands, and then ask you to sell them to him. When you give him a part of your country, he will not be satisfied, but ask for more. In process of time he will ask you to become like him. . . . He will tell you that your mode of life is not as good as his—whereupon you will be induced to make great roads through the nation, by which he can have free access to you. He will learn you to cultivate the earth. He will even teach you his language and learn you to read and write. . . . But these are but means to destroy you, and to eject you from your habitations. HE WILL POINT YOU TO THE WEST, but you will find no resting place there, for your elder brother will drive you from one place to another until you get to the western waters. These things will certainly happen, but it will be when we are dead and gone. We shall not live to see and feel the misery which will come upon you."[19]

Such were the prophecies which the conjurors made while fanning themselves with large wings.

When The Ridge was five or six years old, the prophecies seemed to be coming true. The Cherokees were still preoccupied with warfare. As a Charleston trader had observed: "War is their principal study & their greatest ambition is to distinguish themselves by military actions."[20] As the colonists east of the mountains drifted toward revolt against King George III, the Cherokee warriors sensed an opportunity for scalps and glory, and small bands made forays against white settlements along the frontier. In two days they killed thirty-seven persons along the Catawba River, a single incident among many that aroused the whites to fury.

The governments of Virginia, Georgia, and the Carolinas organized a joint campaign for the purpose of crushing the Indians. In the summer of 1776 four expeditions made up of sixty-five hundred riflemen advanced separately but simultaneously into Cherokee country. Nowhere were the Indians strong enough to repulse the concerted attack, and no aboriginal practice was too barbarous for the white men to adopt. They even developed refinements of their own. Bounties were placed on Indian scalps, and neither women nor children could always escape. More than fifty Cherokee towns went down in utter waste. Men from General Griffith Rutherford's force burned the Hiwassee settlements to the ground. They cut down orchards, ruined fields, killed horses, and plundered personal property. Cherokees who escaped death became fugitives in the woods, forced to exist on nuts and wild game. Many died of hunger and exposure. "The most prominent feature in the early reminiscences of [The] Ridge," wrote McKenney and Hall, "refers to the distressed situation to which the Cherokees were reduced by [these] invasions."[21]

The Ridge's father decided to remove his family from the scenes of destruction and despair. He put them all in large canoes hollowed from poplar logs, and they floated down the Hiwassee to the Tennessee River. They followed the Tennessee to a point beyond the present site of Chattanooga. They could have turned south and joined one of the towns of Cherokees who had migrated with Dragging Canoe, the disaffected secessionist. Instead, they paddled in a northerly direction up a tributary branch, perhaps the stream known as Sequatchie, to Sequatchie Mountain, the "place of the grinning possum," or, as the white men called it, Walden Ridge. This was a nearly unbroken rock wall that trended to the northeast, its top covered with thick stands of trees and shrubs. Several breaks could be found in the steep wall, clefts that wound into the heart of the ridge and were watered by numerous springs.

Here, in one of these sheltered glens, the family settled down, safe not only from the storms that howled across the ridge, but also, best of all, from further white harassments. They escaped John Sevier's campaigns of 1780 and 1781, especially the dire campaign of 1782 when, having destroyed several Chickamauga towns, the white men veered to the Coosa and burned and pillaged until they reached "the region of long-leafed pine and cypress swamp."[22] After Sevier's campaigns the majority of the Cherokees drifted south and west into land formerly held by the Creeks, thus shifting the nation's center of gravity and leaving only a weakened remnant still in the Overhill towns.* Many of the Cherokees were again starving in the forests.

Apparently, however, The Ridge's father kept his family well. Sequatchie Valley was considered one of the best hunting grounds in all the Cherokee domain. It was the haunt of deer and bear and wandering buffalo, with thousands of birds and many kinds of fish in the streams. The Ridge's father not only hunted for his family, he also managed the education of his sons. No doubt, like most Cherokee fathers, he seldom chided them and never punished them

---

*See the map in this chapter for the extent of the Cherokee domain as it shaped up during the early 1780s and as it remained throughout the time span of most of the following narrative, with only minor changes, except insofar as it was reduced by land cessions to the United States.

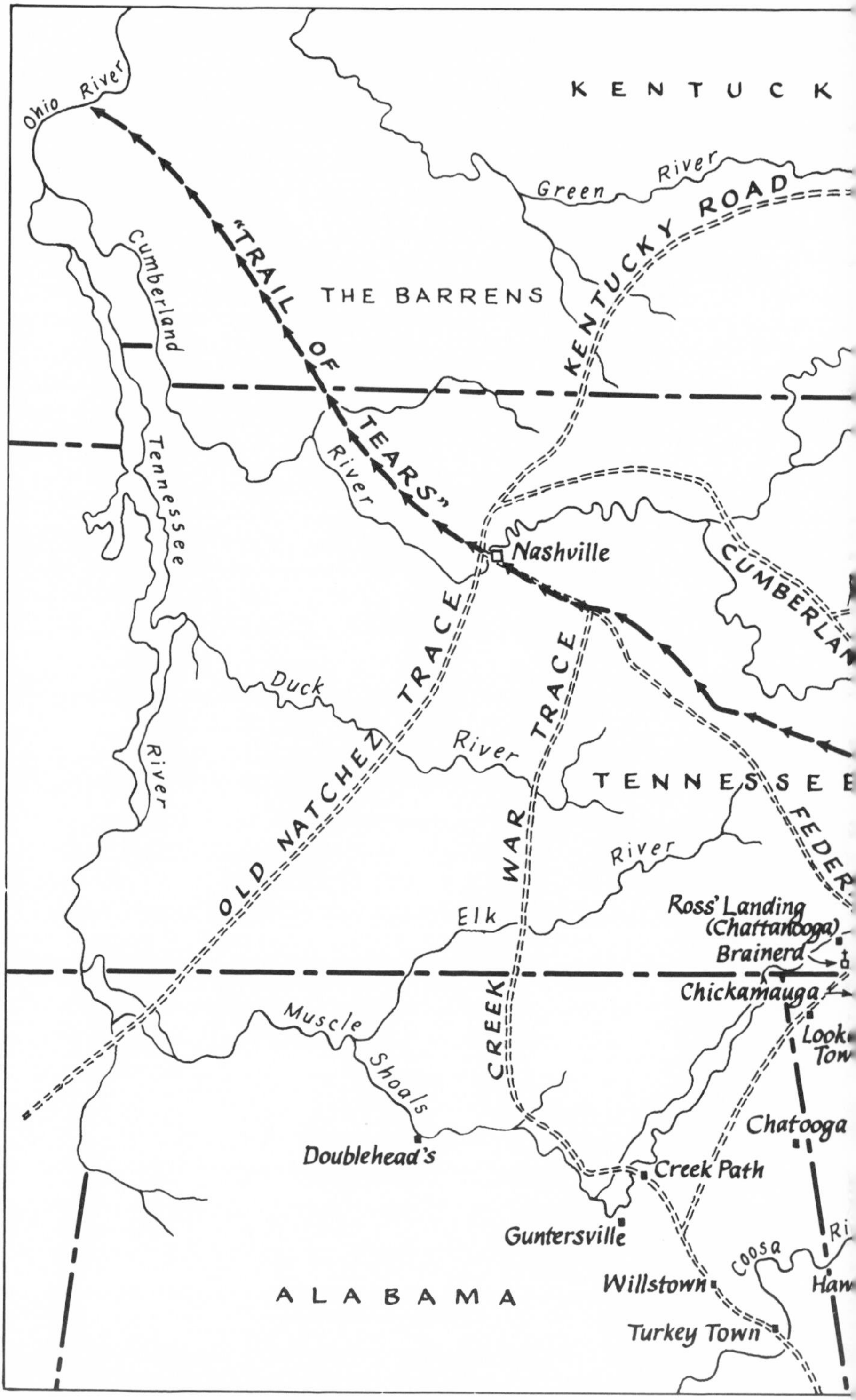

KENTUCK
Ohio River
Green River
KENTUCKY ROAD
"TRAIL OF TEARS"
THE BARRENS
Cumberland
Tennessee
River
Nashville
CUMBERLAN
OLD NATCHEZ TRACE
CREEK WAR TRACE
Duck
River
TENNESSEE
FEDER
River
Elk
Ross' Landing
(Chattanooga)
Brainerd
Chickamauga
Look
Tow
Muscle
Shoals
Chatooga
Doublehead's
Creek Path
Guntersville
Coosa
Ri
Willstown
Haw
ALABAMA
Turkey Town

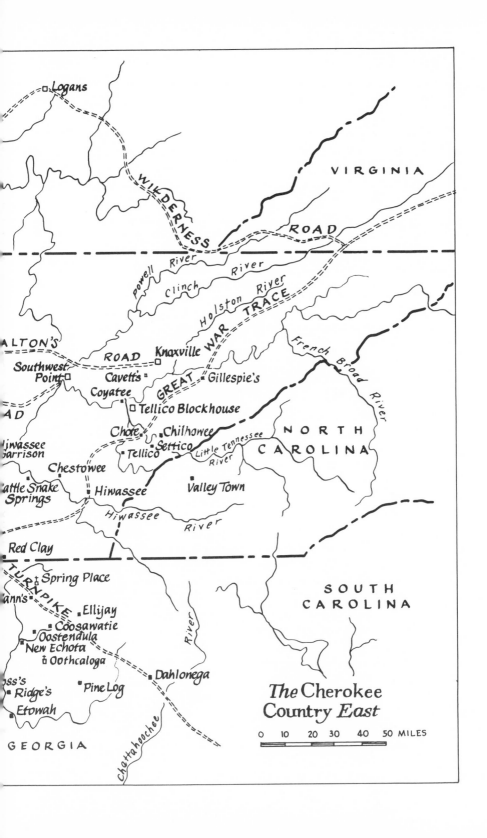

VIRGINIA

Logans

WILDERNESS ROAD

Powell River

Clinch River

Holston River

GREAT WAR TRACE

ALTON'S ROAD

Knoxville

Southwest Point

Cavett's

Gillespie's

Coyatee

French Broad River

Tellico Blockhouse

AD

Chote

Chilhowee

NORTH CAROLINA

iwassee Garrison

Tellico

Settico

Little Tennessee River

Chestowee

Hiwassee

Valley Town

attle Snake Springs

Hiwassee River

Red Clay

TURNPIKE

Spring Place

SOUTH CAROLINA

ann's

Ellijay

Coosawatie

Oostendula

New Echota

Oothcaloga

River

ss's

Dahlonega

Ridge's

Pine Log

The Cherokee Country *East*

Etowah

0   10   20   30   40   50 MILES

GEORGIA

Chattahoochee

with blows, for Cherokee parents believed that physical punishment of children only debased their minds and blunted their sense of honor.[23] While yet an infant The Ridge learned to swim like an otter, and from the age of four or five he had played with a blow-pipe and with a sycamore bow and arrows. At eight or nine his training as a hunter began in earnest. He was allowed to eat only twice a day as a matter of discipline and was sent daily into the forest to absorb its lore.

His father taught him to steal with noiseless tread upon the grazing animal—to deceive the timid doe by mimicking the cry of the fawn—or to entice the wary buck within the reach of his missile by decorating his own head with antlers. He was inured to patience, fatigue, self-denial, and exposure, and acquired the sagacity which enabled him to chase with success the wild cat, the bear, and the panther. He watched the haunts, and studied the habits of wild animals, and became an expert in the arts which enable the Indian hunter at all seasons to procure food from the stream or forest.[24]

The Ridge learned from his father how to pound the roots of the buckeye and how to place the pulp in a basket and wade into a stream, churning the basket through the water till fish rose to the surface dazed from the buckeye juice and helpless against being taken by hand, spear, or net.[25] No doubt he also learned how to build a canoe, how to burn the heart from a poplar log and smooth the wood with scrapers.

Cherokees such as The Ridge's father paid close attention to the ritual side of a hunter's life, the spells and incantations. The son must have learned early the sacred formulas addressed to the two most potent guardians of the hunter, water and fire—how the hunter must "go to water" every evening before the hunt began and then recite: "Give me the wind. Give me the breeze. Yu! O Great Earth Hunter, I come to the edge of your spittle where you repose. Let your stomach cover itself; let it cover itself at a single bend, and may you never be satisfied." And then to the fire: "And you, O Ancient Red, may you hover about my breast while I sleep. Now let good dreams develop. . . ."[26]

He must have also learned how the hunter had to fast in the morning and travel all day without eating or drinking, and how at sunset he must go to water again and recite the sacred prayer before building his fire or eating his supper or lying down for the night. The Ridge must have learned still other hunting rituals from his father—how, for instance, one had to ask permission of every animal before one killed it. He learned the charm that one must repeat while taking aim, to speed his arrow or bullet to the soul of his quarry. He learned how one must sacrifice the tongue of every deer he killed by giving it to the fire, or how one had to pass his moccasins over the flames to protect his feet from snakes.

In time The Ridge became an expert at hunting, and that is how he earned his final name. It is recorded that "after arriving at the age of a hunter" it was his custom to reply, when asked by which way he had reached camp, "I came along the top of the mountain." Frequently repeated, the answer seemed to suggest a characteristic bent, and as a result, the youthful hunter received the name Kah-nung-da-tla-geh, "the man who walks on the mountaintop."[27] Hence "The Ridge," the name he would bear among the white men. It implied that one who walked a mountain ridge could see far. "And those of us who knew his history from his own personal life," wrote a white acquaintance after Major Ridge's death, "are ready to agree that he walked along the mountain top in regard to integrity, high resolve, and purity of character."[28]

Meanwhile, on reaching the age of puberty, when Cherokee boys began to wear clothes, he was ready to leave the "parental school" and begin the training that would make him a warrior. According to Cherokee custom, such training must start with a formal initiation, a ceremony that would dedicate the youth to a warrior's life. It would involve an invocation to the Great Spirit to make him brave and bring him a strong heart in the face of danger. In this undertaking The Ridge's father secured the tutelage of a venerable chief who had made a mighty reputation on the war trail.

"*Gatlun hi a-sgá si-ti,*" the ancient war chief said to The Ridge, "I shall make you *dreadful.*" *A-sgá si-ti*—the Cherokee expression for "dreadful," "ugly," "mean"—was the most emphatic statement the Indians had to indicate formidable or terrifying qualities.

McKenney and Hall wrote:

The ceremony took place immediately. The hoary brave, standing upon the brink of a mountain stream, called upon the Great Spirit to fill the mind of the young warrior with warlike inclinations and his heart with courage. He then, with the bone of a wolf, the end of which terminated in several sharp points, scratched the naked boy from the palm of one hand along the front of the arm, across the breast, and along the other arm to the hand—and in like manner lines were drawn from the heels upward to the shoulders, and from the shoulders over the breast downward to the feet—and from the back of one hand

along the arm, across the back, and to the back of the hand. The lines
thus made each covered a space of two inches in width, and consisted
of parallel incisions which penetrated through the skin, and caused
an effusion of blood along their entire extent. He was then required
to plunge into the stream and bathe, after which the war chief washed
his whole body with a decoction of medicinal herbs.[29]

The Ridge was then ordered not to associate with girls, sit near
women, or allow himself to be touched by any female for seven
days. On the eighth day the old chief came and said a prayer to
the Great Spirit. Then he gave the neophyte some mush and roasted
partridge. The partridge had been chosen because in flight its wings
made a noise like thunder, while it was quiet and hard to detect
when sitting or walking. "Thus were indicated the clamour of the
onset, and the cautious stealth which should govern the movements
of the warrior at all other times."[30] And so at the age of twelve
The Ridge was dedicated to the warrior's life. But several years
were to pass before he followed the warpath.

The frontier had enjoyed nearly a decade of relative peace since
John Sevier's expedition of 1782. Dragging Canoe's seceding Cherokees, who had come to be known as Chickamaugas, remained recalcitrant, but only minor border troubles occurred, sporadic raids by
small parties, and the frontier was spared any major instance of
rapine or pillage. Sometime during that period The Ridge's parents
decided to backtrail to the Hiwassee River, though not to their
former home in the town of Hiwassee. Instead, they went to the
adjacent settlement of Chestowee, the "Rabbit Place." It was a town
of some forty or fifty lodges, a former Yuchi village located near
the ford where the great war trail to the North crossed the river.
There The Ridge's family was living in 1788, the year the comparative
border peace was shattered by what a son of John Sevier called "the
hottest Indian war I ever witnessed."[31]

The Cherokees could not forget that six years earlier Sevier's
men had blazed out tomahawk claims in Cherokee lands, or "improvements" as they were brazenly termed. In that way the Unakas
had made it clear they hoped to establish ownership by conquest
rather than purchase. Such claims were invalidated by subsequent
pacts, including the Treaty of Hopewell, which the Cherokees had
signed in 1785 with delegates from the Congress of the United
States. Congress passed a resolution warning the white intruders
to vacate Cherokee lands. But the white settlers, especially those

who had squatted on land between the Holston and the French Broad, refused to leave the Cherokee domain. By the spring of 1788 the Cherokees were in a furor, and it was all the principal chief of the Upper Cherokees, Old Tassel, could do to maintain an uneasy peace.

When in June that year a fanatic settler shot the chief in cold blood under a flag of truce, all hope of peace ran out. The war spirit surged especially strong among the Chickamaugas in the Lower Towns, whose leaders included Doublehead and Pumpkin Boy, brothers of the murdered chief. By July, war was unavoidable, no matter how much the responsible leaders wanted to keep the peace. Drums beat in every Cherokee town. The Upper Cherokee council chose Little Turkey to succeed Old Tassel as principal chief, and the capital was removed to Oostanaula on the river of that name. With the entire nation seething with the war spirit, Dragging Canoe recognized Little Turkey as head chief of all the Cherokees, and thus an eleven-year schism was healed on what amounted to a war basis. Numerous war bands, often no larger than twenty or thirty men, poured from the Lower Towns and up the great war trace, fanning the war fever of the settlements through which they passed.

Chestowee did not escape the mounting hysteria. A leader there announced his aim of going to war and called for volunteers. A party began to form. Those who volunteered began to dance the warrior dance, their faces painted vermilion with one eye circled with white, the other with black. Each brandished a red and black ceremonial club, the red symbolizing blood, the black fearlessness. Soon the dance gained in tempo, the warriors pretending to strike the enemy. They chanted in monotonous tones and finally ended with four loud whoops. The dance was repeated over and over, the number of participants increasing as the blood pressure of the younger men rose.

The Ridge, now large and strong, though only seventeen, succumbed to the excitement. He declared for battle against his father's wishes and in spite of his mother's tears. Neither parent was well, and he was their major support, but the lure of the warpath with its prospect of glory was more than he could resist. He purified himself according to Cherokee custom. He shaved his head except for a scalp lock, in which he tied red feathers tipped with white. He painted his face and made himself ready for the trail, and when the time came to depart, he filed off with his comrades dressed in moccasins and a breechclout and carrying only his weapons and a pouch of dried corn meal. "In this expedition," wrote McKenney and Hall, "he endured, without a murmur, great hardship and dangers."[32]

According to Indian custom, the party fasted the first day out. Thereafter a cup of meal was the daily ration of each. Along the way the Chestowee warriors joined forces with other Cherokees, and the war band eventually numbered two hundred men. They planned to destroy Houston's Station, a small fortified settlement of five or six families. It was an isolated outpost sixteen miles south of White's Fort, later known as Knoxville. On learning that Indians were advancing against it, General Joseph Martin garrisoned the station with a small force under Major Thomas Stewart. The major detailed thirty-one scouts under Captain John Fain to reconnoiter along the Little Tennessee and search for Indian signs.

The Cherokees had their own scouts out, and on learning of the white men's sally, they prepared an ambush at the deserted town of Setico,* where an old orchard stood, full of ripe apples. Carefully hidden, they watched the mounted Unakas cross the river. The Cherokees waited until the soldiers, tempted by the fruit, scattered among the trees. Some of them laid their rifles carelessly aside. The Indians erupted from their ambuscade, with war whoops and nerve-wracking turkey gobbles. They divided into two groups, one surrounding the orchard, the other taking possession of the ford. Thus they caught their foes in a double trap. Their first volleys killed six soldiers among the trees and wounded four others. The troops panicked and fled toward the ford, as the Cherokees had anticipated. Ten white men were killed in flight, and several were wounded, some while swimming their horses through deep water. Half the band succeeded in crossing the river and rode their horses up a steep bank. There a Cherokee brave overtook a soldier. They grappled in combat.[33]

"The white man being the stronger," wrote McKenney and Hall, "threw the Indian, when a second came to the assistance of the latter, and while the gallant Tennessean was combating with two foes, [The] Ridge, who was armed with only a spear, came up and dispatched the unfortunate white man, by plunging his weapon into him. This affair was considered highly creditable to [The] Ridge,

*The older settlement named Setico—or Citico, which means "big fish there"—was located on the Little Tennessee at the mouth of Citico Creek, Monroe County, Tennessee. It should not be confused with the younger village of Setico on the present site of Chattanooga.

the Indians regarding not courage only, but success, as indicative of merit, and appreciating highly the good fortune which enables one of their number to shed the blood of an enemy, in however accidental or stealthy a manner."[34] Thus in his first campaign The Ridge became an Outacite or Man-killer. He had taken his first scalp, *uska-na-gili,* his enemy's hair.

Only lust for scalps prevented the Cherokees from annihilating Captain Fain's force. According to one observer, it cost the most adept scalper about two minutes to take his trophy. The time consumed in the heat of the fray for the victors to acquire their prizes was probably all that sixteen desperate white men needed to make their escape.[35]

But the Cherokees had time enough to wreak their hatred on the dead. They ripped bellies open and left bowels to float on the water. They decapitated one corpse, cut out its heart, and strewed its intestines about the ground. If thoughts of avenging Old Tassel had heightened their frenzy, the irony is that among the soldiers who had escaped was the man who had killed the old chief. It was later learned that, wounded though he was, he had managed to swim the river and crawl into a hollow log, where he was overlooked in the boisterous confusion.[36]

The Cherokees pursued the fleeing soldiers to within five miles of White's Fort. They killed several more and took one prisoner. On the following day they returned to their first objective, Houston's Station. They put it under seige and, notwithstanding its defense by several of the best riflemen on the border, it might have fallen had not Sevier come to the rescue with a large force. The Cherokees withdrew, full of glory for the Setico massacre, if not for the consummation of their original plan. Their initial success had satisfied their lust for blood, and they were now eager to return home, with scalps mounted on green pine branches, to sing the death song and sound the shrill death whoop and boast of their deeds of valor. Certain knowledge that the whites would strike their homes in a massive retaliation cast the only shadow on their triumphant return.

Soon indeed came word that General Martin had mustered five hundred men at White's Fort, and a fierce attack on the towns along the Hiwassee appeared inevitable. In concern for his ailing parents, especially his father, The Ridge decided to take his family to a safer place, one remote from the probable scenes of battle. He chose the thinly populated community of Pine Log, which sprawled between the Oostanaula and the Etowa rivers, toward the southern edge of Cherokee settlements in northern Georgia.* It numbered about twenty lodges, scattered for a mile along a creek of the same name. The surrounding land was fertile, the town thrived, and The Ridge was pleased with his choice of new home. Leaving his parents there, where they were safe from the white offensive, he again prepared for the warpath.[37]

General Martin's force swept through Hiwassee late in August, 1788, and made for the Chickamauga towns, only to be repulsed by Dragging Canoe's warriors at Lookout Mountain. The whites became so demoralized that they refused to proceed, and Martin dropped back after burning his dead in an Indian town house. The Cherokees determined to follow up the victory, Dragging Canoe having mobilized an army of three thousand warriors, including a thousand Creeks.[38] The Ridge had joined this force, which followed Martin's men in retreat, and when the Cherokee army separated into smaller units, for forays against the frontier, he went with the contingent led by John Watts, or Young Tassel, nephew of the murdered chief. Watts was a large, portly mixed-blood, known as a "generous and honorable enemy."[39] His party, hundreds strong, harassed Sevier in September when he moved against the Middle Towns of the Cherokees, burning lodges and ruining crops.

The Ridge was still with Watts in October, 1788, when that chief led his warriors against the white settlements. White's Fort, at what the Cherokees called the Place of the Mulberry Grove, was the main objective. But because of a disagreement among the chiefs— Watts, The Glass, Bloody Fellow, and Kitegisky—the fort was spared the attack. As the Indians started home, they surprised Captain John Gillespie's station on the Holston. They had waited so long to make their appearance that the men of the station had concluded that Dragging Canoe had forgone revenge for Martin's invasion, so most of them had left the stockade to work in the fields. The Indians captured several of the settlers, then moved against the station itself. It was fiercely defended by those inside until their ammunition ran out. As the gunfire ceased, the warriors clambered up the stockade, The Ridge probably among the rest, and ran across the roofs and dropped inside the enclosure. They killed all the men there and many of the women, and took twenty-eight women and children prisoners. They burned the station to the ground, then near the

*Pine Log was located in what is now Bartow County.

smoking ruins the four chiefs left a defiant ultimatum addressed to Martin and Sevier.[40]

Ordinarily, after such a victory, the warriors would have returned home to boast of their valor, but Watts was an enterprising leader, and success encouraged him to attack again. His force moved at last against White's Fort, as well as Houston's Station, "and while these attacks were beaten off, the Holston settlements were never in greater danger of extinction."[41]

Later that year Watts took his men into winter quarters on Flint Creek* at the edge of the Appalachian Mountains. There they built rough huts of logs and bark, a semipermanent encampment from which to harry the Holston settlements during the cold season. It was true that Hanging Maw, head chief of the Upper Cherokees, was eager to reestablish peace and had come among the Indian forces with the assurance from General Martin that Congress was at last determined to enforce the Treaty of Hopewell and make the white settlers withdraw from Cherokee lands.[42] Watts received such pledges with skepticism and held his warriors poised for attack.

Sevier learned of their presence from his scouts, however, and one bitterly cold day in January, 1789, the Cherokees found themselves surrounded by Unakas, who also held the only means of retreat, the pass behind the camp. Sevier had arranged a line of "grasshopper" guns to mow the Indians down, but the Cherokees returned such deadly fire against the exposed artillerymen that Sevier ordered a mounted charge. A series of desperate hand-to-hand encounters followed, and the Indians suffered a severe defeat.[43]

The Cherokee losses at Flint Creek were frightful. "We have buried 145 of their dead," wrote Sevier, "and by the blood we have traced for miles all over the woods, it is supposed the greater part of them retreated with wounds."[44] The Ridge seems to have escaped unhurt, but his movements are unknown; the record shows only that he returned to Pine Log (probably in March, 1789) after seven months on the warpath.

He found that both of his parents had died in his absence. Their deaths left him responsible for two younger brothers and a sister, for whom he had to provide. It was in order for The Ridge to assume such a duty, for according to ancient ways of Cherokee clanship, an elder brother held more authority over younger siblings than even

*John P. Brown (*Old Frontiers*, p. 297n) identifies Flint Creek with the stream now called South Indian Creek, in Unicoi County, Tennessee.

their own father, for he was of the same clan as they, their mother's, invariably different from their father's. Nevertheless, The Ridge was only a youth in 1789, and the responsibility was a burden. "Under these depressing circumstances," wrote McKenney and Hall, "he spent several years in obscurity, but always actively engaged either upon the warpath in predatory excursions against the whites, or in hunting expeditions to remote places where the game abounded."[45]

Among such places was the Cumberland Plateau, still one of the finest hunting grounds in the Cherokee domain. It was a vast upland prairie covered with luxuriant grass, where deer, elk, and buffalo grazed. But there was also what remained of Cherokee hunting grounds in Gan-da Giga-i, or Kentucky,* covered for the most part with primeval forest, bowered with wild grapevines, and interspersed with brakes of giant cane. Buffalo still ambled along wide traces between the trees; deer, elk, and bear flourished, not to mention wolves and wildcats. Kentucky was a hunter's dream, and The Ridge went there on long hunts with parties of friends.

One such trip ended in an incident of the sort that corroded relations between the whites and Indians. The Ridge had joined a party led by Tah-cung-tees-kee, The Remover (not that such was his name at the time, for he earned it later by becoming one of the first Cherokees to migrate beyond the Mississippi),[46] and they passed beyond the Cumberland Plateau and into Kentucky after buffalo and bear. When the band ran out of tobacco, Tah-cung-tees-kee proposed they replenish their supply by killing a few Unakas. They left The Ridge and an old man to look after camp. In a short while they returned with scalps and tobacco taken from the pockets of their victims. McKenney and Hall wrote: "We know not who were the unhappy victims; they might have been hunters, but were as probably the members of some emigrant family which had settled in the wilderness. . . . We are told that [The] Ridge was so greatly mortified at having been obliged to remain inactive, far from the scene of danger, that he actually wept over the loss of honour he had sustained, and that his grief was with difficulty appeased."[47]

Such border raids continued, though the white settlements and the Indians were nominally at peace for several years. Even the signing

---

*Gan-da Giga-i, the Cherokees' name for their northern hunting lands, means "bloody ground." A truncated form of it (Gan-da Gi) evolved into the present name Kentucky.

of a new treaty—the Treaty of Holston, in July, 1791—failed to ease the tension, for the Cherokees soon began to feel that they had been tricked. Many young men agitated for a new war against the whites, and a few Cherokees joined the northern Indians ranged against General Arthur St. Clair, whom they defeated on November 4, 1791. To forestall more Cherokees from joining the enemy in the Northwest Territory, the United States welcomed a company of their warriors for a new campaign against the Indians in the North. Still, the settlers in Tennessee and Kentucky remained the prime targets of Cherokee resentment, and in May, 1792, John Watts, after succeeding Dragging Canoe as war chief and while still himself in favor of peace, notified the governor of Tennessee that "it was beyond his power to restrain" certain warriors from making hostile raids.[48]

The recalcitrant braves included The Ridge. He may have declared for the warpath in the early summer of 1792 when the Lower Towns withdrew from the commitment to the United States.* It was a rousing occasion when even Watts changed his mind during the annual council at Willstown in September, 1792, and announced, "We will all go to war together." Many young bloods from the Upper and Middle Towns followed the lead of the Lower Town hotheads and cast their lots for war. And The Ridge himself may well have been with the army of Cherokees, Creeks, and Shawnees that Watts led shortly thereafter against the Cumberland settlements, in a campaign that failed.[49]

The record is clear, at any rate, concerning The Ridge's implication in a border depredation early the next year, an event with dire consequences. He and his associates were unaware that peace had been made while they were on the trail. On May 25, 1793, some eighteen miles from Knoxville they killed a white man and his son— Thomas and James Gillum—and stole some twenty horses. Beside the bodies they left two war clubs of another tribe, to suggest that the killings had not been done by Cherokees.[50]

The Ridge and his comrades then drove the horses to Coyatee, the town of Hanging Maw, where certain principal men were gath-

---

*Cf. Arthur Campbell's statement of July 19, 1792: "We have alarming intelligence that all the lower Towns of the Cherokees have seceded from their late engagement to the United States; that a large party of warriors had set out to intercept the Boat carrying the goods for the Treaty, and . . . it is to be feared they have succeeded" (*Calendar of Virginia State Papers*, V: 634).

ering to proceed to Philadelphia for a talk with the whites. The
Ridge's party sold two ponies to the chief's son. Then they resumed
the trail, eager to reach home to boast of their exploit. They were
detained, however, when one of their number fell ill. Accordingly
they arrived at Pine Log several days after their ill-considered act
had provoked a grim reprisal. They found the village in mourning.[51]

The ruse involving the war clubs had failed in its purpose, and
the whites were sure that the marauding warriors had been Cherokee.
The governor of Tennessee had ordered John Beard, a "rash and
inhuman" captain of militia, to follow their trail with fifty horsemen,
but under no circumstances to cross the Little Tennessee, then the
boundary between the whites and Cherokees. Beard advanced to
where The Ridge's band had forded the stream for Coyatee. There
he violated his own orders and led his men across the river. They
attacked the town, killed eleven chiefs and warriors, and wounded
Hanging Maw. There was an irony here in view of Hanging Maw's
incessant efforts to promote peace.[52]

The Ridge and his comrades received no welcome at Pine Log.
McKenney and Hall wrote:

The relatives of the slain were incensed, and disposed to take revenge
for their loss upon the young men who had occasioned the misfortune,
nor were there wanting accusers to upbraid them openly as the authors
of a great public calamity. Having no excuse to offer, [The] Ridge,
with a becoming spirit, proposed to repair his error as far as possible,
by warding off its effects from his countrymen. He raised the war
whoop, entered the village as is customary with those who return victorious, and called for volunteers to march against the enemy—but
there was no response; the village was still, no veteran warrior greeted
the party as victors, and those who mourned over deceased relatives
scowled at them as they passed. The usual triumph was not allowed,
and the young aggressors, so far from being joined by others in a new
expedition, fell back abashed by the chilling and contemptuous reception
which they met.[53]

Only one old conjuror acted in a friendly manner, and that was
because he had prophesied that The Ridge and his friends would
bring scalps to adorn the war poles. He did what he could to change
the sentiment of Pine Log and succeeded in swaying a chief, who
publicly condemned the idea that relatives of the slain could think
of revenging themselves upon friends. If blood must flow, the chief
declared, let it be Unaka blood. He then began to chant the war
song, to such effect that the young braves of the town began to

volunteer, and The Ridge was the first of all to act.[54]

Pine Log was not the only town to form war parties. After the first shock, John Watts found that at last he was war chief of a unified nation. By September, 1793, he had a thousand warriors, including Creeks, ready to move against the white settlements, with Doublehead as second in command. This was a new experience for The Ridge: John Watts believed the Indians could fight in the white manner and had his warriors march abreast like British soldiers. They crossed the Tennessee on the twenty-fourth and advanced all night toward Knoxville. It was Watt's plan to surprise that settlement at dawn. To do so required that the Cherokees avoid all smaller stations along the way, lest they raise the alarm; but Doublehead was loath to leave such prizes behind. The argument that followed delayed the march. On reaching Cavett's Station, Doublehead prevailed in his counsels. The Indians heard the Knoxville garrison fire its sunrise gun and assumed their approach had been detected. Since the chance seemed lost to take the garrison by surprise, Watts ordered his warriors to attack the smaller station.[55]

Just one family occupied the blockhouse, that of Alexander Cavett, numbering thirteen, only three of whom were men. They made a fierce resistance, dropping five Cherokees with their fire. But the Indians so outnumbered them that further defense was hopeless, and Cavett agreed to surrender on liberal terms. Watts promised to exchange the prisoners for the same number of Indians in white hands.[56]

During the truce Doublehead looked on in silence. He was a vengeful man, now implacable since his brother Pumpkin Boy had fallen in the campaign. No sooner had the gates of the blockhouse opened and the Cavetts come forth than he gave the war whoop and drew his tomahawk in defiance of Watts. "[The] Ridge has since frequently related the fact," wrote McKenney and Hall, "that the women and children ... were hewn down by the ferocious Doublehead, who afterwards became ... a tyrant in the nation; [The Ridge] spoke of this foul deed with abhorance, and declared that he turned aside, and looked another way, unwilling to witness that which he could not prevent."[57]

Watts ran to the rescue, but was in time to save only one member of the family, Alexander Cavett, Jr. Doublehead demanded that the boy die too, but Watts refused to yield him up and had him spirited away by some of his Creek allies. Not that he succeeded in his act of mercy—three days later a Creek chief killed the boy

and scalped him. Meanwhile, the Indians plundered Cavett's house
and stables, then burned the buildings down.[58]

Dissension among the leaders brought the campaign to an end.
After the Cavett massacre, the army marched to the Tennessee,
crossing it at the same ford by which they had come. Then they
headed for a village near the mouth of the Etowah River.[59] During
this time John Sevier prepared to strike the Cherokee towns in retaliation. Collecting a force of six or seven hundred men, he crossed
the Tennessee and pushed as far as Oostanaula, where he learned
the whereabouts of Watts's army and hurried in pursuit.

Hearing of Sevier's approach, the Cherokees entrenched themselves on the Etowah. Sevier's scouts appeared downriver half a mile
from where the Indians waited, and the warriors rushed from their
entrenchments to meet the white men, thus leaving the main ford
unguarded. A principal part of the white force erupted there and
caught the Indians by surprise. The warriors rushed back and engaged
the Unakas in a hot skirmish. Superior numbers were no match for
the firepower of the American rifles, and Sevier's forces drove the
Indians back before they had time to collect their dead. They lost
not only their encampment but also a large number of guns, supplies,
blankets, and horses. They fell back before Sevier as he crossed the
Coosa and marched down the river to the region of Turnip Mountain, destroying towns and food deposits in his path. "The party
flogged at Hightower [Etowah]* were those which had been out
with Watts," the white leader reported. "I have great reason to
believe their ardor and spirit were well checked."[60]

Sevier was right. The battle of Etowah was the Cherokees' final
large-scale engagement with American forces. A year passed without
any serious outbreak on the frontier, except for the destruction of
two Cherokee towns in September, 1794, by a force of white volunteers. On November 7 practically every chief of the Upper Cherokees met the governor of Tennessee at Tellico Blockhouse to confirm
the peace that the United States had offered a Cherokee deputation
in Philadelphia.[61] There George Washington had given the delegation a large silver pipe as a memorial of his warm and abiding
friendship, and Silas Dinsmoor, the newly appointed agent to the

---

*The village of Etowah, whose name means "deadwood place" and was early
corrupted to "Hightower," was located near the present site of Rome, Georgia.
The name was applied to the nearby river, which joins the Oostanaula to form
the Coosa.

southwest Indians, would soon be writing: "Peace is the general talk in this country & I believe it is really the desire of the Cherokees to bury the old red hatchet & not shed any more blood."[62] Indeed, the Cherokees could live now, as Little Turkey said, "so that [they] might have gray hairs on [their] *heads*."[63] Meanwhile, The Ridge had returned to Pine Log. There the border warrior settled down to the ways of peace and soon became a rising young chief.

2 • YOUNG CHIEF

During the new era of peace The Ridge's abilities were recognized by his neighbors, and he was chosen to represent Pine Log at the tribal council at Oostanaula. He attended probably for the first time in 1796.* He had not yet accumulated any property, except for a few silver ornaments and an aged, ugly white pony. His clothes were old and worn, not at all in keeping with his new position. In general the Cherokees valued ceremonial show. It was expected that on important occasions a man would appear well mounted, that he would parade his possessions, especially "horses, weapons, trinkets, and the trophies of war and hunting."[1]

Consequently, when The Ridge rode up to the council grounds so poorly dressed and ill mounted, he was coldly received. The younger men wished to bar him from the council. Maturer and wiser heads, however, were less disturbed by his broken-down horse and his lack of personal adornment. McKenney and Hall wrote that "the old men invited him to a seat near them, and shook him by the hand, and the younger members one by one reluctantly extended to him the same sign of fellowship."[2] At this council he was content merely to observe and learn. He listened closely to the speeches of the chiefs and headmen, but remained silent.

As a matter of fact, nothing of much significance occurred. As usual, however, the proceedings were conducted with great solemnity. It was the Cherokee way for orators to speak one at a time, in a deliberate voice, slowly and calmly. No one interrupted, though the speeches were sometimes long. Sometimes, too, owing to the large

*McKinney and Hall give The Ridge's age as twenty-one on his first attending the Cherokee council, but here, as elsewhere, they seem to make The Ridge younger than was the actual case.

28

number of syllables with similar sounds, the speeches had the effect
of monotony, in spite of short sentences, rising inflections, and
strong accents on concluding syllables. Often a deep grunt sounded
at the end of a sentence, resembling the hard breathing of a man
chopping trees. Everyone waited politely for an orator to conclude.
Then the next speaker would rise and without gestures give his
arguments, sometimes in a voice so low he was asked to repeat
what he had said. Orators always spoke in a standing position. Complete courtesy and good manners prevailed, and every man could
have his say. Then all would sit down together and deliberate at
length on the proposition before the house.[3]

As Jedidiah Morse, the distinguished geographer, later described
a Cherokee council: "Indian chiefs are generally . . . the ablest
and wisest men in the nation; more frequently they are old men,
and manage their councils, and the affairs of the nation, with sober
dignity, great order, deliberation and decorum. They proceed slowly,
but surely. Nothing is permitted to interrupt their business after they
engage in it; and when they have finished it, the Council breaks up."[4]

The Ridge's native abilities included oratorical talents of a high
order, and if nothing of moment happened at his first council, and
if he remained silent then, the same could not be said for many
later ones. Indeed, The Ridge distinguished himself the next year
by suggesting to his peers that certain aspects of the traditional
Blood Law be abolished.

The Cherokee Nation was divided into seven clans—Wolf, Deer,
Bird, Paint, Blue, Long Hair, and Kituwah—each with a distinct
genealogy traced through the female line of descent, and at that
time the influence of clan tradition on Cherokee life reached into
every sphere. It dictated much about the council, even to the char-
acteristics of the council house, whose seven-sided shape symbolized
the number of the clans. Each clan had its separate seating area,
and many council members were chosen as clan representatives.

Among the rights and responsibilities of the clans was the administration of the Blood Law, the Cherokee version of the Mosaic
decree of an eye for an eye—*lex talionis*. Blood must be forfeited
for blood, and if the man who had taken a life should flee, his
nearest relative might fall in his place, a victim of the revenge
taken by the clan to which the slain one belonged. It made no
difference whether the death was accidental or not; blood must be
spilled in retaliation. Sometimes such a convention destroyed up-
standing men who had the ill luck to cause another's death by ac-

cident or who, owing solely to relationship, were sacrificed for the deeds of kinsmen.

Such a practice seemed abhorrent to The Ridge. The revulsion that had overcome him at the excesses of Doublehead at Cavett's Station suggests that a sense of compassion had grown in his heart even while he was on the warpath. He had begun more and more to sense the value of human life and come to feel that the laws and institutions of the whites, in insuring more protection for the individual, were clearly superior in many respects to the ways of the Cherokees. Such an insight in one so forceful and energetic as The Ridge quickly aroused in him the impulse to overhaul the Blood Law and make it more humane in its intent and application. In a moving speech he excoriated the injustice of those parts of the law which made accidental homicide a crime and which "substituted a relative for a fugitive murderer, and successfully advocated [their] repeal."[5] The action so impressed Benjamin Hawkins, the Creek agent, that he remarked: "The Cherokees are giving proof of their approximation to the customs of well regulated societies; they did in full council, in my presence, pronounce, after solemn deliberation, as law, that any person who should kill another accidentally should not suffer for it, but be acquitted; that to constitute a crime, there should be malice and an intention to kill."[6]

To enforce such a statute, which meant flouting an immemorial custom, proved to be no easy task. But as sponsor of the law, The Ridge was determined to see that it was carried out. To that end he secured the pledge of every chief to punish its violation, and soon a chance came to put the integrity of all such promises to a test, when a murderer fled from justice. McKenney and Hall wrote:

The relations of the deceased were numerous, fearless, and vindictive, prompt to take offence, and eager to imbue their hands in blood upon the slightest provocation. They determined to resent the injury by killing the brother of the offender. The friends of the latter dispatched a messenger to [The] Ridge, to advise him of the intended violation of the new law, and implore his protection; and he, with a creditable promptitude, sent word to the persons who proposed to revenge themselves, that he would take upon himself the office of killing the individual who should put such a purpose into execution. The threat had the desired effect, not only in that instance, but in causing the practice of substituting a relative in the place of an escaped homicide to be abandoned.[7]

Thus, early in his public career The Ridge became a civilizing influence upon his fellow Cherokees.

He would likewise become an example of the progressive spirit in his domestic life. Sometime in his early twenties, possibly in 1792,[8] he married Susanna Wickett, whose last name was given now and then as Wicked. Her Indian name seems to have been Sehoya.[9] She was described as a "handsome and sensible" girl "who possessed a fine person, and an engaging countenance, and sustained through life an excellent character."[10] As The Ridge still followed many old Cherokee customs at that time, he possibly effected the engagement in the traditional manner, by killing a deer and taking it to the lodge of Susanna's parents to indicate that he was a good provider. In that case she would have accepted his suit by cooking him a meal. The pair probably went before a conjuror for a prediction on the course of the marriage, and his words presumably were favorable.

As for the marriage itself, the traditional rite was simple. With several companions, the groom received a ceremonial meal in a lodge on one side of the town house, while the bride, similarly waited on, was feted in a house on the other side. At the close of the banquets the men and women of the village took their respective places at opposite sides of the town house. Then the attendants led the bride and groom into the council chamber, where they stood as far apart as possible. A woman relative of the groom, in the absence of his mother, handed him a ham of venison and a blanket. At the same time the bride's mother gave her an ear of corn and a blanket also. The two young people then walked slowly toward each other and, on meeting, exchanged the venison and the corn and put the blankets together, an act which symbolized their promise of living together in the same house, the man providing the meat, the woman the corn. It was customary then for the town chief to pronounce "the blankets joined"—that is, the couple were married.[11] When The Ridge led Susanna from the town house, they both held ends of the blankets, while he carried the corn and she the venison. Tradition would decree that he lead her to a new cabin—in Pine Log, no doubt a typical Indian shelter made of logs with a bark roof and an earthen floor. The fireplace would have lain in the center of the room under a hole in the roof to serve as sole chimney. And doubtless the corn that Susanna tilled grew in the common fields of the town, along with pumpkins, squashes, muskmelons, sweet potatoes, cabbages, and beans. Like other women of Pine Log, she also started to cultivate cotton.

Benjamin Hawkins had encouraged the Cherokee women to learn how to spin and weave, promising that the United States would supply the nation with spinning wheels and looms, and in the fall of 1796, while the men of Pine Log were out in the woods for their autumn hunt, the agent visited the women and found them eager to turn their cotton into cloth. They promised to plant larger crops thereafter "and follow the instructions of the agent and the advice of the President."[12] And The Ridge's experience on coming home may well have paralleled that of the chief who found that the cloth his women had made during his absence exceeded in value the entire result of his six months of hunting.[13] Who convinced whom—The Ridge or Susanna—as to the desirability of adopting the white man's ways is not clear, but in any case the two agreed about the matter. According to McKenney and Hall, "[The Ridge's] wife zealously seconded his views, and though bred in a wigwam, learned after her marriage the domestic arts appertaining to good housewifery, and became as skillful in housekeeping and agriculture as she was industrious and persevering."[14] Susanna, whom a Moravian missionary later described as "naturally high-spirited" and "much bent on riches and greatness,"[15] was clearly a powerful driving force behind her husband.

The American agents not only encouraged the Cherokee women to spin and weave; they also advised the men to give up the chase, which was now failing in results, and turn to agriculture and the raising of livestock. To accomplish this end, they suggested that the Cherokee families scatter from the villages into the forest and open individual farms, where they could grow more grain and cotton and raise more horses, cattle, and hogs than could be done while they were crowded together in their towns.[16] The policy was so successful that within a few years a Moravian missionary could report that "at present only that portion of the Cherokee nation which is confessedly the most indigent and degraded continues to live in towns. The greater and more respectable part live on their plantations, and thus acquire those habits of industry and sobriety which are uniformly counteracted by their congregating together."[17]

The Ridge was one of the first Cherokees to take such advice. Sometime after his marriage he decided to clear land like a white man's farm and build a house like those he had seen while on the warpath. He left Pine Log and located his "improvement" in a

rich valley that lay along Oothcaloga Creek,* so named for the
many beaver dams that could be seen there. In time Oothcaloga
Valley was to become the home of a large number of Cherokees,
including such prominent figures as "Black Wat" and "Red Wat"
Adair, two turbulent half-blood cousins, as well as William Hicks,
later a principal chief of the nation.

The Ridge erected a log house, complete with "the luxury of a
chimney." It also had a roof of boards, split from logs, all held in
place with weight poles—"and thus was completed the usual log
cabin of the frontier settler, an edifice which ranks in architecture
next above the lodge or wigwam. And here . . . the Indian warrior
and his bride, forsaking the habits of their race, [set] themselves
to ploughing and chopping, knitting and weaving and other Christian employments."[18] In time the improvements of The Ridge would
include orchards of apples and peaches, extensive fields of corn and
cotton. He began to raise horses, cattle, and hogs, and to acquire
Negro slaves to do the harder work about the premises.

His views coincided with those of the Indian who remarked before the council:

The hunting is almost done & we must now live by farming, raising
corn & cotton & cattle & horses & hogs & sheep. We see that those
Cherokees who do this live well. The men & women & children are
well cloathed: But there is some who will not work & take care of
the land. They are poor themselves. Their wives & children are not
well cloathed & sometimes they are hungry & have nothing to eat,
they then straggle about . . . to the house of those who work and
eat up the provisions which they had provided for themselves. I now
look around this assembly & see a great many who work & take care
of their farms, they live well, we can all see the good to be derived
from industry.[19]

As for Oothcaloga, owing to the industry of those who settled there,
the valley became known as "the garden spot of the Cherokee country." It was said that the Cherokees lived better there than in any
other part of the nation.[20] Before long The Ridge's brother Oo-watie,
as well as his sister and her husband, followed and settled there on
farms wrested from the forest.

There too at Oothcaloga were born all of The Ridge's children.
Susanna was probably attended by four midwives at each birth, as

*Oothcaloga, the sprawling Cherokee settlement that grew up along Oothcaloga
Creek, was located not far from present-day Calhoun, in Gordon County, Georgia.

Cherokee custom decreed. The first child was a girl, whose English name was Nancy; the second was John, who was born in 1803; the third, a baby who died; the fourth, a feebleminded boy named Walter or "Watty"; and the last, a girl named Sarah, or Sally, who was seven or eight years younger than John. Four living children in all—that number constituted a fair-sized family among the Cherokees, who were not as prolific as the neighboring whites.

As time passed, The Ridge pursued more and more the material comforts of civilization, although he remained illiterate, always signing documents with his mark. He knew almost no English and when addressing the whites had to speak through interpreters, and subsequent observers who claimed that he knew English were invariably confusing him with his son John. Hence the contradictory comments in the records about his knowledge of the white man's tongue. Cherokee remained the speech of his household, and his children knew no English till they were old enough to attend white schools. "My father," Yellow Bird wrote of John Ridge, the elder son, "grew up till he was some twelve or fifteen years of age,* as an untutored Indian, and he used to remember the time when his greatest delight was to strip himself of his Indian costume, and with aboriginal cane gig in hand, while away the long summer days in wading up and down creeks in search of crawfish."[21]

Receiving no Christian instruction during his early years, the youngster absorbed only Cherokee notions of religion from his parents. Later he formulated a general outline of his early beliefs for the statesman Albert Gallatin. The Cherokees, he said, were neither idolators nor worshipers of any of the heavenly bodies.

They believed in a great first cause or Spirit of all Good & in a great being the author of all evil. These were at variance and at war with each other, but the good Spirit was supposed to be superior to the bad one. These mortal beings had on both sides numerous intelligent beings of analogous dispositions to their chieftains. They had a heaven, which consisted of a visible world to those who had undergone a change after death. This heaven was adorned with all the beauties which the savage imagination could conceive. An open forest, yet various, giving shade and fruit of every kind. Flowers of various hues & pleasant to the Smell—Game of all kinds in great abundance—enough of feasts and plenty of dances, & to crown the whole the most beautiful women, prepared and adorned by the Great Spirit, for every individual that

*John Ridge was actually seven years old when he entered a missionary school. See Chapter 5 below.

by wisdom, hospitality & Bravery was introduced to this happy & immortal region. The Bad place was the reverse of this & in the vicinity of the good place, where the wretched, compelled to live in hunger, hostility & darkness, could hear the rejoicings of the happy, without the possibility of reaching its shores.[22]

Certain Cherokees, John Ridge added, pretended to supernatural powers and were known as witches or wizards. They were thought to change themselves into birds and animals and go on nightly journeys in search of human victims, especially among the sick, and it was necessary to hire "witch shooters" to protect the weak and the ill from their visitations. "Such characters were the dread of the Country & many a time have I trembled at the croaking of an owl or gutteral hoarseness of a Raven by night in my younger days."[23] No doubt the beliefs John Ridge described were much like those of his parents at this early period.

"Christian employments" did not mean that The Ridge had yet renounced all Indian ways, all Indian ideas, or that he was ready to embrace the Christian religion as preached among the Cherokees by several missionaries. that step would come only after many years; it would be taken first by Susanna, and in The Ridge's case not until after a residence of three decades at Oothcaloga. Though the Indian festivals had lost in seriousness, and were degenerating into mere "frolics," he continued to observe them, especially the Green Corn Dance, which seemed to be the most important Cherokee observance. He also enjoyed watching "the heathen ball-play," a strenuous racquet game that enthralled the Cherokees, a kind of peacetime equivalent to war, when in putting the ball between the goalposts the players were liable to be punched, mauled, kicked, or even killed.* Yet for all its residue of Indian attitudes and customs, The Ridge's life at Oothcaloga tended to a steady transformation into a country gentleman's way of living—that of a small southern planter.[24]

His life as a planter, however, "did not withdraw him from his public duties. He continued to be an active member of the council, in which he gradually rose to be an influential leader, . . . the orator

---

*Variant forms of the ball-play, which the Cherokees called *anet'sa*, have been found among numerous North American tribes, from the Seminoles of Florida to the Crees of Canada. In its early forms the game was almost invariably employed as a training for war. As played among the northern tribes, it evolved into lacrosse, the national sport of Canada, now standardized with fixed rules. For a discussion of the game as played by Cherokees, see James Mooney, "The Cherokee Ball Play," *American Anthropologist*, III, No. 2 (April, 1890): 105-32.

usually chosen to announce and explain to the people the decrees of that body."[25]

Among his political allies and models were James Vann and Charles Hicks, both of mixed blood. The latter had built a log house of two stories on an old Indian fortification a few miles from Oothcaloga. He was mild and gentle, with a warm disposition. In spite of a crippled hip, his principal occupation was that of a farmer, though he also served at this time as interpreter for Col. Return J. Meigs, the American agent to the Cherokees. Meigs, an old soldier who had fought against the French and who was known as White Eagle among the Indians for his thatch of silvery hair, had the knack of judging character, and he appreciated Charles Hicks, whom he would later call "a man of as much information as anyone in the nation."[26] Hicks also received warm praise from a Moravian missionary who described him as "a very sensible and cultured half Indian. He is well versed in English literature and quite familiar with the better English authors. . . . He has a small library of English books. He is an able judge of matters pertaining to the political affairs of the Indians and has an understanding of their ways and seems to know what is best for them. His concept of matters spiritual and his sympathetic approach to them is unusual in this country."[27] Hicks reciprocated the esteem of the Moravians and became in time their first convert. Meanwhile his early political activities associated him with the faction led by James Vann.

Vann, the son of a white trader among the Cherokees, was one of the most intemperate characters in the nation. He ran a prosperous trading post and could support more than one wife, but his disposition showed a savage streak, and before his coming to a violent end, his hands would drip with blood, including that of a brother-in-law whom he shot in a duel. He hog-tied the next man who presumed to live with his sister and gave him seventy lashes. On suspecting that a certain white woman had stolen from him, he extracted a confession by having her strung up by the thumbs. In all he was a thoroughly godless man, and yet he approved of the civilizing influence of the Moravians; he had even helped them in 1801 to found a school in Spring Place. Three years later he built the most imposing house in the Cherokee country, a double-story red-brick mansion, with fireplaces at both ends and with elegant porticoes in the front and rear. Here he kept gargantuan supplies of brandy and whiskey and dealt drinks like a lord to his followers.

He was himself frequently in his cups and when drunk was liable to turn vicious and become as deadly as a water moccasin.

Vann was only a town chief, but he had "great private influence on the nation,"[28] and was therefore cultivated by the federal government. He doubtless received a "gift" from Colonel Meigs in connection with the treaty that opened a federal pike through the Cherokee country, a road which passed his holdings and from which he profited greatly. Still, as John Howard Payne would later observe, "With all his errors, [Vann] was . . . a patriot." His faction favored civilization and the advancement of the Cherokee Nation and jealously opposed the exploitation of the Indians by the whites. The Ridge joined this group, and some of his most notable deeds during the first decade of the nineteenth century—or what Payne would call his "more Roman days"—were done under Vann's influence.[29]

Meanwhile, the precarious unity of the Cherokees, which the murder of Old Tassel had produced and which the death of Dragging Canoe had furthered, seemed in danger of foundering on the issue of civilization versus the old ways. The crack-up became more imminent when the controversy assumed a geographical alignment, the Upper Cherokees accepting American help and advice while the Lower Towns shunned it except where it concerned the raising of livestock. The Lower Cherokees suspected that, in pressing their program, the Americans had an ulterior purpose—the acquisition of land. Some of them suggested that migration across the Mississippi, beyond the reach of civilization, might be the solution to their dilemma, and in taking that tack, redheaded Will of Willstown snorted that "Congress was scratching after every bit of rackoon skin in the nation that was big enough to cover a squaw's ———; that their hunting was nearly over, and after that their land was the next object."[30] Even proponents of civilization like The Ridge could see that the land was always the object of the Americans; that Congress wished to civilize the Indians not so much for the Indian's welfare as to replace his hunting and fishing with agriculture and stock raising so that, needing less country for hunting grounds, he would have more to cede. Each new treaty meant new cessions of land.

Three cessions were made in 1798—a tract in North Carolina and two in Tennessee, including hunting grounds between Clinch River and Cumberland Mountain. In 1804 the Cherokees signed away a small parcel in Georgia known as Wafford Settlement. All these surrenders aroused resentment in a large number of the Indians. But the dealings between the commissioners of the United States and certain Cherokee chiefs in October, 1805, set less well with the people than did any prior arrangement. Prominent in all the negotiations was the chieftain Doublehead, who had become Speaker of the Nation in 1796. His aggressive personality overshadowed that of Little Turkey, then the principal chief, and he became a spokesman for the Cherokees in the talks with the federal government.[31]

It was common knowledge that Doublehead had prospered as a result of the transactions of 1798. He had acquired a stable of blooded horses, and about two dozen slaves worked his lands. He had probably received another bribe in 1804, and his public image was not improved by his insolence. Thus his popularity was low when he entered talks with the U.S. commissioners at Tellico, Tennessee, in 1805. It would have been even lower had the Cherokees known that the secretary of war had instructed his agents to deal specifically with Doublehead, on the assumption he could always be bought.[32] The land cessions he and his deputation made on this occasion were highly unpopular. The major portion was a vast territory north of the Tennessee, stretching from the Hiwassee to Muscle Shoals. It contained the best hunting grounds in the Cherokee domain—the "wilderness," including the Cumberland Plateau and parts of Kentucky.

The resentment grew more bitter still when news leaked out that a secret agreement, unsanctioned by the Cherokee council, had reserved two tracts for Doublehead's use at the mouths of the Clinch and Hiwassee rivers. To make matters worse, a similar reserve at the mouth of Duck River was held for Tahlonteskee, Doublehead's kinsman. As a result, many Cherokees considered Doublehead a traitor. His leasing of farmlands to white men on the tracts he had secured at Muscle Shoals through the treaty he had signed at Washington in December, 1806, added fuel to the fire.[33]

Moreover, another land deal with Colonel Meigs was brewing in the summer of 1807.[34] But Doublehead's land manipulations were only one reason for his having become the most abhorred chief in the nation. "As he sought office with selfish views," McKenney and Hall wrote, "he very naturally abused it, and made himself odious by his arbitrary conduct. He not only executed the laws according to his own pleasure, but caused innocent men to be put to death who thwarted his views. The chiefs and the people began alike to fear him."[35]

Certain influential men—the Vann faction led the movement—determined that he should die for his crimes. The Ridge, Alexander Saunders, and James Vann were "selected" as his executioners. The Ridge had detested Doublehead since the outrage at Cavett's Station, but Vann had a family score to settle. Doublehead had married the sister of his favorite wife and had treated her brutally, having beaten her while pregnant till she died. The Vanns regarded the death as murder; revenge became a paramount issue in their household. Vann's wife had even vowed to seek vengeance with her own hands, and she pushed her husband to act. He was still incensed over a row he had had with Doublehead in Washington when he had called the Speaker a traitor. "High words [had] ensued," according to Payne, "and dirks were drawn; but the parties were separated and no blood was shed."[36] Now, however, Vann volunteered to execute the "traitorous murderer" with the help of Saunders and The Ridge. The three decided to stage the execution at the August meeting of the Cherokees to collect the tribal annuity from the American agent.

On the way to the agency at Hiwassee, Vann fell ill and could not proceed. He yielded "the honor of destroying Doublehead." to Saunders and The Ridge,[37] and they decided to eliminate the chief not as a wife-killer but as a traitor and a lawless speculator in Cherokee lands. On reaching Hiwassee, The Ridge went with Saunders to McIntosh's tavern to wait for Doublehead's arrival. While they waited, the chief paddled up to Hiwassee in his canoe and, without their knowledge, rode off on horseback to a ball-play three miles away. He did not return to town till long after dark, and when he entered the tavern, he seemed excited, half drunk. There was a bandage on his hand. An old white man named John Rogers began to revile him.

Doublehead replied: "You live by sufferance among us. I've never seen you in council or on the warpath. You have no place among the chiefs. Hush and interfere no more with me."[38]

Suddenly someone seized a candle that flickered on the table and held it close to Doublehead's face. A moment later The Ridge darted up and, blowing the candle out, shot Doublehead through the jaw near the lower part of the ear. In the darkness he and Saunders slipped from the tavern, thinking their purpose had been achieved—that the traitor was dead.

Soon they heard that Doublehead had killed another man that afternoon. The ball-play had drawn a large crowd, and at dusk while the spectators had milled from the field, excited over the bloodiness of the game, "the whiskey kegs of the whites [had] met them in every direction."[39] Many were soon tipsy, including Double-head and a warrior named Bone-Polisher,[40] who had approached the chief as he sat astride his horse and, grasping the bridle, had called him traitor. Doublehead ordered him to go away or he would kill him, but Bone-Polisher became more abusive. Doublehead drew his pistol; he threw the priming out, intending merely to snap it at his assailant to intimidate him. But enough priming remained to discharge the pistol. Bone-Polisher retaliated with a blow from his tomahawk, chopping off one of Doublehead's thumbs, "all but some skin by which it hung."[41] After that Doublehead lashed out with his pistol and drove the cock so deep into Bone-Polisher's skull that the warrior died. And so more blood had flowed to justify The Ridge's act, if it needed vindication.

But The Ridge and Saunders also learned that Doublehead was still alive, though his jaw was shattered, with the ball lodged in his neck. They heard that during the night the tavernkeeper had moved the chief to his house, thrusting him in secret through a back window; that, later still, Doublehead was spirited off to a safer place. It took Saunders and The Ridge till after dawn to find the new hiding spot—the loft of a Mr. Black, who taught in Gideon Blackburn's school. With war whoops they rushed into the room where Doublehead lay, two men of Bone-Polisher's clan joining their company. As they approached, the wounded chief sprang up, drew a dirk, and caught at a pistol, but "the sheet clung to his limbs & clogged his heels."[42] The Ridge and Saunders leveled their guns at him, but both missed fire. Doublehead sprang on The Ridge and grappled at him with a desperate strength, till Saunders drove his tomahawk into the chief's forehead with such force that it took two hands and a foot against the cloven skull to pry it loose. A third Indian pounded the head with a spade and crushed it to a pulp.[43]

After the killing, The Ridge "addressed the crowd who were drawn together by this act of violence, and explained his authority and his reasons."[44] No one mourned the slaughtered chief, unless it was Meigs, who had a treaty to conclude; nor was there any re-taliation. The consensus was that, however crudely, justice had been done.

Doublehead's death on August 9, 1807, benefited the Cherokees in a number of ways, including increased tribal unity. It led to the

entire abolition of clan revenge at the Council of Broomstown on
September 11, 1808, which abrogation was reaffirmed in 1810 at
Oostanaula. As most Cherokees felt that the destruction of Doublehead was justified and that his relatives should not be forced by
clan responsibility to take revenge, there was an incentive to remove the question from the jurisdiction of the clans and base punishment on a sounder principle than mere retaliation. Gideon Blackburn, spurred by the fact that "the execution" had taken place in
the house of one of his teachers, encouraged sentiments for reform
among a number of principal men. And when the Cherokees came
together at Broomstown, they took pains to negate blood revenge
by the clans. In reporting the reform to Jedidiah Morse, Blackburn
declared that "All criminal accusations must be established by testimony; the infliction of punishment is made a governmental transaction." This provision in itself proscribed clan retaliation. But the
question was resolved even more specifically. "One law," wrote Blackburn, "is that no murderer shall be punished until he has been
proved guilty before the council."[45] Thus, The Ridge was legally
immune from retaliation from Doublehead's clan, though enforcement of the new provisions was another matter.

That there was no disposition to bring The Ridge to account
before the National Council for Doublehead's death was demonstrated by his appointment to the Lighthorse Guard. This consisted
of two "regulating companies" of six men each—a captain, a lieutenant, and four privates.[46] The guard's duty was called "riding the
judicial circuit," to enforce the laws of the nation as "the judges,
jurors, and executioners of justice." Such responsibilities were not
easily assumed in a primitive society, and the Lighthorse Guard
necessarily consisted of persons of courage and judgment. "Major
Ridge," wrote McKenney and Hall, "was placed at the head of this
corps, whose duty it was to ride through the nation, to take cog-
nisance of all crimes and breaches of law, and to decide all con-
troversies between individuals. In the unsettled state of the community, the want of forms, and the absence of precedent, much was
left to their discretion; and after all, these decisions were enforced
rather by the number, energy, and physical power of the judges,
than through any respect paid to the law itself."[47]

One incident, perhaps apocryphal, illustrated the necessity of
acting on rapid judgment. While hunting turkeys one day, The
Ridge stole quietly through the woods near a spring a mile or so
from his house. Suddenly, while looking through a screen of foliage,

he recognized Colonel James Blair, a law enforcement officer from Oconee Station, South Carolina, approaching on horseback and leading an extra horse on leash. At the spring were two half-bloods, Wiley Hyde and Tom Phillips, both notorious lawbreakers. The Ridge watched the colonel tether his horses and approach the Cherokees where they drank the cool spring water. Suddenly the half-bloods covered him with their rifles.

Colonel Blair threw up his hands. The Ridge heard him exclaim, "Don't shoot! I'm a friend with some whiskey on my hip."

The Indians relented for a moment. Then the one named Hyde raised his rifle, cocked it, and was about to shoot Blair in the chest. The Ridge made his decision in an instant, raised his own gun, and fired. Hyde fell on his face in the water, and instantly Colonel Blair covered Phillips with his pistol. When The Ridge came up, his intuition was confirmed: Blair had trailed the half-bloods from Oconee Station, where they had stolen two horses from a settler. They would have added murder to their crimes had The Ridge refrained from shooting first. In this instance he had to act as judge and executioner at the same moment.

He helped the colonel tie Phillips and place him on one of the stolen horses. The dead man they buried 150 yards from the spring. The Ridge then watched the colonel start for South Carolina with the prisoner. "This act," according to Judge John W. H. Underwood, "gained for Major Ridge an honorable name among the pale faces, who ever after looked at him to redress wrongs committed by members of his tribe."[48]

Meanwhile Colonel Meigs, who had reasons for feeling that "Doublehead's death . . . had a greater effect on the concerns of the white citizens than that of any other Indian,"[49] proceeded to promote the treaty he had planned with the dead chieftain. He succeeded in reaching a secret agreement with none other than Black Fox, the principal chief, who accepted a "gift" of one thousand dollars, a new rifle, and an annual allowance of one hundred dollars. Several other chiefs were "influenced" also, and on September 7, 1807, Meigs and his fellow commissioner, General James Robertson, met the Cherokee headmen at Chickasaw Old Fields, near Muscle Shoals, to adjust the boundaries of the land ceded by the treaty signed in Washington during the previous December. The chips flew in favor of the United States, and Meigs cynically wrote the Secretary of War that the chiefs "well deserved [the] silent consideration" they had received in view of the explanations they would have to make to their tribesmen.[50] The Cherokees were not long in learning that the treaty was a "cheat put upon the chiefs,"[51] and their suspicions extended to another plan that would have doubtless worked in their favor. Vann's faction, including The Ridge, was in the forefront of the objectors.

The arrangement involved the establishment of an ironworks inside the Cherokee domain. Earlier in the year, Colonel Elias Earle of South Carolina had proposed to the War Department that he was prepared to build and manage the works if the Cherokees would cede the land. He had prospected through the nation and found a suitable site, a tract at the mouth of Chickamauga Creek, convenient to waterpower, iron ore, and limestone. Negotiations were therefore opened with the chiefs, and some perceived the advantages that Earle's project would have for the nation. At a meeting held at the agency on December 2, Colonel Meigs secured an agreement for a cession of six square miles to be made to the federal government. It was planned that Earle would in turn lease the land from the United States and erect the buildings for the works.[52]

Believing all would go according to speculation, Earle gathered workmen at Greenville, South Carolina, and started them out for Chickamauga with a wagon train of supplies and equipment. He did not count on the spirit of resistance that worked in such men as Vann and The Ridge, who imagined sinister motives behind the project. No sooner had word arrived that the train was rolling over the federal pike than The Ridge resolved to intercept it.

With a band of thirty horsemen he lay in wait along the turnpike, and when the wagons failed to appear, he led his followers along the road. Not far from the house of Vann's sister he found the caravan where another party of Cherokees under a half-blood named Will Crittington had stopped it. The wagons, manned by eight Negroes, had been detained for three days, but the leader, a white named William Brown, had refused to turn back, in spite of a secret warning from Vann's sister. She had told him that his life was in danger from her brother's men.

The Ridge stepped up to Brown and snatched his gun and fired it into the air. Then one of his braves brandished a tomahawk in Brown's face, striking the white man's cheek, but the blade was dull and no blood was drawn. Crittington caught the brave's arm before he could strike again, then stood ready to serve as interpreter for The Ridge, who said "he intended to have a good deal of talk with the white man."[53] The Ridge ordered Earle's foreman to proceed no farther. He said that most of the Cherokees opposed the building of the ironworks and were determined that the train should not pass through their country.[54]

Brown asked leave of the Indians to proceed as far as Coosawatie, where he expected to find a passport from the agent awaiting him. But The Ridge was adamant. He insisted that the train turn back. In the face of such determined opposition, Brown's will crumbled. He sold the tools and equipment at a sacrifice to anybody who would buy, then began to retrace his way.[55]

An ironworks would have doubtless served Cherokee progress. The State of Tennessee, however, refused to ratify the treaty ceding the land at Chickamauga to the federal government, and the entire scheme collapsed. Colonel Earle filed a claim with the secretary of war for losses suffered when The Ridge turned back his wagon train. He did not hesitate to pad his accounts, but they were pared down at the insistence of Colonel Meigs. Six years after the train was intercepted, Earle collected $985 in Washington, and the amount was charged against the Cherokee annuity.[56]

Meanwhile the difference between the Upper and Lower Cherokees continued to grow. As the Lower Towns had secured control of the tribal organization, they were favored in the distribution of annuity funds. The exasperation of the Upper Towns became so acute that early in 1808 a deputation of chiefs went to Washington to place their complaints before the president. "They state," the secretary of war summarized to Colonel Meigs, "that for several years their part of the nation has received scarcely anything from the U.S., either as annuities or for lands sold; that the great chiefs generally live in the lower part of the Nation, and after receiving the Annuities, &c., they divide nearly the whole among those of their own neighborhood."[57] The Great Father, Mr. Jefferson, explained that the distribution of the funds, once the agent had turned them over to authorized representatives of the tribe, was purely a Cherokee affair, and he could only instruct the agent to use his good offices to suggest redress of grievances to the principal chiefs.

As an answer to the dilemma, Alexander Saunders had proposed that the nation be formally divided into two parts, an idea the deputation placed before the president. "[An] object of their journey," the secretary of war reported, "was to propose a division of the lands of the Nation between the upper and lower Cherokees

by a fixed line; and then to have certain tracts, for farms, laid off
for each family to be farmers; to be under the jurisdiction and laws
of the U.S. & to become actual Citizens."[58] The agent was instructed
to explore the possibility of fixing such a line, but the president
also raised the question of exchanging lands for territory across the
Mississippi for those who were still inclined to follow the hunt.

The agent let the first proposal languish; he was correspond-
ingly assiduous in pursuing the second. While the Upper Cherokees tried to reach an agreement with the Lower Towns on the
dividing line, Meigs promoted the idea of removal to such chiefs as
Black Fox, The Glass, Tahlonteskee, and John Jolly. He was so
successful in his sales campaign, employing his usual means of per-
suasion—quiet bribery—that at a clandestine council of those in
favor of emigration Black Fox appointed a new delegation composed
of river chiefs to visit Washington. Their purpose—to sign a treaty
for the exchange of land. At the fall council of the nation, held at
Hiwassee, Black Fox brought the scheme into the open, having first
entrusted to Tahlonteskee, leader of the recently appointed deputation, his message to the president. In substance it ran: "Tell our
Great Father, the President, that our game has disappeared, and we
wish to follow it to the West. We are his friends, and we hope he
will grant our petition, which is to remove our people towards the
setting sun. But we shall give up a fine country, fertile in soil,
abounding in water-courses, and well adapted for the residence of
white people. For all this we must have a good price."[59]

All that was needed was a council vote to sanction the purpose
of the deputation, and Black Fox hoped that by taking the people
by surprise, a vote of approval might be engineered. He seemed to
be gaining his objective. The council sat in silence, "apparently
awed or cajoled into compliance." The Ridge looked on with indignation, and when he saw the old men fixed in their seats, he knew
that someone else must speak, or the day would be lost. In great
excitement he rose from his place among the younger chiefs and
spoke:

My friends, you have heard the talk of the principal chief. He
points to the region of the setting sun as the future habitation of this
people. As a man he has a right to give his opinion; but the opinion
he has given as the chief of this nation is not binding; it was not
formed in council in the light of day, but was made up in a corner—
to drag this people, without their consent, from their own country, to
the dark land of the setting sun. I resist it here in my place as a man,

as a chief, as a Cherokee, having the right to be consulted in a matter of such importance. What are your heads placed on your bodies for, but to think, and if to think, why should you not be consulted? I scorn this movement of a few men to unsettle the nation and trifle with our attachment to the land of our forefathers! Look abroad over the face of this country—along the rivers, the creeks, and their branches, and you behold the dwellings of the people who repose in content and security. Why is this grand scheme projected to lead away to another country the people who are happy here? I, for one, abandon my respect for the will of a chief, and regard only the will of thousands of our people. Do I speak without the response of any heart in this assembly, or do I speak as a free man to men who are free and know their rights? I pause to hear.[60]

Black Fox had counted on no one's raising an objection. Now he knew by the cheers that greeted the close of The Ridge's speech that his efforts to stampede the council were doomed to failure— and not merely that. Three chiefs—The Glass, Tahlonteskee, and Black Fox himself—were broken on the spot, and though Black Fox was reinstated at a later council, he felt disgraced for the rest of his life.[61]

The council proceeded to choose a new delegation, six men, of whom The Ridge was one.[62] They started for Washington City sometime in November, probably on horseback. The first lap of their journey was over the Georgia Road. They struck through South Carolina by way of Greenville, through North Carolina via Salem (the settlement of the benign but industrious Moravians, where a peculiar dialect of German was heard more often than English), then across Virginia to the straggling, marsh-bound capital beside the Potomac River. They put up at one of the boarding-houses at the foot of a grassy hill where sheep grazed between the paths climbing crookedly up to the Capitol. Though still unfinished, it was doubtless the most imposing building The Ridge had ever seen, with its marble walls gleaming in the pale winter sunshine. A mile or so away the miry course of Pennsylvania Avenue ran perilously close to a swamp, past the Executive Mansion, a bland-looking building with walls plastered pink and with pillars of white hugging the front wall in half relief. The center of the Cherokees' interest, however, was the War Department building, where presided Henry Dearborn, a not-too-competent senior general momentarily at the helm. No doubt the Cherokees were much more knowledgeable about affairs at Washington than officials there conceived. As an acute observer later wrote:

Many of them feel much interest in the affairs of the government of the United States, particularly such as the election of the President, for whom they entertain much respect and veneration. [They] hail him as their "Great Father" and actually look to him for the exercise of parental care over their future destiny as a nation. They also feel a deep interest in the appointment of the Secretary of War—that officer being required in the course of his official duties to have a supervision over the affairs of the Indian tribes connected with the government of the United States. . . . To such of the members [of Congress] as they consider to be friendly to the Indian interest, they feel a most sincere gratitude, and become enthusiastic in their praises. But to those who, from their acts on the floor of Congress, appear to be unfriendly to the interest and welfare of the Indians, they feel a bitter indignation; and they are slow to forget either an injury or a benefit.[63]

Such sophistication had already begun to show itself among the Cherokee leaders, to a lesser degree at first, but had officials in Washington taken as shrewd an interest in the Cherokees as the Cherokees did in them, they would have suffered less surprise at the competence with which these Indians conducted their affairs.

The deputation, like the people it represented, was split into two factions, each with a separate purpose. The delegates from the Lower Towns sought to exchange the lands they occupied for a wilderness tract on the Arkansas River. Those from the Upper Towns, including The Ridge, looked to founding an elective government in the eastern part of the nation. They anticipated adopting such laws of the United States as were best suited to their current condition. "The parties who made these objects their choice," wrote Colonel Meigs, who was with the group in Washington, "pursued them without anxiety, or any kind of collision either on the road or in the city. . . . They had no written instructions to my recollection. They had therefore plenipotentiary power—the interest of the nation was confided, & safely confided, to their ability and integrity."[64]

On December 21 they prepared a word of greeting for President Jefferson, all of them signing with their marks. The talk was put into English by their interpreter.

Father—The underwritten, chiefs of the Cherokee Nation instructed by their national council to come to the city of Washington & there to take by the hand their father the President, & express to him in behalf of their nation their sincere sentiments of gratitude and to say to him—that, for nearly eight years they have experienced his protecting and fostering hand, under which they progressed in agriculture & domestic manufactures much beyond their own expectations or the

expectations of their white Brethren of the United States & that by the
schools many of their children have made great advancement in the
usefull facts of english education, such as reading, writing, and arithmetic—that by means of these acquisitions the desireable work of civilization advances & will in future be accelerated & knowledge diffused
more easily and widely amongst their people provided the same measures
shall be [pursued] by your successor in office, which they please themselves will be the case, & that he will also hold them fast by the hand
& that the magnanimity of the U. States will not suffer ten thousand
human beings [to] be lost between whom & the white people the great
Spirit has made no difference, except in the tint of their skins, for they
believe that the great Spirit loves his red children as well as his white
children & looks with equal eye on the works of his hands, & that
their final destination is the same.

Father—

When you retire from the Administration of the great business which
has been committed to your hand by our white Brethren, a conscious-
ness of upright intentions will be your reward: a reward beyond the
lash of contingencies—that the great Spirit will add yet many years to
your usefull life & that it may be happy is the affectionate wish of the
red people whom we represent.[65]

A postscript stated that they would communicate their "particular objects" through the secretary of war. This they did. The
president replied in writing, though not before he had granted the
deputation a personal audience. The long, gaunt figure of the president, with reddish hair grown gray, left a deep impression on The
Ridge, as did the city itself and the civilized towns through which
the deputation had passed. As his second term drew to a close,
Jefferson maintained a solicitous attitude toward Indians of every
tribe, and many delegations had been called to Washington to hear
his parting words. He liked to remind them of how he had tried
to check the flow of liquor into their midst, the firewater that was
so dangerous to their welfare, and of how he had always fostered
peace and friendship, and looked on the red men with the same
goodwill that he held for his fellow whites. What he said in person
to the Cherokees on this occasion was doubtless mirrored in the
dignified replies to their proposals which he committed to them in
writing.

To his "children," the delegates from the Upper Towns, he
gave assurance that he had carefully considered the talks they had
delivered through the secretary of war. "You inform me," Jefferson
wrote, reviewing their words, "of your anxious desires to engage in
the industrious pursuits of agriculture and civilized life; that finding

it impracticable to induce the nation at large to join in this you wish a line of separation to be established between the upper and lower towns so as to include all the waters of Hiwassee in your part; and that having thus contracted your society within narrower limits, you propose, within these, to begin the establishment of fixed laws and regular government." The president made it clear that he approved these goals, but he also emphasized the need for the division to rest on the mutual consent of both parts of the nation. He offered, if necessary, the services of American surveyors to run and mark such a boundary line.

The regular administration of laws, adapted from those of the United States, struck him as more difficult to achieve than the establishment of a dividing line. "Who," he asked, "is to determine which of our laws suit your condition, and shall be in force with you? All of you being equally free, no one has the right to say what shall be law for the others." He then gave the delegates a succinct explanation of the American system of representative government, and suggested that each Cherokee town, along with the surrounding countryside, elect delegates to a central council by means of a majority vote. The Cherokees had, of course, their National Council; the new feature in the president's suggestions pertained to the method of choosing the members, more regularly democratic on the whole than the usual haphazard means employed by the Cherokees. Further, he advised the deputies to be guided by the counsel of Colonel Meigs, who should be invited to attend the council as a consultant on American law. Meigs, he added, would instruct the delegates in parliamentary procedure, "so as to preserve order, and obtain the vote of every member fairly." The president advised further: "This council can make a law for giving to every head of a family a separate parcel of land, which, when he had built upon and improved it, shall belong to him and his descendants forever, and which the nation shall have no right to sell from under his feet. They will determine, too, what punishment shall be inflicted for every crime."

But once such laws were adopted, who would execute them? It might be best, Jefferson thought, if each town and neighborhood surrounding it were to choose by majority vote the best and wisest men "to be judges in all differences, and to execute the law according to their own judgment." The president closed by saying his words were only suggestions for the consideration of the Upper Towns, but he wished the delegates success in their "laudable endeavors to save the remains of [their] nation by adopting industrious occupations and a government of regular law."[66]

All in all, however, he was more interested in the proposal of the Lower Towns, since, if brought to pass, it would mean more land for white settlement. He gave the "river delegates" his solemn pledge that, should their people choose to migrate beyond the Mississippi, they would never be bothered there again; their new homes would be theirs forevermore.[67]

Both groups were pleased with Jefferson's replies and returned home in January, 1809, to bring his messages to their people. As for The Ridge, McKenney and Hall noted: "The advantage of traveling through the United States was not thrown away upon this intelligent and liberal-minded Indian. . . . He returned with a mind enlarged by travel, and with a renewed ardour in the cause of civilization."[68]

He now found that Vann's faction was leaderless. Vann had grown more captious, more irresponsible, more homicidal when in his cups. He had killed one white man and wounded another, making him a cripple. He had even turned on his best friend, Alexander Saunders, saying slanderous things about him. "The bottle was in one hand," according to reports of Vann's last hour, "and he was lifting the cup of whiskey to his lips with the other. The door, which swung loosely, was silently pressed open by the point of a rifle. In an instant James Vann was dead, and no one [knew] his slayer."[69] No one moved to discover or to punish the killer. In all probability Vann's friends felt relief that he would no longer cause them anxiety. Charles Hicks assumed leadership of the faction, having been recently fired as agency interpreter on the grounds of "insolence" in the wake of certain Meigsian manipulations of the river chiefs. The Ridge could work with Hicks, a quiet and reflective man, and they formed a close and lasting alliance to promote their people's advancement.

Meanwhile no agreement could be reached concerning the proposed dividing line. The majority of the Lower Cherokees developed a sudden love for their present homes and voted against migration to the wilderness on the Arkansas. Only a small number decided to leave at this time, under the leadership of Tahlonteskee, who, in view of Doublehead's fate, thought of removal as an expedient good for his health. In the fall council of 1809, at Willstown, the Upper and Lower Cherokees mended their differences and notified the agent of their solidarity. "Friend and Brother," the chiefs wrote on September 27: "It has now been a long time that we have been much confused and divided in our opinions but now we have settled our affair to the satisfaction of both parties and become as one— You will now hear from us not [as] from the lower Towns nor [as from] the upper Towns but [as] from the whole Cherokee nation." The chiefs explained that, since it was so hard to accomplish results in a gathering so cumbersome as the entire council, they had appointed a National Committee composed of "thirteen men to manage [their] national affairs."[70] The Ridge's name was third on the list.*

Under the new dispensation The Ridge continued in his office as judge in charge of the Lighthorse Guard. Meanwhile he also became an ambassador to the Creek Nation and had, along with the aged interpreter Chulioa, the status of a chief in the Creek council. His several offices placed him in a strategic position to help shape the destiny of the Cherokees in the following months, as the threat of war intensified between the United States and Great Britain. Such a development would have grave consequences for the Indian tribes of both the North and the South, especially for the Creeks and Cherokees in the South.

*The other names: John Lowrey, John McIntosh, Richard Brown, Turtle-at-Home, Charles Hicks, John Walker, George M. Waters, Thomas Pettite, Doghead, George Lowrey, Tur[key?] Cock, and Sour John. Two years later the committee was altered to include a few more older men. The new list included the names of Chulioa, Sour Mush, Wasausee, Duck, John McLemore, John Lowrey, John Walker, George Lowrey, John McIntosh, Seekeekee, The Ridge, and Charles Hicks.

3 · THE CREEK WAR

I N 1811 rumors of war made the Cherokees and their Indian
neighbors apprehensive, for wars between the whites inevitably
affected the tribes in the forest. The Creeks were especially
restless.

As ambassador to the Creeks, The Ridge was one of forty-six
Cherokees who attended a council in September at Tuckabatchee,
the Creek capital on the Tallapoosa. Ostensibly the Cherokee mission was to arrange a truce in the mutual horse stealing that irri-
tated both tribes. Without question the real motive was to hear the
talks of a delegation from the North led by the Shawnee chief
Tecumseh, who had just spent several weeks among the Chickasaws
and the Choctaws. As his mother was a Muskogee, Tecumseh was
always welcome among the Creeks. He had won their respect while
fighting beside them in the border wars. He had returned in 1809
to prepare the ground for an ideal scheme that filled his mind, a
confederation of tribes to match the "seventeen council fires" of the
Americans. Now in 1811 he was in the South again, and rumors
that he would attend the Creek council had brought five thousand
persons to Tuckabatchee, including Choctaws and Chickasaws as
well as The Ridge and his fellow Cherokees.[1]

On arriving, Tecumseh and his company filed into the town
square in a dignified procession. They were a mixed lot—six Shawnees, two expatriot Creeks, six Kickapoos, and six from a tribe in
the far Northwest, probably Sioux.[2] Tradition would later picture
Tecumseh and his Shawnees as all dressed alike. They wore buck-
skin hunting shirts, loincloths, leggings, and moccasins with beads
and fringes. Each one's hair was plaited in strands. Their temples
were shaved, and hawk and eagle feathers adorned their heads—all,
that is, except Tecumseh's. The chief had chosen crane feathers

for his hair, one white, one stained vermilion. All wore silver bands around their arms. Under their eyes semicircles of vermilion flared toward their cheekbones; a dot of red was daubed at each temple, while large smears glistened like blood upon their chests.[3] They silently took their places in the council.

That night, around a fire in the center of the square, they danced the Dance of the Lakes, a wild and rousing exhibition, a spirited pantomime of war, in which Tecumseh himself took part in spite of his lamed and bowed leg. He was naked now, as were his comrades, except for breechclout and moccasins of deer hide. The dance was a fit prelude for incendiary oratory, but Tecumseh did not speak that night, nor the next day, nor even the next. Indeed, the normal business of the council delayed the talk for more than a week. Then Colonel Hawkins, the aged and ailing agent, left for his home on the Flint River, a move he could make without missing anything important, since the council was riddled with his spies. Finally, about September 30, the time for Tecumseh's talk arrived. He chose to counter the pleas of the Sioux chiefs, who proposed that the Creeks take the warpath at once against the Americans.[4] His hazel eyes shone; his resonant voice was eloquent.

Tecumseh's oratory, according to Lewis Cass, later Secretary of War, revealed his genius: "It was the utterance of a great mind. . . . When he spoke . . . on the glorious theme that animated all his actions, his fine countenance lighted up, his firm and erect frame swelled with deep emotions, which his own stern dignity could scarcely repress; every feature and gesture had its meaning, and language flowed tumultuously and swiftly, from the fountains of his soul."[5]

He spoke in Shawnee before the multitude at Tuckabatchee, and Creek disciples turned his talk into Muskogee. He declared the time was not yet ripe for war, whatever his brothers the Sioux might say. He advised the Creeks to keep the peace, though it was plain he hated the whites. He reminded the Creeks how the whites had usurped their lands, and he dwelt on the pressures that the United States exerted for more land and the consequences of that steady encroachment for the Indian—the diminution of his numbers and possibly even in time the extermination of the race.[6] His answer to this fateful dilemma was not immediate, uncoordinated war, however, but the formation of a comprehensive confederation of tribes so that the red men could face the whites with solidarity whenever the proper time should come.

"I do not want to be at war [now] with the Americans," he
said in substance, "but to be at peace with them." He counseled
the Creeks to do no injury to the whites, "to be in friendship with
them; not to steal even a bell from any one of any color. Let the
white people on this continent manage their affairs their own way.
Let the red people [also] manage their affairs their own way." This
he told them "in the name of the British."[7] The great burden of his
talk was of his conversations with the Great Spirit—as well as the
revelations his brother Tenskwatawa the Prophet had received—
about how the Indians should manage their affairs. The principal
message Tecumseh preached was veiled behind his talk of peace.
In essence it was a call to reaction, a plea to return to the Indians'
ancient ways. Only then, and only after the Indian tribes had been
welded into an effective confederacy, would they be able to resist
the whites with any hope of success.*

After the speech, The Big Warrior, head chief of all the Creeks,
the hugest man in the nation and "as spotted as a leopard,"[8] tried
to learn more precisely what Tecumseh meant. And after further
conversation he reached the conclusion—or so he reported—that the
emissary was either a madman or a liar whose talk deserved to be
forgotten, save insofar as it called for peace.[9] To The Big Warrior
it was unthinkable for the Creeks to abandon the road to civilization.
It was also unthinkable for the Creeks to go to war, and he needed
no Shawnee to tell him that. It was said that Tecumseh took offense
at The Big Warrior's skeptical attitude. It was also said that he
looked The Big Warrior in the eye and declared his blood was
white—that since The Big Warrior did not believe the Great Spirit
had sent Tecumseh, he would leave for home at once, and when he

---

*It is often stated that Tecumseh preached war and that his doctrines propelled
the Creeks, as well as the northern Indians, into immediate war with the whites.
But that his utterances to the Creeks in 1811 were peaceable and cautionary in
tenor is shown by the résumé of his talk, as forwarded to Colonel Meigs by the
Creek council, and especially by such a passage as: "It is probably that Guns
will be fired at the Northward but we advise you to lie still. If there should be
any attempts to take away your lands it may be that some of these will help you
but we advise you to live in peace and raise your children." Meigs to Secretary
Eustis, 4 Dec. 1811, in National Archives, RG 75, Records of the Cherokee Agency
in Tennessee (M-208, Roll 5). It was instead Tenskwatawa the Prophet who,
during Tecumseh's absence in the South, led the Shawnees into battle contrary
to Tecumseh's plans. Once his people had begun to fight, however, Tecumseh
found it expedient, though against his better judgment, to follow the course set
by the Prophet. He accepted a brigadier generalship from the British and led the
northern Indians until his death at the battle of the Thames on October 5, 1813.

arrived there, he would stamp his foot and the earth would shake, and the tremors would jar down every house in Tuckabatchee.[10] But he would leave Seekaboo, his Creek interpreter, a prophet who would spread his gospel among the Creeks.

For all of Tecumseh's oratory concerning peace, the question remained about what his gospel really meant or where at least it would lead. That question Colonel Hawkins later raised, while at the same time he framed its answer: it meant little more, as events would finally prove, than

kill the old chiefs, friends to peace; kill the cattle, the hogs, the fowls; do not work, destroy the wheels and looms, throw away your ploughs, and everything used by the Americans. Sing "the song of the Indians of the northern Lakes, and dance their dance." Shake your war clubs, shake yourselves; you will frighten the Americans, their arms will drop from their hands, the ground will become a bog, and mire them, and you may knock them on the head with your war clubs. I will be with you with my Shawanese, as soon as our friends the British are ready for us. Lift up the war club with your right hand, be strong, and I will come and shew you how to use it.[11]

Such was the deeper meaning behind Tecumseh's talk. And its reactionary spirit, its antagonism toward the civilization the Indians had acquired, and the danger of its leading in the end to war with the Americans, repelled the Cherokee visitors. They refused to associate Tecumseh's coming with the great comet that swept slowly across the sky, lighting up the heavens at night, a spectacle which held the backward and more ignorant Creeks in awe and doubtless prepared the way for Seekaboo's secret machinations. The Cherokees remained as skeptical as The Big Warrior of Tecumseh's claims and plans. As The Ridge and five other chiefs later informed President Madison: "We turned away our ears and never listened a moment to the orations of the enemies of our father."[12] Moreover, according to a later tradition, the Cherokees advised Tecumseh never to come to their people with his message or they would put him to death.[13] And without regret they watched him leave Tuckabatchee with his band.

On December 16, when they had returned home—in time to hear Colonel Meigs deride the Shawnee's presumption in advising the southern tribes about their lands—an earthquake struck at half past two in the morning. Never before in any man's memory had such a quake occurred. It damaged buildings; springs belched muddy or clouded water. Fantastic reports arrived from the West—for the disturbance seemed to focus near the settlement of New Madrid on the Mississippi—about how the water in the river had risen and fallen like a tide; how lake bottoms were elevated above the surrounding land; how the earth cracked in gigantic fissures and sulfurous fumes fouled the air; how flashes of lightning streaked from the earth, with noises like cannon fire; and how the ground felt hot to one's foot.[14] Many Cherokees were in a panic.

Even The Ridge worried lest the "prophets"—conjurers, wizards, or witches—had worked mighty spells that had affected the earth, or even lest the world were coming to an end. As the tremors returned at intervals week after week and month after month, he grew so concerned that he sought advice from Charles Hicks and then from John Gambold, the Moravian brother who ran the school at Spring Place. The missionary described the nature of earthquakes, which he asserted were part of God's plan, and his explanations allayed The Ridge's anxieties. Father Gambold had other arguments to puncture the claims of the prophets. How could their spells disturb the earth when they lacked the power even to improve their own condition? But the missionary could not forgo a short sermon, in which he said that quakes should serve as reminders to sinners and bring them to repent for their transgressions. Gambold wrote in the Spring Place diary:

After a period of meditative silence The Ridge exclaimed, "We are just too worthless." He then continued, "Now I will tell you what happened at Tellico, where Indians are killing each other in cold blood." He told us of a respected Cherokee . . . who had invited several Indians to his home for drinks and for dancing. An exhausted old man lay down on the floor to one side of the room and fell asleep. With a club the host killed him and then dragged the body to the fire and broiled it. For no special reason another one's skull was crushed with a club and his brains spilled out on the floor. Then he asked, "What do you think of this?" We told him the evil spirit had taken possession of the man. This afforded us the occasion for further conversation.[15]

After Gambold's reassurance The Ridge rode from Spring Place with his mind at comparative ease. He was all the more convinced that his people's future required civilization, more and greater civilization—not its vices but its virtues. Yet the continued quakes strengthened the hands of the more conservative Cherokees, and the enemies of civilization grew bolder in their agitation. Their stand received support from the hysteria that was now sweeping through the Creek Nation. At first the Dance of the Lakes had not appealed to even the most reactionary partisans, for under Creek custom, war dances were held only after battle, not before. But by Christmas of 1811, during the earthquake shocks, which the gullible took as reverberations from stamps of Tecumseh's heel to the north, small numbers of Creeks began to dance—numbers that grew as self-styled prophets made their influence felt. The movement flourished among the Alabamas to the south, and its power to affect others spread throughout the Creek confederacy.

The prophets were nurturing a plan of action brought from the North and covertly imparted by Seekaboo. They kept it secret from the chiefs but "let it mature among the opposers of Civilization and the young people," as Alexander Cornell, the Creek interpreter, observed when the frenzy had reached its peak. "From the confidence with which the prophets speak to their power and the source of it, their ability to punish all who reveal their secret, which they have ways of knowing, prevents the young people from communicating anything to their own families."[16] The agitators claimed command over lightning; their spells could change dry ground to bogs to swallow up their enemies; a wave of their hands could turn away bullets; the magic rings they made spelled death to all who wandered inside them.[17] With such means of inspiring dread, their movement was a vast, secret, dark intrigue, working toward explosive ends.

Aware of the fears and hatreds building up among the Creeks, and afraid lest they should lead to war against the United States, the Cherokee council assured Colonel Meigs of the abiding friendship of the Cherokees. At the same time, The Ridge induced the council to instruct Charles Hicks to send a friendly warning to the Creeks.[18] This Hicks managed to do sometime in April, 1812, saying that "the rumors of war which surrounded [them] would soon be verified, and if the Indians joined Great Britain against the United States, they would lose every foot of land; and if they joined the United States against Great Britain, they would lose no land, but would secure the friendship of the United States forever." It was sensible advice, to which the headmen of the Creeks, in ignorance of the prophets' plans, replied that "they were determined not to interfere in the wars of the white people, and should prepare the minds of their young people to be neighborly and friendly."[19] Neither progressive Cherokees nor the Americans were deceived by such professions, and few believed that all was well in the Creek Nation. The common feeling was soon expressed by Governor Willie Blount of Tennessee, who wrote to Andrew Jackson: "The chiefs hold peace councils, and the wild young men use the tomahawk."[20]

Certain Cherokees who balked at the advancement program had meanwhile proved responsive to the Creek contagion. "Some of the Cherokees dreamed dreams," wrote McKenney and Hall, "and others received, in various ways, communications from the Great Spirit, all tending to discredit the scheme of civilization."[21] Conservatives had arranged a great medicine dance at Oostanaula the year before, and after "a grand savage feast" the women began to dance with tortoise shells fastened to their ankles. Pebbles inside rattled in unison with their movements and with the beat "of their wild uncouth songs." One ancient warrior chanted about the glories of former days; many were doubtless awed by a feeling that the Great Spirit moved among them.

At that psychological moment a delegation from Coosawatie introduced a half-blood prophet called Charley, perhaps the conjuror pictured by John R. Ridge as the "old Cherokee magician, contemporary with Tecumseh, [who] inspired great dread from the fact that two demons attended him in the shape of . . . ferocious black wolves."[22] Hailing from the mountains, Charley insisted that he brought a message from the Great Spirit. The assembly received him with hushed respect, and he was led to a seat not far from the bench where The Ridge sat. The people were eager to hear what Charley had to say; all were silent when he rose. The Great Spirit was displeased, he cried, that the Cherokees had taken up the white men's ways. "They had mills, clothes, feather beds, and tables— worse still, they had books, and domestic cats! This was not good— therefore the buffaloes and other game were disappearing. The Great Spirit was angry, and had withdrawn his protection."[23]

One evening He had sent His warning to Charley and his friends. In the darkness they had heard a noise in the air and thought a storm was ready to break. They stepped outside the house to look at the clouds, and there in the sky they saw gigantic Indians riding on black horses. The leader was beating a drum. He approached close to Charley and his friends, who wanted to run and hide. Suddenly the leader called:

Do not be afraid. We are your brothers and have been sent by the Great Spirit. He is displeased with you for accepting the ways of the white people. You can see for yourselves—your hunting is gone and you are planting the corn of the white men. Go and sell the same back to them, and plant Indian corn and gather it according to the ways of our ancestors, and do away with the mills. The Mother of the nation has abandoned you, because the grinding breaks her bones. She wants to come back to you, if you will get the white men out of the country and go back to your former ways.

And then the voice added: "You can see for yourselves that the whites are different from you, for you were made of red clay, and they from white sand. . . . Now I have told you the will of the Great Spirit, and you must pass it on. But if you don't believe my words, look up into the sky."[24]

This they did, and they saw the clouds part, and from the sky came a bright light. Within that light they saw white houses—houses which the leader told them they should build for certain white men who would help them if they returned to their ancient ways. The leader repeated that they must tell their people all they had seen and all they had heard. And it would go ill with any man who disbelieved.

"The [Cherokees] must return to the customs of their fathers," Charley cried. "They must kill their cats, cut short their frocks, and dress as became Indians and warriors. They must discard all the fashions of the whites, abandon the use of any communication with each other except by word of mouth, and give up their mills, their houses, and all the arts learned from the white people."[25]

The prophet promised his silent audience that the game would then return and the whites would go away. Therefore the Cherokees must believe his words and obey his appeal. Let them paint themselves as in former days, let them hold feasts, let them dance, let them listen to the whispered inspiration of the Great Spirit in their dreams. And then Charley ended with an ominous threat. If anyone denied his message, the Great Spirit would strike him dead.

The harangue produced an awesome effect, especially on those who disliked the new ways. The talk was good, they cried. But The Ridge foresaw what mischief might come of Charley's agitation, and he determined to counter it with all his might. He rose and shouted to the company: "My friends, the talk you have heard is not good. It would lead us to war with the United States, and we should suffer. It is false; it is not a talk from the Great Spirit. I stand here and defy the threat that he who disbelieves shall die. Let the death come upon me. I offer to test this scheme of imposters!"[26]

At The Ridge's defiance, excited Cherokees rushed upon him.

But he was ready for their assault. He struck them down until their numbers overwhelmed him. They threw him to the ground. They might have killed him, but a friend, Jesse Vann, and others rushed to his aid. Together they beat the crowd back, and The Ridge sprang up again to hold his assailants at bay until an influential old chief exerted enough personal magnetism to stem the violence. The Ridge had won his point; he had defied the prophet. Although battered and bloody, he continued to live.

His stand shook Charley's credibility for many of the aroused Cherokees. Others retained their belief in the prophet. They rallied round him when he set a judgment day for those who spurned his doctrine. On that day, Charley claimed, the Great Spirit would send a storm with hailstones as large as hominy mortars. The ice balls would destroy all but the faithful, provided they collected on the highest peak of the Smoky Mountains. There a consecrated ground of ten acres would remain secure for them, a haven of peace in a fury of ice. In the wake of Charley's prophecy hundreds of Cherokees left their homes. They deserted "their negroes, their orchards, their bees and almost everything about them that came from, or savored of the *pale-faces;* they tore themselves, amid entreaties and tears, from their unbelieving friends and started for the 'reservation'"[27] on a mountaintop in western North Carolina. The hailstorm failed to materialize, and Charley was at last disgraced conclusively. From that time on, the furor of the prophets waned among the Cherokees, though not among the Creeks.

By now The Ridge was recognized as one of the staunchest defenders of civilization among his people. No one appreciated more clearly than he how cordially the United States had fostered the program to which he was committed. It was natural then, as war clouds thickened, for him to express sympathy for the American cause. At the spring council of 1812, when the chiefs in general favored a neutral policy, he joined forces with John Lowrey and John Walker (both liberal leaders notwithstanding the silver rings in their ears), and the trio offered Colonel Meigs a plan for a force of Cherokees to serve the United States on a par with American volunteers. Meigs did not feel authorized to accept the offer, but admitted that the "expression of their good will . . . would . . . give satisfaction to the Government." The agent promptly sent the proposal of The Ridge and his friends to the secretary of war. Meigs added: "It is my opinion that several corps of Infantry or Cavalry might be furnished & being particularly under the direction of the General-in-chief, might render valuable service in an active campaign & might be considered as a pledge of fidelity of the nation and with proper impressions on their minds might be restrained from acts of barbarity. I mention Cavalry because they are real horsemen, they are remarkable for the ease with which they ride & manage their horses. . . . The Government can employ them at any point, either Northward or Southward."[28]

The secretary of war held the matter under advisement.[29] General Jackson, intent on raising volunteers in Tennessee, considered the Cherokee proposal and decided in favor of "the policy to enlist Lowry [sic], Walker, and The Ridge in our service and make them furnish a sufficient number of pilots to the Creek towns."[30] The matter rested there for months, even after June 18, the day war was declared. It was true that Jackson made ready to move against the Creeks, who clearly needed a sound drubbing. He instructed a liaison officer to tell Lowrey, now addressed as Colonel, "that when we march I want as many of his men together with himself as will be sufficient for guides, that if any plan can be devised so that in time of action, our friends and brothers the Cherokees can be distinguished from the Creeks I would rejoice to have him and his regiment in the field."[31] In a bustle of activity the Cherokees made ready to join the Tennessee volunteers in spite of the lukewarm feeling of many chiefs. But official sanction for the campaign failed to come from Washington.[32] The War Department was loath to set one tribe against another, fearing a troublesome aftermath. The first U.S. response to the Cherokee offer was to encourage the Indians to make saltpeter from the bat dung abounding in the caves of their country. Colonel Meigs appointed Gideon Morgan, the white husband of Margaret Sevier, a mixed-blood granddaughter of John Sevier, as supervisor of such operations.[33]

That fall The Ridge attended the Creek council in a dual capacity, as ambassador of the Cherokees and as a petitioner in his own interest. He had purchased the "chance" to several Negro slaves inherited by the Cherokee chief Shoe Boots at the death of a relative living among the Creeks. The Ridge applied to Colonel Hawkins for possession of the blacks, but they were retained by certain Creeks of Coweta "on the claim of blood." A nephew of The Pathkiller, who had succeeded Black Fox as principal chief of the Cherokees, had killed a Creek. The relatives insisted on keeping the slaves in payment for the death instead of revenging themselves on The Pathkiller's clan. As The Pathkiller was present with the Cherokee delegation and was himself in danger, he requested The Ridge to withdraw the papers from Colonel Hawkins, lest the Creeks invoke clan retaliation, which was still very much in effect with them. As a result, The Ridge lost his chance of securing the slaves that autumn. Two of them came into his possession the following spring, but the rest would not until 1816.[34]

At the council, meanwhile, the Creek chiefs issued "an unqualified and unanimous profession of friendship" for the United States.[35] The Ridge was in a position, nevertheless, to see how divided the nation was—indeed, how those who called themselves the Red Sticks, from their vermilion war clubs or from the magic sticks manipulated by the prophets, were preparing for war. He was therefore not surprised when word reached the Cherokee Nation in July, 1813, that civil war had erupted among the Creeks—that the adherents of the prophets had burned several towns friendly to the American agent; had slaughtered horses, hogs, cattle, sheep, and goats; and had destroyed every mark of civilization they could find. Nor was he surprised when the violence spread from civil war to war against the Americans.

The new developments started with a skirmish in lower Alabama when a band of Americans surprised a Creek pack train transporting arms and ammunition from the Spanish fort at Pensacola. The whites sacrificed their first advantage in a scramble for mules and plunder and, when counterattacked, were shamefully beaten.[36] This action at Burnt Corn Creek was merely a prelude, however, to the real beginning of the Creek War. That came on August 30, when a thousand Red Sticks under William Weatherford surprised Fort Mims, a poorly guarded stockade on Tensaw Lake some forty miles north of Mobile.

The stockade sheltered not only white refugees but also a number of half-blood families who had fled down the Alabama River during the Creek uprising. It was to take these mixed-bloods that the Red Sticks charged the fort, but once the assault was under way, no restraints could be maintained. The prophets who were present, their faces painted black, brandished medicine bags and magic sticks to urge the warriors on. The naked horde rushed a gate left open through the negligence of the commanding officer, and though the garrison made a courageous stand, it was overwhelmed in hand-to-hand fighting. The buildings were fired, and most of the occupants massacred, nearly four hundred men, women, and children. The soldiers who came from Mississippi ten days later to bury the dead found buzzards and starved dogs feeding on the bodies, all of which had been scalped, with many mutilations.[37]

The news of Fort Mims reached the Cherokees while a friendly Creek named William McIntosh, the headman of Coweta, visited in their midst enlisting aid against the Red Stick insurgents.[38] One of his wives was a Cherokee, and McIntosh had much the same status among the Cherokees as The Ridge enjoyed among the Creeks. It was his privilege, though a Creek, to sit as a chief in the council at Oostanaula. His popularity was immense with the Cherokee head-men, who feared for his safety, since the Red Sticks aimed to kill him on sight. When the time came for his departure, The Path-killer instructed The Ridge to raise a band of warriors and escort McIntosh across the hostile country between the Cherokees and his home.

At Coweta they found the Creek council in emergency session. With The Big Warrior present, the friendly chiefs worked to devise means of resisting the insurgents. They had already asked the United States for help. The Big Warrior now entrusted The Ridge with a talk addressed to the Cherokee council, along with a diplomatic token comprising a sheaf of tobacco tied with a string of wampum. The tobacco was to be smoked in the Cherokee council, and the import of the talk was to implore aid against the Red Sticks.[39]

The Ridge hurried back to Oostanaula with his articles of diplo-macy, and the council met in September to weigh the issue. The Ridge delivered a vigorous speech in favor of The Big Warrior's request. As McKenney and Hall wrote:

He maintained that the hostile portion of the Creeks, in making war against the whites, had placed the Cherokees in a condition which obliged them to take one side or the other; that in the unsettled state of the country no distinction would be known but that of Indians and white men, and a hostile movement by any tribe would involve the whole in war. He insisted further that if the Creeks were permitted to put down their chiefs, and be ruled by the prophets, the work of civilization would be subverted, and the Red Sticks, in their efforts to re-establish a state of barbarism, would destroy all the southern tribes.[40]

The chiefs listened in silence and respect, but as a neutral atti-tude still prevailed among most of them, the council voted for a course of nonintervention.

"Then," The Ridge said, "I will act with volunteers. I call upon my friends to join me."[41]

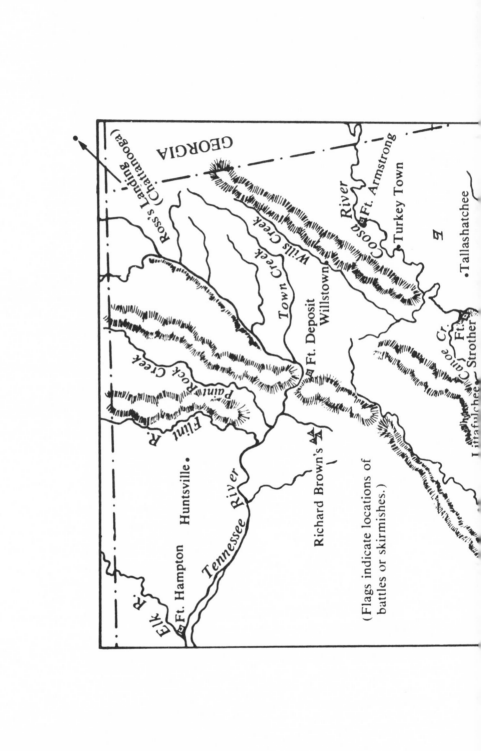

GEORGIA

Ross's Landing
(Chattanooga)

Ft. Armstrong

Coosa River

Turkey Town

Wills Creek

Town Creek

Ft. Deposit

Willstown

Tallashatchee

Paint Rock Creek

Flint R.

Canoe Cr.

Ft. Strother

Emuckfaw

Littafutchee

Huntsville.

Tennessee River

Ft. Hampton

Elk R.

Richard Brown's

(Flags indicate locations of battles or skirmishes.)

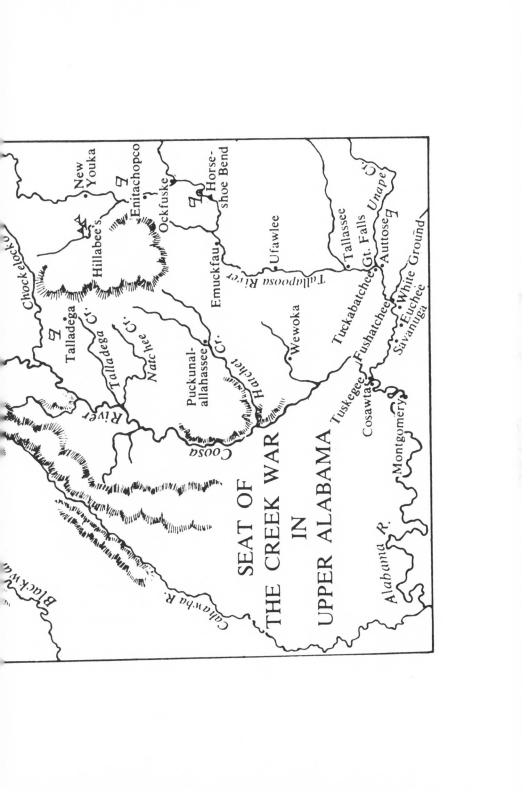

SEAT OF
THE CREEK WAR
IN
UPPER ALABAMA

New Youka
Enitachopco
Ockfuske
Horse-shoe Bend
Hillabee's
Chockelock
Talladega
Talladega Cr.
Natchee Cr.
Puckunal-allahassee Cr.
Emuckfau
Ufawlee
Tallapoosa River
Wewoka
Tallassee
Gt. Falls
Unape
Auttose
White Ground
Tuckabatchee
Fushatchee
Savanuga
Euchee
River
Coosa
Hatchet
Tuskegee
Cosawta
Montgomery
Alabama R.
Cahawba R.
Black Wa

So many younger men responded to his plea that the chiefs requested another vote and reversed their decision. They declared war on the Red Stick rebels. Meanwhile the secretary of war had ordered Colonel Meigs to confer "with the Governors of Tennessee and Georgia relative to a co-operation against the hostile Creeks with such force as [might] be organized in [the Cherokee] agency."[42] On September 16 The Ridge and several fellow chiefs learned of this development from Meigs himself at Hiwassee Garrison. "They had been concerting measures to aid the friendly Creeks," the agent recorded. "On my communicating to them the [wishes of] the War Office, they appeared exceedingly pleased and observed that they could bring a much larger number into the field than I had mentioned provided arms could be had. . . . Rifles would be preferred, but . . . muskets would be well received. . . . They are sensible that if the hostile Creeks should put down the friends of the United States, they would ruin the Cherokees if in their power."[43] Meigs proposed that the Cherokees, when armed, should join with the Tennessee volunteers well before they entered Creek territory.

As plans took shape, the Americans readied a multipronged campaign under the overall command of Maj. Gen. Thomas Pinckney, who led troops from the Carolinas. The Georgia militia, under Brig. Gen. John Floyd, would drive from the east to fight alongside the friendly Creeks under McIntosh, who received the rank of major. Some help could be expected from the volunteers of Louisiana and Mississippi under Brig. Gen. F. L. Claiborne. But the main thrust was to come from Tennessee, which put three forces into the field. General Jackson, in command of the combined Tennessee operation, directly led militia from the western part of the state. East Tennessee supplied the two other contingents, an advance brigade under Brig. Gen. James White and a division that followed under Maj. Gen. John Cocke, commander of the joint forces from the eastern part of the state.

As the campaign opened, the Cherokees found themselves attached to the forces of all three Tennessee generals, though most were to serve with General White's brigade. On paper they constituted a regiment nearly five hundred strong. In reality they represented no such compact organization. The warriors were embodied in several smaller bands under various chiefs, and Jackson's white liaison officer suggested their basic lack of unity when he reported that "each chief calculated on commanding his own party under the direction of the commander in chief of our army only." Colonel Meigs issued supplies and clothing to the amount of $3,362, which he charged to the secretary of war, and The Pathkiller appealed to General Jackson for additional arms.[44]

How many braves The Ridge himself recruited remains a question, but in view of his vast enthusiasm it must have been a respectable number.[45] Ready for war, mounted on a large horse, his shoulders powerful and erect, he made a commanding figure. Informed conjecture shows him accoutered partly as an Indian, partly as a white. He doubtless wore two feathers in a headband with a deer's tail in back, in line with the measure adopted to distinguish friendly warriors from the hostile Creeks. Some of the Cherokee officers wore swords, and perhaps The Ridge did too, along with a large hunting knife. Whatever else his uniform, almost certainly he wore moccasins, perhaps even deerskin leggings. At the back of his saddle was a rolled blanket of military issue, and somewhere too were hunting pouches stuffed with pipe and tobacco, flint and steel, and a supply of lead bullets. From his shoulder hung a powder horn, and he managed to carry a rifle while holding the reins of his horse.

The Ridge seems to have brought his band to Hiwassee Garrison, just as Walker did, to join General White's thirteen hundred volunteers dressed in coonskin caps, in stained and grimy buckskins, or in homespuns dyed with butternut juice. Like Walker, The Ridge may have started on October 16 for Turkey Town on the Coosa River, for The Pathkiller's village was in danger of a Creek attack, and the principal chief had issued a call for help. General Jackson had received the appeal and ordered General White to make all haste toward the town and secure it from assault. With warriors constantly swelling his brigade, the general from "the mulberry place" reached his destination in early November, preceded by some two hundred Cherokees, including The Ridge.[46] The Cherokees formed a various company that ran the gamut of appearance from mountain tribesmen who looked like warriors of a former age to mixed-bloods indistinguishable to the eye from white men.

While gathered in Turkey Town, the Indians received a talk from Colonel Meigs, commending their cooperation. "Brothers," the colonel wrote:

I flatter myself that, in the just & necessary war now commencing against the hostile Creeks your Battalions will be considered as a respectable part of the Army, according to your numbers. The Generals Jackson, Cocke & White will consider you as entitled to their care & friendly attention [and will see] that you have provisions, ammunition & medical aid when necessary: in all these you will have equal advantages with other troops: and of course it will be expected that you will be obedient to every order & regulation that may be made for the government of the whole.

Meigs cautioned that the United States did not make war on "women & children, the aged & helpless." Soldiers in the American service spared unresisting prisoners, he explained; "and I am much pleased," he added, "lately to hear similar sentiments from several Cherokee officers who are now arming."[47]

The Pathkiller, as principal chief, was commissioned a colonel, more as a matter of policy than as a practical measure, for he was too old to take an active part in the coming campaign. His personal staff officer, Charles Hicks, was made a captain. Command of the Cherokee regiment fell not on John Lowrey, as originally planned, but on the Indian countryman Gideon Morgan, who was named a full colonel. Lieutenant Colonel Lowrey was appointed second-in-command. Richard Brown, who led no more than sixteen warriors but who was attached to Jackson's headquarters, was made a lieutenant colonel, though Meigs had recommended that he be commissioned as only a major, the rank Walker received. Thus field grades went to men of mixed blood with a fluent command of English. The Ridge received the lowest rank among the chiefs who had made the original proposal of Cherokee service. No doubt because of his lack of English, he was commissioned as only a first lieutenant, and listed as "aborigine" in a mounted company under his old friend Captain Saunders.[48] But as Meigs declared in his exhortation: "The war in our part of the Union is just commencing. There may yet be time enough for every man of ability and a military turn to have such rank . . . as he has a right to expect."[49] Before the Creek War was finished, The Ridge would rise to the grade of major and thereafter adopt his military title as his first name.

Meanwhile the men at Turkey Town learned of a concentration of hostile Creeks at a village called Talleshatchee in an open woodland twenty-five miles away. Without waiting for instructions from Jackson's headquarters or for reinforcements from General White's lagging columns, Colonel Morgan ordered all available Cherokees, including The Ridge, to take the trail on November 4, their heads ornamented with the white feathers and deer's tails that served to distinguish them from the enemy. They reached their objective to find that a detachment of mounted Americans under General John Coffee had already reduced the town to desolation. The Creeks had made a determined stand; Coffee's force had mowed them down to the last man. If Colonel Meigs had beguiled the Cherokees with words about white soldiers forbearing to kill women and children, here was a view to disenchant them.[50] Davy Crockett, one of Coffee's men, would later describe how a squaw had fallen with "at least twenty balls blown through her" because she had shot a soldier with a bow and arrow in front of a building that sheltered numerous braves. "We now shot them like dogs," Crockett went on, "and then set the house on fire, and burned it up with . . . forty-six warriors in it. I recollect seeing a boy who was shot down near the burning house and the grease was stewing out of him. In this situation he was still trying to crawl along; but not a murmur escaped him." Crockett also told how the white men later broke into the burned-out cellar and gorged on potatoes basted in drippings of oil from the roasted warriors.[51]

One hundred and eighty-six corpses, not counting slaughtered women and children, were strewn about the devastated town. "The joy which the sight produced among the Cherokees," wrote Gideon Morgan, "was such as to baffle every attempt to preserve . . . order." They ran about among the dead, seeking for scalps overlooked by Coffee's force. In addition they rounded up nineteen prisoners, all women and children, whom they led to Turkey Town, where wounds were dressed and they were shown all "other attention."[52]

The following morning General White forded the Coosa with a thousand men. It was Jackson's wish for White's brigade to advance to the Ten Islands and to hold Fort Strother while Jackson's army, reinforced with Cherokees, moved against the Creeks.[53] But General Cocke, some distance behind on White's trail, was jealous of Jackson's early success and countermanded the order. "Let us . . . share some of the dangers and glories of the field," was the sentiment Cocke expressed when he ordered White's brigade, on November 7, to join his own division near the mouth of Chatooga River, and with it all the Cherokees under Gideon Morgan.[54] This sudden move left Jackson's rear troops without protection, but the men from western Tennessee had nearly reached their destination, a town called Talledega, when White's runner overtook them with the news of Cocke's astonishing order. Jackson refused to hesitate in his headlong drive against the Creeks. He surrounded the enemy on November 9 and in fifteen minutes produced a rout, the surviving Red Sticks fleeing pell-mell to the surrounding mountains.[55]

The victory at Talledega so crushed the spirit of the Creeks that those assembled at the Hillabee towns on the Tallapoosa decided to sue for peace. They sent an envoy to Jackson, who accepted their offer. Meanwhile General Cocke, eager for a victory, heard of the warriors gathered at those towns and, unaware of their wish to surrender, ordered White to move against them, with the Cherokees and a troop of Tennessee mounted men.[56] With provisions for three days, the force rode quickly toward the principal Hillabee town, spreading devastation in their path. On the way they burned two deserted villages and reached their objective on the eighteenth, the very day the Creek envoy arrived at Jackson's headquarters. Having surrendered, the Creeks at the Hillabee town expected no violence and made little resistance when White ordered his men against them. The Cherokees slaughtered 61 Creek warriors and took 250 prisoners, all "without the loss of a drop of Blood."[57]

Afterward Morgan reported to Colonel Meigs that he could not

do justice to all who [had] signalized themselves by their cool & deliberate bravery, but it would be doing injustice to the character and probably cool the ardor of the Cherokees, to withhold [notice of] the most prominent characters. Major John Walker, having been ordered with several others on an elevated ground to prevent the escape of the enemy, was unable from its quick termination to distinguish himself in Battle; he proposed to Captain Saunders & Lieutenant Ridge to accompany him to a small town six miles distant to which they consented; they were joined by some others and pursued their route. On their way they . . . killed three of the enemy & on their arrival at the town discovered a house & yard filled with women & children, 40 in number, whom they made prisoners.[58]

Thus was the character of military glory; it made little difference in the bragging of the Cherokees that they found their exploits had involved a people who had already sued for peace.

The drive against the Hillabee towns had one hapless consequence: it prolonged the war. Not comprehending the split in the white command, the Creeks assumed that Jackson had made a treacherous mock of their offer to surrender. As a result, no other Red Stick town would ask for peace; indeed, the hostiles, with no hope of quarter at American hands, were to battle doggedly on to utter exhaustion.[59]

The Red Stick warriors the Cherokees had taken prisoner were detained at Hiwassee Garrison, while the women and children were distributed through the Cherokee Nation. "I have impressed on [the Cherokees] to treat them well," wrote Colonel Meigs, who advised that all such prisoners must necessarily be surrendered "if required by the Government. These last," he added, "cannot perhaps be better disposed of at present."[60] The Ridge sent home a young Creek girl, who would live for years in his household and become almost a member of the family. He also took several Negro slaves as spoils of war, valuable acquisitions in his drive to become a Southern planter. Jackson later requested him to restore the slaves to their rightful owner, an Indian countryman friendly to the Americans. But it took several emphatic letters from the general to move Major Ridge to make the restoration.[61]

Meanwhile the combined forces under General Cocke had settled down to build a strong stockade on the Coosa River. Cocke named the post Fort Armstrong after the secretary of war. And in writing to the War Department he begged leave "to suggest the propriety of keeping a regular force stationed [there]."[62] He left it garrisoned largely by Cherokees, however, when he marched his troops to Fort Strother on Decemeber 12 to join up with Jackson's command. This was in reality a futile move, for the term of service for most of Cocke's men was due to expire in a few weeks, and faced with a dearth of supplies in a hostile country, the troops were restless, unruly, and eager to rush home. At the same time, Jackson was faced with a mutiny of his own soldiers; he put the trouble down with an iron will, but it was clear that he could expect to continue the offensive only after fresh men were supplied to him. He knew furthermore that victory depended on him and an army from Tennessee. General Pinckney seemed only able to give impossible orders. The expedition from Louisiana and Mississippi had come to nothing, and after meeting the Creeks, General Floyd's militia from Georgia was in retreat. Only Jackson held firm, but he needed fresh men, with new terms of service.

Consequently he sent General Cocke back to eastern Tennessee with a large part of his command, including White's brigade, under orders to raise fifteen hundred new troops and bring them on to the Creek Nation.[63] On December 18, Colonel Morgan read a talk to the Cherokees assembled on the Coosa near Fort Armstrong. Their services were "for the present dispensed with." But let them hold themselves in readiness for further orders, Morgan added: "Fifty nights shall not pass ere your swords, your lances, and your knives shall drink the blood of your enemy. Your valor shall shew them the imbecility of their Prophets and instil fresh fear in their hearts. You are requested to hold yourselves in the best possible state of preparation."[64] It was at this time that The Ridge returned to Oothcaloga to raise more warriors. "On his reaching home," declared McKenney and Hall, "Major Ridge sent runners through the nation to collect volunteers for another expediton."[65]

He continued in such activity for a month. On January 16, 1814, at Colonel Meigs's promise of reimbursement, he agreed to furnish the men collecting in the Hightower (or Etowah) area "with fifty weight of powder at the price of three quarters of a dollar." The force requested a hundred pounds of lead from Meigs, and The Ridge added a statement to their letter, penned by someone barely literate. "This is a phew wordes from your friend the Rige," wrote the scribe: "Sir when eye saw you last fall eye had taken up my gunn against the hostile Creekes but itt was because the[y] done bad and eye went against them and taken a good maney and have taken up my gunn to gow against them again and expect to have a lairg [number] of my people with me this time. Wee will gow with our oaldes brothers the whites like a band of brothers and Sir wee want to heare from you when Morgan our gide will bee ready to gow and when wee will see Ginneral Cock[e]."[66] Cocke was still in Knoxville, raising his division, but Morgan had returned to Fort Armstrong, held now by a handful of whites and sixty Cherokees.

During Jackson's worst extremity his army had dwindled to 130 men, but when requested by Governor Blount to retreat, he had answered that he would perish first. A drought earlier in the year had left the rivers at their lowest stage, preventing boats from crossing the shallows and seriously thwarting the transport of food to Jackson's headquarters. A shortage of supplies had hampered the campaign from the start. Colonel Meigs had carefully made it of record that "the Cherokees [had] cheerfully supported the Army with Beef and Pork and nearly all the corn they had,"[67] but now they too were hungry. At one point the general himself, in spite of his gastric ailments, was forced to a diet of acorns. He rode constantly between Fort Strother on the Coosa and Ditto's Landing on the Tennessee to hasten supplies for the army he expected from home.

As soon as two regiments arrived, he determined to move into Creek territory. He marched to the recent battleground of Talledega, where two hundred Cherokees and friendly Creeks joined his command on January 20. The move had occurred too suddenly, however, for The Ridge and his warriors—indeed for the majority of the Cherokees—to join the columns for action. Hence they missed the battle glory at Emuckfau, where Jackson failed of a decisive victory and thought it prudent to abandon his attempt to destroy the main Red Stick encampment on the Tallapoosa. No doubt, had the Cherokees arrived in great force, the issue would have been more positive, both there and at Enitachopco, where Jackson snatched a narrow victory from apparent defeat. His force retreated to Fort Strother, where those who remained in service began constructing flatboats for the transportation of supplies down the river once the contractors had brought them thus far.

The second period of The Ridge's service, when he bore the rank of major, began officially on January 27. He assembled his warriors on February 8 with the intention of leading them at once to Fort Armstrong in spite of rain, high water, and muddy roads. At Jackson's request, however—for the general was not yet prepared to advance—The Ridge delayed his march, and over a week passed before he brought his warriors to the fort. He left for Turkey Town on the twenty-second. Four days later, along with Lowrey and Walker, he reached Fort Strother "with upwards of two hundred warriors," the core of the Cherokee regiment. Jackson sent at once for Gideon Morgan "to organize and command them. . . . I wish you here," the general added, "to keep the Cherokees employed untill I get up my army."[68] Richard Brown and Lowrey again served as lieutenant colonels under Morgan, with The Pathkiller still a colonel for the sake of policy. There were four majors: Walker, James Brown, Saunders, and The Ridge. The Ridge was the fourth major in order of rank. A dozen Cherokees, some of them of mixed blood, served as captains, and John Ross, a rising young man, seven-eighths white, who had received his education at Kingston, Tennessee, acted as adjutant with the rank of second lieutenant.[69] The Cherokees continued to arrive in bands of various sizes, and when the full body had assembled, they numbered more than five hundred fighting men, many of them mounted, armed with muskets and rifles, lances and tomahawks. As identification signs, they continued to wear white feathers in their hair and deer's tails.

It is known that Major Ridge made the personal acquaintance of Jackson during these early years. Perhaps it occurred during the days when Jackson's forces were building up at Fort Strother— the days when Jackson, lean of body and thin of face, with red, rough skin, unruly hair, and piercing blue eyes, circulated ceaselessly among his men, his left arm now in his coat sleeve but still nearly useless from the wound he had received in a duel before the cam-

Andrew Jackson. From a painting attributed to Thomas Sully. United States Signal Corps photograph in the National Archives.

paign. His health was on the mend now, though he still suffered from occasional paroxysms of that intestinal disorder whose distress would cause him to prop his lank body against a sapling trunk, freshly chopped, his arms dangling over the horizontal pole. No suffering seemed to daunt his implacable will; he was a man so tough-grained, so unyielding, that he had earned the nickname of "Old Hickory."

Jackson's forces continued to build, and when they reached their maximum strength, they numbered five thousand men, mostly militia, hastily raised and poorly equipped. But they also included the regulars of the Thirty-Ninth U.S. Infantry, and these, Jackson believed, "will give strength to my arm and quell mutiny."[70] The buildup was complete by March 13, and sufficient supplies had arrived from Tennessee so that Jackson felt no longer haunted by the spectre of famine, and on the next morning to the roll of a single drum (for only one drummer could be found in the entire army) the general ordered his forces to march. As almost all of the Cherokees were mounted, they were attached to General Coffee's troop of cavalry and moved forward with the white horsemen.

The army forded the river, and pushing through thick forest, marsh, and canebrake, arrived on March 21 at the mouth of Cedar Creek, where the barricades of Fort Williams were hastily thrown up. Major Ridge and other Cherokees accompanied the detachment Jackson sent to scour the surrounding country. On the twenty-second they burned two deserted towns some twelve and fifteen miles down the river, then returned to the fort.[71]

Supplies had meanwhile arrived in flatboats down the Coosa, and with his rear secured, Jackson ordered his men forward the following morning. The advancing columns now consisted of two thousand infantry and four hundred cavalry, plus five hundred Cherokees and a hundred friendly Creeks, the latter including a band of Cowetas under William McIntosh. They cut a passage across the ridge that separated the Coosa Valley from the Tallapoosa, and they splashed through marshes more mucky than ever, a hard advance of nearly fifty miles, till on the evening of the twenty-sixth they came to a campsite within six miles of their destination: that is, a sharp bend in the Tallapoosa that formed a peninsula of about one hundred acres known as Tohopeka (or the Horseshoe), where the population of six Creek towns were then enforted for a last stand.[72]

The Americans advanced with their Indian auxiliaries early next morning, and by ten o'clock they were in battle position. The Red

Sticks had thrown a breastwork of logs across the neck of Tohopeka to protect the encampment behind. It was arranged to subject any frontal assault to cross fire; hence Jackson proposed to bombard it with his artillery. Meanwhile he sent the mounted men under Coffee, including both Cherokees and friendly Creeks, to ford the river two miles below and to station themselves along the eastern side of the bend to cut off any Creek retreat. Thus, the enemy was surrounded in the Horseshoe, the houses visible from where Major Ridge and the Cherokees lurked. They could see a line of canoes moored along the peninsula's shore.

Coffee sent up signals as soon as his men had taken their places, and Jackson ordered the cannonade, the guns emplaced on a slight rise some eighty yards from the breastwork. The cannons poured grapeshot into the center of the fortification, while the rifles and muskets laid down a blistering fire whenever the Creeks showed themselves behind the logs. The volleys persisted for two hours, with little success. Meanwhile, beyond the river, the Cherokees had grown impatient for action. Covered with a brisk fire, three privates, including Charles Reese, the brother-in-law of The Ridge's brother Watie,* plunged into the river and swam to the Creek canoes. There one of them, a warrior named The Whale, was wounded, so they brought only two canoes, but these were filled to capacity for the return trip, each warrior securing a new canoe.[73]

"Major Ridge was the first to embark," wrote McKenney and Hall, "and in these . . . boats the Cherokees crossed, a few at a time, until the whole body [as well as Captain William Russell's spies] had penetrated to the enemy's camp."[74] Soon their bullets drove the Red Sticks from out of the huts toward the breastwork that Jackson bombarded, and they set fire to several of the buildings. They themselves advanced in the direction of the barricade, firing on the Creeks who lay behind it. Spurred by the prophets, who danced and howled their incantations, their faces blackened and their heads and shoulders decked with feathers, the Red Sticks battled fiercely, and seeing that the Cherokees and Russell's spies were not strong enough to displace them, Jackson determined to take the breastwork by storm. His men hurled themselves against it. Creek bullets were flattened against the bayonets the soldiers thrust through the portholes. The Cherokees redoubled their attack,

---

*In time the double *o* was dropped from the spelling of Oo-watie's name. In pronunciation the sound of *w* swallowed up the sound of double *o*.

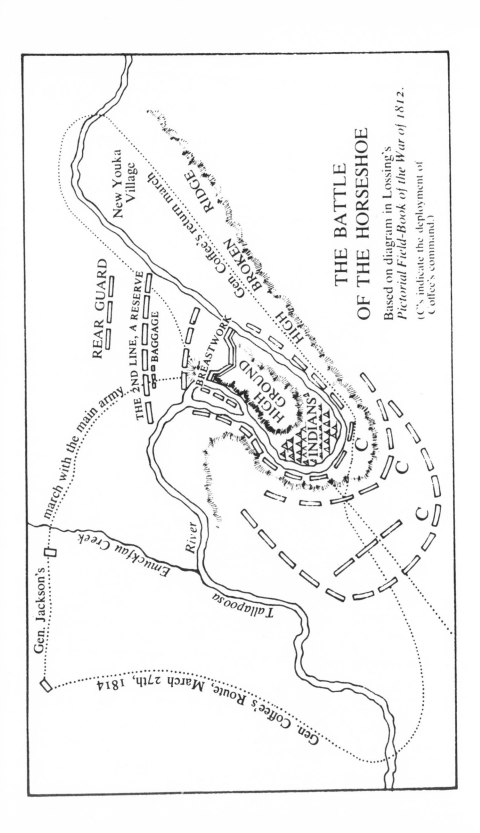

THE BATTLE
OF THE HORSESHOE

Based on diagram in Lossing's
Pictorial Field-Book of the War of 1812.

("C"s indicate the deployment of
Coffee's command.)

REAR GUARD

New Youka
Village

Gen. Coffee's return march

BROKEN RIDGE

HIGH

THE 2ND LINE, A RESERVE

BAGGAGE

BREASTWORK

HIGH GROUND

INDIANS

C

C

C

march with the main army

Emuckfau Creek

Gen. Jackson's

River

Tallapoosa

Gen. Coffee's Route, March 27th, 1814

diverting the attention of the Creek defenders, giving the white soldiers a chance to swarm across the barricade, Sam Houston among them, cheering on the men behind him.

The fight continued for five hours, no Red Stick begging for his life, and when more than half of the Creeks lay dead among the smoldering ruins, the rest plunged into the river. It was then they found the opposite shore lined with Coffee's mounted men, who poured a deadly fire down on the swimmers, closing all chance of escape.[75]

According to the account of McKenney and Hall:

[The] Ridge was a distinguished actor in this bloody drama, and we are told that he was the first to leap into the river in pursuit of the fugitives. Six Creek warriors . . . fell by his hand. As he attempted to plunge his sword into one of these, the Creek closed with him, and a severe contest ensued. Two of the most athletic of their race were struggling in the water for life or death, each endeavoring to drown the other. [The] Ridge, forgetting his own knife, seized one which his antagonist wore and stabbed him; but the wound was not fatal, and the Creek still fought with an equal chance of success, when he was stabbed with a spear by one of [The] Ridge's friends, and thus fell a hero who deserved a nobler fate.[76]*

Some of the Red Sticks hid themselves behind thick piles of brush and timber. Not wishing to annihilate the Creeks completely, Jackson sent an interpreter in their direction with a message of clemency provided they would surrender. The Red Sticks shouted in defiance and fired their muskets, shooting the messenger, whereupon the whites set fire to the timber and, as the Red Sticks fled from the inferno, gunned them down. The firing did not cease till late at night. "The carnage was dreadful," Jackson wrote.[77]

The next morning he detailed a squad to count the dead. To make sure no corpse was counted twice, they snipped off the nose of each dead Creek as soon as he was counted.[78] This practical operation constituted by no means the most barbaric atrocity inflicted upon the bodies, and the greatest responsibility was held by white men, not the Indians, who merely scalped the dead. The whites

---

*While The Ridge was thus engaged at the Horseshoe, Colonel Meigs was recommending him to the favor of the Secretary of War (March 27, 1814, in National Archives, RG 75, Records of the Cherokee Agency in Tennessee): "Ridge is a respectable young chief, strongly attached to the Government and has distinguished himself in raising men and carrying on the war."

flayed corpses to make belts, and some secured hide for bridle reins.*
The work of the squad detailed to count bodies resulted in Jackson's report that, out of 1,000 Red Stick warriors, 557 lay dead in
the ruins of Tohopeka. Coffee estimated that his men had killed
350 more in the water, leaving only about 100 who could have escaped, many of them direly wounded. It was learned later that
Menawa, the Red Stick leader, had dressed himself in woman's
clothing as soon as he was wounded and had lain in a pile of dead
squaws till night came on, when he fled to safety.[79]

In contrast to the Creek toll, the Americans had lost only
thirty-two in death, with ninety-nine wounded. Of the Cherokees
eighteen were dead and thirty-six were wounded, while the friendly
Creeks counted but five dead and eleven wounded. Thus stood the
casualty figures for one of the most decisive Indian battles on the
continent. The power of the Creeks was broken at the Horseshoe.
From that day on Old Hickory's fame began to grow, the ground
swell of popularity that would eventually sweep him into the White
House. And in his first great military success, as he himself acknowledged, the Cherokees played a decisive role, one that Jackson would
prefer later to forget. The record prompted Meigs to write: "The
Cherokee warriors have fought and bled freely and according to
their numbers have lost more men than any [other] part of the Army."
And later when Jackson, in the White House, was inclined to forget
his debt to the Cherokees, John Ridge publicly reminded him:
"The General, as a soldier, has admitted the valour of my honored
father in that campaign."[80]

Meanwhile the Americans returned to Fort Williams. There
Jackson discharged the Cherokees in triumph, and they made their
way home, a wet ordeal, the rains falling continually. At the same
time, the commander marched south to the junction of the Coosa
and the Tallapoosa. Fort Toulouse he rechristened as Fort Jackson.

---

*The latter objective, according to an eyewitness, was accomplished in the
following manner: "They began in the lower part of the leg, near the heel, and
with a knife made two parallel incisions through the skin, about three inches or
more apart, running these incisions up the leg and along the side of the back to
the shoulder blade and thence across to the other shoulder, and from there down
the other side of the back and down the other leg to the heel. The strip between
the incisions was then skinned out, and the soldier had a long strap of human
skin, which he used as a bridle rein. So in the Creek War all the barbarity was
not committed on the Indian side" (H. S. Halbert quoting W. S. Williamson in
Lyman Draper Papers [transcript, Western History Collection, University of Oklahoma Library], Volume X, 44).

Opposition melted before him, and William Weatherford, supreme
military leader of the Red Sticks, came to his headquarters to lay
down his arms.

General Pinckney reached Fort Jackson on April 20 with soldiers from North and South Carolina. In view of the general sub-
mission of the Creeks, he pronounced the war over and, except
for troops needed for garrison duty, he ordered the volunteers from
Tennessee to return home. They marched north without delay,
crossed the Tennessee River, and at Fayetteville Jackson bade them
goodbye in a stirring address. When the Cherokees, including The
Ridge, reached home, they found their country had been ravaged
and despoiled during the passage through it of the white volunteers. The militia, disorderly and irresponsible, had stolen horses,
killed hogs and cattle, destroyed corncribs and fences, and taken
corn and maple sugar, even clothing, from the Indian residents.
Indeed, the Cherokees found their homes and families had suffered
more at the hands of their white allies than from their enemies,
the Creeks.[81]

4 • CHEROKEE DIPLOMACY

T HE Cherokees had much at stake in whatever peace treaty the United States should make with the defeated Creeks. For half a century Cherokees had occupied country along the Coosa as far south as Will's Creek, but they were acutely aware that a boundary line between themselves and the Creeks had never been fixed. Therefore in the spring of 1814 the National Council requested Colonel Meigs to advise the secretary of war of the Cherokee interest in the treaty soon to be made. The agent complied; the secretary apprised Jackson of the Cherokee concern; and the general invited his recent allies to send a delegation to the treaty conference.[1]

Jackson had just been made a major general in the U.S. Army and named commander of the Seventh Military District, with headquarters in Mobile. He planned to conclude the treaty on his way to the new command, and the Cherokees, on learning of his departure from the Hermitage, sent a delegation, including Major Ridge and accompanied by Colonel Meigs, to meet the general as he traveled south. They overtook him at the log stockade of Fort Strother on July 5, 1814, and the following morning the agent presented a memorandum.[2] It made clear that the Cherokee chiefs desired a boundary to be fixed in such a way that no Cherokees would be included in the Creek Nation, and that the line should be run to the westward of the Chattahoochee "so as to pass below the Ten Islands and so continue as to meet the boundary adjoining the Chickasaws."[3] Impatient, Jackson requested that the Cherokees and the Creeks settle the matter between themselves, before the treaty, and set August 10, 1814, as the convention date. Then he left for Fort Jackson to complete arrangements for the council.

The Cherokees, some sixty strong, followed a little over three

81

weeks later, making camp about four miles from the fort.[4] Jackson addressed them in general council along with the friendly Creeks, all assembled within Fort Jackson, an abject structure only half completed, with a stockade of small round pines unstripped of bark.

Jackson outlined the terms of the treaty, then withdrew to allow the two delegations to thrash out their differences over the boundary. No agreement could be reached during several days of discussion. Colonel Hawkins attempted to break the deadlock by suggesting the use of an old tradition for the solution of such disputes; that is, "each nation should establish the distance they had carried their tomahawk into each other's country and between the extreams [sic] should be the line."[5] The measure seemed to meet with approval. The Creeks claimed that they had invaded as far as Coosawatie, thirty miles north of the Etowah River. The Cherokees, on the other hand, had forged as far south as the Hickory Ground within eight miles of Fort Jackson. All that remained was to reach a compromise between the two limits, but when the debate was resumed the next day, the Creeks abandoned the plan outright. They argued that they could not think properly on the subject, owing to "the distressed state of their affairs."[6] Later The Big Warrior confessed they had hoped by this device to secure an extension of their lands below the zone where Jackson proposed to limit them by treaty.[7]

Meanwhile it was during the hot and sickly season that the Creeks and Cherokees debated. Tempers flared, but finally the two delegations agreed to enter into a "voluntary and friendly agreement," to be committed to writing, which specified that the Creeks anticipated a settlement at some future date and in the meantime had no objection to the Cherokees' occupation of the disputed territory.[8] Jackson, Meigs, and Hawkins witnessed this bizarre document on August 9, and on the following day the peace treaty was concluded. It was a "treaty of conquest," severe and unequivocal, whereby the United States appropriated twenty-three million acres of Creek land, or half the future state of Alabama. The surge of American migration across the Appalachians was mounting with each passing year, creating pressure for new land on which the pioneers could settle. In seizing such quantities of land, Jackson was acting merely as a figure in an inevitable historic process. To hasten matters he resolved the boundary question by leaving the lines to be spelled out by the U.S. commissioners who were to be appointed by the president. Among the deferred problems was the Creek-Cherokee dispute, a matter that would engage the energies of Major Ridge for some time to come.

Ironically the treaty had been made with Jackson's allies, the friendly Creeks.[9] Hostilities were not really over as long as the belligerent Red Sticks could look to the British. The Big Warrior warned Jackson that the hostiles "were not completely cowed and that they would be yet killing of us." He described them as "a parcel of wolves . . . like wild people in the woods."[10] As a matter of fact, during the Creek negotiations Jackson received dispatches that compelled him to move to his command in Mobile as soon as he could complete the business in hand.[11] The hostile Creeks had reached Pensacola; the Spaniards had welcomed them, and the British had supplied them with arms and ammunition.

War clouds began to lower again. Jackson sent out spies to verify the strength and situation of the enemy. On reaching Mobile he found the trouble emanating from Pensacola even worse than rumor had painted it, and he began at once to organize an expedition to crush it. His plans included his former Indian allies. In September, 1814, both Colonel Meigs and Colonel Morgan received requests from his adjutant general "to enroll the Cherokee Indians and muster them for immediate service—as many as will go."[12] Jackson counted on five hundred Cherokees responding to his call, and he promised "with the presumption of he that rules [to] give them the Regimentals of the Royal Creeks"[13]—referring, no doubt, to the scarlet coats the British had presented to certain Red Sticks during the Creek War.

September 20, 1814, found Colonel Meigs appealing to the Cherokee council. "Nothing will give the General more pleasure," he wrote, "than to see the Cherokee warriors at his Headquarters."[14] Four days later The Pathkiller and Chulioa replied that, though the appeal had been read in council, too many "great warriors" had not been present, making it necessary to defer debating the matter until the tribe gathered at the agency to receive the current annuity.[15] Meigs informed Jackson that the Cherokees showed some disposition to join the campaign, but he was unable to raise the cash to meet the payroll for the former Cherokee regiment and had to disappoint the warriors at annuity time. Enthusiasm for service seemed to evaporate in many cases. But Major Ridge, Major Walker, and Major Saunders, along with Captain James Foster, agreed to meet at Coosawatie on December 6 to make arrangements for collecting men.[16] They were already too late to help Jackson drive the British from

Pensacola—that glory had gone to the friendly Creeks—and before
The Ridge and his fellow officers had their warriors ready for the
field, Jackson had won his brilliant victory at New Orleans. The war
with Britain was over, and there was no further need for a Cherokee
regiment.

The men disbanded and returned home, Major Ridge to his acres
at Oothcaloga. New forces were being felt. The emphasis on cotton
and the advent of the cotton gin were bringing about the plantation
era. As The Ridge returned to the life of a small Southern planter,
he doubtless took some pride in the realization that he had proved
his loyalty and personal attachment to Andrew Jackson, whom he
admired as a great and valiant leader.

In the long course of events, Jackson was to prove less than the
Cherokees' staunchest friend, and almost at once came evidence of
his equivocal attitude—developments that must have shaken Major
Ridge's confidence in the general, though to be sure his faith was
never entirely destroyed. The first bewildering sign was Jackson's
opinion about Cherokee claims for spoliations, for reimbursement by
the United States for nuisances committed against their property by
the troops from Tennessee. After the drought of 1813, when rivers
had been too low to permit food to reach Jackson's army, the Cherokees had shared what food they had, giving of their corn and cattle
freely. Colonel Meigs took care to record what the Cherokees had
done, how they had come to Jackson's aid when all else had failed
and the "spectre famine," as the general named his greatest enemy,
threatened the expedition with utter defeat. As the evidence mounted
about the extent of Cherokee losses, and as their crops continued to
fail from frost and drought, leaving many families destitute, the
agent took measures to file statements of claims against the American
government and requests "for indemnity for losses suffered by the
wanton maraudings and depredations of the Tennessee levies on their
marches and countermarches through the Cherokee country." Meigs
continued:

These depredations may at first sight seem incredible: but I have no
doubt of the justice of the statements: they are well known to thousands.
I received a letter from an officer of high rank in the army, in which
he says, "The return of the Horse thro' their country has been marked
by plunder & prodigal, unnecessary and wanton destruction of their
property: their stocks of cattle & hogs have been shot & suffered to
rot untouched—their horses in some instances shared the same fate;
their cloathing intended to defend them from the wet & cold in the

present campaign has been stolen and in some instances where they remonstrated their lives have been threatened."[17]*

Major Ridge, like other Cherokees, assumed that his people's sacrifice had earned the general's permanent gratitude, and it was hard to understand Jackson's attitude toward Colonel Meigs's spoliations program, especially when the agent made it clear that most of the trouble had come from the "left wing" of the army, under the command of General Cocke and General White, and not from the troops of western Tennessee directly under Jackson. It was true the general had ordered officers returning to the eastern part of the state to "keep up a strict police . . . on [their] line of march" to prevent the kind of havoc "alleged by the Pathkiller to have been committed on the persons & property of his nation."[18] It was naive of Jackson to believe that mere orders could ensure a change of deportment in that unruly collection of white frontiersmen, and it came as a shock to hear him give the lie to Meigs's allegations.

In time he would brand the whole docket of claims as "one complete tissue of groundless falsehood," and he would fulminate that they "exceed all corruption."[19] But Meigs continued to collect evidence and countered Jackson's charges: "I will mention some of the claimants, some of whom I presume have your esteem & in whom on trying occasions you have placed your confidence, and have not been deceived by them." Major Ridge's name figured in the long list he gave, citing some of the most respectable leaders in the Cherokee Nation. "From such men," Meigs added, "I could not with propriety withhold my confidence."[20] But Jackson's persistent opposition delayed settlement of the claims.

Major Ridge was also perplexed by the animus Jackson developed toward a just settlement of the Cherokee's boundary dispute with the Creeks. The general labeled their efforts to protect their lower settlements as "Cherokee intrigue," and if his wishes had been observed, some of the towns would have been included in Creek territory. His line of reasoning seemed to be: the more the U.S. commis-

---

*David Crockett cites an example of wanton destruction from his own experience: "The next day we marched on, and at night took up camp near a large cane break. While here, I told my mess I would again try for some meat; so I took my rifle and cut out, but hadn't gone far, when I discovered a large gang of hogs. I shot one of them down in his tracks, and the rest broke directly towards the camp. In a few minutes the guns began to roar, as bad as if the whole army had been in an Indian battle, and the hogs to squeal as bad as the pigs did when the devil turned barber" (*Davy Crockett's Own Story*, p. 68).

sioners curtailed the Cherokee domain, the more acres there would
be to squeeze from the beaten Creeks. In this contest Jackson was
no negligible opponent, and now it became Major Ridge's chief
objective to help protect the Cherokee domain.

As soon as Congress ratified the Treaty of Fort Jackson, President Madison appointed Colonel Hawkins, Colonel William Barnett,
and General Sevier to run the new boundary and thus set off the
lands ceded to the United States. All the commissioners were old
and ailing, and they delayed for months in getting the survey under
way—so long, in fact, that rumors began to circulate that provisions
in the peace treaty between the United States and Great Britain
in some way interfered with execution of Jackson's treaty. The War
Department sent instructions to the various agents among the southern Indians to scotch such error. And at last the commissioners
came sufficiently to life to call a council with the Creeks in September, 1815, at the ruinous town house of Tuckabatchee. As some
of the lands the Creeks were ceding touched upon the Cherokee
domain, it became imperative to reopen the Creek-Cherokee boundary question. The secretary of war had informed the commissioners
that no record of the Indian boundaries existed in either the War
Department or the Land Office. They depended entirely upon tradition, and the matter would have to be thrashed out with the
Indians themselves. Hawkins pressed The Big Warrior to invite the
Cherokees to send a delegation to the council, and Major Ridge was
among the thirty or forty chiefs and warriors who proceeded to
Tuckabatchee, along with Colonel Meigs.[21]

The council opened on the sixteenth, with only two commissioners present, Hawkins and Barnett; it was explained that General
Sevier was too ill to attend. The Treaty of Fort Jackson was read,
and the Speaker of the Creeks presented objections.[22] The Cherokees felt oppressed by recollections of the Creek procrastinations
of the year before, and Meigs wrote Hawkins that it would be
highly improper for the Creeks to shirk an agreement with their
neighbors on this occasion.

The issue came to a head on September 21, 1815, the final day
of the council. The Cherokees invited Barnett and Hawkins to the
town house to hear the deliberations, but as the Cherokees had
anticipated, no agreement could be reached with the Creeks, and
so, with little reason for the Cherokees to remain longer at Tuckabatchee, Colonel Meigs advised Hawkins and Barnett of their intention to return home. They left without delay.[23]

The commissioners began the line on September 24, 1815, taking several prominent Creek chiefs with them as observers. The party had the protection of a force of eight hundred friendly warriors, who discouraged a threatened attack by the hostiles at the juncture of the Flint and Chattahoochee rivers.[24]

Sevier died almost before the work had begun, and after some delay the president chose General Edmund P. Gaines to fill his place. The Cherokees could not feel sure that the commissioners would honor their claims; in fact, they had definite fears, as they reported to Meigs, that the line when finally run might infringe on their rights. The occasion to explore the matter further came when the people assembled to receive their annuity. To promote friendship the War Department had sent "presents" amounting to the value of nearly a thousand dollars, which Colonel Meigs delivered "to the Cherokee officers who had distinguished themselves in the late expedition"—nine chiefs beginning with The Pathkiller, The Ridge's name appearing fourth on the list.[25] Sentiment in favor of the administration in Washington had risen to a high point, and after the annuity was paid, the chiefs called a council to discuss the possibility of sending a delegation to the capital for the purpose of negotiating with the highest authority such problems as the boundary line.

"They informed me," Meigs wrote William Crawford, the secretary of war, "that seven years had now elapsed since they had made a visit to the President of the United States, and they respectfully now solicit the President to permit them to send on a few chiefs." The council had appointed a delegation of six, all but one of whom had been officers in the late war. With Colonel Lowrey as Speaker, the group included Major Ridge, Major Walker, Captain Richard Taylor, and the warrior Cheucunesee. Lieutenant John Ross, whose intelligent grasp of affairs had impressed The Ridge and whose career the latter sought to advance, was named as clerk, because of the education he had received in English.[26]

Permission for the Cherokees' visit to Washington City arrived from the War Department on December 19, 1815, and the delegation was ready to depart by Christmas Day. The Pathkiller placed a letter of instructions in their hands. He asked them to "take our Father, the President of the United States, by the hand and express to him the satisfaction we feel in having successfully carried through the late war." He confided in their "wise and prudent conduct" in transacting the business committed to their care, especially the delicate task of bringing the boundary question to a just settlement. He recommended that the Cherokees comply with the request of the president that they cede a certain tract of land in South Carolina "for a valuable consideration." He also suggested that the time was at last right for the establishment of an ironworks in the Cherokee Nation, and he instructed the delegates to arrange for such a works "by the advice and with the consent of the United States." He also gave them carte blanche to transact any other business that might be deemed important to the Cherokees and their white brothers.[27]

The deputation traveled by way of Knoxville, Major Ridge accompanied by a Negro servant. Their progress was slower than the mails, especially in the mountains, so Colonel Meigs thought it prudent to forward to the War Department all documents concerning the boundary dispute. This they did at Knoxville on January 10, 1816, before resuming their journey.[28] They reached Washington on February 8. How different The Ridge found it from his first visit! It was still marked by the ravages of war, the Executive Mansion a gutted ruin and the marble walls of the Capitol cruelly defaced by its firing at the hands of the British. The Capitol glowered vacantly down from its low hill over the slope of a muddy sheep pasture. Congress had been obliged to move to other quarters.

The delegation's arrival was noticed by the *National Intelligencer* with the comment: "These are men of cultivation and understanding. Their appearance and deportment are such as to entitle them to respect and attention."[29] They were showered with attentions, as a matter of fact, and invited to influential houses. At one party Major Ridge was asked to give some idea of Indian music. He sang a song too racy for translation. Captain Taylor helped him with the performance, and they were much amused at the urgency of the ladies to know its meaning. "Oh, you don't want to know," The Ridge said. "It's just like a white man's song—all about love and whiskey." On that occasion a condescending lady remarked that if she were an Indian, she would prefer to marry a man who had gone to Washington and Philadelphia, for then he could bring her home a calico petticoat. "Oh," The Ridge replied, "Washington husbands are of no use to our women now. They can weave their own petticoats."[30]

The chiefs were a social success, but they also buckled down to work with iron wills. They paid their respects to Secretary Crawford at the War Department, presented a copy of their instructions as credentials, and were welcomed warmly with Southern courtesy and suaveness. Then Colonel McKenney of the Office of Indian Trade, in Georgetown, took them in hand. As was customary with Indian deputations, they were all outfitted with new clothes of the latest cut and fashion.

It was disconcerting to find Jackson also in the capital, making his influence felt. In fact, astute man that he was, the general at once knew the purpose of the delegation and had no intention of allowing them to repossess land he had assigned to the Creeks so that, in turn, he could squeeze more land for the United States in the Creek cession. He set about to undermine their case with both the War Department and the president. Persistent and persuasive, Jackson left the secretary under the impression that he had gained his end and started west convinced that the Cherokees were defeated even before they had begun.[31] But Secretary Crawford had an open mind.

He received the deputation's memoranda to the president. On February 16 Colonel Lowrey sent his credentials to his excellency, Mr. Madison, along with the greeting: "Father, I am directed by the highest authority of the Cherokee Nation to express to their Father the President of the United States that they rejoice at the successful termination of the late war, in which the young Cherokee warriors had the honor to participate with the young warriors of the republic."[32]

The delegation then not only explained the boundary difficulty, but they also described the Cherokee grievances at the hands of the Tennessee troops. They told of how upwards of ten thousand white soldiers had passed through the southwestern section of their country. Their memorandum continued: "We now have to state to our father that a great many of the white young warriors, not feeling the ties that should bind them and make them strong by the principles of subordination—feeling liberty in the extreme, it relaxed into licentiousness—, and they destroyed our cattle, sheep & hogs: & in some instances our horses, for mere sport; or prejudice founded only on the difference in shade of our complexion." They begged the president to have the evidence which accompanied their letter examined by "such persons as you may think proper to direct," either in Congress—"the Great Council"—or elsewhere.[33]

Three days later Lowrey petitioned the president on behalf of the families of the Cherokees killed and wounded in the Creek War, describing their hardships. "We beg leave," he concluded, "to ask whether our people cannot be put on the same footing as our white brothers for relief."[34]

The delegation decided not to send one letter concerning the boundary question, lest its words offend their opponents, especially Jackson, now the national hero since the victory at New Orleans and one whose powerful influence they wisely feared. But it eloquently appealed their case. "Take not from us, oh father, our inheritance; leave us our lands," the memorandum read, and then came the offensive passage:

Father, you have with you, as with us red children, those who make crooked talks; they, like the serpent, speak with a split tongue. Believe not their talks, for they are false; nor their actions, for they are deceitful. The spirit of gain urges them, the laurel of popularity prompts them, and we, your faithful children of the Cherokee nation, who expected nothing but justice, are to fall a sacrifice to their rapaciousness. We therefore pray, oh father, that you will interfere in our behalf, and use your powerful sword for our protection; that sword which is wielded by justice and tempered with humanity.[35]

On the twenty-second the president granted them an audience at the queer octagonal house of Colonel Tayloe's, partly triangular and partly circular in shape, with curving doors and curving glass windows, which the devastation of the Executive Mansion had forced him to occupy. Mr. Madison, his small figure dressed in a plain brown coat and knee breeches, his eyes clear and blue under bushy eyebrows, waited in silence while Colonel Lowrey, as speaker for the delegation, addressed him in dignified formality.:

"Father: I now have the pleasure to be in your presence. I am directed by my nation at council to take you, Our Father, by the hand. This day was appointed by the Great Spirit for us to see one another. It makes my heart as glad to enter your house as it does when I enter my own house."

Madison answered with equal formality: "I was apprised of your coming before you arrived. It always gives me pleasure to receive my friends in my house, especially my red Brethren the Cherokees, who have fought by the side of their white Brethren & spilt their blood together."

After a few more words the president indicated one of the delegation's memoranda. "From this paper," he continued, "I discover you wish to know whether our red Brethren who have lost their friends in the late war & on whom their support depended cannot be placed on the same condition as your white Brothers." The president's answer was yes. "Those that had been crippled by wounds will be provided for with pensions [the same] as our white Brothers."

Then the president mentioned the destruction of Cherokee property during the war. The spoliations, he declared, would be considered favorably—"as much as what is right." As for the iron-works, he did not believe that such an undertaking could at present be underwritten by the United States; ". . . notwithstanding," he hastened to add, "we wish to do everything for the promotion of civilization." He instructed the Cherokees to continue looking to Colonel Meigs, their agent, for supplies of ironware. Then the president mentioned the cession of land in South Carolina which The Pathkiller had indicated in his letter of instruction. The cession would please him, he declared, provided the Cherokees weren't too extravagant in their price. "I have no doubt but that the State of So. Carolina would make you a handsome offer for it. It is probable that the subject will require a consultation before you leave the city."[36] And then the audience came to an end.

The delegation rejoiced. It seemed assured of success in the most important points of its mission. Then a dispatch from home threw the delegates into consternation: the U.S. commissioners had carried the line to Nickajack on the Tennessee, thus relegating a number of Cherokee settlements and over two million acres of Cherokee land to the territory that would be ceded. Again the Cherokees appealed their case. On February 28, Colonel Meigs assured The Ridge and his colleagues that "the President your father will hear and candidly attend to the evidence laid before him and probably will propose such an arrangement as will do justice to you." Bad news continued to come from home, and the Cherokees continued to petition the federal government.[37]

"The voice of the Cherokee people," they wrote the secretary of war on March 12, "now calls loudly to your Government for justice." And for the first time they began to hedge about the cession in South Carolina, suggesting that under the circumstances the American offer of five thousand dollars might be far too low. Two days later the War Department sent instructions to the commissioners to hold up work on running the Cherokee line "until it shall be defined by treaty with the deputation of that nation in this city."[38]

Thus, the Cherokees won their point. On March 22, 1816, they signed two treaties with the United States. The first ceded the land in South Carolina for $5,000, to be paid by the state. The second contained stipulations concerning the boundary line so generous that the Cherokees were assured of almost their entire claim. At the same time they conceded to the United States the free navigation of all rivers in their territory and the right to open roads. For such concessions, and to reimburse them for the losses suffered during the war, the United States agreed to pay $25,000. Soon, too, as a graceful courtesy, the secretary of war presented through the delegation three silver-mounted rifles, appropriately inscribed, to Charles Reese and the two Whale brothers for their valor in capturing the first canoes at the battle of the Horseshoe. Colonel McKenney added some large silver medals.[39]

After rounds of entertainment, Major Ridge was ready to depart along with his servant and Captain Taylor, leaving the rest to follow at a later date. They traveled by way of Baltimore, and Major Ridge was much impressed with that half-Southern city, the home of *Niles' Weekly Register,* which had noticed the presence of the Cherokees in the capital. Baltimore was a busy port which carried on a large trade with the West Indies and Europe, especially in Virginia tobacco. It was also the largest city The Ridge had ever seen, and he would sometimes talk about it with friends and acquaintances at home. From there the travelers took a coach to Knoxville, arriving April 12, 1816.[40] They proceeded home at once, presumably on horseback, to find the nation both concerned at the activities of the U.S. commissioners and jubilant over the success of the delegation at Washington.

On the sixteenth the War Department notified the commissioners to resume running the Cherokee line according to terms reached at the capital. In addition to a copy of the treaty the instructions included the order: "You will be attended by some of the Cherokee chiefs who are acquainted with the point at which [the boundary] is to terminate."[41] The commissioners met the Cherokees at the ford where the military road out of Fort Strother crossed the Coosa. The Indians held a council and chose two commissioners of their own, Major Ridge and Colonel Brown, "to designate the different points at which their line should run." Brown traced a course west of the Coosa that substantially followed that which had been indicated by the Cherokees in July, 1814.

Major Ridge pointed out the landmarks for the line east of the Coosa, leading Gaines and Barnett over aboriginal trails through forest and savanna, past marsh and canebrake, and now and then past lonely Cherokee clearings. The first segment of that portion of the line, as The Ridge demonstrated, should extend from below the Ten Islands to an isolated dwelling on Cedar Creek, a tributary of the Tallapoosa. Then it should strike across country to a point where the Chattahoochee ran calm and deep. The final landmark that he pointed out was the former site of the double-story log building known as Vann's Store beside the Ocmulgee.[42]

Word of the treaties concluded with the Cherokees, and especially of the change in tack ordered upon the boundary commission, stirred up a storm in Tennessee, where the people assumed that "a large and very valuable tract of land ceded by the Creeks [had] been given to the Cherokees."[43] Jackson took Secretary Crawford's policy as a rebuke, indeed as a personal affront; he felt his conquest had been in part annulled and believed himself humiliated in the eyes of the Indians, a bitter draught for such a proud man to swallow. He wrote scathing letters to Meigs, whom he accused of sinning "against the light and knowledge," and he collected affidavits from various Creek chiefs claiming former Creek ownership of all lands south of the Tennessee and threatening prosecution for what he called false damage claims.[44] On June 10, 1816, he protested to Crawford: "On the principle of right & justice, the surrender ought never to have been made. The Government has certainly been imposed on. The convention should not have been ratified, unless we are getting like the nations of old, who, having become so hardened, would not listen to the voice of instruction until brought to repentence by the visitation of some serious calamities." He vowed that it was now the "height" of his "diplomatic ambition [to] restore to the U. States the territory fairly and justly ceded by the Creeks."[45]

His ambition did not have long to wait. Owing no doubt to persistent howls from Tennessee, President Madison appointed Jackson, along with David Meriwether and Jesse Franklin, to a commission to purchase the lands the administration had refused to accept as the doubtful bounty of the Creek treaty. It was a galling chore to Jackson to buy back the land he believed was already the rightful property of the United States, but he would have been even more galled had he not received the opportunity, and he set about the assignment with his usual determined will. He began with an attempt to soften up the hard core of the opposition. On July 21, 1816, he wrote to his crony General Coffee, who had succeeded the ailing Hawkins on the boundary commission: "I wish you and Colo. Barnett would see Colo. Brown, Lowrey, The Pathkiller and The Ridge. You can sound them to the bottom and obtain from them a declaration that they will resign all claim for a very small sum; they know they never had any rights and they will be glad, as I believe to swindle the U. States out of a few thousand dollars, and bury the claim, which they know, if persisted in, might bury them and [their] nation."[46]

Presumably Coffee approached prominent Cherokees at the July council called at the Cherokee agency to collect long-delayed military pay and spoliation dues under the terms of the treaty.[47] Jackson instructed him to inform the chiefs that he expected a full Cherokee delegation at the council he had scheduled with the Chickasaws in early September, 1816, at the Old Chickasaw Council House. Treaties with both nations as well as another with the Choctaws, according to Jackson's strategy, would be concluded then and there.

The Ridge bowed out of the intrigue. The deputation of fifteen chiefs and warriors (including Sequoyah, not yet famous) which the Cherokees chose at Willstown on August 20 was instructed flatly to sell no land. But at the council in September Jackson hammered away at his contention that the Chickasaws, who disputed the Cherokee claim to the lands south of the Tennessee, were disposed to sell. Then he presented his impressive array of affidavits swearing that the disputed lands belonged to neither the Cherokees nor the Chickasaws but in reality to the Creeks. If in the face of the general's persuasiveness the Cherokee delegates began to feel their claim was weak, the really telling arguments were the "presents" Jackson thought it "well and polite" to offer. These the fifteen warriors and chiefs, including Toochalar, Speaker of the deputation, could not resist, and notwithstanding their instructions, twelve of them made their crosses on the treaty Jackson presented. It ceded 1,300,000 acres south of the Tennessee to the United States in return for five thousand dollars, plus six thousand dollars a year over the span of a decade. To escape the inevitable wrath of the nation, the purchased delegates stipulated that the treaty must be ratified by the National Council, to meet at Turkey Town on September 28. There Jackson proved as persuasive as ever, and the treaty was ratified by the signatures of eight chiefs, including The Pathkiller's.[48] Thus Major Ridge and those who held like views were defeated, to The Ridge's disgust, in their contest with Old Hickory.

But American hunger for land remained insatiable. The new cession whetted more appetite than it satisfied. Even before Congress could ratify the treaty, moves were instigated for another cession. The opportunity arose from the plight of Tahlonteskee's band in Arkansas, where they had settled on White River with the understanding that a proportionate acreage in the East would be exchanged for the tract they occupied. This exchange had never been consummated, and when The Ridge and his colleagues had received a reminder at the capital, they had retorted that Tahlonteskee had better come home.[49] Such a move was less than feasible, and now the United States was pressing for an appropriate trade of land. In January, 1817, Colonel Meigs received instructions to open negotiations.

Major Ridge, along with such prominent leaders as The Pathkiller, Charles Hicks, and Sour Mush, boycotted the council ostensibly called to hear proposals for changing the Treaty of Chickasaw Council House but really to enable the agent to outline new measures for the exchange of land. Though a few approved, Meigs's plan touched off violent opposition in others, who threatened to break, or as the Cherokees said, to "make a boy" of Toochalar, Major Ridge's kinsman and now the assistant principal chief, for his sin of having approved removal and land exchange.[50] Meanwhile the president had reappointed Jackson and Meriwether as commissioners, along with Governor McMinn of Tennessee, to arrange another treaty. McMinn infiltrated the Cherokee Nation with a legion of agents who engaged in wholesale bribery to silence opposition to land exchange.

There was another Cherokee boycott when Jackson and Meriwether opened a council on June 20, 1817, at Calhoun, Tennessee, the new site of the agency on the Hiwassee River. Only fifteen chiefs were present, all from Arkansas. The boycott failed, however, to hold firm against pressures, inducements, and tantalized curiosity, so a quorum had gathered within a week. Most of the delegates were thunderstruck at Jackson's main proposals, first, that eastern land be paid for the tract Tahlonteskee had taken on White River, and second, that the rest of the Cherokees remove west, exchanging their ancient home for country beyond the Mississippi. All who migrated could draw "a rifle gun, ammunition, a blanket, and a brass kettle or in lieu of that a Beaver trap."[51]

The Ridge joined sixty-six other chiefs in signing a remonstrance against the entire removal policy; they damned it as contrary to the tribal will, besides originating in fraud.[52] But Jackson persisted with a bluff that he would conclude a pact solely with the Arkansas delegation — a bluff that the council could surely have called had it remained firm. It was crumbling with dissension, however, and by July 8, 1817, Jackson had found a sufficient number of chiefs ready to join "their western brothers" in foisting a treaty onto the nation. The general had largely failed in his second objective, but his first was attained through secret bribery to the amount of $5,225 — an end that comprised two cessions of land, one in Georgia, the other in Tennessee, for which the Cherokees received no compensation other than securing Tahlonteskee's home in the West. The inducements to stimulate removal, though largely ineffective, were retained, and the federal government agreed to defray the cost of travel. The treaty provided also for a Cherokee census both east and west of the Mississippi.[53]

After a period of shock and daze the Cherokee committee vented its wrath on September 3, 1817, by voting to break Toochalar. The treaty he had favored had been so cynically negotiated, so obviously obtained by fraud and corruption, that even the acting secretary of war expressed his doubts that Congress would accept it.[54] But the Senate discovered fraud too profitable to rectify. And thus the cause for which The Ridge labored went down in defeat at the hands of a future president of the United States. The Ridge's destiny and that of his people would remain entangled with Jackson's during the fateful years ahead, but in 1817 only the general lines of the future seemed clear: that the American drive for land would inexorably shape the destiny of the Cherokee Nation.

Meanwhile Major Ridge had placed his faith in education as the instrument to ensure his people's salvation—education that would furnish the younger generations with a more equal basis on which to compete with the whites and would prepare them to withstand the pressures of white encroachment with a better chance of success. He had become one of the staunchest champions of education in Cherokee history.

5 • THE TORCHLIGHT

B
Y 1816 two or three hundred Cherokees had been exposed to English instruction in "the three R's" at Gideon Blackburn's schools or that conducted by John and Anna Gambold, or at those spasmodically run by wandering Americans at various native homes. A few Cherokees, like Charles Hicks and John Ross, had gone to white settlements for training. The cause of Cherokee education had thus made modest progress when the Cherokee delegation was approached in Washington by the Reverend Cyrus Kingsbury, a Congregational minister with support from the American Board of Commissioners for Foreign Missions. He dreamed of founding a school on a larger scale than any the Cherokees had yet seen. When he raised the question, the delegates replied that the nation had long desired to establish schools, and the chiefs had thought of even "devoting a part of their annuity to [that] object, but in consequence of some embarrassment had felt themselves unable."[1] Mr. Kingsbury's efforts on behalf of their young people would be most welcome, the delegates declared. They were delighted when he appealed to the president for financial assistance for a definite project.

The secretary of war replied that the president approved the request. Colonel Meigs would be directed to have a schoolhouse built, as well as quarters for teachers and pupils, in whatever part of the nation Kingsbury selected for a school. The agent would furnish two plows, six hoes, and as many axes, in order that the "arts of cultivation" might be introduced among the pupils. For any girl students, he would also furnish "a loom, a half dozen spinning wheels, and as many cards." The War Department would advance partial operating expenses, all of which would be free of strings. The only return the president asked was "an annual report of the state of the school, its progress, and future prospects."[2]

97

Kingsbury reached the Cherokee country in September, 1816. He submitted his proposal to the chiefs during the fall council, and though they were distracted by land cession intrigues, the Speaker replied after a consultation: "You have appeared in our full Council. We have listened to what you have said and understand it. We are glad to see you. We wish to have the school established and hope it will be of great advantage to the nation."[3] So accompanied by a chief appointed to help him locate a site, Kingsbury looked about the country. He chose a spot on the west bank of Chickamauga Creek in Tennessee two miles above the Georgia line. There he bought the farm of an aged Scotsman, and with help hired by Colonel Meigs, he soon had buildings ready for a school he called Brainerd, after a missionary who had done notable work among the northern tribes.[4]

No Cherokee was happier over this development than Major Ridge. He appeared at Brainerd on May 14, 1817, having ridden some sixty miles from Oothcaloga, nor was he disappointed in what he saw: four log cabins for the accommodation of the pupils and the missionaries; several buildings for use as storerooms, corncribs, and stables; and a log schoolhouse which, when finished, would serve as many as a hundred students on the Lancastrian plan. Off in front of the buildings, bordering on higher and more wooded land, were forty-five acres of cleared fields, ready for cultivation. The Ridge looked around and was pleased. This was an important day, one that nearly erased the anxieties of a crop failure at home, for with him were his two older children—Nancy, sixteen, and John, fourteen— whom he had brought to join the score of other scholars there. They were accepted for training, and the diarist of Brainerd described them in the school's journal as "son and daughter of a chief"; also, as "tawny son and daughter of the forest." He added: "[They] have rich clothing, many garments, & some knowledge of letters."[5]

As a matter of fact, they had a fair education already, better than that of most Cherokees then exposed to book learning, for they had studied at the Spring Place school of Father and Mother Gambold since 1810 and had learned much of what that kindly couple were prepared to teach them.

The Ridge had asked the Gambolds to take Nancy as early as January, 1810, but as they ran a school primarily for boys, they had no place for the girl, then eight, unless she lived with a neighbor. The Gambolds suggested that The Ridge secure board and lodging for her at the house of Margaret Vann, a widow of his late notorious friend.[6] She had moved from Vann's huge mansion and was living in a modest house at Spring Place, and there she kept two girls who attended the school. Peggy Vann, as she was called, was a sensible and industrious woman, much appreciated by all who knew her; she agreed to board and lodge Nancy, but The Ridge and Susanna waited six months before they took advantage of the arrangement.[7] On moving to Spring Place, Nancy spent several hours each day of the week, both morning and afternoon, at school, but in return for her room and meals she, along with her two classmates, helped Mrs. Vann "to wash, milk, churn & do other work early in the morn, at evenings & on Saturday, when we have no school."[8]

Meanwhile The Ridge had set his mind on giving John the best training possible for a Cherokee in the white man's tongue. The boy was frail, however; indeed, he had been so since infancy, owing to a scrofulous condition of the hip, an ailment far from rare among the Cherokees:[9] it was the same disease that had bothered Charles Hicks since youth. Susanna made sure that John—or Skah-tle-loh-skee, as he was known in Cherokee—ate no meat from turkeys, whose dewlaps looked so much like scrofulous eruptions, but such denials had not removed the red and purplish mottles or eased the ache in his hip. It was hard for Susanna to let him go and live thirty miles from home, even with such conscientious people as the Gambolds, but The Ridge's ambition was centered on John, especially since Watty, the younger boy, was slow and weak in the mind. The Ridge would later say of Watty, "If the child were to blame for his lack of intelligence, I would be very ill-tempered with him . . . but since it is God's doing, I must have great patience with his weakness."[10] Watty was a good-natured child and gave his parents no trouble. But The Ridge had no hope of his ever taking an education. In that respect his ambitions were fastened on John, whom he dedicated to the future service of the nation.

So on November 12, 1810, The Ridge had taken John to Spring Place and left him there, a slim and delicate seven-year-old, quick and graceful in spite of his limp.[11] His complexion was light, even for a Cherokee, so light that he might have passed for a white child, especially with the tendency of his black hair to wave. But he spoke no English and was imprisoned for the first time in clothes that must be constantly worn, since the missionaries so abhorred nakedness. His dress probably included a small hunting shirt, of cloth Susanna had woven, reaching to his knees and gathered at the waist with a belt or sash. She might have given him breeches in the American style, for such were growing ever more popular among the Cherokees, but almost certainly moccasins, not shoes, covered his feet. The Gambolds welcomed him with gentle solicitude, and soon they were writing to a friend in Salem that he was "quite happy with them and doing well in school."[12] Thus began perhaps the most significant formative period in the life of "John The Ridge's son," years that would modify the entire pattern of his life.

Now that Gideon Blackburn's schools had closed, the Gambolds' house was about the only place in the Cherokee nation where one could gain a white man's education unless one's father were lucky enough to have secured a competent tutor from the white settlements, and that was rare. The Moravians had been at Spring Place since April, 1801, having secured permission from the Cherokee council to build their mission, with help from James Vann and Colonel Meigs. They had located a few hundred yards from where the main road would soon run between Nashville and the white settlements of Georgia—a healthful spot, with fertile soil, abundant woods nearby, excellent pasturage for the livestock, and magnificent springs that purled from the seams of limestone ledges and gathered into a creek that rippled away to the Conasauga. Hence the name they gave the spot: Spring Place. They began at once to erect buildings, of blockhouse style, arranged in a square, to enclose a yard. When they concentrated thus on physical improvements and on preaching the Christian gospel while deferring the opening of their promised school, the council made it clear that the Cherokees wanted practical teachers for their children rather than preachers of a new theology and gave them six months to organize a school or leave the nation.[13]

"[Thus] the Moravians opened their school for the Indians," John Ridge wrote years later to the statesman Albert Gallatin. "[They] cleared a farm, cultivated a garden & planted an orchard" —an orchard of cherry, peach, and apple trees. They also planted catalpa and chinaberry trees about the yard.

The venerable Rev. John Gambold & his amiable Lady were a standing monument of Industry, Goodness & friendship. As far as they had means, they converted the "Wilderness to blossom as the Rose." There the boys and girls were taught to read & write, & occasionally labor in the Garden & in the field. There they were first taught to sing & pray to their Creator, & here Gospel Worship was first established. Never shall I forget father Gambold & mother Mrs. Gambold. By them the clouds of ignorance which surrounded me on all sides were dispersed. My heart received the rays of civilization & my intellect expanded & took a wider range. My superstition vanished & I began to reason correctly

Curious to view the Kings of ancient days,
The mighty dead that lived in endless praise.[14]

It was a busy regime the school followed. When John arrived, there were eight other students, not counting Nancy and her roommates. In winter all rose at daybreak, in summer at sunrise, and when they were dressed, they met for morning prayers, kneeling together. Instruction began after breakfast when the three girls arrived, and the session continued till the noonday meal. After eating, the scholars enjoyed a recess of several hours, during which the boys engaged in physical labor—chopping wood, hoeing the garden, or working under the eye of Mr. Gambold or his brother in the forty acres of cleared fields; or when no work demanded their attention, they were allowed to go with their cane blowguns and bows and arrows to shoot for birds and squirrels. At three o'clock instruction began again and continued all afternoon. Mrs. Gambold, who had gained experience at a Brethren school in Bethlehem, Pennsylvania, taught the secular studies, while Mr. Gambold supervised the training in religion. These tasks were accomplished with a library of fewer than one hundred books. There were fifteen volumes of religious works, including Bunyan; thirteen volumes on scientific subjects; and seventeen of poetry, including *Paradise Lost* and *The Seasons,* by James Thomson, as well as works by Burns, Cowper, and Isaac Watts. There were four books on education and twenty miscellaneous items. As for textbooks, the lot comprised eleven titles, although in most cases several copies of each existed: books for reading, spelling, English grammar, oratory, and accounting. There were fifteen copies of one item: *The Economy of Human Life,* by Robert Dodsley.[15]

Evensong and prayers came after supper, and the scholars went to bed early. John threw himself eagerly into the program. "He learned rapidly," according to his son, "and in the course of a year acquired a sufficient knowledge of the white man's language to speak it fluently."[16] That language was English, of course; the Gambolds taught only English to their scholars, though German was their native tongue. Presumably Nancy made excellent progress too. Both quickly learned to sing in the white man's way, for as John would write, "The school opens and closes with song."[17] On Sunday Mr. Gambold preached in the classroom, and Indians came from miles around to hear him, even on Christmas in spite of the dearth of whiskey in the neighborhood to help them celebrate the holidays.

With John and Nancy adjusting so happily to conditions at Spring Place, and with such satisfactory notices reaching Oothcaloga of their progress, The Ridge had little need to encourage his brother Watie to enroll his bright young son Gallegina, or Buck, as he was called in English. The boy arrived shortly after John and, though a year younger, made as rapid progress. Indeed, his gentle disposition endeared him to the Gambolds even more than John, who showed a colder, more calculating manner, was at times inclined to haughtiness, and was never so likely as Buck to develop that quality so dear to missionaries, the trait they described as "piety." Different as Buck and John were—they even looked different, Buck with a darker complexion, with straight black hair, appearing very much the Indian boy—they drew close together, and here intensified that intimate comradeship that was to identify the cousins with one another for the rest of their lives.

Here too John may have met another boy with whom he became close friends, Jack Bell.* He was not a pupil at the school, but his father ran a "stand" on the public road not far from Spring Place. Whatever the beginning of their friendship, over the years their devotion would grow so strong that they in time became known as "the Damon and Pythias of the Cherokees."18

Meanwhile the regime progressed smoothly, broken only by visits home or by visits of relatives to the school. On January 18, 1811, The Ridge dropped in at mealtime and declared that their custom of singing before and after eating pleased him very much. "We took this opportunity," the Gambolds noted, "to speak of goodness and love of God towards man; and said among other things that it was His will that we should turn to Him in necessity like a child, and that we should heartily thank Him for His good gifts. Thereupon The Ridge remained through the lesson hours, and told the pupils that he wished he were still *their age* so that he would have a chance to *gain understanding*."19 He encouraged them to study hard.

A few months later, on hearing that John had an eye infection, he brought Susanna in great haste to Spring Place. "She could not describe how much she had worried about her son's sight while on the road. Oh, it is beyond telling how the Father of lies keeps busy

*I.e., John A. Bell.

in this country," the Gambolds wrote, "to frighten people and to make everything out worse than it is. . . . How happy both parents were when they learned that the child's eye was not in such a bad state after all. They seemed pleased with what we had done for him, and after they had eaten, they went away much soothed."[20] They felt certain now that their children were in good hands, and later The Ridge told the Gambolds that John was as much their son as anyone's.

The Gambolds regarded John and Buck—especially Buck—as their prize scholars. They taught them not only to speak English, but also to read and write it. The boys studied spelling from Noah Webster's spelling book. They took up arithmetic, and in time progressed to history and geography. They specialized in some degree in academic subjects, in which Nancy, being a girl, did not receive so much instruction, but was instead absorbed in sewing and spinning and weaving. But all in time were encouraged to learn to draw.

One day the Gambolds proudly displayed the scholars to a distinguished visitor, a black-garbed Catholic abbé with the impressive name of Correa da Serra. The visitor wrote to an English friend:

Judge of my surprise in the midst of the wilderness, to find a botanic garden, not indeed like that at Paris, or yours at Kew; but a botanic garden, containing many exotic and medicinal plants, the professor, Mrs. Gambold, describing them by their Linnean names. Your missionaries have taught me more of the nature of the manner of promulgating civilization and religion in the early ages by the missionaries from Rome, than all the ponderous volumes which I have read on the subject. I there saw the sons of a Cherokee Regulus learning their lessons, and reading their New Testament in the morning, and drawing and painting in the afternoon, though to be sure, in very Cherokee style; and assisting Mrs. Gambold in her household work or Mr. Gambold in planting corn. Precisely so in the forests of Germany or France, a Clovis or a Bertha laid aside their crowns, and studied in the hut of a St. Martin or another missionary.[21]

Three years passed at Spring Place, years that witnessed the anxieties of the earth tremors, when the buildings shook as if they would collapse and the springs spouted muddy water; years that witnessed the uncertainties of the Creek War, with soldiers marching across the nation destroying stock and property; years of drought and famine when many Cherokees went hungry. In January, 1814, John received a message from The Ridge, who had come home for a short time from the Creek campaign, to return to Oothcaloga because Susanna his mother was ill. She refused to see a native conjuror or to have anything to do with "Indian sorcery." So The Ridge, involved in the throes of raising men for the new campaign, asked his nearest neighbor, William Hicks, to call at Spring Place for medicinal herbs from Mrs. Gambold's garden, since Susanna would be treated with nothing except what the missionaries advised. She grew better, but her mother, the old Mrs. Wickett, who suffered from the same complaint as John, worsened and died, perhaps owing to the incessant rains. The weather was so bad, in fact, that John's ailment also grew worse, and his return to Spring Place was postponed, especially since The Ridge had to leave again for the Creek War. By the time Major Ridge returned in April, full of honors for his valor at the Horseshoe, John had recovered his health, and Major Ridge took him back to Spring Place, much against Susanna's wishes.[22]

The Gambolds always welcomed Major Ridge, whom they appreciated as "an honest Indian." It was his custom to stop at Spring Place whenever passing to or from the Cherokee agency, and his children saw him several times the following year, always occasions for solemn admonitions for them to study hard and mind the Gambolds. These were also times for solemn conferences with the missionaries, for the Gambolds never lost a chance to tell the gospel story or to exhort The Ridge to piety for his soul's sake. Once on returning from the agency, where he and Susanna had met Colonel Hawkins and his son and accepted their company for the road, he was embarrassed to find the Creek agent under the Gambold's displeasure for drunkenness the previous spring and "blasphemy against the Lord." Father Gambold met them "with a serious mien" and declared he was surprised that Colonel Hawkins could show his face again at Spring Place. When the agent tried to excuse his profanity on the grounds of drunkenness, the missionary took the occasion "to represent to him the sin and shame of that vice and its terrible consequences, with the effect that the wretched fellow got up in silence and left the house. The Ridge apologized that this man had come to us in his company."

"At the same time," Mrs. Gambold wrote, "the honest Indian offered to leave, but we restrained him, saying that the scoundrel who had blasphemed our God had this time forced his company on him as he had last time on our friend Chulioa; for this we sympathize with them both; he, as our honest friend, should with his wife join us for breakfast, and we would feed the others too, but not at our table."[23]

Another visit of The Ridge was the occasion "for serious talks about the fall and salvation of man." The major's manner grew more serious. "I myself would like to hear what is good. When a young man, I killed a wicked Indian, and have often wondered since then whether God would not punish me for that deed one day. I've resolved never to do such a thing again, unless the Council orders me to rid the world of a bad man, as the case was with Doublehead."

The Gambolds assured him God forgave all sins if one prayed to Him from the heart. "Major Ridge paid close attention," Mrs. Gambold recorded. "He seemed to understand our meaning perfectly."[24]

At about this time, however, the Moravian couple heard that Major Ridge was planning to take his children from their school. They received, unfortunately, a rather distorted report that keenly disappointed them in The Ridge. They wrote:

He was here only last month and engaged in conversation with our pupils, and repeatedly reminded them that we had surely come to teach them what was good and that they must therefore pay the strictest attention to everything we told them, and must obey us faithfully, just as he always told them at each visit. Would you have concluded from this that this man is not very far from the Kingdom of Heaven? Now read on. Last week his next-door neighbor, William Hicks, was here, and said that The Ridge is taking a school master into his home and will take his son away from here, *because he is not being treated well by us.* . . . This was told us in front of the pupils, and John Ridge was asked if he knew anything about it. The latter paled visibly, but confessed nothing of having made such a complaint against us. Such is our thanks for . . . long faithful service and care, giving him of our best.[25]

The truth was that The Ridge did not really want to take his children from Spring Place, nor was he dissatisfied with the pains the Gambolds had taken with their education, but he was hard pressed by Susanna, who wanted her children at home, especially John with his ailing hip. Therefore The Ridge was trying to make arrangements for their education to be continued at their house at Oothcaloga. He had taken John on a trip to the white settlements in Georgia, perhaps in connection with the project.[26] Then one day in April he and Watie drove up in a rented carriage to convey the boys and Nancy home. Major Ridge addressed the Gambolds through Peggy Vann, thanking them for the care they had spent on John. Now he wanted to take him home to have him taught by a teacher he had hired for the purpose. "He begged especially that we should not regard this as if he desired to break up the friendship that had existed between us hitherto; he would always feel affection for us and come to our house as before whenever he came into the neighborhood."[27] He confessed, too, as a kind of apology, that the new teacher did not strike him as being so capable as the missionaries, but he was obliged to try the experiment.

The Gambolds reminded him that their object was larger than the mere teaching of reading and writing: they aimed to instruct the children about the Savior and their souls and salvation, and it hurt very deeply to lose them to the care of "a false white man."

The Ridge was silent, and so was Watie.

Much affected, the Gambolds said farewell and, taking each child by the hand, exhorted him to remember their teachings. John received their words quietly; Buck began to weep. It was a sad leavetaking, even though it meant a ride in a splendid white carriage. Later Mrs. Gambold confided to the Spring Place diary: "Since we have seen only too often what kind of people the white-skinned are who press their services on the native Indians, we felt rather apprehensive for the children, especially about our promising little Buck."[28] They felt that Buck was too trusting, too innocent, too eager to please for his own safety, while John was shrewd and circumspect, taking little on faith and revealing skepticism for the gospel story. Indeed, they confessed to their superior in Salem, North Carolina: "That The Ridge was taking his son away we did not mind too much, because with all his skill for learning he is real proud *to be a savage.*"[29] The sentence was in German, except for the final phrase, which appeared in English as if to make it stand out.

Time proved the Gambolds right about one thing. Major Ridge's schoolmaster turned out to be a profane man, a drunkard who taught his pupils little of value and who decamped from his responsibilities within three months. The whole development filled Major Ridge with dismay; he felt especially contrite concerning his brother, whom he had urged to take Buck from Spring Place so that he could join John with the tutor at home. One warm day in August, while returning from the Cherokee agency, he stopped at the school with letters for the Gambolds.

"He seemed very low in spirits," Mrs. Gambold recorded. ". . . and he pleaded in his brother's name, very humbly, that we take back Watie's son Buck, which we promised to do—that is, if the boy's childlike simplicity had not suffered through the bad example."[30]

Though John and Nancy were never to re-enroll at Spring Place, they saw the Gambolds again in October at a convention of former scholars. Mrs. Gambold recorded on the sixteenth: "We received a visit from The Ridge, with his two children—our former pupils, John and Nancy. With them we spoke most seriously and warned them against evil company. The Ridge asked to have our speech repeated to him in his language, and thanked us for our words. Nancy cried loudly. John, however, remained unmoved. The mother, whose fault it was that the children had been taken away, would not come in, but hurried away *alone*."[31]

Watie arrived the next day with Buck.

The father said his son could hardly wait to see us again. Late at night he had demanded that they keep on traveling, but Watie had refused to do so because of a dangerous creek. He promised not only to bring Buck back to our school, but also to enroll his younger brother Stand.* Watie told us frankly that he had soon recognized that the runaway schoolmaster was a bad character; and Buck added that he had cursed us. We told Watie, frankly too, our opinion of such people; and in our hearts we thanked the dear Savior that He had brought back to us our Buck, about whose removal we had sorrowed so greatly. The boy was just as before, childlike, warm and loving.[32]

John continued to read at home from books that Major Ridge ordered on the advice of Charles Hicks. But such a program was only marking time, The Ridge felt, and when he went to Washington as a delegate, his private aim was to explore the possibility of a school for John to attend among the whites. Meanwhile the Reverend Cyrus Kingsbury appeared with his plan, to The Ridge's delight, and hardly had Brainerd opened for students than he was knocking on the door with John and Nancy at his side.

The missionaries at Brainerd described John's character as "thoughtful," and they assigned him and Nancy to the "oldest and highest

*Stand Watie, a late bloomer, figures prominently only at the close of this narrative. Circumstances brought him to the fore in 1839, and he led the Ridge faction, later the Southern Cherokees, until after the Civil War. For his story, see Kenny A. Franks, *Stand Watie and the Agony of the Cherokee Nation.*

class." There were about twenty scholars, but every week or so someone new appeared, including two grandchildren of Colonel Meigs. Most of the students were of mixed blood, some so light they could pass for white and some even with blond hair and blue eyes.[33]

The schedule had something in common with that at Spring Place. A half hour before sunrise the blast of a horn roused the pupils from bed, and just as the sun appeared they collected for morning worship. After prayers the boys and girls would file off separately to various chores till eight o'clock. On one morning John might be assigned to cleaning fish from the weir in Chickamauga Creek, on another to milking cows. On still other mornings he might be sent to hoe in the garden or to pound corn. At eight another blast of the horn served as a breakfast call, and the boys and girls sat down at separate tables to wait for a long prayer to end before they began to eat.

Then the school would open, with the reading of a piece of Scripture, the singing of a hymn, the saying of a prayer. The class-work was conducted on the Lancastrian plan, the greatest virtue of which was that it enabled one teacher, Mr. Moody Hall, to keep a class going, though it was composed of all degrees of accomplishment. More advanced students instructed the less advanced in what they had just learned from the monitor above them or from the master himself, and young John Ridge, the quickest student there, with as many years of schooling as any, doubtless received considerable practice in teaching others. They read from hornbooks and readers; they wrote on sand, slates, and paper; they spelled; they worked problems in arithmetic; and the most advanced pupils studied English grammar and committed to memory the Sunday school catechism. Before the noon meal came a short play period, the only opportunity the scholars had to amuse themselves, except for a second recess at dusk. After eating they resumed classwork, the session lasting throughout the afternoon. Evening prayers were held after supper, and at nine o'clock another blast on the horn signaled the hour to go to bed.[34]

Before two months had passed, John's haughty spirit caused him trouble. The oldest class had been practicing spelling, but as they had missed several words, Mr. Hall told them to take a shorter lesson. John replied "in a hasty & petulant manner" that he would not be held to such a brief assignment, but would study the usual number of words. Laudatory though his aim, his demurrer was "spoken in such a way that it could not be passed over," and he was reprimanded. "He burst into a flood of tears," according to the Brainerd diarist, "—said he meant no harm & was sorry he had given us so much trouble & pain.—We could freely forgive him."

Some gossip, however, when informing Major Ridge, so magnified John's offense that it seemed the Ridge children were running wild. Agitated by the account, Major Ridge rode to Brainerd by the nearest route, reaching there two days after John's trouble while the school was at its evening meal. The children could see that something troubled his mind. After dinner he spoke to the missionaries:

"I heard my children were so bad you could not manage them. I came to see if it was true. If they misbehave, it won't be good to keep them at school." He added that he had a little Coosa girl he had taken in the war and would leave her instead. There was no need for that, the missionaries said. They were "generally pleased with the conduct of his children."

Major Ridge clapped his hands at their assurance, and raised his eyes, as if struggling with strong emotion "at the happy disappointment."

"Never was I so glad!" he exclaimed. "As I was coming, I often said to myself, can it be that my children, after all the advice I have given them, could conduct themselves in such a manner?"

Before leaving, he talked to John and Nancy, and the missionaries were impressed by his frank affection. "You know I have often talked with you," he concluded, "and gave you as much as a father ought to give his children. I hope you will listen to it. I now leave you with these people; they will take care of you, and you must obey them as you would me."[35]

But even if the report about John's misdemeanor had been exaggerated, Major Ridge was shrewd enough to see the situation at Brainerd in its proper light. He perceived that the school had little to offer his children that Mr. and Mrs. Gambold had not already given. John's protest had been essentially correct. It was ill advised to hold the quick and able back to keep pace with the dull and slow. The Ridge's ambitions saw in John a future headman of the Cherokees, the principal chief if the Great Spirit were willing, and the time had come when the principal chief should have an education equal to any white man's. Nothing less would satisfy. It was clear that Brainerd, worthy as the experiment was, could not produce the results he wished. But before Major Ridge withdrew his children from its classes, an event occurred that caused considerable stir in the nation: the arrival of Elias Cornelius, a young divine connected with the American Board of Commissioners for Foreign Missions.

He arrived on horseback in September, 1817, stopping at Brainerd, where John first saw his tall, spare figure and reflective face. Cornelius was pleased with what he found there, but conceived of it as only the beginning of a program that would place the Cherokees on a mental and spiritual par with white men, and to promote goodwill he requested the privilege of speaking before a council. The Cherokees invited him to a meeting on the nineteenth at the house of Charles Hicks. The chiefs had been called to draw up instructions to govern a delegation they were sending to Washington City to protest the idea of removal and the iniquities General Jackson and his fellow commissioners had perpetrated against them.

The gathering filled the large ground floor of Hicks's house, the chiefs sitting on chairs that formed a semicircle in front of The Pathkiller, who reclined on a rug at one end of the room. A considerable number of common Indians stood behind the chairs against the walls, listening with respectful attention to the conversation of the chiefs. Cornelius noticed that the appearance of most seemed less civilized than that of Charles Hicks, who looked like a white man. "Their ears were slitted after the Indian manner," he wrote, "with pieces of silver attached to them. Their dress was the hunting shirt, vest, turban, deer-skin leggins, with silk or other garters, and *moccasons*. Some of them had hats. One of them showed me a pair of silver spurs, made by a native [perhaps Sequoyah, or George Guess, whose patron was Charles Hicks]. The price of them was eleven dollars. They were a true specimen of native ingenuity. The chiefs were all well provided with horses, and saddles, and blankets. Their appearance was that of the utmost contentment." Cornelius, who talked to them through an interpreter, found them extremely friendly: "More good nature," he declared, "I never saw displayed in any meeting than this."[36] Yet they had serious business before them which they conducted with dispatch, and Major Ridge joined The Pathkiller and Charles Hicks, along with fifteen other chiefs, in signing the instructions they drew up. To the order to protest the idea of removal to Arkansas they added a request that the delegation petition President Monroe for aid to Cherokee education. Cornelius was so favorably impressed that he asked for a copy of the paper to send to the American Board for Foreign Missions in Boston.[37]

The chiefs obliged him. They were interested in hearing of his mission, but learning that they had called a general council with the Creeks, to meet in Hightower (or Etowah) on October 17, he asked to postpone his talk until that time in order to reach both tribes at the same time.

The council assembled by one o'clock on the specified date, the chiefs sitting on benches under an enormous roof supported by pillars, around which a railing ran, the common people standing in the open sides outside the railing. With Charles Hicks as his interpreter, Cornelius opened his talk with the chiefs by showing his credentials. Then he explained his mission. According to his own account:

I had travelled far from the North to see them on a subject of highest importance to them and their children; that in this I was not acting as a private man, but, as I had shown them, I had been sent to them by a society of great and good men at the North who loved them and wished to do them good; that it was their belief that in no way could they do the Cherokee so much good as by sending wise and good men among them to teach their children; to instruct them in the arts of agriculture; and in the knowledge of their great Creator; by means of which they might be made happy and useful in this life, and which would lead them to happiness when they should die. I assured them that none but good men would be sent among them; that these would never seek to deprive them of any of their lands, but would be entirely satisfied if they could teach the Indians how to cultivate them in the best manner to themselves. I stated the plan, which would govern the society in the establishment of school; and according to which they had already, by consent of the Cherokees, established one school at Chickamaugah [sic], and might yet establish more.[38]

The Indians listened attentively to the address, for Cornelius was a rousing speaker "with tongue of silver and soul of fire." Then they consulted together, and while the Creeks refrained from committing themselves, the Cherokee chiefs approved unanimously. The Pathkiller requested Major Ridge, as the champion of learning and civilization, to proclaim the sense of their deliberation to the council. The Ridge rose in the center of a large circle of Indians and made a speech that lasted for fifteen or twenty minutes. "He spoke with great animation," according to Cornelius, "in a loud tone of voice, and in true native style"[39]—which meant, among other things, that he punctuated his talk and emphasized important points by mighty grunts from the bottom of his diaphragm. At the same time he held his powerful hands folded immobile against his chest:

I am going to address the council of the Cherokee nation, and each representative will inform his own town respectively the result of our deliberations on the subject of what we have heard from the northern good people who have sent this man to us; of their offer to pity our people, and that we have taken hold of their offer. We have thought right to accept of their benevolent object, that our children may learn to act well in life, and their minds be enlarged to know the ways of our Creator. For we have been told that by education we may know, that at death our spirit will return to the Father of it. It will also promote our children's good to labor for their living when they come to years of manhood. I am sensible the hunting life is not to be depended on.

These good people have established one school at Chickamauga and sent us teachers to educate our children. Whereupon the council requires all persons to treat them friendly, and not to disturb anything they have. And as there is now a deputation of warriors to start immediately to visit the President of the United States, the chiefs are also requested to instruct them to ask our father, the President, for his assistance to educate our children.[40]

No other Cherokee could have put more heart into such a talk; Major Ridge spoke with such fullness of feeling because no subject had more engaged his devotion. Though Cornelius could understand no Cherokee and depended on Charles Hicks for a rough translation, Major Ridge's words so moved him he remarked in his report: "From this speech, judge for yourself whether the harvest among these [people] is not ripe, and the time come when Christians everywhere should open wide to them the hand of Charity."[41]

Cornelius proposed to extend his mission to the Choctaws next, but planned to revisit the Cherokees before returning home. He offered to take certain selected pupils with him to attend the new Foreign Mission School that had recently opened its doors at Cornwall, Connecticut, for the purpose of training "foreign youth" as missionaries, schoolmasters, interpreters, and doctors among the peoples ordinarily designated "heathen" by the whites. One of the first students to enter the school, according to the minister, was a young Kanaka from the Sandwich Islands. Several Indian boys from northern tribes had been accepted, and the American Board for Foreign Missions was eager to include students from the southern tribes as well.

The Rev. Elias Cornelius, who selected John Ridge and Elias Boudinot to attend the Foreign Mission School in Cornwall, Connecticut. Courtesy of Columbia University Library.

Cornelius invited Major Ridge to send John, as the best student at Brainerd;[42] Buck, who had graduated from Spring Place, received the same honor. Watie accepted for his son. The reason Major Ridge declined the offer is not clear; it seemed to provide an exemplary solution for John's educational quandary. Perhaps the boy's chronic hip trouble made a long journey inadvisable at that time; perhaps Susanna objected for other, more personal reasons (and among the Cherokees of that day the mother always claimed final authority where her children were concerned). Whatever the explanation, Major Ridge arranged, on taking his children from Brainerd toward the close of 1817, for John to study at an advanced academy in Knoxville, probably that of James M'Bath, rather than at the Mission School at Cornwall.[43]

Another explanation of John's failure to go to Cornwall at this date may merely have been his father's absence when the final decision came due. Another flare-up had occurred among the wild Indians to the south—the insurgent Creeks and Seminoles across the border in Florida, where the prophets had fled after the British debacle at Pensacola—and Jackson had issued a further call for Cherokee assistance. Ever aware that the fortunes of the Cherokees were bound to those of the United States, Major Ridge now helped to raise a band of two hundred warriors on the assumption that Colonel Morgan would again command, and all went well until Morgan resigned his commission for business reasons and Colonel Meigs replaced him with Major John Lowrey, not the Cherokee of that name, but a white man from Tennessee. Lowrey proved unpopular, perhaps because of his attitude toward removal, and many Indians balked at serving under him. The Pathkiller X-ed a letter of explanation at Major Ridge's house on February 17, 1818, declaring that in spite of wholesale withdrawals a few Cherokees were still ready for service. "Major Ridge who is my son and warrior will join you," the ancient head chief promised the general; and so would Chulioa, his "interpreter to the Creeks," and with them a diminished band of mounted men.[44]

The Cherokees, seventy-two of whom constituted a company under The Ridge, who served as captain, joined Jackson's army around Fort Scott near the Florida border early in March, 1818, and seem to have been attached to the friendly Creek force under McIntosh, now a brigadier general. The Seminole campaign that followed was pure opéra bouffe, with provisions almost nonexistent at times and roads made quagmires by the heavy rains. But at the expense of a single soldier killed, Jackson not only achieved his ostensible purpose of cowing a few bedraggled Creeks, Seminoles, and refugee blacks and hanging the prophet Francis, but also his real design of wresting Florida from the palsied grasp of Spain and presenting a conquest to the president, in certainty that American diplomats could seal the outrage without a declaration of war.[45]

The brevity of the Seminole campaign—far from "the savage war" that Jackson called it in his reports—permitted Major Ridge to return to his family soon after Elias Cornelius had reappeared from tour of the Choctaw and Chickasaw nations before starting for home in the North. With the young divine was a Choctaw youth named Folsom bound for the Foreign Mission School. By the last week in May they were ready to travel north with Jeremiah Evarts, treasurer of the American Board, who had visited Brainerd in the meantime. Buck Watie prepared to go with the company, along with Leonard Hicks, son of the assistant principal chief, and Redbird, a former scholar at Brainerd who had taken John's place in the plans of Elias Cornelius.[46]

The small party rode horseback through Tennessee into western Virginia, the ministers preaching along the route, and in time reports reached Oothcaloga of their triumphant progress: how they had stopped at Monticello with its graceful half-dome to pay respects to the venerable Mr. Jefferson, who showed great interest in the Foreign Mission School, fascinated as he was with the question of higher education, as shown by his zeal to establish a college at Charlottesville; how they also stopped at Montpelier with its classic portico to call on Mr. Madison, who was as small as Mr. Jefferson was lank and tall, who met them with little twinkling blue eyes in a drawing room whose walls were covered with paintings, and who invited them to dine with him; and how indeed, when reaching Washington, they even stopped at the White House and shook hands with Mr. Monroe, whose powdered locks were pulled back in an old-fashioned hairdo. The president was easy and gentle with them, his manners as informal and simple as the plain and common furniture that a niggardly Congress had thrust into his reception room.[47]

While still in the capital they rode down to Mount Vernon and visited Washington's tomb, and Mr. Calhoun, the secretary of war, who had studied law at Litchfield a few miles from Cornwall, promised that the War Department would pay a hundred dollars a year against the expenses of each of the three young Cherokees at the Foreign Mission School. Buck and his Indian friends were flattered and petted everywhere they went in Washington, Baltimore, and Philadelphia. And when they reached Burlington, New Jersey, and stopped at the home of the ancient president of the American Bible Society, who had also been president of the Continental Congress, the old man took such an interest in Buck that he invited him to adopt his name, which Buck did, so that on arriving in Cornwall on August 15 he was enrolled at the Foreign Mission School as Elias Boudinot.[48]

Meanwhile John had found the Knoxville school much as Brainerd had been, not really suited to his needs, and so he was home again with the completion of his education a bothersome question. Major Ridge inquired at Brainerd if arrangements for special tutoring might be made. They could, he learned. But if John must live away from home, as the plan required, why not at Cornwall? And so in September The Ridge requested permission from the missionaries to send his son there.[49]

While the debate proceeded on the feasibility of sending John north on the strength of an earlier invitation, tragedy struck at Oothcaloga. Nancy, who had married an Indian named Ricky, was now dead in childbirth. The body was buried in a wood not far from the Ridge house, and the family sat in mourning before their doorway, Indian-fashion, when Daniel Butrick, a Brainerd missionary, arrived to discuss John's case. He spent several days with the grieving family, finding The Ridge's home a gracious one, to which he was glad to return after visits to others in Oothcaloga Valley. He liked to walk with The Ridge and converse on various subjects such as geography and note the intelligent responses. Butrick gave a concise account of the heathen of Asia after a certain "Mr. Buchanan." He spoke too of Africa and the treatment of Negroes when taken as slaves. On another occasion he and Major Ridge spent some time in looking at the stars, calling their names. How pleased The Ridge seemed to note that sometimes the sense of the white man's name coincided with that of the Cherokees'. There was the case of the Seven Sisters, which the Indians called the Seven Brothers: six had made medicine to elevate them in the sky to punish mothers who had given them stones for bread, but the seventh had been pulled back to earth, to become the father of pine trees.[50] Then The Ridge's words seemed to take a religious turn. "Anyone can see," he said, "that the stars never made themselves." And then he called in his Negroes, eight or ten of them, and asked Brother Butrick to talk to them and pray in their presence. One old woman especially caught the preacher's eye; she seemed "remarkably attentive." The Ridge said she was a slave he had captured in the Creek War. She was a "pious mother" who had her family "repeat their prayers morning & evening & learns them some beautiful lines about the crucifixion of our Savior."

One evening Susanna asked about the nature of sin, and her question gave Butrick an opportunity for "a long conversation." He recorded the gist of it later in his journal: "I first shewed them what kind of actions & words were wicked, & how we conduct [ourselves] and speak if we would please God, and was frequently stopped to answer important and very interesting questions. I told them what thoughts were wicked, & how we must keep our hearts if we desire to please God, or dwell with him above."

And when Sunday came and the preacher was ready to give a sermon, Major Ridge asked him to preach it in the woods beside his daughter's grave. He had prepared seats there. Several neighbors arrived, and The Ridge told them how to behave. As Butrick had knelt in the intimacy of family prayer, the chief had assumed that it was customary for people to kneel during public worship, and he warned his friends that they must do so, and showed them how. Such a popish touch startled the young Congregationalist, but Butrick refrained from interfering, seeing that Major Ridge acted from the heart. "As he told them this," the preacher wrote, "I concluded to kneel. Thus we had a congregation of 40 or 50, principally Cherokees, kneeled before God, in the wilderness, & in a place where the gospel was never preached before."

Meanwhile the missionary had talked to Major Ridge and Susanna concerning John's future. He told them that Mother and Father Gambold had advised that the boy be sent to Cornwall, but he stressed the rigors of the journey. He turned to Susanna and asked if she would be willing to send the boy under such difficult circumstances. It was hard to let him go, she confessed, since her daughter had just died. But she knew he needed knowledge for his own good, and for their people's good.[51] So she was resigned.

"She expressed a great desire to have him go," Butrick recorded, "—said she could not keep him alive if at home, & if any accident befell him on the way she would not blame the Missionaries."[52]

John was eager to take the risk. There was no question of Major Ridge's attitude, an unshakable desire for his son to receive the finest training possible. He wanted John to stay at Cornwall until he had received *"a great education."*[53] He hoped, besides, that the Great Spirit would give him a good heart, so that when he did come home, he could be useful to the nation. And so Butrick gave his consent on behalf of Brainerd. He suggested that all go there to settle details and make arrangements for the trip. A Dr. Dempsey, with credentials from the mayor of New York, was ready to leave for the North and had agreed to conduct to Cornwall any boys the missionaries wished to send. John's parents resolved to commit him to the doctor's care, and once the decision was made, The Ridge gave his heir "stern advice" on how to "conduct himself amongst the 'pale-faces.'"[54]

6 • CORNWALL

THE journey for John Ridge in the fall of 1818 began at Spring Place. Susanna said goodbye to him under a great tree near the spring. While the water murmured, she explained that if she believed he were going to the distant country to make a great fortune, she would not let him go. "No, you could never obtain my consent," she said. But because he wanted "further knowledge in good things"—that reason induced her to let him go.[1] She repeated her farewell and left him with the missionaries.

Father and Mother Gambold had recommended Dr. Dempsey as the escort, and they had taken a deep interest in all arrangements. Before these were completed two more of their former pupils joined the party: Darcheechee, a full-blood Cherokee boy who would soon take the name of David Steiner, and John Vann, more familiarly known as George, a son of James Vann by another wife than Peggy. Darcheechee had no suitable white man's clothes, but the problem was solved when Brother Butrick removed his coat and gave it to him. The Gambolds offered him two shirts, and John Crutchfield, former overseer of the Vann estate who had courted and married Peggy, contributed a vest and trousers. The Brainerd missionaries had voted John and Darcheechee sixty dollars apiece for traveling expenses, and the Gambolds added ten, while young Vann had one hundred dollars from his brother "Rich Joe." It was agreed that all the funds were to be entrusted to Dr. Dempsey's care.[2]

The Gambolds had written a letter of introduction for John to a Moravian dignitary at Salem, where the little party would pass, and just before they set forth, the missionaries did the same for Darcheechee. To the first letter Mrs. Gambold added a postscript: "John looks forward greatly to seeing Salem, and Dr. Dempsey is no

less excited. . . . Perhaps our dear good John may hear some of your
sacred music."[3]

The four travelers mounted their horses on October 3 and trotted
along the Georgia pike. They rode in easy stages, stopping at "stands"
or at private homes when no public shelter was available. In time
they turned into South Carolina, riding northward in a vast loop
along the piedmont, beautiful with fall. At Union, George Vann's
horse kicked Darcheechee's small bay mare, making her lame, and
Dr. Dempsey had to trade her for another mount before they could
resume their journey.[4]

After three weeks of riding they came to Salem, North Carolina,
a neat, industrious town on a rising slope, surrounded by rich
meadows, well-cultivated fields, and woods aflame with the colors
of autumn. They passed sturdy houses on either side of the main
street, low-eaved buildings with tiled roofs and massive chimneys,
the people watching them with interest, and now and then the sound
of German reached their ears. Though their appearance was unexpected, they were warmly welcomed, the letters from the Gambolds
opening the doors of friends.

"They remained three days," it was noted in Moravian records,
"and every attempt was made to see that their visit was as pleasant,
useful, and instructive as possible." They heard the sacred music
Mrs. Gambold had begged for John, for Salem had gained renown
for its music, with a chapter of the Collegium Musicum, the chamber music society the Moravians had organized in Bethlehem,
Pennsylvania, and the Brothers delighted in entertaining visitors
with music, including songs and chorales composed by citizens of
the town. "On their account," it was recorded, "the evening service
was a *Singstunde* with musical accompaniment."[5] The travelers heard
not only the choir in church, but also the organ, a wondrous new
experience for John and his companions.

They were taken to the Female Academy fronting the square,
the school John's sister Sarah would attend years later, and were
shown through all the rooms and heard young ladies play the piano.
They also visited the cemetery, where men and women were buried
in separate sections of the yard, and the waterworks which had been
in operation for forty years, the water flowing by gravity from a
spring outside of town through hollow log mains to the square,
where a series of valves directed it into several public buildings.
In fact, they saw "so many other things," John wrote to Spring Place,
"that I cannot mention them on one Sheet of paper."[6]

On their last evening in Salem, Brother Steiner, whose name Darcheechee would adopt, met with the boys "and admonished them to love the Saviour above all things and remain true to him." They resumed their journey on the twenty-sixth, traveling into Virginia and on to the capital. Dr. Dempsey lacked either the entrée of Dr. Cornelius or the boldness, for the boys saw only the White House, not the president. But on their reaching Philadelphia, the son of Father Van Vleck of Salem took them in charge and showed them about the city.[7] There John bought a watch, though he could ill afford it, a gesture that would raise several eyebrows when he arrived at Cornwall, especially when it was learned that his expense money had given out and he had to borrow from Dr. Dempsey to finish the trip. It had been arranged for the doctor to draw on a New York bank in such a contingency, which Dempsey did to recover the debt. But his allowing John to injudiciously spend his money annoyed the Cornwall authorities as much as the doctor's occasional lapses into profanity. Otherwise they thought he had discharged his responsibilities well enough.[8]

The term was several weeks old when John and his comrades reached the school toward the end of November. It was so late in the season that the maple tree in front of the schoolhouse was bare and ceased to be a shelter to the small gambrel-roofed building of one and a half stories that stood near the Cornwall green. Long known as the "Academy," the building had been given to the American Board of Commissioners by the town in the previous year, along with fourteen acres of land that centered on the "Commons" or steward's house on West Road and eighty-six more that lay on the northerly slope of Colt's Foot Mountain. The town of Cornwall, which sprawled at the mountain's base, was an agricultural community, a cluster of neat, trim houses about the village green some three miles east of the Housatonic. The place had been selected for the Foreign Mission School because of its sheltered location and its reputation for general healthfulness. An English visitor would describe its location as "a deep retired romantic valley" whose southern approach, "for three or four miles, lay through a natural grove of hemlock, spruce . . . and cedar."[9]

The Reverend Herman Daggett, a frail man of fifty-one who had taught Elias Cornelius in his youth, had lately become the school principal, having been called from the neighboring village of New Canaan. He took his job with great seriousness, a charge for which he was well suited, for he was "remarkable . . . for simplicity and

The Foreign Mission School, Cornwall, Connecticut. Courtesy of Columbia University Library.

sincerity in what he said or wrote. Never would he use words without meaning. What he expressed, he believed and felt."[10] He got along well with his boys, of whom there were twenty or so enrolled, including one Abnaki Indian, two Choctaws, two Chinese, two Malays, one Bengalese, one Hindu, several Hawaiians, two Marquesans, and three white Americans—not to mention Cousin Buck, now known as Elias Boudinot, and the other Cherokees. Mr. Daggett reported that the boys were "harmonious, punctual and well behaved," and he was pleased by their air of "seriousness," by which he meant an inclination to piety.[11]

But after the arrival of John and Vann, and especially of Jim Fields, a mixed-blood Cherokee who was related to John on his mother's side and who came soon after, Mr. Daggett noticed a change—a subtle diminishing of seriousness. It might well be that a boy so vain and worldly as to indulge himself in a watch was to blame in some degree. But doubtless a larger cause was the flightiness of Fields, suggested by the gay description of him as he would look shortly after his return from Cornwall: "dressed in fine calf boots, blue cloth pantaloons, silk velvet vest, fine beaver hat, with silver band. His gown was made of red flowered calico, reaching nearly to the ground, with a cape over the shoulders trimmed with a blue fringe."[12] Jim Fields was full of fun and levity and, like his relative Ridge, refrained carefully from professing any faith in the Savior. And so Mr. Daggett concluded that "his appearance, progress, & behaviour" were "not at all promising." It seemed to him that Fields as well as Ridge and Vann were too self-centered, and in none of the recent arrivals, except Darcheechee, was there much "appearance of seriousness."

The whole school, Daggett complained, had put on a different look:

... the pious scholars are grieved, & come to me expressing their fears that the school will not prosper. I endeavor to use every means to instruct, counsel, and restrain: but unsanctified nature will act like itself. If it be the design of the guardians of this school to fill it up with youths of the above description, I confess that I am disappointed. When heathen youths are cast upon our shores, & are taken up to be instructed, we may hope for a blessing upon our labors. But perhaps we are not equally warranted to select or receive youth who are not pious, or even serious, from places where they can enjoy the privilege of a common education, & of religious instruction, & place them in a mission school.

Perhaps his most disturbing observation: "Elias, I fear, is also losing his hopeful impressions."[13]

But the principal's pessimism was short-lived, and early in the new year he assumed a more optimistic tone about his students. And except "for the influence of a few," he wrote, there would have been even a more remarkable improvement. If John knew of Mr. Daggett's previous discontent, he failed to mention it when writing to the Gambolds — his "Beloved Parents." After indicating the number of students and the ten different languages spoken, he concluded: "I am very well satisfied with the School, & the instructors; and am now studying Geography and English Grammar."[14] He did not mention that he was also writing verses — short, tight lines with moralization that must have pleased his teachers. His watch, in which he still took obvious delight, was one of the themes:

Little monitor, by thee,
Let me learn what I should be:

Learn the round of life to fill,
Thou canst gentle hints impart,
How to regulate the heart.
When I wind thee up at night
Mark each fault and set thee right,
Let me search my bosom too,
And my daily thoughts review,
Mark the movements of my mind
Nor be easy when I find
Latent errors rise to view,
Till all be regular and true. [15]

These lines—"Upon a Watch"—he signed and dated February 4, 1819. Others—"On the Shortness of Human Life"—he signed and dated "February 30, 1819" and added "Cornwall Connecticut" with a flourish:

Like as a damask Rose you see,
Or like the blossom on the tree,
Or like the morning to the day,
Or like the Sun, or like the Shade,
Or like the Gourd which Jonas had:
Even such is MAN! Whose thread is spun,
Drawn out and cut, and so, 'tis done.
Withers the Rose, the blossom blasts,
The flower fades, the morning hastes,
The sun is set, shadows fly,
The gourd consumes, —so mortals die. [16]

Perhaps the verses indicated a genuine self-conscious examination of his inner being, stimulated by the exhortations of his instructors. The Gambolds had told him of his mother's new religious concern, and he replied: "I am happy that my dear Mother ... wants to get some Knowledge of that Great Being who made all Things, & that it is her wish that I should return a good Man. Beloved Friends, You know I have been very careless about my Soul. Yet that great God has not taken me away, as He did my sister, I have abundant reason to thank him for it. Truly it is my desire that He would shew me my bad Heart, & make me feel it. Then pray for me, my dear Friends."[17] John Ridge thus created the impression of "hopefulness," and though he would never claim conversion, his teachers were satisfied and ceased to complain. It was reported to the American Board in Boston that among those students who were not "public professors of religion" several seemed to "entertain a hope in Christ."

With Cousin Elias, on the other hand, the instructors were unreserv-
edly delighted. "Elias Boudinot, in particular," Daggett declared,
"is promising both as to piety and to learning."[18]

The program at the Foreign Mission School was designed to
allow the devil no chance through idleness. After rising early in
their quarters under the gambrel roof, the boys would gather for
morning prayer at the ringing of a bell at 6:00 A.M. They would
first read a chapter in the New Testament, each taking a verse in
turn. Then an older student would lead the devotions of the group.
After breakfast in the Commons came the morning stint of work in
the garden near that building, matched by another before the evening
meal. The students had practice also in mechanics and other manual
work. The boys, though probably before John's arrival, had laid
"with odd crookedness" the pipe to conduct water from a nearby
spring to the Commons and the principal's house. There were also
fields to be ploughed, for which the townspeople lent plows and
spans of oxen, the Reverend Mr. Stone of the First Congregational
Church saying a prayer before the first furrow was begun. In summer
the boys chopped wood on the side of Colt's Foot Mountain for the
winter months ahead. Physical labor thus formed a definite part of
the school's program.

Several hours before noon and most of the afternoon were devoted
to study and recitations in the classroom. The students worked at
various levels, on varying subjects, with differing rates of speed.
Because of their groundings at Spring Place and Brainerd the
Cherokees forged ahead, and before long John and Elias were studying the most advanced subjects in the curriculum. In 1821, Daggett reported to Dr. Jedidiah Morse, the eminent geographer at
Yale College, that the two Cherokee cousins had "studied Geography extensively, Rhetoric, Surveying, Ecclesiastical and Common
History, three books in the Aeneid, two orations of Cicero, and
are attending to Natural Philosophy."[19]

Much of each evening was devoted to prayer. Mr. Daggett felt
deeply "the vast responsibility of a minister of Christ," and the
boys' souls were as much the objects of his attention as their minds.
There was no relaxation of the religious emphasis. After a week of
prayer and Bible reading the boys were expected to hear Timothy
Stone's sermons twice on Sunday at the First Church, where they
were restricted to one far corner, possibly the same corner in which
the back of a gallery pew recorded a critical evaluation of the young
man who had recently become the assistant principal:

The eloquence of Herman Vaill
Would make the stoutest sinner quail.

The couplet was followed by another of firm dissent:

The hissing goose has far more sense
Than Vaill with all his eloquence. [20]

At the church one day in May each year the Foreign Mission
School would hold an anniversary exercise in which the students
were exhibited to the townspeople. In 1820 there were thirteen
declamations in a half-dozen languages, John leading off the program
with a speech in English, followed by Elias. A young lady of the
town would later remember: "The Indian pupils appeared so genteel
and graceful on the stage that the white pupils seemed uncouth
beside them. The Indians sang and prayed in their native tongues;
when they prayed they knelt, clasped both hands and held them up.
When they sang, they sat in a row, and all waved their hands
simultaneously." The Cherokee youths completed the program of
1820 with a dialogue concerning the problem of removal to Arkansas.
In 1821 they climaxed the anniversary by staging a war council of
the Arkansas Cherokees ready to fight their Osage neighbors. [21] They
won additional friends for the school, creating favorable impressions
even among those who had hitherto looked askance at the program.

Inducements were held out to students to confess in public that Jesus
was their Savior: restrictions were lightened concerning their walking
about the town; permits were issued allowing "professors of religion"
to roam through a radius of two miles and talk to people and tell
them what Jesus had done for them since coming into their hearts.
To those who wavered Mr. Daggett held up the hopeful example of
Henry Obookiah.

Everyone who came to Cornwall heard sooner or later of Obookiah, the Sandwich Islands youth whose strange experience in
America had led to the founding of the Foreign Mission School.
Obookiah had died of typhus only a few months before the arrival
of the Cherokees, and though the boys were hampered in their
rambles about the town, the cemetery was not off limits, and John
may well have seen the recent grave. He knew too about Obookiah's memoirs, published by the Reverend Mr. Dwight, who had
been the first principal prior to Mr. Daggett's arrival. It was a
pamphlet that fascinated people with missionary sympathies. It was

being turned into other languages and was making Cornwall known around the world. Before long there would even be a Choctaw version, and all the scholars at the school were aware of the general pattern of Obookiah's life: how he had suffered as the victim of tribal wars in the Sandwich Islands, becoming an orphan forced to watch his aunt hurled over the edge of a cliff; how the boy had run away from the hut of his uncle, an ancient kahuna who made sacrifices to grinning idols of wood, and had become a cabin boy on an old square-rigger out of New Haven—a ship that eventually brought him to its home port, where he was grounded like a piece of jetsam.

All the students at Cornwall, especially the Cherokees so homesick for their native hills, could sympathize with Obookiah's loneliness as he wandered along the waterfront or about the city. They could sympathize with his standing before Yale College, yearning for the education white students were gaining there. Here he was found by Mr. Edwin Dwight, a relative of Timothy Dwight, then president of Yale College and the most important divine in all Connecticut. The younger Mr. Dwight took up the stranded boy's predicament with his eminent relative, with the remarkable result that President Dwight invited Obookiah to live with his family, which the young Kanaka did long enough to impress the great man with his worthiness for education. President Dwight had him placed in the home of a clergyman in Litchfield County, who improved his English speech and taught him how to read and write.

The clergyman also tried to convert him to Christianity, which impressed Obookiah as no more sensible than the superstitions of his uncle. However, the seeds were sown for a later overwhelming experience. Meanwhile, Obookiah moved from the clergyman's house to a recently founded center of missionary zeal, the Andover Theological Seminary, where he became the object of ministerial experimentation. Next he hired out to a farmer, and while working alone in the woods, he was filled with a haunting dread. He seemed to see a crater of fire yawning at his feet. "I thought that if I should then die," he wrote, "I must certainly be cast off forever." A voice seemed to say in his ears, "Cut it down, why cumbereth it the ground?" He dropped his ax, fell to his knees, and looked up at the sky for help. "I was but an undone and hell-deserving sinner."

Thus the seeds sown by the clergyman had thrived. Obookiah became a Christian, and as the years passed, he tried to turn the Bible into his own language, to help other Polynesians who had

come to America on ships that sailed the Pacific. He longed to
return to his native islands, to carry his new religion to the people
there and impart to them the sense of assurance and peace that
had replaced his fear of hell. And then his path again crossed that
of Edwin Dwight, and soon a cause developed—the founding of a
school for training youths like Obookiah so that they might minister
to their people at home. With Obookiah as a living symbol of what
such a seminary could accomplish, the backers of that philanthropic
dream found money rolling in. The school opened its doors in May,
1817, but Obookiah, one of its first students, a gentle, serious, optimistic young man of twenty-six, was dead from fever within a year.
Dr. Lyman Beecher of Litchfield, the leading clergyman of the
state after the death of President Dwight, preached a funeral sermon
that amounted to canonization, and Obookiah dead became more
useful to the Foreign Mission School than Obookiah living.[22]

The fame of the Puritan saint had carried knowledge of the
school beyond the confines of New England, even beyond the
boundaries of the United States. Adam Hodgson, an English merchant, had heard of it in Liverpool and when touring America in
1821 made a point of stopping at Cornwall. He spent the night at the
house of Colonel Benjamin Gold, an agent of the school, and early
the next morning met with the boys at their prayers. Later in the
day Elias, along with a young Hawaiian and David Brown, the half-
brother of Colonel Richard Brown and a recent arrival at the school,
went to see the traveler at his room—at Colonel Gold's request,
of course, for foreign students could not approach the houses of
townspeople without specific invitations. They sat with Mr. Hodgson
for half an hour, and he asked on coming to the classroom to see the
trigonometrical copybook that Elias kept. And he wrote about the
visit in his *Letters*, which were published two years later.[23]

Meanwhile at the end of 1820 Baron de Campagne, who had
heard of the school in Basel, Switzerland, sent a gift of one hundred
ducats. Mr. Daggett chose Elias and David Brown to write letters
of thanks, and as good publicity they were printed in the *Religious
Intelligencer* and the *Missionary Herald*. The baron was so pleased
to hear from two Indian youths who were "far from [their] native
country, brought [to Cornwall] by the kind providence of God,"
that he transmitted the even greater sum of fifteen hundred florins,
trusting it to arrive at Cornwall "before the departure of the two
friends Brown and Boudinot." But if the honor of corresponding
with the baron had fallen on Elias, Mr. Daggett chose John to write

to President Monroe, the letter to be delivered by Dr. Morse when he went to Washington to present his monumental report on the condition of the American Indian. "The letter of John Ridge is without any correction," Mr. Daggett explained, "[so] some of the pointing is erroneous, and two or three words are misspelt."[24]

John wrote on March 8, 1832:

> Honored Sir, . . . I am happy to understand that Doct. Morse is about to visit the seat of government, to exhibit to you, his report, relative to the Indians, whom he has visited. We their sons, who have the advantage of instruction in this seminary, hope that it may meet your cordial approbation, and that assistance may be profered to [our] long-neglected and despised people. . . . I rejoice that my dear nation now begins to peep into the privileges of civilization—that this great and generous government is favorable to them, and that ere long, Congress will give them the hand of strong fellowship—that they will encircle them in the arms of love, and adopt them into the fond embraces of the *Union*. . . .
>
> It is a known fact, that those Indians who have missionaries among them, and who live on this side [of] the Mississippi, are coming up, with faster steps to civilization, than those who have been enticed to remove to the west. An instance of this may be found in viewing the condition of my dear people. I left them about two years ago; when they were at work the tools of the whites were used—some possessed large farms; cattle, horses, hogs, etc. Their women were seen at the wheel, and the weaver's shuttle was in motion. How different is the condition of that part of my nation, who have been enticed by their foolish imaginations, and particularly by the allurement of the white men, to remove to the Arkansas. The equipage of a hunter, viz. a brass kettle, gun and knife were offered to them, which mortified at the sight, we saw them eagerly receive and depart. They are now in pursuit of game, in which employment we have reason to apprehend, they would have continued, or perhaps have sunk into oblivion, were it not that teachers have been sent to them by Christian benevolence.

John concluded on a more personal note. "My father and mother are both ignorant of the English language," he explained, "but it is astonishing to see them exert all their power to have their children educated, *like the whites!*"[25]

At this time Mr. Daggett entrusted to Dr. Morse a calculation which Elias had made of a lunar eclipse, perhaps the most sophisticated showpiece that could be elicited from the class.[26] Obviously the teachers and agents were proud of the progress made in the school, and in 1822 it could be described as in a flourishing condition.

John, however, was having a painful time now. The sleeping

quarters under the gambrel roof were cramped and poorly ventilated. They were too hot in summer, too cold in winter.[27] He had
found his second winter at Cornwall harder to bear than the first,
and the third brought trouble. The "scrofulous condition," as he
explained to President Monroe, had again attacked his system, and
it was aggravated by the intense cold and great quantities of snow.
He placed himself under the care of Dr. Samuel Gold, the Cornwall
physician, and informed his parents, who were so concerned at the
news that they suggested he come home in the spring or as soon as
he could travel. He considered doing so, especially if he might
attend some college in the South as soon as he was better.

Meanwhile the Cherokee students met together once a week to
talk, sing, and pray in their own language, and John's health became
an object of their prayers. But as time slipped by, the disease grew
worse, making it necessary for John to miss much classwork, and the
doctor removed him from his regular quarters to a special room
in the Commons, where he could be nursed by Mrs. John Northrup,
wife of the steward who had joined the staff the previous year. In
the spring of 1821 John, who was now eighteen, was still too ill
to travel home, even by ship from Boston or New York, and when
summer came, a thousand-mile journey was unthinkable because of
the intense heat. Moreover, Dr. Gold found his ministrations of no
help and recommended that his patient place himself in the hands
of a specialist in New Haven. This was done. John spent three
weeks or a month there without improving, and Daggett reported
to Boston that he feared the youth would "never see his native
country again."[28]

On hearing of John's turn for the worse, Major Ridge, grew
alarmed. Earlier he had consulted with the Gambolds on the advisability of his going to Cornwall. They had in effect counseled against
it because of the expense, especially in view of his need to take an
interpreter along.[29] But now only one course seemed open: he must
go without delay. He left on September 4, 1821, and riding overland, he reached his destination toward the end of the month.[30] With
his instinct for the proper impression he hired for the last lap of
his journey a coach-and-four, "the most splendid carriage . . . that
ever entered the town."[31]

He attracted universal attention, "a large, tall man in white top
boots" and in a "coat trimmed with gold [braid],"[32] for most people
in Cornwall had never seen an Indian chief as impressive as The
Ridge. He received immense respect from all, including even the

sage of Litchfield, Lyman Beecher, who was just then turning farmer out of consideration for his dyspepsia. He was full of the subject, involved as he was in the problems of clearing his acres. "[Major Ridge] was welcomed [under] the parental roof . . . ," noted a daughter of Beecher, "and his tall and athletic form and noble bearing bespoke him as one of the princes of the forest."[33] But of all the people The Ridge encountered on the trip, he liked "the chief of Litchfield" least: he talked too much about the land, and The Ridge distrusted all white men who showed such greed for land.[34]

He was comforted, however, to find John improved and able to serve as his interpreter when he paid his respects to Dr. Gold. The call so impressed the doctor's son, the future historian of Cornwall, that he later wrote in his volume about the town: "No memory of my boyhood is clearer than that of a visit to my home in my sixth year of . . . John Ridge and his father, Major Ridge, the Cherokee chief. The latter wore the uniform of a U.S. officer, and I was deeply impressed with his 'firm and warlike step.' I called him 'the nice, big gentleman.' My father exchanged presents with him, giving him a small telescope and receiving in turn from him an Indian pipe carved in black stone, with the assurance that it had often been smoked in Indian councils."[35]

Major Ridge remained two weeks in Cornwall, lionized every day except Sundays. On those days he retired to his room at the tavern and refused to be seen because—or so reports ran—Sunday was set aside for worshiping the Great Spirit, and if he should go to church, he would attract too much attention and divert concern from the purpose of the moment. He would meet the people of Cornwall every day except the Sabbath.[36]

John, though better, was not thought well enough to travel yet, and so on starting home The Ridge was accompanied by only Leonard Hicks, who had gained his father's consent to enter a school in South Carolina and bask again in a southern climate. In New York City they secured passage to Savannah on the coasting schooner *Caravan*, aboard which Major Ridge became a center of interest, much the same as at Cornwall. Before the packet reached port on October 21, 1821, seven Georgians invited him to add his mark to their card expressing "grateful acknowledgements to Captain Timothy Stevens for his polite attention and gentlemanly conduct."[37]

John Ridge had reasons meanwhile for wanting to stay at Cornwall. Mr. Northrup, the steward, had a fourteen-year-old daughter, "a beautiful blonde with blue eyes and auburn hair,"[38] whose gracious character would prompt McKenney and Hall in later years to hail her as "this truly excellent lady."[39] Her mother found herself so busy in looking after the other students, in fixing their meals and taking care of their clothes, that she sometimes sent her daughter Sarah Bird—or Sally, as family and friends more often called her—to do the chores in John's sickroom. A nurse so young and attractive quickly aroused the patient's interest. Her presence gave intense color to everything around him, and he could feel a great vitality stream through his body. New reserves of strength seemed to curb the ailment in his hip. Dr. Gold took note of his vigorous rally, presumably after The Ridge's departure, but he also noted violent reactions that impressed him as the profoundest troughs of dejection, and during a morning visit he discussed the matter with Mrs. Northrup. He pointed out John's great improvements—so marked, indeed, his medicine might be discontinued. But something troubled the young man, the doctor added. "Some deep trouble." And he suggested that Mrs. Northrup try to uncover what it was.

Perhaps the doctor had suspicions of something more than he admitted and anticipated some cruel and ugly crisis that his forewarning might forestall. At any rate, he nudged Mrs. Northrup into action. That afternoon while school was in session and Sarah was away from home, she carried an apronful of stockings into John's room and began to darn them while she sat beside his bed. The early part of the conversation dwelt on impersonal matters. Eventually Mrs. Northrup raised the point of Dr. Gold's concern.

"John, if you have some trouble, you ought to tell me. You have no mother here, and you've always confided in me."

With a half-suppressed scowl he denied that anything was wrong. Mrs. Northrup persisted with gentle firmness. He met her appeals with a frigid silence, but soon her insistence overcame his reluctance to speak. He confessed with mingled hope and despair that he was in love with Sarah, but if he expected Mrs. Northrup to relieve his anxieties, he was wrong. After a few vague and fluttering objections she left the room, and when her daughter arrived at home, she asked a single question, direct and laconic:

"Do you love John Ridge?"

Sarah gave an instant reply. "Yes," she said. "I do."

Bigots later accused Mrs. Northrup of having abetted John's suit. In reply she always claimed that both she and her husband had only felt dismay on first learning that Sarah was drawn to an Indian, even such "a noble youth [as John Ridge], beautiful in appearance, very graceful, a perfect gentleman everywhere."

The Northrups adopted a course that parents often do when disapproving of daughters' choices. They bundled Sarah off to her grandparents' care in New Haven, with instructions to hold "parties and introduce her to other gentlemen and try every way to get her mind off of John Ridge." Though the old people complied, the whirl of New Haven failed. Sarah took no notice of others; her appetite deserted her; she lost weight. Her grandparents, fearing she might come down with consumption, brought her home after three months.[40]

John was determined to marry Sarah, but on his writing home for permission, his mother showed the letter to Daniel Butrick and asked for his advice. "I told her," the missionary wrote, "that a white woman would be apt to feel above the common Cherokees, and that . . . her son would promise more usefulness to his people, were he connected with them in marriage."[41] This was exactly the counsel Susanna wanted, for she and Major Ridge cherished plans for John to marry the daughter of some chief.[42] So she asked that a letter be written refusing her consent. John answered with a more urgent appeal, and when he described his love for Sarah, his mother relented.

On receiving Susanna's permission, John asked Sarah to marry him. He spoke not in shame or a sense of racial inferiority, for he had been raised in pride of his Cherokee heritage: the men of his nation had fought the whites for generations, and within his own lifetime their performance in battle had equaled that of General Jackson's best white soldiers, the conduct of his own father having been recognized as among the most valiant of all. Moreover, the Northrups had overcome their first aversion to the thought of an interracial alliance for their daughter. Their objection now seemed only that John was a cripple—that he was forced to hobble about on crutches.

Sometime in 1822 Mrs. Northrup told him frankly that he must go home and regain his health in the milder climate of the South. He would have the family's consent only if he could return in, say, two years without his crutches. Then and only then, under that condition, could he marry Sarah. John accepted that commonsense position, especially since the Northrups' stand was reinforced by a decision of the American Board in Boston that his continued stay in Cornwall could not be encouraged as long as his hip gave trouble. He made plans to return to Oothcaloga at the end of summer, along with his Cherokee friends.[43]

Cousin Elias wavered whether to return or not. Mr. Daggett would like to see him receive a more finished education, and at home Brother Butrick urged upon Dr. Evarts the desirability of his grounding himself in theology before returning to the Cherokees. Butrick pleaded so earnestly that the treasurer of the American Board was won completely to his point of view. Provisions were made to send Elias and David Brown as special students to Andover for a year—provided Boudinot's health permitted. He had lately developed a bilious complaint and was often racked by fever.[44]

The question of how the Cherokees should travel was settled by John's infirmity. His doctor ruled out riding horseback or travel by wagon or stagecoach. Mr. Daggett was convinced the prognosis for his lameness was poor, that "the nature of his disorder [was] such that he might continue lame for years," and that in any event only a water passage was feasible.[45] After a poignant parting with Sarah, with promises that he would get well at any cost, he rode with his friends to Middleton, Connecticut, and boarded a schooner for Charleston.

John's companions included Darcheechee, James Fields, Thomas Basel, and young Vann, as well as a Delaware known as Adin C. Gibbs on his way to the Choctaw Nation, and they were taken in charge by the Reverend Reynolds Bascom, who was going to the Indian country as a missionary. They reached Charleston on November 6, 1822, and there they soon met Boudinot, whose health had precluded his going to Andover after all and who had sailed from Boston on the ship *Mount Vernon*. He arrived on the eleventh, and they found him shielding himself from the autumn sun under a brand-new silk umbrella.[46]

Charleston was a picturesque city, with numerous coaches and footmen in sumptuous liveries, and it was said that a dueling club flourished there in which precedence was set by the number of times each member had "gone out." But the cavalier city also had its puritan side, and that was the side that took the travelers in tow. They were invited on the first Sunday evening after their arrival to a meeting at the Circle Church, where Gibbs the Delaware and John spoke to a large audience. Gibbs confined himself to remarks about the Foreign Mission School, and John about the Cherokees. He spoke of their early possessions in the Carolinas, and of their wars with the whites. He had harsh names for those who scoffed at the practicality of Indian civilization and gave examples of Cherokee advancement. He described the Cherokee government: he described the agricultural improvements of his people and the extent of their livestock holdings; he spoke of the accomplishments of Cherokee men "in the arts of husbandry" and of the women in domestic life. And his talk along with Gibbs's moved the audience to give two hundred dollars for missionary work among the southern tribes.[47]

The local newspaper reported that John "had a fine spirit and excellent talents, and that he only required the benefits of a more complete education to prepare him for great usefulness and high distinction." The editor commented on his "taste for legal and historical pursuits" but otherwise had reservations about his character: "He is not a professor of religion," it was observed, "nor have we any reason to think that his character and temper, like that of Gibbs, have ever been regulated and softened by the influence of that Spirit upon his heart without which the native corruption will show forth, in spite of all the influence of philosophy or literature."[48]

Another meeting occurred the following Friday at the same church, and John spoke again. He scotched the Rousseauesque notion of the superior happiness of uncivilized peoples. He declared:

I question whether the gentlemen who support this argument would be willing to renounce the privileges of polished society and voluntarily adopt the manners of savages, and take their abode in the wilderness, far from civilized people. Will anyone believe that an Indian with his bow and quiver, who walks solitary in the mountains, exposed to cold and hunger, or the attacks of wild beasts, trembling at every unusual object, his fancy filled with agitating fears, lest the next step should introduce his foot to the fangs of the direful snake, or entangle it "amidst his circling spires that on the grass float redundant," actually possesses undisturbed contentment superior to a learned gentleman of this commercial city, who has every possible comfort at home? Can anyone convince me that the degraded Hottentot in Africa, or the wild Arab in the desert of the Sahara, whose head is exposed to the piercing rays of a meridian sun, entirely dependent on his camel for safety, enjoys more real contentment of mind than the poorest peasant of England? Will anyone compare the confined pleasures of the Hindoo, whose mind is burdened with the shackles of superstition and ignorance, who bows before the car of the Juggernaut, or whose wretched ignorance compels him to invoke the river Ganges for his salvation—Will anyone, I say, compare his pleasures to the noble and well regulated pleasures of a Herschel or a Newton, who surveys the regions of the universe—views the wisdom of the Deity in forming the lights of heaven with all the planets and attending satellites revolving in their orbits, irradiating infinite space as they move around their common centres—and who demonstrates, with mathematical exactness, the rapid flights of the comet, and its future visits to our solar system!

I have made this contrast to shew the fallacy of such theories, and to give you a general view of the wretched state of the Heathen, particularly of the aborigines of this country, who are gradually retiring from the stage of action to sleep with their fathers. It is on the exertions of the benevolent that their safety depends, and only the hand of charity can pluck them from final extermination.[49]

Again the people were roused enough to contribute another $200 for missionary work. They also gave books, and to pay for the young men's journey home they subscribed $184, not counting the value of a wagon one man contributed. "The Indian young men from Cornwall" were sent from Charleston with praise and good wishes.

They reached Augusta in about ten days. They lay over for four days and held another meeting "in Mr. Brantley's church." John spoke on "the mutual change of feeling between the whites and Indians; the good effect of missionary efforts; and the desirableness of continuing them with increased zeal." Gibbs and Boudinot led in prayer and made "a solemn and tender impression by their hearty appeals." Brother Bascom was so affected by the efforts of his charges that he wrote: "Wherever they go, they will put to silence all objections to the practicability of civilizing and Christianizing their too long neglected countrymen."[50]

The health of John and Elias had improved on the trip, and their spirits were high, and when they arrived in the Cherokee Nation early in December, 1822, they were welcomed like young heroes. They reached Spring Place on the ninth and Brainerd a few days later. "The dear youths from Cornwall," as the Brainerd journal referred to them, spent some time in riding circuit with a minister— all, that is, but John, whose hip restricted his movements—and they served as interpreters and spoke before gatherings and led in prayer. The Brainerd diarist found they "bid fair for extensive usefulness among this people," and he trusted they were "chosen instruments for great good."[51] After several weeks of such activity, with his health improved still more, Boudinot retired to his family's house to spend the rest of the winter with his mother.[52]

Meanwhile John had seen many people, for Major Ridge's house was a popular place, and his father received guests of every status.

They looked on John as the finest flower of the younger generation, and as a white friend was to comment, he became, "from the time of his return from college, . . . a leading man in the Nation. He was the idol of the half-breeds, and well respected by most intelligent Cherokees."[53]

He saw at first hand the surprising changes which had occurred in the four years of his absence, the nation having experienced a great awakening. The revival spirit was at work, with Christianity spreading. The teachings of the Moravians were having success in Oothcaloga, where nine or ten prominent citizens moved into the fold, including William Hicks, the brother of Charles. Major Ridge had told the Gambolds he himself was not yet ready to embrace Jesus as his Savior, but he had carefully passed their instructions on to Susanna, whose growing religious fervor had climaxed in her embracing the Brethren's faith in 1819 and receiving "Catherine" as her second name. She was baptized on November 14, the day the new church house was consecrated at Spring Place. As a result, her high spirits had grown more amiable.[54] The Ridge liked to say: "Susanna has chose the *good* part. I am glad. I am not so yet, but when we get missionaries [in Oothcaloga], I shall go to hear, and be instructed by them."[55] To Brother Butrick he seemed "convinced of the truth and importance of the Christian religion, and determined to seek after God."[56]

He joined his brother Watie and William Hicks in begging that the Moravians open a mission in Oothcaloga. The Brethren in Salem approved the petition, appointing the Gambolds to go there as soon as replacements could be sent to Spring Place. Just before the move, however, Mother Gambold's heart gave out, and she was racked by the agonies of angina. The Ridge came by the mission one day and saw her suffering, but she smiled and asked him to bear a message to her "dear friends" at Oothcaloga.[57] He knew on leaving that he would never see her again.

Her death was a crushing blow to Father Gambold. But when he sojourned in Salem, his superiors there decided that he must marry again for the sake of his work. He arrived in Oothcaloga shortly after John, with a new wife, to found a new mission there in a raw, unfinished building that Joseph Crutchfield had made available. A frail old man with silvery hair, he prospered yet in his work and would soon lead into the fold John's aunt and uncle Watie. There were also plans to start a mission school, plans that pleased The Ridge. He wanted schools, more schools; the Cherokees could never have too many schools. He talked of education every time he met a missionary. "He appears very anxious that all his people should receive instruction, and come into the customs of the whites," reported William Chamberlin.[58] He wanted education for them in English, and he had voted for English to be adopted as the official language of the Cherokee government and to have all official records put into that tongue. Meanwhile something had occurred which made it possible for Cherokees who, like himself, could speak little or no English to become literate in their own tongue.

Perhaps the most interesting guest who had ever come to The Ridge's house, had they only known it at the time, was a distant cousin named George Guess, or Sequoyah, as his name was called in Cherokee—a middle-aged man with one lame and shrunken leg who wore a turban and smoked incessantly on a long-stemmed pipe.[59] Many Cherokees had scoffed when, convinced that "talking leaves" were not just magic reserved for the white man, he had determined to draw up a system of writing for the Cherokees.

"He was a poor man," John Ridge later explained, "living in a retired part of the nation, and he told the head men one day that he could make a book. The chiefs replied it was impossible, because, they said, the Great Spirit at first made a red and a white boy; to the red boy he gave a book, and the white boy a bow and arrow, but the white boy came round the red boy, stole his book and went off, leaving him the bow and arrow, and therefore an Indian could not make a book. But George Guess thought he could. He shut himself up to study." He wrote on bark with pokeberry juice. He worked year in, year out.

His corn was left to weeds and he was pronounced a crazy man by the tribe.—His wife thought so too, and burned up his manuscripts whenever she could find them. But he persevered. He first attempted to form a character for every word in the Cherokee language, but was forced to abandon [that approach]. He then set about discovering the number of sounds [that is, syllables] in the language, which he found to be eighty-six, and for each of these he adopted a character . . . and these characters combined like letters formed words. Having accomplished this he called together six of his neighbors, and said, "Now I can make a book." They did not believe him. To convince them, he asked each to make a speech, which he wrote down as they spoke, and then read to them, so that each one knew his own speech, and they then acknowledged he could make a book.[60]

Sequoyah, inventor of the Cherokee Syllabary. A McKenney and Hall lithograph from an 1828 painting by Charles Bird King. Smithsonian Institution, National Anthropological Archives, Neg. No. 991A.

The eighty-six characters,* some adapted from the Greek, some from the Roman script (for Sequoyah owned one of Noah Webster's blue-backed spellers), including a character for the sound of *s* to combine with certain syllables, proved so efficient that anyone speaking Cherokee could read or write the language after a week of study. One was reading as soon as he had learned his ABC's: to read, all one had to do was to say the names of the characters, one after another as they stood on paper—just as by naming the letters *x p d n c* one pronounces the word "expediency" in a rough way.†
The operation was so simple that the vogue of Cherokee writing began to sweep like wildfire through the nation, and it would soon be common for one, in traveling about the country, to see directions for different paths inscribed on the trees in Sequoyah's characters.[61] Sequoyah himself had taught the syllabary in both Arkansas and the East.

The next logical step was printing. The National Council would soon be involved with the idea, both for English and for Cherokee. Just when Major Ridge along with other Cherokees received the notion of a Cherokee press (and how or from whom) is not clear, but he included it in his conversations with the missionaries as early as 1822. Butrick recorded in his journal the importance his friend attached to "a printing press in the nation, for the diffusion of council information. . . . Major Ridge seemed sensible of the great benefit which might result from the circulation of a newspaper."[62] Why not a paper in both English and Cherokee? The idea would then have compelling currency, with The Ridge and other enlightened Cherokees pushing it in council.

Meanwhile, however, the question of land had assumed a new urgency, absorbing the political energies of the Cherokees. Political developments during John's absence in the North had been as remarkable as social and religious ones. The machinery of government had been improved; a new capital had been established at the

---

*Later one character was dropped, making a final total of eighty-five. What made the syllabary feasible was that Cherokee, like Japanese, was composed mostly of unclosed syllables, hence their manageable number.

†Cf. John Pickering in the *North American Review*, XXVIII (Apr., 1829): 501: "As soon as the characters are learned, the whole written language is acquired; and as the same characters invariably represent the same sound, there can be no such thing as an error in orthography or spelling, and both children and grown persons actually acquire the art of reading in the course of a few days!" In view of the simplicity of Sequoyah's system it is surprising that Major Ridge, advocate of education and civilization, should have remained illiterate even in Cherokee.

D a	R e	T i	Ꮼ o	O u	i v
S ga O ka	F ge	Y gi	A go	J qu	E gv
Ꮻ ha	P he	Ꭿ hi	F ho	Γ hu	Ꮝ hv
W la	Ꮯ le	P li	G lo	M lu	Ᏻ lv
Ꮙ ma	O me	H mi	Ꮩ mo	Y mu	
O na Ꮫhna Gnah	Λ ne	Ꮒ ni	Z no	Ꮔ nu	O nv
T qua	Ꮺ que	P qui	V quo	Ꮻ quu	E quv
U sa Ꮻ s	4 se	Ꮟ si	Ꮠ so	8 su	R sv
L da W ta	S de Ᏼ te	J di Ꮧ ti	Λ do	S du	Ꮩ dv
Ꮪ dla L tla	L tle	C tli	Ꮰ tlo	Ꮱ tlu	P tlv
G tsa	V tse	Ir tsi	K tso	J tsu	C tsv
G wa	Ꮻ we	Ꮼ wi	Ꮼ wo	Ꮫ wu	6 wv
Ꮿ ya	B ye	ᏸ yi	ᏺ yo	G yu	B yv

Sounds represented by Vowels.

a, as a in father, or short as a in rival.   o, as aw in law, or short as o in not.
e, as a in hate, or short as e in met.   u, as oo in fool, or short as u in pull.
i, as i in pique, or short as i in pit.   v, as u in but, nasalized.

Consonant Sounds

g nearly as in English, but approaching to k. d nearly as in English but approaching
to t. h k l m n q s t w y, as in English. Syllables beginning with g, except Ꮫ have sometimes the
power of k, A, S, O, are sometimes sounded to, tu, tv, and Syllables written with tl, except Ꮱ
sometimes vary to dl.

Cherokee syllabary invented by Sequoyah. Courtesy of Columbia University Library.

confluence of the Coosawatie and Conasauga rivers—New Town, soon to be superseded by New Echota. Major Ridge was now the Speaker in council. His protege John Ross had become president of the National Committee, and they worked closely together to promote the welfare of the nation and protect its interests.

On a splendid tall horse, in the fall of 1819, The Ridge had led the procession that ended at the new council house, two open pavilions facing each other with a log house for the clerks of the nation. Brother Abraham Steiner, on a visit from Salem, later wrote:

> I was at the opening of the council, which was on Sunday. . . .
> It was past noon, the council had convened, and a multitude of people gathered. Nothing was done, and all seemed to wait with anxious solicitude. All at once a troop of horsemen were seen coming along the road, thro' the vista of the trees, with a stately looking person in front. A little way from the council they alighted, marched two in a file towards the council house with the stately person before them, whom I observed on drawing near to be the Cherokee *Ridge*, the speaker of the people, and who is reported to be the greatest orator in the nation. Coming up before the council, who were seated, all ranged in fine order around Ridge, who made a speech of some length.

After Going Snake's reply, The Ridge handed about a twist of tobacco, from which every chief cut a small piece. The Pathkiller made a short speech, and then Steiner was asked to preach. Charles Hicks translated the substance into Cherokee. "The great multitude were so orderly and silent during the transaction," Steiner added, "that you might have heard a pin fall. They were much rejoiced at the translation, and called it the dedication of their council house."[63]

So far only a single family or two lived at New Town, and there were few accommodations for the crowds at council time, so that Oothcaloga, just four or five miles away, was overrun at that season. But to feed the multitudes, large open sheds had been built not far from the council house where an abundance of food could be had at reasonable prices—bread, beef, venison, pork, and fowl. There thirty cooks, employed by the nation, supplied refreshments free to anyone who chose to call for them. Nine separate oxen were set apart for the chiefs, besides all kinds of other provisions.[64]

In 1819 the Cherokees had sent delegates to Washington City, led by Charles Hicks, and a fringe of land along their entire northern border was ceded to the United States as payment for past and future emigration to Arkansas. The Americans proved insatiable: the state of Georgia was now clamoring for the United States government to make good a commitment given in 1802 to extinguish in Georgia's favor the Indian title of all lands within the boundaries of the state, in return for the claim on western lands that Georgia had ceded to the federal government, the lands that now composed Mississippi and Alabama.[65] Since the bulk of what remained of the Cherokee domain lay within the chartered limits of Georgia, the Indians felt more pressured than ever. The issue came to a head in the annual council of 1823, at which John was asked to serve as interpreter, thus receiving his first real taste of Cherokee politics. "Since the organization of a code of laws now in operation in this nation," he wrote, "I had the first opportunity of acquainting myself with the manner of the proceedings . . . of the Cherokee legislative Council.

"The appointed time for the commencement of business," he continued, "was the 1st of October 1823, whose dawn was the prelude of transactions the most essential and important to the Nation . . . at once solemn and pregnant with conjectures. . . . The whole confidence and talent of the Nation was now seated. The Agent of the United States [Joseph McMinn, temporary successor of Colonel Meigs, who had died from a chill the previous January] was expected, and the Commissioners on the part of the United States and Georgia were to come. These arrived, and were received with a respect equal to the importance and weight of their commissions."[66] Major Ridge, as Speaker of the Council, addressed them in tones of congratulation and friendship, and U.S. Commissioner Campbell answered with polite compliments to Cherokee civilization.

The commissioners went about their business in a leisurely manner. They needed time in which to make judicious applications of funds at their disposal, their purpose to detach the more susceptible chiefs from the opposition and to split the council into factions. At length those from Georgia presented the object of their mission in writing, the Cherokees having insisted that the negotiations could proceed only if reduced to writing, an expedient they deemed necessary on recalling misrepresentations in the past. "Its whole drift and motive," John Ridge wrote, "was to impress the Cherokees with the conviction that the State of Georgia had just, but longstanding claims against the Nation, which they attempted to authenticate by quotations from some old treaties . . . entered into by the United States with this nation." In the formal maneuvers which followed, the Cherokees remained firm in their resolve never to part with another foot of land. The U.S. commissioners, no more successful in their manipulations than those from Georgia, grew harsh and threatening and then, by turns, suave and wheedling. "Gentle, brilliant, and forceful periods of eloquence, strongly backed by large sums of money as presents, were spent in vain."[67] The chiefs remained firm.

At this point the Creek ambassador, General McIntosh, arrived with six or seven Creek chiefs and received a rousing welcome. He was hailed as "Beloved Brother." As Butrick explained in his journal, "He was the Creek King in the Cherokee council as Major Ridge was the Cherokee King in the councils of the Creek Nation,"[68] and he was escorted to the White Bench, reserved for dignitaries held in highest esteem. In private conversation the general favored cession and emigration, saying in substance: "The white man is growing. He wants our lands; he will buy them now. By and by he will take them and the little band of people, poor and despised, will be left to wander without homes and be beaten like dogs. We [should sell now and] go to a new home and learn like the white men, to till the earth, grow cattle and depend on these for food and life."[69]

Soon he sent John Ross a letter dictated to his semiliterate son Chilly. In broken English it raised the question of a treaty. In case Ross could bring himself to favor it, two thousand dollars would be given to him as a present. The same amount would be available to the clerk of the council, Alexander McCoy, and to Charles Hicks three thousand dollars "for present." And "nobody shall know it," the general promised. In addition the amounts would be paid before the treaty was signed, "and if you got any friend you want him to receive they shall receive the same amount." If the offer were taken, the commissioners for Georgia had promised to pay McIntosh seven thousand dollars for his services.[70]

Astonished, Ross confided the matter to several close associates. They decided that Major Ridge and Alexander McCoy should confer with the general and verify whether his proposal had been made with the sanction of the U.S. commissioners. McIntosh revealed that it had, and added he would be glad to address the council and press for a compliance with the commissioners' views. He was sure, he said, that if the National Committee fell in line and said they despaired of holding out longer against the United States, The Pathkiller could be induced to yield. He ended by glibly trying to galvanize them with descriptions of his spoils from former treaties.

The committee convened in secret early the next morning to

receive the letter and a report of the interview. It resolved to invite the general before an immediate meeting of both houses, and on his appearance the Cherokees received him with customary deference. Major Ridge opened the session. Then Ross, a small man only five feet six and a half inches tall, arose with the letter in his hand. After explaining the reason for the joint meeting, he concluded by informing the chiefs that "a gross contempt" had been offered his character, "as well as that of the General Council. This letter . . . will speak for itself. Fortunately the author has mistaken my character and my sense of honor."[71]

He handed the general's letter to the clerk, silence having fallen over the house. Sentence by sentence, McCoy read and interpreted its contents. No one seemed more thunderstruck than The Pathkiller. Slowly he rose, and when he addressed the council the whole tenor of his speech was that of mourning. McIntosh stammered out a lame reply. The Pathkiller ordered: "Set him aside."[72]

The headmen whispered in a short consultation. Then The Ridge arose. "As speaker for the Cherokee Nation," he began, in obvious sorrow, for McIntosh had been his comrade-in-arms, "I now address the Honorable Council"—his brief remarks stressing the maxim "trust placed in our hands is a sacred trust" and, in that vein, leading to the denunciation of McIntosh, who had "stood erect, encircled with the generous confidence of the people and the authorities of his own Nation." "I now depress him," Major Ridge concluded. "I cast him behind my back. I now divest him of trust. . . . I do not pretend to extend this disgrace in his own Nation. He is at liberty to retire in peace . . . [and] resort to the bosom of his family to spend his sorrows and revive his wounded spirits. He has been the concern of my warmest friendship and still carries my sympathies with him."[73]

The general left the council in great agitation and rode his horse until it dropped. The National Committee sent a letter to the chiefs of the Creeks that the Cherokee council had decreed William McIntosh "discharged from ever having any *Voice* in [Cherokee] *Councils* hereafter as a chief connected with this Nation."[74] The committee also advised the Creeks to keep a strict watch over his conduct lest he ruin their nation.

The several commissioners left the council grounds without delay. Those who had acted for the United States complained that the president would "have to learn his children better manners" before they would visit them again.[75] Thus, The Ridge's faction enjoyed

a triumph on a position—"Not one more foot of land to the whites!"—
with which father and son would be identified for nine years to come.
But realizing that the United States would never relax in the drive
for more territory, the Cherokees decided to take the initiative. On
the heels of their firm stand in council the chiefs appointed a deputation of four—Major Ridge, John Ross, George Lowrey, and Elijah
Hicks—to carry the Cherokee case to Washington City.

During his year at home, John Ridge's health had so improved that
he secured permission from his parents to go north and press for
Sarah Northrup's hand. Not that he was completely cured; he
limped yet, just as he would do for another decade. But he had
accomplished what the Northrups had demanded—thrown his
crutches away. In December, 1823, he accompanied Major Ridge
with his sister Sally, now thirteen, as far as Washington City. Sally
had spent several years at Spring Place, and Major Ridge had hopes
the War Department would send her now to some good finishing
school in the East. John paused several days with them in the capital, then traveled on to Cornwall, where the Northrups found him
suitably sound.

His welcome was otherwise less than satisfactory. When the reason for his return became known, the people of Cornwall went into
collective shock. The news of John's courtship, according to J. F.
Wheeler, who heard the story from the couple themselves, "spread
like wildfire—the papers proclaimed it an outrage, and preachers
denounced it in the pulpit—that an *Indian* should go into a civilized community of New England and marry and carry away one
of the finest daughters of the land."[76] But no amount of calumny
could discourage John Ridge, and he found Sarah more in love with
him than ever.

The wedding took place at the steward's house on January 27,
1824, with the pastor of the Second Congregational Church, Walter
Smith, officiating. After the ceremony, according to Wheeler's account, "Ridge came near to being mobbed." The bride and groom
thought it wise to leave Cornwall at once, and Mr. and Mrs. Northrup found it just as desirable to keep them company on the first
stage of their journey. At almost every stop the couple had to face
aroused crowds who had learned of their marriage from the papers—
"excited throngs denouncing [Ridge] for taking away as wife—a
white girl."[77]

But John Ridge could match the scorn of his detractors. Proud of his Indian heritage, he had written bitterly that race prejudice was

the ruling passion of the age, and an Indian is almost considered accursed. He is frowned upon by the meanest peasant, and the scum of the earth are considered sacred in comparison to the son of nature. If an Indian is educated in the sciences, has a good knowledge of the classics, astronomy, mathematics, moral and natural philosophy, and his conduct [is] equally modest and polite, yet he is an Indian, and the most stupid and illiterate white man will disdain and triumph over this worthy individual. It is disgusting to enter the house of a white man and be stared full in the face with inquisitive ignorance. I find that such prejudices are more prevalent among the ignorant than among the enlightened.[78]

But John's experience now, from Cornwall on, must have shaken even this last conviction. Intermarriage in New England had revealed that prejudice was pervasive, from the elite down.

To be the object of such scorn was galling to John's proud spirit. Interrupting an impassioned denunciation at a stage station, he admitted that he *had* trespassed in white country "and plucked one of its finest flowers." But he refused to admit that "he was her inferior in any respect."[79] And again he barely escaped manhandling from the mob. He felt as popular among these hissing, growling, cursing whites as the Seminole chief among the Cherokees in the "legend of the Cherokee Rose."*

There was poetry in the tale, and aside from the observation that

---

*Indeed the pattern of Ridge's story had much in common with the legend's archetypal plot—of how a heroic young Seminole chief, who had suffered a weakening ailment on the eve of battle, was taken captive by a Cherokee foe and condemned to torture. But as no self-respecting Cherokee would dream of torturing one so grievously ill, "it became necessary to wait for his restoration to health before committing him to the fire; and as he lay prostrated by disease in the cabin of his Cherokee captor, the daughter of the latter, a young dark-faced maid, was his nurse"—or so ran Wheeler's version of the tale. "She fell in love with the young chieftain, and wishing to save his life, urged him to escape; but he would not do so unless she would flee with him. She consented. Yet before they had gone far, impelled by soft regret at leaving the land of her fathers, she asked permission of her lover to return for the purpose of bearing away some memento of it. Retracing her footsteps she broke a sprig from the white rose which climbed the poles of her father's lodge, and preserving it during her flight through the wilderness planted it by the door of her new home in the land of the Seminoles." That was how, asserted the legend, that lovely white rose which blossomed among the glades of Florida and throughout the Deep South had come to be known as the Cherokee rose (*Fort Smith Herald*, Aug. 13, 1870, p. 4, col. 2).

John Ridge was bringing his own white flower home, well-wishers discovered poetry in his own story; it soon became a theme for admiring verse, as, for instance, Silas H. McAlpine's sentimental ode:

> *O, come with me, my white girl fair,*
> *O, come where Mobile's sources flow;*
> *With me my Indian blanket share,*
> *And share with me my bark canoe;*
> *We'll build our cabin in the wild,*
> *Beneath the forest's lofty shade,*
> *With logs on logs transversely piled,*
> *And barks on barks obliquely laid.*
>
> *O, come with me, my white girl fair,*
> *Come, seek with me the southern clime,*
> *And dwell with me securely there,*
> *For there my arm shall round thee twine;*
> *The olive is thy favorite hue,*
> *But sweet to me thy lily face;*
> *O, sweet to both, when both shall view*
> *These colors mingled in our race.*
>
> *Then come with me, my white girl fair,*
> *And thou a hunter's bride shalt be;*
> *For thee I'll chase the roebuck there,*
> *And thou shalt dress the feast for me:*
> *O, wild and sweet our feast shall be,*
> *The feast of love and joy is ours;*
> *Then come, my white girl fair, with me,*
> *O, come and bless my sylvan bowers.* [80]

The poet's intent was amiable, but all he knew of the matter was that John Ridge was a Cherokee, though with "bark canoe" he might have been a Cree in Canada, or with his "sylvan bowers" a swain smitten in Arcadia. Much the same could be said of the more ambitious effort of Edward Coote Pinkney of Charleston, where John had called attention to himself on his first trip home. Pinkney, son of the U.S. minister to Great Britain, had written some of the best verse in America between Freneau's and Bryant's, but "The Indian's Bride" was surely not among his best works:

> *Why is that graceful female here*
> *With yon red hunter of the deer?*
> *Of gentle mien and shape, she seems*
> *For civil halls designed,*
> *Yet with stately savage walks*
> *As she were of his kind.*

The poem went on like this for ninety-eight lines, hardly more realistic in its concept of the Cherokees' "sylvan life" than McAlpine's briefer song. Its idyllic vision of noble contentment in the aboriginal life rested on precisely the kind of assumptions, mingled with patronizing sentimentalities, that John had denounced months before in the Circle Church:

> *She humanizes him, and he*
> *Educates her to liberty. . . .*
>
> *With naught of dread, or to repent,*
> *The present yields them full content.*
> *In solitude there is no crime;*
> *Their actions are all free,*
> *And passion lends their way of life*
> *The only dignity;*
> *And how should they have cares?—*
> *Whose interest contends with theirs?—*
> *The world, or all they know of it,*
> *Is theirs. . . .*[81]

But how preferable the stance of the poets to the malignant reaction of some who were scandalized by the thought of interracial marriage. A number of rumors were set flying: that Mrs. Northrup had wooed the young Indian for her daughter, that the wedding had been performed secretly, that Mr. Northrup had gone mad and deserted his family. On March 9 Herman Daggett wrote a letter to refute such falsehoods, and it was published in the *Religious Intelligencer.*[82] No doubt the scandalmongering in Cornwall would have languished had not Isaiah Bunce, the opinionated editor of the Litchfield *American Eagle*, who scorned all missionary activity, especially the pampering of young barbarians practically on his doorstep, published a blast in his paper against intermarriage as an attack on the Foreign Mission School. It was not a subject for irony, he wrote—"this subject of INERMARRIAGES with the Indians and blacks of the missionary school at Cornwall. . . ."

The affliction, mortification and disgrace of the young woman, who is only about sixteen years old [and "who has thus made herself a *squaw*"] . . . will, it is believed, on examination be found to be the fruit of the *missionary spirit*, and caused by the conduct of the clergymen at that place and its vicinity, who are agents and superintend the school. And though we shrink from recording the name of the female thus throwing herself into the arms of an Indian yet, "daring to do all that may become a man or a christian," we hesitate not to name those believed to be mediately or immediately the cause of the unnatural connection; they are—[and here Bunce named five men, beginning with Dr. Beecher and ending with Mr. Daggett]. . . . And the relatives of the girl, or the people of Cornwall, or the public at large, who feel indignant at the transaction, some of whom have said that the girl ought to be publicly whipped, the Indian hung, and the mother drown'd, will do well to trace the thing to its true cause, and see whether the men above named, or their system, are not the authors of the transaction as a new kind of *missionary machinery.*[83]

The agents of the school made no move to defend themselves against the Bunce diatribe. Indeed, they agreed with its point of view, condemning mixed marriage, claiming the union of John and Sarah was an isolated phenomenon, and forbidding any further weddings across racial lines by anyone connected with the Foreign Mission School. Bunce reprinted his attack and made additional ones on the school, and when at last eight family heads at Cornwall sent a declaration to the *Eagle* that Bunce's articles were "base fabrications," he lacked the sportsmanship to print it. It made its appearance months later in the *Connecticut Journal.*[84] At this point the uproar might have subsided, except for a new crisis involving the daughter of Colonel Benjamin Gold, agent for the school and one of the fathers who had signed the protest to the editor.

While still at Cornwall, Elias Boudinot had joined the First Congregational Church and so had received invitations to visit the Gold home. He had conceived an interest in Harriet, youngest daughter in a family of fourteen children, and she had responded. They had said nothing of their mutual feelings, but when Boudinot went home to the Cherokee Nation, they had continued to correspond. Two years passed. Harriet Ruggles Gold decided she could not go on with the correspondence unless she was prepared to accept Boudinot's hand. Early in the fall of 1824 she confessed to her parents her desire to marry him. They were dumbfounded. The idea of her joining her life with an Indian's was unthinkable—granddaughter that she was of Hezekiah Gold, Congregationalist minister, with two Yale-bred uncles and with two sisters married to clergymen and another to a general in the state militia. But nothing her parents could say would change Harriet's mind.

She replied that she was determined to become a missionary to the Cherokees and knew no better way than as the wife of a leading man of the nation. The Golds remained so adamant in their opposition that they sent Boudinot a letter of refusal, and that autumn

Harriet fell into a decline; she became so ill that Dr. Gold, Benjamin's nephew, feared she would soon die. It slowly dawned on her parents that she had lost the will to live and they were "fighting against God" in denying her appeals, and so with winter coming on, they relented. Colonel Gold sent another letter to Boudinot, which fortunately reached him before the one that bristled with refusal and rejection.

Harriet's health began to mend, but during the winter the Golds found it necessary to keep the promised marriage a secret till the rest of the family could be prepared. They delayed an announcement until Harriet had fully recovered. Then, when General Brinsmade, Harriet's brother-in-law, heard the news, he hurried to Cornwall and, as an agent of the school, laid the facts before his fellow members of the Board, making them "as white as sheets." Three days later the Reverend Joseph Harvey of Goshen, himself an agent, called on the Golds and demanded whether they had given their consent to such an alliance. The matter lay in Harriet's hands, they replied. On Sunday the minister delivered the girl an ultimatum to be answered within three days: the agents would guarantee to hold the affair in complete secrecy if she chose to give Boudinot up. If not, they would publish the banns in whatever way they deemed appropriate. Harriet refused to be pressured. She answered Mr. Harvey as she had answered her parents.

Her letter left the agents, especially Dr. Beecher, completely flouted, completely frustrated. On June 17, 1825, they published the banns in such a way as to hold the Gold family up to public censure. They stressed the secrecy of the negotiations between Boudinot and Harriet, as if to imply something underhand. They declared their "unqualified disapprobation of such connections" and branded those who had condoned or assisted in the negotiations as "criminal; as offering insult to the known feelings of the christian community; and as sporting with the sacred interests of this charitable institution."[85]

A storm then broke in Cornwall. It was thought unsafe for Harriet to remain at home, and she was hidden in the chamber of a neighbor's house, from which she could see a depressing scene of mob action on the green. There was displayed an enormous painting of a young woman and an Indian and, in addition, an older woman depicted as the instigator of Indian marriages. As evening fell, with the church bell tolling, two young men of the town laid Harriet's effigy on a funeral pyre—a barrel of tar—which her brother Stephen set on fire. The bell continued to toll till ten or eleven o'clock.[86]

When Harriet took her place in the choir the following Sunday, she was turned from the singer's seat to shield the other girls from disgrace. The pastor's wife even asked the choir to tie bands of black crepe around their arms. Church communion was delayed. Harriet was made to feel completely isolated. "I have seen the time," she wrote, "when I could close my eyes upon every earthly object, and look up to God as my only supporter, my only hope; when I could say to my Heavenly Father with emotion I never felt before, 'Other refuge have I none, so I, helpless, hang on Thee.'"[87]

Her conduct in the ordeal won the admiration of her sister Mary, who wrote: "Harriet never appeared more interesting than she does at present. It is a time of great commotion in Cornwall, still Harriet is meek though firm as the hills. . . . My feelings are in unison with the multitude of my Christian friends, who tell me to comfort Harriet."[88] In time all objecting members of the Gold clan were reconciled, and the divided family was unified.

Meanwhile Boudinot had his harassments too. He saw the lurid newspaper stories of the burning in effigy on the Cornwall green and received letters with pictures of a gallows. One letter from Boston threatened his life if he dared return to New England, and another claimed that the whole state of Connecticut was ready to rise against him. The uproar dismayed his friends—David Brown for one.[89] It was hard for the Cherokees to understand why their *friends* could so object to an Indian asking to marry a white woman. After all, scores of white men, including missionaries, had taken Indian women as wives. Major Ridge, still smarting from the disapproval John's marriage had aroused, and angry at the violence of the opposition to Boudinot, approached William Chamberlin "with a plain question" and said he wanted "a plain answer." Did their friends in the North have anything in the Scriptures—or anything else—to justify their reactions to the marriage of Indian men to white women? Chamberlin said nothing in the Bible prohibited mixed marriages. He was in favor of them, and so was President Monroe.[90] Perhaps he echoed *Niles' Weekly Register*, which made the same point:

Why so much *sensibility* about an event of this sort? A gentleman who was thought fit, by many thousands of people, for the office of president, openly and frankly recommended an incorporation of the Indian race with the citizens of the United States, by intermarriages,— and we could never see any reason why, on account of *that* recommendation, his claims to the office should have been lessened. The proudest man, perhaps, in America, and as great a stickler for *dignity* as can be met with, boasts of the Indian blood in his veins. But the rev. doctor, who is at the head of the school, rudely exposes the name of the young lady who had found pleasure in the society of an Indian youth, and makes the affair "criminal." It is a strange world. If the persons are free to do as they please . . . we do not see why this fuss is made about them.[91]

The fuss did not stay Boudinot. When the proper time came, he went north, pausing only on the last lap of his journey to assume a disguise in case a lynching party awaited him. But Cornwall was quiet.

The wedding took place on March 28, 1826, at the Gold house, with a new minister from Goshen officiating.[92] The Golds rode with the bride and groom as far as Washington, Connecticut. True to prediction, the doors of the Foreign Mission School closed the following autumn, though the American Board in Boston explained its demise on grounds other than the Indian marriages. Conditions had changed so much since its founding that it was now more advantageous to train foreign youths in their own homelands. As time passed, Cornwall would reconcile itself to the marriage of two of its daughters to the Cherokee cousins. The townspeople even came to think of Sarah Northrup Ridge as a kind of princess who dressed in silk every day and had fifty servants to wait on her. "She simply said to this one, go, and he goeth, and to another one Come, and he did so."[93] In reality John Ridge was to have only twenty-four slaves at the height of his prosperity.

7 • AGENTS FOR THE CREEKS

THE Cherokee delegation, having arrived in Washington shortly after New Year's Day of 1824, settled down at Tennison's Hotel. They found the city not much changed from Major Ridge's last visit. The Executive Mansion had been rebuilt and painted a dazzling white, and the Capitol was also restored, with a dome considerably smaller than the one it was destined to bear in later years. Otherwise the city seemed pretty much the same, a place of "magnificent distance," as one traveler described it that same year. "On [its] common pastures were hundreds of cows, owned by the citizens." In wet weather "the depth and adhesiveness of its mud" was nearly incredible.[1] Its streets were sometimes virtually quagmires. In such conditions the Cherokees found that to go about the city cost as much as lodgings did.

On January 5, John C. Calhoun, the suave and able secretary of war, acknowledged receipt of their first communication, saying he could receive them at noon the following day. At that meeting Major Ridge, as delegation head, requested an audience with the president, and the reception was arranged for three days later.[2] Calhoun presented the deputation to James Monroe, tall and rawboned and dressed in a fastidious blue coat with buff vest and white top boots. Possibly the delegation had met him before—in 1819 when he had visited the Cherokees during a western tour. With John Ridge interpreting before he traveled on to Cornwall, Major Ridge addressed the president "in the figurative style of savage oratory, with frequent recurrence to the idea of the Great Spirit above," or so John Quincy Adams, secretary of state, noted in his diary. Adams, short and balding, showed such interest in the Cherokees that they gave him "some account of their institutions."[3]

The visit was principally a matter of form. Calhoun made it

154

clear that all matters for negotiation must pass through his office. Early in the talks the convention of 1802 was read, and the Cherokees said they understood its provisions. Then through Calhoun's office on the nineteenth they advised the president of the Cherokee resolve to make no further cessions of land and requested him to intercede with Congress to authorize "an adjustment" between the United States and Georgia for the release of the federal government from the compact of 1802 "so far as it respects the extinguishment of the Cherokee title to lands within the chartered limits of Georgia."[4]

The request led to further interchanges between Calhoun and the Cherokees. The secretary declared it incompatible with the American system for the Indians to remain indefinitely as a separate entity within the limits of Georgia, that they must plan either to become integrated with the social and political fabric of the state or to emigrate beyond the Mississippi. On this point the secretary put on a great show of firmness. The Cherokees were equally adamant: "Sir," they answered on February 11, ". . . we beg leave to . . . remind you that the Cherokees are not foreigners but original inhabitants of the United States; . . . that the states by which they are now surrounded have been created out of land which was once theirs; that they cannot recognize the sovereignty of any state within the limits of their territory. . . . An exchange of [land] twice as large west of the Mississippi, as the one now occupied by the Cherokees east of that river, or all the money now in . . . your treasury, would be no inducement for the nation to exchange or sell their country."[5]

The effect was an explosion among the representatives of Georgia. They were afflicted by the spectacle of an apparent "diplomatic correspondence" between the Cherokees and the War Department. They were especially incensed when Calhoun addressed the chiefs as "gentlemen," imputing some "deep design" to his word choice.[6] "These misguided men," they fulminated at the president, "should be taught by the general government that there is no alternative between their removal beyond the limits of the State of Georgia and their extinction. The government of the United States will deceive them grossly if they are led to believe that, at this day, their consent is necessary to the fulfillment of its obligations to the State of Georgia. Their will must yield to the paramount duties of the general government to *itself* and to *each member* of the confederacy."[7]

President Monroe privately characterized the Georgians' letter as an insult. Adams described it as a "most acrimonious reproach

against the United States, whom it charges almost in terms of fraud
and hypocrisy, while it broadly insinuates that the obstinacy of the
Cherokees is instigated by the Secretary of War himself."⁸ In preparing his message to Congress on the subject the president consulted with his cabinet, who sustained his conclusions. His message
opened with a lucid review of the situation, outlining the negotiations before and since the Cherokees had come to the city. He
stated Georgia's position, but added: "I have no hesitation . . . to
declare it as my opinion, that the Indian title was not affected in
the slightest circumstances by the compact with Georgia, and that
there is no obligation on the United States to remove the Indians
by force."

Not that he thought it best for the Cherokees to remain in
Georgia. "My impression is equally strong," he resumed, "that it
would promote essentially the security and happiness of the tribes
within our limits, if they could be prevailed on to retire [to lands]
procured for them by the United States, in exchange for those on
which they reside." He pointed out the difficulties of the Indians,
hemmed in and pressured as they were on every side, and lamented
that they were liable to lose their moral character under such conditions. "But all these evils may *be avoided*," he wrote, "if these
tribes *will consent* to remove beyond the limits of our present states
and territories."⁹

Whatever the president's sentiment regarding the wisdom of
removal, he recognized the justice and legality of the Cherokee
position, and his words carried much weight with Congress. On
April 15, the Cherokees themselves delivered a memorial to the
Capitol, restating their case and appealing to the magnanimity of
the American people to protect their interests.¹⁰ Secretary Adams
was impressed at how aptly they expressed themselves on paper.
"They write their own state papers, and reason as logically as most
white diplomats," he noted,¹¹ as if to gainsay aspersions by the
Georgians that they used the services of a white ghost-writer. Such
charges (in connection with one of their letters to Calhoun) the
Cherokees themselves scotched in the *National Intelligencer:* "[That]
letter and every other letter," they pointed out, "was not only *written*
but dictated by an Indian. We are not so fortunate to have such
help. The white man seldom comes forward in our defense. Our
rights are in our own keeping . . . our letters are our own—and
if they are thought too refined for 'Savages' let the white man take
it for proof that . . . Indians can think and write for themselves.

We refer the Georgia delegation . . . to our correspondence with their own Commissioners in our own country."[12]

The dapper secretary of state was also impressed with the apparent prosperity of the Cherokee delegates. "Each of the chiefs," he added, ". . . possesses from fifty to a hundred thousand dollars [in] property."* As they had come to the capital at their own request, the War Department had not followed the usual custom of outfitting them in the uniforms of army officers, or in civilian dress of the latest fashion, but it had not escaped the attentive eye of Mr. Adams that they were clothed as well as most white gentlemen. "They dress like ourselves," he noted on one occasion, "except that Hicks, a young and very handsome man, wore habitually a purfled scarf." Their manners, according to the secretary, differed in no way from those of "well-bred country gentlemen."[13] Mrs. Adams did not hesitate to invite them to her decorous Tuesday evenings, and they attended almost all of her receptions, gatherings of fifty to a hundred guests. Also, representatives of the War Department took them on an excursion to Baltimore, the country's third largest city, where gas streetlamps had just been installed to the Cherokees' surprise and delight.

They attended a party at the home of Mr. Calhoun, where Major Ridge's "fine figure and handsome face made a great impression."[14] They were present, too, at several Wednesday evening levees at the White House, giving an exotic touch to an affair that some thought was edging in the direction of a capital disgrace. As the *National Intelligencer* viewed the balls,

The secretaries, senators, foreign ministers, consuls, auditors, accountants, officers of the army and navy of every grade, farmers, merchants, parsons, priests, lawyers, judges, auctioneers, and nothingarians, all with their wives, and some with their gawky offspring crowd to the President's house every Wednesday evening; some in shoes, most in boots, and many in spurs; some snuffing, others chewing, and many longing for their cigars and whiskey punches which they had left at home. Some with powdered head, others frizzled and oiled, and some whose head a comb has never touched, half hid by dirty collars reaching far above their ears as stiff as pasteboard.[15]

The Cherokees enjoyed themselves thoroughly, not only when

---

*Adams had an exaggerated notion of their wealth. The property of neither Ross nor Major Ridge, the richest members of the delegation, would be found by federal appraisers to equal the lower figure that Adams cited.

going out, but also when dining at home at the Tennison House. On one occasion they found at their table a congressman from Georgia, who on the floor of the House had referred to the Cherokee people as "savages subsisting upon roots, wild herbs [and] disgusting reptiles." George Lowrey pointed to a dish of sweet potatoes and, in a loud voice, asked the black waiter to bring him "some of those roots." He took only a small portion, but managed to catch the attention of the dining room. Several times he asked for more of "those roots," adding at each request, "We Indians are very fond of roots," while diners all about burst into laughter.[16] On reporting Major Ridge's conversation about the same time, a correspondent of the *National Gazette* called him "fluent and facetious."

When he was told of the contents of a communication of the Georgian delegation to the president, The Ridge remarked, "It is a very hot talk—I suppose it was intended for the people at home."[17] But the Georgians pressed their arguments long and hard and without relenting, and though in the opinion of Adams the Cherokees had "sustained a written controversy against the Georgia delegation with great advantage,"[18] they lost in the end the immediate object of their campaign. Congress appropriated another fund to send commissioners to treat for Indian lands. The view seemed to prevail in the Capitol that the Cherokees could be dispossessed as arbitrarily as the whites had dispossessed the seaboard tribes. The bittersweet mixture of success and failure extended to other objectives of the Cherokee mission. It was to no avail that the delegates petitioned for the relocation of their agency and for the dismissal of Governor McMinn as agent for misrepresentation and other misbehavior. Their request that the light horse be paid for the expulsion of white intruders met with no better success, though their plan to tax white traders was upheld.

Perhaps their most clear-cut success involved their request that the United States start paying the one-thousand-dollar annuity, plus interest, stipulated by the Tellico Treaty of 1804. Startled, Calhoun at first denied the existence of such a treaty, but the chiefs produced their copy of it, signed and sealed. A hurried combing of War Department files brought to light the American copy, long lost, and the federal government at once complied with its terms.[19]

As for Major Ridge's personal mission, plans for Sally's further schooling came to naught. In his need (for though a man of property he had no ready cash) he had turned his hopes toward the Indian Office, but Colonel McKenney now dashed them with an

Major George Lowery, Assistant Principal Chief of the Cherokees at the time of removal. From a painting attributed to John Mix Stanley. Smithsonian Institution, National Anthropological Archives, Neg. No. 44654.

announcement that "the fund for Indian civilization" had no money presently available for the education of "female children at the metropolis."[20] Furthermore the Quakers, having heard of certain things John Ridge had said in defiance of Georgia and interpreting them as indications of active hostility on the part of Cherokees in general, failed to make Sally welcome at "Mrs. Corbett's school," which she had hoped to attend. At the same time no vacancy developed for her at the Moravians' academy for girls at Salem.[21] So reluctantly The Ridge prepared to take her home as the Cherokee negotiations drew to a close.

The delegation called on the president on June 3, 1824, to say farewell, and in the presence of Calhoun and Adams, Major Ridge made a short speech in Cherokee, which Lowrey and Ross turned into English. Adams noted: "It was merely an expression of thanks for the reception and treatment they had met here, and assurances that they would remember it after their return home. There was less of Indian oratory, and more of the common style of white discourse, than in the same chief's speech on their first introduction. The President answered briefly."[22] The Cherokees took their leave immediately, reaching home "after a passage of sixteen days from Baltimore."[23]

They found their people in the grip of a famine caused by drought. Many families were forced to live on greens and roots, their plight underscoring with bitter irony the jibe of the congressman from Georgia. In addition, there was an epidemic of smallpox, which the unenlightened thought was caused by a snake as thick as a man's body, with an ugly white head and a smell so poisonous that a single whiff meant possible death. The conjurors were doing a brisk business, holding physic dances and praying to an immense eagle they claimed to see, or to a black dog in the north, a white dog in the east, a gray dog in the south, or a red dog in the west.[24]

At this period of national distress The Ridge solved a vexing personal problem, the question of Sally's schooling. The Brainerd missionaries had opened a branch outpost at Turnip Mountain, renamed Haweis—it was located a few miles downstream from the Head of Coosa, close to which The Ridge maintained a ferry and a second home. When a school was opened at Haweis, under the direction of Frederic Ellsworth, Major Ridge sent Sally there. She was joined by three of Watie's daughters, and all of them lived with the Ellsworth family. The cost of board and schooling was small, and Major Ridge paid in corn, beef, and other foodstuff for the mission. In order to be close to the school, he and Susanna spent much time at Ridge's Ferry, where John and his bride now occupied a separate apartment. The ferry was located on the Oostanaula, about a mile from its junction with the Etowah to form the Coosa. It serviced the road between New Town and Alabama, as well as a converging toll road that Major Ridge had opened at his own expense. The Ridges were frequent guests at Haweis, where they listened while Brother Ellsworth expounded the gospel, and Sally often came home to Ridge's Ferry.[25]

Meanwhile the time had arrived for the fall council of 1824. The Ridges returned to Oothcaloga, so convenient to New Town, and families from every part of the nation converged on the capital. The Cherokees asked William Chamberlin, the Brainerd missionary, to preach a sermon in the council house, and according to his record, "The King, his councillors and the members of the National Committee were present. The ladies were very neatly dressed and seated in front and the gentlemen on the right and left." John Ridge, newly elected to the National Committee, "interpreted the discourse with a great deal of animation." Then before the audience filed out, Major Ridge, as national Speaker, "made [a spirited] speech in favor of religion."[26]

Afterward Major Ridge walked with Chamberlin through the town, while the people returned to their temporary lodgings, with many candles and flaring pine knots to light the way. "I fancied myself in some of our larger towns at the north," wrote the missionary; and the sight reminded Major Ridge of the many gas street-lamps he had seen on his journey earlier in the year. "Baltimore *i tsu la ha*," he said in lively tones. "This is like Baltimore." The Ridge expressed satisfaction at the meeting "and with the general appearance of his people." He was glad that so many of them had become Christians, and he solemnly declared that he would do all he could to encourage them. He hoped that soon the council, like Congress in Washington, would have a chaplain to open deliberations with prayer. Chamberlin approved and later jotted in his diary: "When I reflect on the astonishing change that has taken place among this people within a few years, I cannot but exclaim, Lo, what hath God wrought? . . . The Chiefs are indeed generally enlightened men and are doing what they can for the improvement of their people."[27]

At this time the council resolved to establish a national academy at New Town. The chiefs planned to house it in a brick building forty feet square and two stories high, with four chimneys and eight fireplaces. And it was planned that the lower room would be furnished with seats and desks to accommodate a goodly number of students. Associated with the academy would be a small museum, and almost at once people began to rummage through their houses for old relics and curios to bestow there, in Boudinot's care—ancestral peace pipes, strings of wampum, and headpieces decorated with buffalo horns. The council also remembered the phenomenal spread of Sequoyah's syllabary and took steps to honor the inventor. A silver medal, suitably inscribed, "was presented to him, as a testimonial of [Cherokee] gratitude."[28]

Scarcely had the council come to an end than several prominent people assembled in the council house to make still another move for the stimulation of Cherokee culture. After considerable discussion they decided, on November 5, 1824, to establish the Moral and Literary Society of the Cherokee Nation. The objective of the organization, according to its constitution, was "the suppression of vice, the encouragement of morality, and the general improvement of the nation." The society also entertained the aim of uniting "in *fidelity* the citizens of this nation to the true interests of their country, and for supporting the government and laws thereof." Dues were set at one dollar a year, and five dollars or more entitled one to a life membership—provided that he practiced "the strictest morality." A board of officers was decreed, under whose direction a library was to be formed of books treating of "Morality, History, Religion, Jurisprudence, and general Literature."[29] A full meeting of the society was to be held every year at council time in New Town, and David Brown, just home from Andover, was appointed to deliver the address in 1825, with John Ridge named as a substitute in the case of illness on Brown's part or any other contingency. Those present passed John Ridge's motion that the president be empowered to appoint agents to solicit donations, in money or books, and Boudinot proposed that his cousin be asked to reduce the constitution to writing and publicize the society in American newspapers. This Ridge did, sending a column to the *Boston Recorder,* from which the story was picked up by several other journals and papers. As corresponding secretary, Boudinot also did his part in spreading word concerning the organization, appealing for "Books on travels, Histories, both ancient and modern, Maps, and in fine, books of all descriptions tending to the objects of the Society."[30] John Ridge wrote:

The word *Literary* is used as a part of the Society's denomination. As it is not intended, it is presumed it will not be expected that eloquent dissertations on general science, or literary discoveries, will emanate from the infant society. Its disposition to improve, and hold the fond connection of *fraternity* with other societies in the U.S. of the kind, will be an excitement to its members to drink as plentifully as their means will admit, from scientific fountains already opened, and as others shall flow in future times. . . .

Civilization has shed the beams of gladness among this people. Religion's lamp is seen to luminate the darkness of ignorance. The Indians know their value, and with fond delight, anticipate a time when liberality will place them on a footing with other nations whose merits have not been sacrificed by prejudice on oblivion's altar.[31]

Plans for the society had met with approval in the October council, where the question of improvement had been so much to the fore, but the topics of land and emigration had been the principal concerns of those deliberations. The council had reiterated the Cherokee stand against removal and voted to return the deputation to Washington City to carry on their campaign there—the same men, with the exception of Major Ridge, who was busy then with his own affairs. Yet January 10, 1825, found him in the federal capital well ahead of the arrival of Ross, Lowrey, and Elijah Hicks. On that day he went to the Gadsby Hotel, the newest and most lavish caravansary in the city, to pay his respects to Andrew Jackson, who was now serving as senator from Tennessee after having organized the territorial government of Florida. Old Hickory was probably the most popular man in the United States, much more so than President Monroe, and was now an active candidate for the presidency, his quarters the destination of multitudes of callers. His shocks of hair were more unruly than ever; his blue eyes were still sharp and keen. Major Ridge saluted him in Cherokee, and when *Niles' Weekly Register* reported the speech, the editor found that its figurative beauty suggested a poem by Ossian:

"My heart is glad when I look upon you," The Ridge said:

Our heads have become white. They are blossomed with age. It is the course of nature. We ought to thank the Great Spirit who has taken care of our lives. When first we met we were taking the red path. We waded in blood until the murderers of our women and children had ceased. In the land of our enemies we kindled our war fires. We sat by them until morning, when battle came with the yells of our enemies. We met them; they either fled or fell.

War is no more heard in our land. The mountains speak peace.

Joy is in our valleys. The warrior is careless and smokes the pipe of peace. His arms lay idle; he points to them, and speaks to his children of his valiant deeds; his glory will not depart with him, but remain with his sons.

We have met near the house of our great father, the president. Friendship formed in danger will not be forgotten, nor will the hungry men forget who fed him. The meeting of friends gladdens the heart. Our countenances are bright as we look on each other. We rejoice that our father has been kind to us. The men of his house are friendly. Our hearts have been with *you* always, and we are happy again to take the great chief by the hand.[32]

Major Ridge addressed General Jackson as a diplomat, whatever his real purpose in coming to Washington City. As he was no longer a member of the Cherokee delegation, and as the Cherokees were now making common cause with the Creeks, a statement published years later by his grandson, John R. Ridge, seems to the point: "Ka-nung-ta-claga, a war chief of the Cherokees," wrote Yellow Bird, "possessed influence at Washington; and his son John Ridge, afterwards chief of the Ridge Division of the Nation, then a young man of twenty-two or twenty-three years of age, could speak the English language fluently. The Creek chiefs applied to them to act as their agents. . . . The Ridges accordingly proceeded to Washington and set the ball in motion."[33] They were probably in the company of The Big Warrior, principal chief of the Creeks, who, old and ailing, was to die in the capital a few weeks hence.[34] Such work on behalf of the Creeks, whatever it might be, agreed with the policies of the Cherokees ever since McIntosh's authority had been "washed away" by the Cherokee council in October, 1823. John Ross had written to the Creek chiefs, unmasking McIntosh's aims, proposing a concert of action between the two tribes, and appealing to the Creeks to follow "the pattern set by the Cherokees" and to refuse to make any further cessions of land. This they had resolved to do in two councils in 1824.[35] The Cherokees appealed to them again in December, Major Ridge probably taking the message to their council at Broken Arrow, and their stand was so firm that the U.S. commissioners complained to Governor Troup of Georgia that "for some time past the Cherokees [had] exerted a steady and officious interference in the affairs of [the Creeks]."[36]* Because of his

*Cf. Gov. Troup to John Forsyth, April 6, 1825, Georgia Department of Archives and History: "When the treaty is holden at Broken Arrow, the Cherokees

furtive midnight meetings with the commissioners, the Creek chiefs summarily broke McIntosh of all authority, and doubtless out of pique he proceeded to sign a treaty with the U.S. commissioners on February 12, 1825, at Indian Springs, Georgia—a treaty that ceded to the United States all of the Creek lands in Georgia and several million of acres in Alabama and provided for the removal of the Creeks beyond the Mississippi. He was induced to do so, and to persuade his adherents to do so also, by large bribes including reservations of land on the Chattahoochee. At the same time, he was reported to have said that, in doing so, he forfeited his life under the laws of the Creek Nation.[37]

On that score he proved right. At daylight on the morning of April 30, 1825, a band of about two hundred Creek warriors surrounded the buildings owned by McIntosh on the bank of the Chattahoochee. It was a company of executioners sent by the Creek chiefs to avenge the Creek Nation. They spread bales of kindling wood at the foot of the walls, and soon the buildings were burning briskly. Chilly, the son of McIntosh, made his escape through a window and swam the river to safety, and the wives and children of the general were allowed to escape. McIntosh was left alone in his burning house; he could be seen at a window on the second floor with a rifle in his hands. Then as he came down the burning stairs, he was met by a volley of bullets and fell and would have been burned in the building had not several warriors rushed inside and grasped him by the legs and dragged him down the steps to the ground. "While lying in the yard," according to one report, "and while the blood was gushing from the wounds, he raised himself on one arm, and surveyed his murderers with looks of defiance. At that moment an Ockfuskie Indian plunged a long knife, to the hilt, in the direction of his heart. He brought a long breath and expired."[38] The warriors continued to fire at his body until they had put more than fifty balls through his head. His lieutenant, Etome Tustunuggee, was discovered in the second burning building, a public stand which the general had operated, and was executed with equal barbarity. Then the warriors fell to slaughtering stock and destroying property. They would not allow the wives of McIntosh even a suit in which

---

are present, by their emissaries, under the eye of the agent, busied to defeat, by the most wily machinations and contrivances, the object of the treaty. They witness the failure of the treaty and by these means."

General William McIntosh, a Creek chief killed by his own people. A McKenney and Hall lithograph from a painting by Charles Bird King. Smithsonian Institution, National Anthropological Archives, Neg. No. 45111B.

to bury their husband, and he was lowered naked into the ground.

Major Ridge, along with most of the Cherokees, approved of the execution.[39] According to John R. Ridge, it became the object of the Ridges to secure the abrogation of the McIntosh treaty. How they proceeded, and the extent of what they did in pursuit of this purpose, can only be surmised now. But, in point of fact, suspicion of the treaty was sown in the mind of the new president, John Quincy Adams, who had been chosen upon the vote being brought to Congress, though Jackson had received more votes in the electoral college, and after a preliminary investigation General Edmund P. Gaines was sent to Georgia with federal troops to prevent the Georgians from taking forcible possession of the territory in question. He was also instructed to secure from "the hostile Creeks" their side of the story in that explosive situation. He met the Creeks first in July, 1825, and according to the *Savannah Georgian*, "Two Cherokees [and] a deputation from their tribe attended the Council of the Creeks at Broken Arrow, and . . . these Cherokees . . . wrote the talks to General Gaines, . . . with his knowledge and approbation. One of the Cherokee deputation (Major Ridge) avowed the fact to a citizen of this state who lately stopped at his home while travelling through the Nation."[40]

The Cherokees who wrote the Creek talks were John Ridge and David Vann, whom Opothle Yoholo had named his secretaries "through the influence of [Major Ridge]."[41] The position taken by the Creeks conformed to "the Cherokee pattern," and General Gaines reported:

They protest against the Treaty—they refuse to receive any part of the consideration money, or to give any other evidence of their acquiescence in the treaty. But they have in the strongest terms deliberately declared that they will not raise an arm against the United States, even should an army come to take from them the whole of their country— that they will make no sort of resistance, but will sit down quietly and be put to death, where the bones of their ancestors are deposited; that the world shall know the Muscogee nation so loved their country that they were willing to die in it rather than sell it or leave it. This was their mode of expression, as interpreted in the presence of B. Hawkins* and several instructed to state whether or not the public interpreter did his duty.

---

*Not the former Creek agent, who was now dead, but a mixed-blood descendant.

Thus, the Cherokees had counseled a course of passive resistance twenty-four years before Henry Thoreau, the Massachusetts Yankee, published his essay on civil disobedience. "The Council. . . ," Gaines concluded, "has thus appealed to our magnanimity."[42]

The general—sometimes called "Granny Gaines" because of his caution—judged the temper of the Creeks correctly, and after lengthy negotiations he reached agreement with them that promised to satisfy even Georgia. It had not been easy, for as Gaines declared, "They had been operated on and embarrassed in such a manner by their *professed* friends, and secret enemies, [that they] oppose every proposition connected with the late treaty."[43] The Creeks agreed to sign a new treaty in place of that signed by McIntosh at Indian Springs, to relinquish all the Creek lands east of the Chattahoochee, and to allow the McIntosh faction reparations for losses and let them migrate beyond the Mississippi. Gaines would have at once concluded a treaty had not some of the principal chiefs already started for Washington. The chiefs wished to include John Ridge and David Vann in that part of the deputation that was to leave later, but the general objected, claiming that the president would never accept the Cherokees as Creek chiefs. The Creeks insisted on having someone in Washington of their own race, able to read and write English and thus prepared to protect the rights and interests of the Creek Nation, and if Ridge and Vann were not acceptable as fully accredited chiefs, then they must go as secretaries. Surely the United States could not object to that. The general agreed.[44]

Oddly enough, it was the Cherokee council who objected, disturbed by reports that Cherokees were interfering in the internal affairs of their neighbors. It was argued that Ridge and Vann might represent the Creeks as private citizens, but not as long as they held seats in the National Committee; hence they were dropped from that body, with others named to serve the rest of their term. This move was publicized as official punishment by those who opposed John Ridge's activities. It was nothing of the sort, he retorted, but merely a move on the part of the council to disclaim any responsibility for his actions.[45]

His sharp tongue and forthright manner, as well as his calculating and aggressive personality, had made enemies, and some were circulating false reports about him, even about his personal life. He was accused of abusing his wife and of bringing squaws into their house—and the reports would grow more vicious as time went on. It was said that Mrs. Ridge had fallen into melancholy, with thoughts

David Vann, Cherokee. A McKenney and Hall lithograph from an 1826 painting by Charles Bird King. Smithsonian Institution, National Anthropological Archives, Neg. No. 45113D.

of suicide. Indeed, the myth would develop that she had killed herself by jumping into the Oostanaula. Friends defended Ridge against such calumnies; Brother Butrick wrote to the Northrups to refute the rumors of John's cruelty and Sarah's unhappiness, and the letter was printed in the *Religious Intelligencer:*

> Little did any of us think that by this marriage [John Ridge] would expose himself to the hatred and slander of thousands who bear the Christian name, in a Christian land. The father of Mr. Ridge is, at home, just what you saw him to be at Cornwall, a gentleman. His mother, a pious devoted Christian, is also a lady. They live, not like *common* white people in the southern country, but rank among the first. J[ohn] Ridge and his wife live with them. They have an apartment by themselves. And as I have understood by the Cornwall students, your daughter dresses richer, and appears more like a lady, than when at Cornwall. I am confident . . . that she is not called to engage in any manual labour further than what she pleases; and she has universally appeared cheerful and contented, whenever I have seen her at their house.[46]

This was verified by Jeremiah Evarts, treasurer of the American Board for Foreign Missions, when he visited Ridge's Ferry. "As to the inquiry whether young Mrs. Ridge is contented and happy," he wrote, "it is certain that she often says she is; and surely she ought to know."[47]

Under such a distressing cloud, John Ridge left for Washington early in November, 1825, with David Vann and the Creek chiefs. They traveled by way of Milledgeville, then capital of Georgia, where they "arrived in full Indian regalia," which they soon changed to white men's clothes. They stayed, according to news reports, "in a small building near the market, by themselves, and appear[ed] very adverse to communication of any kind with the whites."[48] Doubtless they sailed from a Georgia port, reaching the federal capital later in the month, as *Niles' Weekly Register* noted, "with a young intelligent speaker by the name of Ridge."[49] A party of seventeen—thirteen Creek chiefs, their interpreter, the two Cherokees, and the young son of one of the chiefs—they took quarters in the Indian Queen Hotel of Jesse Brown, "the prince of landlords," where a lurid sign with the portrait of Pocahontas creaked in the wind, and Brown in a white apron met them affably at the curb. At mealtimes the Prince of Landlords, according to Nathan Sargent's description, would escort the newly arrived to seats, "and then [go] to the head of the table, where he carved and helped the principal dish. The excellence of this he would announce, as he invited those at table to send up their plates for what he knew to be their favorite portions; and he would also call attention to the dishes on other parts of the board, which were carved and served by the guests who sat nearest to them. Brandy and whiskey were placed on the table in decanters, to be drunk by the guests without additional charge."[50] The delegation found the Indian Queen a comfortable and convenient shelter. At about the same time, a deputation of the McIntosh faction, angry and hostile, settled down at Tennison's Hotel. Soon Colonel McKenney had provided both delegations with new clothes, and negotiations were ready to start.

The initial interview was held on November 30 with James Barbour, the secretary of war. Opothle Yoholo, the head chief, announced that he was prepared to talk with the government. "I expect all the transactions of the late disturbances have been laid before our Great Father," he said. "I know writings were entered into in our nation on both sides. I doubt not the President has seen them all. He can judge. . . . I look for protection to the United States. I expect the late treaty to be cancelled."

The secretary of war reminded him of the preliminary agreement that General Gaines had reached with the Creeks, showed him a copy of the general's report, and verified the names of the chiefs listed in it. Then the secretary ventured that Opothle Yoholo, he supposed, had "no objection to carrying the agreement into effect."

"The subject is embarrassing . . . ," the chief replied. "Clouds rest upon it. Our nation expects us to act under a clear sky. We must reflect well, and counsel about what is to be done. We will give you an answer tomorrow."[51]

John Ridge wrote a reply on December 3, 1825, the deputation signing it with their marks. The Creeks were willing to treat, the letter stated, but there would be no exchange of territory, only a sale—for money—of their land east of the Chattahoochee. "We respectfully suggest to you our determination not to cede any more than the Lands east of the river and to have the east bank, up to high water mark, as the boundary between us. The acknowledgement of that line on your part will afford facility to an arrangement with you. On no other conditions will the Delegation consent to enter into an agreement. We may as well be annihilated at once

as to cede any portion of the land west of the river."[52] Thus, the
basis for a new treaty was laid; only the details remained to be
worked out.

Snags developed in the final steps, however. The United States
insisted on acquiring all Creek lands within the chartered limits of
Georgia in order to satisfy the aroused citizens of that state; the
Creeks refused to surrender any land west of the Chattahoochee.
They did not understand the white men's "lines"; they refused to
yield in their stress on a natural boundary, as dictated by their
great Council Fire at home. Opothle Yoholo won admiration for
the dignity with which he stood his ground. He asked for an interview with President Adams, but his request was denied. Then the
Creeks, by means of Ridge's pen, took refuge in the arguments of
passive resistance they had directed at General Gaines:

> In our first letters, in the spirit of reconciliation & loyalty to the U.
> States, we agreed to surrender all the lands east of the Chattahoochy
> River. This ought to convince the genl. Government that we are not
> incapable of Reciprocating, in proportion to our ability, the Liberality
> of the U. States. Further concessions cannot be made and after the
> reasons first assigned, more you cannot demand. We now appeal to the
> magnanimity of the United States. We have travelled a long road to
> perform this duty. It is ordained by the Great Creator that we are so
> reduced as to be dependent on your power and mercy: and if the huge-
> ness of Strength you determine to decide by power and not by right,
> we shall return to our friends and live there, untill [*sic*] you take pos-
> session of our country. Then shall we beg Bread from the whites and
> live the life of vagabonds on the soil of our progenitors. We shall not
> touch a cent of money for our Lands thus forced from our hands, and
> not a drop of white man's blood will be spilled. And as fast as we are
> knocked in the head—the throats of our wives and children are cut,
> by the first tide of population that know not law, we will then afford
> the United States a Spectacle of Emigration, which we hope may be to
> a Country prepared by the Great Spirit for honest and unfortunate
> Indians.[53]

For weeks the issue remained at an impasse. The secretary of
war had the rough draft of a treaty drawn up, but neither side
would retreat from its position. On January 17, 1826, when the
deputation left the War Office convinced that the talks were at a
definite end, Opothle Yoholo retreated to the Indian Queen and,
feeling his honor had been besmirched, attempted suicide in his
room. That evening Colonel McKenney saved the negotiations by
writing privately to John Ridge and prevailing upon him to con-

vince the Creeks that a small compromise was necessary. This Ridge did, and Opothle Yoholo and his colleagues agreed to depart from the Chattahoochee boundary at the Big Bend and to take from there a more westerly branch of the river for the border as far as the Cherokee line.[54] Thus, agreement was reached and the treaty was signed on January 24, 1826, in the office of the secretary of war.

The first article repudiated the McIntosh treaty. Lands along the lines agreed upon were ceded, leaving almost nothing to the Creeks within the bounds of Georgia. In return, the Creeks received $217,600 in cash and a perpetual annuity of $20,000. For their part they agreed to make financial restitution to the McIntosh faction in accordance with the findings of a special agent appointed by the War Office. The United States promised to pay for the emigration of the McIntosh party, to subsist them for a year in the West, and to pay them $100,000, or less, depending on the size of the emigration. The Creeks agreed to relinquish the ceded land by January 1, 1827.[55]

In April, 1826, Colonel McKenney gave the deputation a kindly commendation. "Write to Little Prince and Tuskenaha [the principal chiefs]," he suggested, "and say, their Father has paid great attention to the talk of his children; and that his children have conducted themselves well since they have been here, and made by their good conduct many friends."[56] He failed, evidently, to foresee a certain trouble that would erupt in Congress when the treaty was sent by the president for ratification. After it was signed, Ridge and Vann had brought to McKenney a paper with a couple of dozen people indicated as those to whom the chiefs had agreed to pay sums from the treaty money. Every chief on the delegation was to receive from five to ten thousand dollars. The listed included several favored chiefs at home, including Little Prince and Tuskenaha, each slated for ten thousand dollars. In return for their services Ridge and Vann were asking fifteen thousand dollars apiece, and they specified ten thousand dollars for Major Ridge. McKenney indicated that the United States was obliged only to pay the treaty money to the chiefs of the Creek Nation; their distribution of it was their own affair.

Then he asked if every member of the deputation understood the distribution proposed.

"No," Ridge answered frankly. "But Opothle Yoholo and Charles Cornells know, and that's enough."[57]

Disconcerted, McKenney took the matter to Secretary Barbour, who called the delegation to the War Office after a supplementary article ceding the rest of the lands in Georgia had been signed and sent to Congress. "They came," McKenney wrote, reviewing the incident. "The list of payments was read and interpreted to the whole Delegation, the [Cherokee] secretaries being absent, after a full explanation by the Secretary of War as to the possible effects such an apportionment might have upon the nation at home. He was told that they would disclose every transaction in full council, and that there need be no apprehension whatever."[58] Barbour wanted to know whether they had all agreed to the distribution as indicated. They answered, "Yes," repeating that it was their own arrangement and that the secretary need have no fears. They would see to it that the distribution was ratified at their Great Council Fire. So assured, Barbour washed his hands of the matter.[59]

But when knowledge of the proposed distribution reached Congress, cries of outrage hurtled toward the dome. The representatives of Georgia were certain that the affair smacked of fraud, and in pressing their arguments, they seized especially on the payments slated for the Cherokees. Barbour retorted that the Creeks, as long as they were treated as independent people, had the right to select their own agents.[60] And Senator Tazewell of Virginia came to the defense of Ridge and Vann with an astringent statement. The Creeks, he said, "had manifested more skill in diplomacy than the United States. They had completed their affairs more dexterously than we had ours; and . . . these two Cherokee boys sent here had completed a treaty on better terms for the Creeks, and worse terms for the United States, than all the diplomatic functionaries [we] employed. . . . We have nothing to do with that affair except to place the money in the hands of the Creek nation, and let them distribute it according to what they consider justice on their part towards the Cherokees."[61] This attitude prevailed; the treaty was ratified and the purchase money appropriated, with the stipulation that it be delivered to the Creek Nation for whatever disposition the chiefs deemed fit.

Meanwhile Ridge and Vann, angered at the accusations of fraud and aware of the danger such allegations might create for them in the Creek Nation, wrote to the War Department in the name of the deputation. They complained of slander in Congress and requested a testimonial as to their good faith during the deliberations. Colonel McKenney wrote the delegation on behalf of James Barbour: "I am directed to reply that, in the intercourse had with you in negotiating the treaty, the Secretary discovered nothing improper in your conduct, but esteemed you to be men of correct principles. The mode of distributing the money as submitted by you was an arrangement of your own, and . . . the Secretary . . . considered you as acting with such a knowledge of the whole matter as led him to hope . . . that the consequences he had apprehended would not take place."[62] McKenney's reply was not as positive a voucher as Ridge had hoped to receive, but with skillful explanations he could make it serve as protection in the Creek Nation, should the contingency arise.

The delegation would return home with the trappings of success. The Indian Office had issued medals of the largest size, each of the chiefs receiving one, and Opothle Yoholo was entrusted to carry one home to Little Prince.[63] Moreover, McKenney had arranged to have portraits painted of several members of the delegation, including Ridge and Vann, to hang on the walls of the Indian Office in Georgetown along with the pictures of other Indian visitors. They sat for the affable artist Charles Bird King under the trees of his home on Twelfth Street. A native of Newport, Rhode Island, who had studied with Benjamin West in London, King was an artist of grace and skill who painted portraits for the government at twenty dollars a head. His picture of John Ridge showed a slim young man with a sensitive and intelligent face who could have passed for a white man of brunette complexion, with eyes dark and animated and with hair cut rather short and curling at the ends. About his throat was a high white collar, and he was dressed in a trim coat and vest of latest fashion. A sheet of writing paper lay curled under his left hand, and in his right was a long, white, graceful goose quill, the symbol of his calling. Bird not only painted original oils for the government; he was also commissioned to make copies for the sitters, "of a size more convenient and portable, but just as true and perfect."[64]

Three or four years later Mrs. Frances Trollope, the vinegary English visitor, saw the room in which McKenney hung the pictures and devoted a passage to it in her book of travels:

The walls are entirely covered with original portraits of all the chiefs who, from time to time, have come to negotiate with their great father, as they call the President. These portraits are by Mr. King, and, it cannot be doubted, are excellent likenesses. . . . The countenances are full of expression, but the expression in most of them is extremely similar; or rather, I should say that they have but two sorts of ex-

John Ridge. A McKenney and Hall lithograph from an 1826 painting by Charles Bird King. Smithsonian Institution, National Anthropological Archives, Neg. No. 45113A.

pressions; the one is that of very noble and warlike daring, the other of a gentle and *naive* simplicity, that has no mixture of folly in it, but which is inexpressibly engaging, and the more touching, perhaps, because at the moment we were looking at them, those very hearts which lent the eyes such meek and friendly softness were wrung by a base, cruel, and most oppressive act of their *great father*.[65]

In writing those words Mrs. Trollope may have had the Cherokees in mind.

The portrait gallery was in a sense an ethnological museum. McKenney claimed that he had conceived of the project for the benefit of posterity, to transmit some notion of how the aborigines of America looked at this particular time.[66]* And while in the city John Ridge associated himself with another ethnological venture when Albert Gallatin, Swiss-born secretary of the treasury in Thomas Jefferson's time, asked for his help in securing vocabularies of the Uchee and Natchez tongues. Two of the chiefs in the Creek delegation spoke these languages, and Ridge recorded words and sentences from them after a scheme supplied by Gallatin. He also provided Cherokee vocabularies and wrote a short sketch on the progress of civilization among his people. Gallatin advised McKenney: "Of the favorable effects which, if published by [Baron Alexander von] Humboldt, this essay written by a native Indian may have on public opinion both here and abroad I have already verbally conversed with you; and I may add that it gives an opportunity to Mr. Ridge to obtain a general reputation which he may not again meet with."[67] It is uncertain whether Ridge's sketch, written with grace and high spirits, was published,[68] but Gallatin included his vocabularies, along with one compiled by Boudinot, in "A Synopsis of the Indian Tribes of North America," which he published in the *Transactions and Collections* of the American Antiquarian Society. Concerning a collective tussle with Uchee, Gallatin wrote: "The Uchee language is the most guttural, uncouth, and difficult to express with our alphabet and orthography of any of the Indian

---

*Cf. the *Savannah Georgian*, June 3, 1826, p. 2, col. 5: "Communicated.—I wish to know whether the Cherokee *interpreters* or *Secretaries* Ridge and Vann, who wished to feather their nests at the expense of the Creek tribe, to the tune of $15,000 apiece, have had their portraits taken at the expense of *our nation:* along with the portraits of the other disinterested Indian parties to the late treaty. Were *their* portraits also taken for the benefit of posterity? I hope, if they have been taken, that they may be preserved: in order that the People may see how their money goes—and that posterity may have the benefit of the portraits of two as arrant, cunning and mercenary diplomatists as ever graced the Council Boards."

languages within my knowledge. The vocabulary here given is extracted from one taken by Dr. Ware, in Mr. Duponceau's Collection, and from another obtained by Mr. Ridge from a Uchee chief at Washington. Mr. Ridge had probably the best Indian ear, but was not so correct in his English orthography."[69]

The majority of the delegation had started for home after the treaty was signed. They left Ridge and Opothle Yoholo in the city to take care of miscellaneous matters. Ridge himself reached home by the end of May or early June, 1826. By the middle of August he found it necessary to attend the Creek council called near Fort Mitchell, in eastern Alabama, for the purpose of receiving the treaty money. The council convened on the sixteenth, and the ceremony of the black drink led the agenda. It involved boiling leaves of a small holly bush which the Creeks called *arsee* and which the whites called "Carolina tea" or *Ilex vomitoria*. The nauseous brew was poured into large gourds, each holding nearly a gallon, and was thus passed around for all to drink as much as their stomachs could hold. Acting as an emetic, the drink was vomited up, cleansing and purifying all who underwent the ceremony — or so the Creeks contended. With evidences of the rite covering the council ground, the Creeks felt purged and ready for official business. Ridge and Vann took part in the council.[70]

Those senators who supposed that delivery of the purchase money to the chiefs in open council would circumvent the proposed distribution were proved wrong. It was true that certain chiefs felt grave dissatisfaction and made an abortive attempt to break the authority of Opothle Yoholo. Ridge and Vann had the correspondence between the War Department and the delegation read and "interpreted as best suited their purpose," reported the agent, Colonel John Crowell, "and made such other statements as were calculated to appease the chiefs."[71] "I know the chiefs of this nation, their feelings. . . ," John Ridge would later write,[72] and now he proved his point. He knew that they had come to expect such special grants as the distribution involved; "that they used such money to purchase adherents, and to carry on the legitimate expenses of their government, and to feed and clothe the needy members of their tribe. They had never developed a sense of accountability in the handling of public funds, but they did feel a patriarchal responsibility for the welfare of their people."[73] And as for their employment of the Ridges and Vann — of John Ridge especially — they felt in great need of skilled and knowing agents of their own race, in particular of educated men in whom they could place their trust, to help them deal with federal agents whom inevitably they regarded as much their enemies as the most aggressive frontiersmen. In the end Opothle Yoholo was sustained, and the division of cash was made. Major Ridge apparently received the entire amount slated for him. John Ridge and Vann, however, received only a part of their claims, five thousand dollars apiece.[74] They would never receive the full amount promised them. But ten years later, after several petitions to the federal government, the War Department exerted influence on the Creek chiefs to pay them another five thousand dollars apiece—a transaction that caused such high feeling among the Creeks that one man was killed, whereupon his family seized the assailant and, lashing him to a tree, stabbed him to death and left his body hanging from the branches.[75] The Creeks could well afford to make the payments, Yellow Bird would later argue, since the Ridges and Vann in working for the abrogation of the McIntosh treaty had helped to rescue several million acres of Creek land from "the greedy maw of the Federal government."[76]

When the supplemental article had been signed in Washington, it was supposed that the Creeks were at last surrendering all lands in Georgia, but the western boundary of Georgia had never been surveyed. "In undertaking to lay down the boundaries from an office map," Colonel McKenney explained, "wrong lines were assumed, and the Creeks [were] left in possession of a tract which they were afterwards induced, by the advice of indiscreet friends, to insist on retaining."[77] These friends were Ridge and Vann, who remained advisors to Opothle Yoholo. The federal government made repeated attempts to buy the land in question, "about 192,000 acres of pine barrens,"[78] but the Creeks, on Ridge and Vann's advice, remained firm in their refusal to sell. In the face of these rebuffs the secretary of war threatened the Cherokee council with unspecified reprisals unless the chiefs restrained the activities of Ridge and Vann among the Creeks.[79] The chiefs did nothing; they tacitly approved the success of the young men. At last in 1827 the president instructed McKenney, as commissioner of Indian affairs, to include the Creek country in a proposed western tour, there to meet the Creeks in council and do whatever necessary to break the impasse.

McKenney spent some time in the Upper Lake country, meeting tribes and making treaties. He reached the southern Indians in the fall of 1827 and approached the Creeks in November. The Upper Towns of the Creeks had called a council relative to the collection of taxes and the counting of the money prior to its being placed in the treasury, an operation in which John Ridge took an interest. He enjoyed much prestige among the Upper Towns; indeed he had the status of a chief, a kind of counselor in their councils, for on February 17 of that year the chiefs had decreed: "John Ridge in consideration of his former services and our great friendship to his Nation shall be allowed to sit and give his opinion in Council when he chooses. We wish this to be known by our father the President of the United States and our agent is hereby requested to transmit this paper to the Secretary of War."[80] Hence Ridge's interest in the council relative to taxes.

"I was invited by letter to attend that Council," he wrote. "I set out for the Creek country in company with Mr. David Vann, and having joined the Chiefs of Chejahla and Talledega, . . . moved on toward Tuckabatchee." Two days from their destination they learned of the expected arrival of "Land Buyers," along with chiefs from the Lower Towns. "We reached the town after Col. McKenney, and took lodgings with Opothle Yoholo."[81]

On his arrival Colonel McKenney had requested an interview with Opothle Yoholo, who had been named prime minister of the nation, and on whose decision the issue would doubtless rest. A general council was agreed upon, in place of that restricted to the Upper Towns, and runners were sent out to invite all chiefs to Tuckabatchee. Fifteen hundred Indians assembled at the appointed time, but for three days Opothle Yoholo had delayed opening the council till Ridge and Vann had arrived. "These persons," wrote McKenney and Hall, "having learned the white man's art of talking on paper, were much esteemed by the chief, who expected to be able to protect himself from any artifice that might be practiced in the phraseology of the treaty that would be proposed, while they used their advantage, on this and other occasions, to thwart the designs of the Government, and keep alive the existing agitation."[82]

After the ceremony of the black drink, the council opened. "I was invited . . . to attend," wrote John Ridge, "and take a seat . . . near their most distinguished chiefs, [and] a speech was delivered, announcing our arrival. . . . The Council composed of the Upper and Lower Towns arose, and individually took me by the hand and expressed their pleasure at my arrival."[83] Then the chiefs sent an invitation to Colonel McKenney and the agent Crowell to appear. When they arrived, Opothle Yoholo had them seated in front of him and the principal chiefs, Little Prince excepted, for his

Opothle Yoholo, Prime Minister of the Creek Confederacy. A McKenney and Hall lithograph from an 1826 painting by Charles Bird King. Smithsonian Institution, National Anthropological Archives, Neg. No. 45111F.

conjurer had forbidden him to enter the square as long as he was ill. The council, otherwise full, had power to do any business the chiefs thought proper.

Both Ridge and McKenney left accounts of the proceedings — accounts that are slanted, acrimonious, hard at points to reconcile; indeed, it seems that the whole truth can be found in neither. With Ridge there, McKenney doubted he could achieve his purpose, "for it was ascertained," he wrote, "that during the previous night the proposition of the commissioner had been debated, and a negative reply decided upon. It was believed that the two half-breed Cherokees had prevailed upon Opothle Yoholo to refuse to make the transfer of the disputed territory until a government could be organized, like that which had been established by the Cherokees, after which the sale was to be made, and the money put into the Creek treasury — one of the half-breeds [John Ridge] being the prospective minister of finances."[84] Without much hope of success, McKenney determined to spare no effort to push his cause. He made a prodigious effort and produced a talk that Ridge found suitable, in style and manner, for "Chippeways, Kickapoos, Menominees, Sioux, etc." Ridge made a satiric résumé of it:

That the Great Father told him [the commissioner] to go and visit his red children in the cold country at the lakes, then to his children who live where the Sun sleeps, then those who live in the warm country, and by all means his Creek children. He obeyed and went in stages and traveled far — then got into the great canoe that carries fire in its bottom and sends its smoke to heaven, and traveled to the great lakes, where the winds live and where cold dwells and makes the waters to freeze hard so men & cattle can pass over dry shod. He left the big canoe and entered a bark canoe and went up a river whose rapids were like the falls of the Tallapoosa, and found Indians. They were sitting in darkness and had not heard their father's talk for a great while. Their paths were choked up with briers and their feet were bleeding. He gave them their father's talk, and with it the light, and the Indians were glad, but said when you go away the briers will grow again, and again our feet will bleed — he asked them why? Because, they said, we have bad birds among us and they make the briers to grow. Then he drove away those bad birds from their country, and left a mouth with them, & told them they must listen to that mouth alone, it would talk the voice of wisdom from Washington and if the birds come back again to listen to them no more. They promised him they would do as he told them, and then he shook hands with them and went to another river to which he had his canoe carried — went down that river to the great father of rivers, the Mississippi.[85]

He saw other Indians; the rest of his speeches were similar to the one he had given; how after clearing the briers from the paths of the Indians and healing their bleeding feet, he left "a mouth to speak the voice of wisdom from Washington." And so on until he came to the Creeks. This talk was, for the most part, Ridge noted, "irrelevant to . . . his object, consisting in gross Indian and disgusting flattery."[86]

"There was a small strip of land," the commissioner said, "which the treaty of Washington did not embrace, and as the Georgians wanted it, & as the Delegation promised, if the treaty lines did not reach it, that they would throw it in, he wished them to carry their promise into effect, and give up the land, and he would pay them well for it. He understood that some people regretted that this strip was not included in the new treaty; for his part he was glad of it, as now the Creeks would enjoy from it an additional consideration in money."[87] This was the substance of his talk about the strip of land which the Creeks called E-kan-nah-sil-kee.

McKenney waited then for the decision of the council, and when he received the prime minister's emphatic no, he attributed the turn to the influence of Ridge and Vann—especially Ridge. He determined now to strike at the man he considered his archenemy. He boldly used his information of the "intrigue" and unveiled a plan of Ridge's and Opothle Yoholo's to the gathered Creeks. It was a shot in the dark, but the shot reached its target.

Opothle Yoholo, no doubt acutely aware of the jealous and vengeful temper of his people, and uncertain of their reaction to the disclosed plan, not yet matured, grew alarmed "for perhaps," McKenney surmised, "the first time in his life." He hesitated, and the commissioner pressed his advantage, holding forth until the chief instructed the interpreter: "Tell him he talks too much." But the intended effect had been produced: a hum of voices sounded through the council. McKenney knew that Little Prince was camped somewhere in the neighborhood, and he closed his talk by saying that he would appeal in that quarter, and if Little Prince spoke the language of the council, "their talk would be reported to the President for his decision."[88]

No doubt McKenney enjoyed the benefit of intelligence furnished the secretary of war by a special investigator who had found Little Prince "imbecile with age . . . infirm and . . . wrought upon by those near him."[89] The commissioner disclosed everything to the principal chief, who had never been as dependent on John

Colonel Thomas L. McKenney, Commissioner of Indian Affairs, painted by Charles Loring Elliott. In the Collection of the Corcoran Gallery of Art, Bequest of James C. McGuire.

Ridge as Opothle Yoholo. When Little Prince learned of Ridge's ambition to become treasurer of the Creek Nation, with the connivance of the prime minister, his suspicions were aroused, and the commissioner played upon them artfully, implying that Ridge had plans to "feather his own nest" at the expense of the Creeks. But the most telling blow was McKenney's repudiation of Ridge as spokesman for the Creeks. No letter in which he had a hand would be considered by the War Department or by the president. Thus, the commissioner struck where Ridge had been of greatest value to the Creeks and with one blow shriveled his worth.

"I now leave you and your people," McKenney said. "I shall return immediately to Washington, and report what I have seen and heard."[90] He went to the agency at Fort Mitchell to spend the night, fearing he had failed in his appeal. Little Prince had seemed apathetic and withheld his opinion till he could deliberate.

At Fort Mitchell a runner from the head chief arrived at midnight. "Tell the commissioner not to go," ran the message. "In the morning the Little Prince will come to him and make a treaty." He came the next day with a number of chiefs, excepting Opothle Yoholo, and when the agreement was signed, Little Prince instructed McKenney: "Take a paper, and write to the Cherokee chief that if his young men come among my people again I will kill them!"[91]

Thus, McKenney could write in triumph to the secretary of war that he had broken John Ridge on the spot. But it was not all easy sailing for him. Certain members of Congress demanded by what right or authority he could take it "upon himself to depose a chief acknowledged as such by the Creek Indians."[92] It was necessary for McKenney to submit an elaborate report to the secretary of war in justification of his actions against John Ridge[93]—a report which, in spite of its intricate and self-righteous argumentation, left the impression that Washington bureaucrats had come to hate John Ridge, as a historian of the Creek Nation would later write, "not for his exploitation of the Creeks, but for his ability and independence."[94] But the fact remained, McKenney had won his point, and Ridge had lost. This defeat closed his more active participation in Creek affairs, though he still remained in close contact with Opothle Yoholo. Hereafter, except for certain brief excursions into Creek matters, he turned his energies back to Cherokee concerns, a much more canny politician for his experience among the Creeks.

8 • "NOT ONE MORE FOOT OF LAND"

T HE money Major Ridge received from the Creeks enabled him to make improvements at Ridge's Ferry. Over the original log house, "neatly underpinned with rock,"[1] was built a more up-to-date dwelling of sawed lumber.* General Daniel Brinsmade later described it as "an elegant painted mansion with porches on each side as the fashion of the country is." The general added, "We saw in the house the likeness of John Ridge, Esq., accurately painted in the position of writing which was his principal business."[2]

The building work was done by a carpenter from Tennessee, but John Ridge supervised the operation and may have actively helped on the job. At any rate he later informed Dr. Gold of Cornwall that, before leaving his parents, he had built them "a fine house," one that "would look well even in New England."[3] It "resembled in no respect the wigwam of an Indian," McKenney and Hall noted — "it was the home of the patriarch, the scene of plenty and hospitality."[4] It was two stories high. Its foundations measured fifty-four by twenty-nine feet. There were four brick fireplaces, and eight rooms, ceiled and paneled with hardwood. The outside walls were weatherboarded and painted white. Verandas stood in front and back, and over the front porch rose a balcony supported by turned columns, with a glass door opening onto it. There were thirty glass windows, set in facings of walnut, each with blinds and painted shutters.[5] "The arched, triple window at the turn of the staircase

*The Ridge house still stands, renovated and modernized. It is known as the "Chieftain," and its address is 80 Chatelaine Road, Rome, Georgia. The bronze marker on the grounds assumes that the original structure was built by The Ridge about 1794. The present researches, however, can document neither that claim nor any date before the early 1820's for Major Ridge's occupation of the premises.

Major Ridge's house in Rome, Georgia, as it looks today. Courtesy of the Celanese Fibers Company.

looked out on a line of poplars, then on to the shining Oostanaula, with its fringe of reeds and lilies."[6] The parlor, where the portrait of John Ridge hung, was located on the second floor. So too was Sally's room.

Two kitchens of hewed logs stood close to the back door. Nearby was a smokehouse for the family's meat supply. Farther away were stables with watering troughs and mangers for the horses, and there were various sheds and cribs, including a lumber house. Some distance farther still stood cabins for the slaves.[7] The whole establishment, shaded by enormous oaks and sycamores, crowned an embankment that overlooked the Oostanaula and through which a shallow cut sloped down to the ferry. The boat was tethered at the shore when not in use, a broad, shallow, flat-bottomed affair with a double floor of thick planks. It was large enough to float a wagon with its team. A rope tied to a tree and stretching across the river was the means by which the boat could be drawn through the water.

"My father has a plenty," John Ridge wrote—"a fine plantation, orchards, etc."[8] At the height of The Ridge's prosperity his Oostanaula orchards contained 1,141 peach trees. There were also 418 apple, 11 quince, 21 cherry, and an unspecified number of plum trees. There were eight different fields, comprising 280 acres of open ground, both river-bottom and upland clearings.[9] The principal crop was probably corn, but Major Ridge also grew cotton, tobacco, wheat, oats, indigo, and potatoes. There were also a vineyard and a nursery, and a garden which contained a variety of ornamental shrubs as well as vegetables. In a pasture grazed cows that furnished milk and butter for the table and beef for the smokehouse. Hogs rooted half wild about the plantation and in the neighboring woods among the pine, ash, beech, and oak trees, and there were sheep to furnish wool for Susanna's weaving. As McKenney and Hall remarked, The Ridge "went forward in the march to improvement, until his farm was in a higher state of cultivation and his buildings better than those of any other person in that region, the whites not excepted."[10]

A short distance up the river, under immense trees, stood a building that measured fifty-four feet by seventeen, with a brick chimney and an adjoining shed. This housed the trading post in which Major Ridge was a silent partner. It was operated by George M. Lavender, a young white man who had come from Knoxville as a boy and got his start by working for Lewis Ross, brother of John, at Ross's Landing, soon to be known as Chattanooga. Lavender was a serious man who tended strictly to business, and under his management the store flourished; yet he was forced to remain dependent on The Ridge. In 1819, some three years before they established their partnership, the National Council had prohibited white men who were not Cherokee citizens from becoming resident traders.[11] Lavender had satisfied the letter of the decree by taking Major Ridge as his partner, a profitable arrangement for both, for The Ridge's presence in the company drew hosts of Cherokees to trade there, confident in his upright character. The trading post did "a land office business," selling numerous articles procured in Augusta. No doubt John Ridge was thinking of his father's business when he wrote: "calicoes—silks— cambricks—ect.—handkerchiefs and shawls—are introduced by Native merchants, who generally trade to Augusta."[12] It was said that Lavender kept his money in a keg, and that it was always stuffed with currency, or gold and silver coins. Doubtless Major Ridge's profits from the store handsomely augmented the income from his ferry, estimated at $1,200 a year—income that he must have plowed back into his estate, for he seldom seemed to have much cash on hand (the Moravians had to dun him repeatedly for what he owed them for the education of his children). In time his improvements at Ridge's Ferry—the ferry itself, the plantation buildings, clearings and orchards, and the structure that housed the trading post—were valued at over $22,000, a large amount for that day.[13] The figure excluded the value of his thirty slaves and of his interest in the trading business other than the worth of the building, as well as his scattered improvements elsewhere, so that in all he was worth considerably more. Indeed, he came to be numbered among the half-dozen richest men in the nation, and Yellow Bird could remember his grandfather as having "become wealthy by trading with the whites and by prudent management."[14]

Meanwhile John Ridge, gaining in prosperity, had set up for himself. He had become a gentleman of the green bag, as a lawyer was called in the backwoods; indeed he was one of the first lawyers in the Cherokee Nation. And the National Council had granted him a partnership with Alexander McCoy in the ferry at New Town. Leaving his father's house with his family and eighteen slaves, he settled some six miles to the northeast, where The Ridge's toll road ran through a fertile vale that would later be known as Ridge's Valley.[15] John's son, Yellow Bird, would remember the home he built there: "a large, two-storied house, on a high hill, crowned with a fine grove of oak and hickory, a large clear spring at the foot of the hill, and an extensive farm stretching away down into the valley, with a fine orchard on the left."[16] The beautiful spring, whose crystal stream purled away to the Oostanaula, was called Tanta-ta-rara, or Running Waters, and gave the estate its name.

The house, not as large as Yellow Bird remembered, measured fifty-one feet by nineteen, with a one-story addition thirty-one feet long and twenty wide. Both floors were neatly laid, the upper story was ceiled, and the whole structure was meticulously chinked and plastered. The roof was shingled even to the spacious porch in front, and there were three chimneys with six fireplaces and a brick baker attached. In the walls were twenty-four glass windows. There was an outside kitchen, as the custom was in that region; also two smoke-houses and a corncrib. Not far away stood a two-storied stable with an adjoining shed, and there were quarters for the Negroes, who were invariably called servants, never slaves. At the height of development the plantation would include seven fields, totaling 419 acres of cleared upland, as well as a 10-acre woodlot. John Ridge would sow much the same crops as his father, emphasizing corn; and in his orchards were planted 493 peach, 100 apple, 9 cherry, 6 quince, and 7 pear trees.[17] Running Waters was not as splendid an establishment as Major Ridge's, but John Ridge might well have boasted that his home, too, would "look well in New England."

Later he added a smaller farm to his holdings. He would serve as the executor of The Pathkiller's estate, and in 1828 he bought from the heirs of the dead chief a ferry near Turkey Town as well as the adjoining improvements on either side of the Coosa. The cleared land amounted to a hundred acres, ninety-six of which lay in the river bottom, under cultivation. An orchard contained sixty-six peach trees and twenty-two apple trees, and there were seven houses, the principal one measuring fifty feet by eighteen, with walls of peeled logs and floors of sawed planks. A piazza eight feet wide ran the entire length of the structure, and there were two log chimneys. Besides the houses, some of which were mere huts set aside as slave quarters, the improvements included a smokehouse, two stables and three corncribs. Located on the main Alabama Road, the ferry earned four dollars a day.[18] The plantation could scarcely compare with Running Waters, yet it added considerably to the status of John Ridge as a man of property.

Major Ridge and John were not alone in making improvements on their farms; a vast enthusiasm for progress had settled over the nation, and the result spelled "civilization," as Colonel McKenney was quick to tell his superiors in the federal government. "The Cherokees on this side of the Mississippi," he wrote in 1825, "are in advance of all other tribes. They may be considered as a civilized people."[19] To illustrate his point he could do no better than call attention to a letter from David Brown that was enjoying currency in the national press.

It was a rhapsodical letter, dashed off at white heat and filled with pride in Cherokee progress. Brown mentioned the translation he was making of the New Testament into Cherokee, but that was not the real purpose of his letter. He wanted Americans to know how far the Cherokees had gone in making a good life for themselves. He began by describing the appearance of the country they occupied, with its "range of majestic and lofty mountains" and its fertile plains and valleys, partly covered with tall trees and watered by gliding streams. There herds of cattle flourished; horses were plentiful, and there were flocks of sheep and goats and herds of pigs. Brown described the crops the Cherokee farmers raised—the Indian corn, wheat, oats, potatoes, cotton, indigo, and tobacco. "The natives carry on considerable trade with the adjoining states; and some of them export cotton in boats, down the Tennessee to the Mississippi, and down that river to New Orleans. Apple and peach orchards are common: and gardens are cultivated with much attention paid to them." He mentioned the butter and cheese on every Cherokee table.

"There are many public roads in the nation, and houses of entertainment kept by natives. Numerous flourishing villages are seen in every section of the country. Cotton and woollen goods are manufactured here. Blankets of various dimensions [made] by Cherokee hands, are very common. *Almost every family in the nation grows cotton for its own consumption.* Industry and commercial enterprise are extending themselves in every part. Nearly all the merchants in the nation are native Cherokees. Agricultural pursuits, the most solid foundation of our national prosperity, engage the chief attention of the people." Nevertheless the Cherokees pursued various branches of mechanics. Their material prosperity paralleled an increase in population, Brown asserted, citing statistics from a recent census. He noticed the 1,217 African slaves, but denied much intermixture of Cherokee and Negro blood.

Brown also paid attention to religion: the nation had adopted Christianity to a significant extent. "Presbyterians, Methodists, Baptists and Moravians are the most numerous sects. Some of the most influential characters are members of the church, and live consistently with their professions." Education was the corollary of religion. "The whole nation is penetrated with gratitude for the aid it has received from the United States government and from different religious societies. Schools are increasing every year; learning is encouraged and rewarded. The young class acquire the English, and those of mature age the Cherokee system of learning."

At last Brown came to a consideration of Cherokee government. After describing the national capital he mentioned the Cherokee council. "The legislative power is vested in what is denominated in the native dialect, *Tsalagi Tinilawigi,* consisting of a national committee and council. Members of both branches are chosen by and from the people for a limited period. In New Town, a printing press is soon to be established; also a national library, and a museum. Immense concourse of people frequent the seat of government when *Tsalagi Tinilawigi* is in session."[20] Thus one observer summarized

Cherokee civilization as it had developed by 1825. That a native could do so, Colonel McKenney pointed out, was but another indication of the progress the Cherokees had made.

Proud as they were of their improvements, something about the emptiness of New Town most of the year struck the leaders as reprehensible, something that should be corrected. When Tsalagi Tinilawigi met a month after David Brown's letter, steps were taken to change the situation. First the capital was rechristened New Echota, a name reminiscent of the ancient Cherokee town of refuge. It was resolved that the place should be laid off in one hundred lots, each an acre in size, to be sold to the highest bidder on the second Monday in February, 1826. The proceeds were to be used for the benefit of the public buildings to be raised there. The town square would comprise two acres. It was also resolved that the main street should be sixty feet wide, and the others fifty.[21] Thus, in time the Cherokees would have a capital adequate, in their opinion, to the government of which they were so proud.

The same fall council of 1825 took a definite step toward establishing a Cherokee press. It resolved that fifteen hundred dollars should be allocated for that purpose from the next annuity payment. The chiefs intended that the money should also help to found the National Academy, but as matters would develop, emphasis was placed on the press, and the school lost sight of. Fifteen hundred dollars was, of course, inadequate to purchase a press, including two fonts of type, one of which would have to be specially cast. So Tsalagi Tinilawigi named Elias Boudinot as an agent to go among the white communities to solicit necessary funds.[22] As a matter of fact, it was proposed that Boudinot become editor of the projected newspaper, and his nomination had the support of the missionaries, in spite of the temporary lapse that had cost him some of their goodwill.

That summer a national ball-play had been held near the home of Boudinot's parents in Oothcaloga. It was true that the ball-play, the forerunner of lacrosse, had developed into something almost as dangerous and obscene as a Roman orgy. It was equally true that Boudinot, unhappy about the turn of his love affair with Harriet Gold and smarting from the insults aimed at him in letters from the North, had been seen in attendance at the game. Moody Hall, who spread the report, was incensed, having expected "better things" of him,[23] and his reputation among the godly dropped perceptibly. But a new missionary, the tall, gangling, blue-eyed Samuel A. Wor-

cester, who had come to Brainerd to learn Cherokee and who anticipated Boudinot's help in his plans of turning religious works into
Cherokee, later visited "the fallen young man" and was won by his
sincerity and ability. Here was just the person, Worcester decided,
to help him with the protean Cherokee verb, and the missionary
would meet every difficulty that developed, including Boudinot's
own reluctance to accept the editorship when the chiefs proposed to
pay a printer more. At Worcester's insistence, the American Board
of Commissioners in Boston would agree to increase the editorial
salary of three hundred dollars a year by a grant of one hundred
dollars, a sum that was to be tripled as time went by.[24] Meanwhile
Boudinot, who had to go north to marry Harriet in any case, launched
into his fund-raising campaign as the new year opened, while his
cousin, John Ridge, worked for the Creek delegation in Washington.

Boudinot began his solicitations in the South. He stopped in
Charleston, which had proved generous in the past, and began to
give the lecture he would smooth and publish later that year. It
became his custom to say:

You behold an *Indian;* my kindred are *Indians,* and my fathers are
sleeping in the wilderness grave—they too were Indians. But I am not
as my fathers were—broader means and nobler influences have fallen
upon me. Yet I was not born as thousands are, in a stately dome and
amid the congratulations of the great, for on a little hill, in a lonely
cabin, overspread by the forest oak I first drew my breath; and in a language unknown to learned and polished nations, I learnt to lisp my fond
mother's name. In after days, I have had greater advantages than most
of my race; and I now stand before you delegated by my native country
to seek her interest, to labour for her respectability, and by my public
efforts to assist in raising her to an equal standing with other nations
of the earth.[25]

Here Boudinot probably paused for effect, then delivered with
emphasis the following sentence, the theme of his talk: "The time
has arrived when speculations and conjectures as to the practicability of civilizing the Indians must forever cease." The history of the
Cherokees proved without equivocation that civilizing the Indians
was a practicable endeavor. "It needs only that the world should
know," he asserted, "what we have done in the last few years, to
foresee what yet we may do with the assistance of our white brethren,
and that of the common Parent of us all." Boudinot devoted the
rest of his talk to illuminating that proposition. In some respects
his lecture resembled David Brown's letter, though a more finished

performance. Like Brown, he described the domain of the Cherokees in picturesque terms. He also noted the growing population, and its dispersal to individual farms:

The rise of these people in their movement toward civilization, may be traced as far back as the relinquishment of their towns; when game became incompetent to their support, by reason of the surrounding white population. They then betook themselves to the woods, commenced the opening of small clearings, and the raising of stock; still however following the chase. Game has since become so scarce that little dependence can be placed upon it. They have gradually and I could almost say universally forsaken their ancient employment. In fact, there is not a single family in the nation that can be said to subsist on the slender support which the wilderness would afford. The love and practice of hunting are not now carried to a higher degree than among all frontier people whether white or red. It cannot be doubted, however, that there are many who have commenced a life of agricultural labor from mere necessity, and if they could, would gladly resume their former course of living. But these are individual failings and ought to be passed over.

No doubt another pause. Then Boudinot resumed with emphasis: "On the other hand it cannot be doubted that the nation is improving, rapidly improving, in all those particulars which must finally constitute the inhabitants an industrious and intelligent people."

Like Brown, Boudinot had recourse to the census to prove his point, only he was more specific. To indicate Cherokee status for the previous year he cited figures for several categories of livestock and for several items of civilization: 22,000 cattle; 7,600 horses; 46,000 swine; 2,500 sheep; 762 looms; 2,488 spinning wheels; 172 wagons; 2,943 plows; 10 sawmills; 31 gristmills; 62 blacksmith shops; 8 cotton machines; 18 schools; 18 ferries; "and," he added, "a number of good roads." He described the schools, paid tribute to the missionaries, then gave major importance to three items of "late occurrence" that placed the Cherokees in a favorable light: the invention of the syllabary, the translation of the New Testament into the native tongue, and the organization of the Cherokee government. This threefold discussion brought him to the main assertion of his address—indeed, the reason for his tour—that, having reached their present stage of civilization, the Cherokees needed to employ "more than ordinary means" to effect further progress.

"Sensible of this last point," Boudinot said, "and wishing to do something for themselves, the Cherokees have thought it advisable [to establish] a Printing Press and a Seminary of respectable character; and for these purposes your aid and patronage are now solicited."

The appeal brought results, not spectacular ones, but enough that, as the tour proceeded, Boudinot could hope the press, if not the academy, was assured. He went to New York and spoke before interested church groups. Then after his marriage with Harriet Gold in Cornwall, the couple went to Massachusetts, where Boudinot lectured at Salem and Boston churches. By this time his collection amounted to nearly six hundred dollars. On May 26 he spoke before the First Presbyterian Church in Philadelphia, and his address was printed in that city, a sixteen-page pamphlet that left many whites amazed that an Indian could express himself so well. The pamphlet was used to raise funds, and money continued to come in after Boudinot had ended his campaign. Evidently the young couple went home via the Shenandoah Valley with the Blue Ridge visible on their left, then down into Tennessee and at last across Hiwassee Ferry into the Cherokee Nation.[26]

The Boudinots stayed for several months with Watie and his family, who made the bride as welcome as Major Ridge and Susanna had done in the case of Sarah Northrup. While waiting for the press to materialize, Elias taught the mission school at Hightower for the winter of 1826 and '27. The school was not far from Oothcaloga, and he and Harriet saw much of his family during those days when Boudinot's salary was only twenty dollars a month. It was there Worcester visited him and the two began their partnership for Cherokee advancement. They set about systematizing the Cherokee language and searched out rules for the formation of tenses in the Herculean verb, which Boudinot decided must be the most complicated verb in the world, with at least twenty-nine tenses in the indicative mood. They believed they had isolated 178 forms of the verb "to tie" in the present indicative alone. "I have more confidence in Boudinot as a translator than in any other," Worcester wrote to Boston, "and, though I may be deceived, and some have greatly doubted, yet my spending near a fortnight in his family has given me quite a respect for his character."[27] The two decided to conduct their experiment in New Echota, where Boudinot planned to settle. He steadfastly refused to go to Brainerd, with its dampness, on the grounds of his health. Worcester gracefully yielded and made plans to follow him to New Echota.

At last the Cherokees had sufficient money to buy their press, and Worcester agreed to supervise the casting of the type in Boston.

The work was done at the printing shop of David Greene, a commissioner of the American Board for Foreign Missions, and he doubtless gave the Cherokees a bargain, for he was a philanthropist. Boudinot moved to New Echota sometime in 1827, to live in a comfortable two-storied house with glass windows and a rock-walled cellar. Years later a visitor gave its dimensions as twenty-four by thirty feet and wrote that "the sills and sleepers were post oak, hewn out by hand. . . . The weather boarding, eight inches wide, was of heart pine. [There were four rooms downstairs] and three upstairs, with five closets. . . . The chimneys were of brick with large open fireplaces."[28] A front and rear porch completed the dwelling, which was set among luxuriant shade trees. Soon Worcester and his family came to live in a house built on identical lines.

New Echota, for all its being the capital of the Cherokees, did not look more prepossessing than any other country crossroads in Georgia, except for the Supreme Court building with its upraised judge's bench and the hard pinewood seats for jurors, witnesses, and the attending public, and for the new council house—a spacious rectangular log building of two stories, with brick chimneys and fireplaces, glass windows, sawed plank floors, and a stairway that led to upper conference chambers.[29] There were four stores, three empty except at council time, along with a few more houses, where Alexander McCoy lived, and Elijah Hicks, among others. But New Echota was different from the ordinary Georgia crossroads for the spirit brooding there, the spirit of hope and determination that seemed centered on the projected press. Boudinot had prophesied in his *Address to the Whites* that "the Indian must rise like the Phoenix, after having wallowed for ages in ignorant barbarity."[30] Perhaps he was already thinking of the name for his newspaper, although Worcester is said to have suggested *Cherokee Phoenix — Tsalagi Tsu-le-hi-sa-nu-hi,* or something like "I will arise" in the Cherokee language.

The printers arrived a few days before Christmas, 1827—Isaac N. Harris, an opinionated young white Methodist who never succeeded in learning the syllabary and who never got along with Boudinot, and John F. Wheeler, also white, who learned the syllabary in a few days and who got along so well with Boudinot—and with his sister—that he eventually became his brother-in-law.

The press, a "union" model of a size called "small royal," made of cast iron, with springs to hold the platen, had been delayed owing to a hitch in the casting of the syllabary, and did not roll up the Georgia Road from Augusta till sometime in January, 1828.

The Reverend Samuel A. Worcester's house, restored, in New Echota, Georgia. Worcester's house was a duplicate of Elias Boudinot's house, in which the Treaty of New Echota was signed. Courtesy of the Georgia Department of Natural Resources.

Mr. Greene accompanied it to assist in the installation in a cabin "of hewn pine logs, chinked, and the cracks plastered. One log on each side," wrote Wheeler, "was cut out and long windows made, and very low down, which would have been convenient for a shoe-maker's shop, but were too low for printers, and we had to raise them a log higher." They also had to make, after some deliberation, the cases to correspond with the syllabary as systematized by Worces-ter, "and having a couple of rough carpenters, we set them to work."[31] The carpenters made the cases, most of them nearly three feet square, with the characters written at the top. They were heavy and hard to move, but in a few days the office was in order. Then after another delay, occasioned by their having to send to Knoxville for paper, Boudinot and his printers issued the first number of the *Phoenix* on February 21, 1828. It was a day of triumph—the appear-ance of the first Indian newspaper ever published—a newspaper edited by an Indian, partly in an Indian tongue, for Indians to read.

Boudinot had meanwhile circulated a prospectus which he re-printed in that first number. In it he said that

the Editor would, by no means, be too sanguine, for he is aware that he will tread upon *untried ground:* nor does he make any pretentions to learning, for it must be known that the great and sole motive in estab-lishing this paper is the benefit of the *Cherokees.* This will be the great aim of the Editor, which he intends to pursue with undeviating steps. . . . There are many true friends to the Indians in different parts of the Union, who will rejoice to see this feeble effort of the Cherokees to rise from their ashes, like the fabled Phoenix. On such friends must princi-pally depend the support of our paper. . . .

The columns of the *Cherokee Phoenix* will be filled, partly with English, and partly with Cherokee print; and all matter which is of common interest will be given in both languages in parallel columns.

1. The laws and public documents of the Nation.

2. Account of the manners and customs of the Cherokees, and the progress in Education, Religion and the arts of civilized life; with such notices of other Indian tribes as our limited means of information will allow.

3. The principal interesting news of the day.

4. Miscellaneous articles, calculated to promote Literature, Civil-ization, and Religion among the Cherokees.[32]

Boudinot held true to his word. In a four-page spread of super-royal size, with five columns to the page, he published exactly what he had promised to. It was slower work to set type in Cherokee, just as it was slower work to write in it, and with only Wheeler to set the syllabary, the columns in Cherokee averaged only three a week as compared to seventeen in English. but as every Cherokee character but one represented an entire syllable and took up no more space than an English letter, and as it was possible to express an idea in fewer words in Cherokee than in English, the difference was not so great as it appeared.*

Boudinot was devoted to his responsibility, and no slave worked harder. Every week he wrote an editorial and translated it into Cherokee. He selected exchanges to reprint from other periodicals, which required much searching through their pages. He wrote feature articles, Cherokee news items, accounts of developments in the several fields he had promised to cover. He selected Cherokee laws to print, and since they were often framed only in English, the "official" language of the nation, it was necessary to turn them into the native tongue for his Indian readers. He rummaged through the archives of the nation and reprinted correspondence between the Cherokees and the federal government from Washington's day to the present. At the same time, he welcomed communications from his readers. John Ridge, for instance, kept the nation posted on developments among the Creeks and early published a long letter giving his side of the controversy with Colonel McKenney.[33]

Boudinot read proof, which even Wheeler agreed was sometimes "very foul," and in addition to his editorial duties, he served as business manager for the paper. All the while he continued to collaborate with Worcester, turning the religious literature of the whites into Cherokee. Since the Indians had taken to singing with such passion at their services, there was a need for hymns, and the pair turned to translating the texts of religious songs. A hymnal of some fifty pages became, in Boudinot's words, "the first Cherokee book ever published."[34] But even before it was off the press the two had begun to prepare a Cherokee edition of the Gospel of Saint Matthew.

And all the while Major Ridge looked on the work with keen pleasure. He could hardly have been more pleased if his son John had been at the helm of the Cherokee press.

---

*Cf. Worcester's explanation in the *Phoenix* for August 20, 1828: ". . . a single word in Cherokee requires often several English words to translate it. Fewer words are required in Cherokee than in English to express the same ideas, for the reason, that what we express by pronouns, adverbs, and prepositions is, in Cherokee, expressed chiefly by variations of the verb."

Elias Boudinot, Editor of the Cherokee Phoenix. Courtesy of the Oklahoma Historical Society.

"The Prodigal Son," in Cherokee. Courtesy of Columbia University Library.

Meanwhile important events had taken place in Major Ridge's life, some of them of significance to Cherokee history. When the health of Mr. Ellsworth had failed, forcing him to close his school at Haweis late in 1826, The Ridge had taken Sally to Salem, and she was accepted by the Moravians to finish her schooling at the Female Academy. On his way home he stopped at Spring Place on January 22, 1827, and found the mission in mourning. During his absence the Cherokees had lost in quick succession their principal chiefs: the aged Pathkiller had died first, and two weeks later Charles Hicks lay in a walnut coffin at Spring Place. Hicks had attended the council at New Echota the previous fall, though badly ailing. On his way home he was forced to camp in the woods and had taken cold from the dampness. He had gone to bed with dropsical complaints and had never risen again. Major Ridge, on taking a last look at his friend, learned that he had died gently on January 20, as though he had merely fallen asleep. The Ridge delivered an impressive exhortation at the funeral.[35]

He felt troubled in spirit as he reached home. The government had temporarily devolved upon him as Speaker of the Council, and on John Ross as president of the National Committee, but the Cherokees were restless, for the deaths of the chiefs had roused new hopes among the Georgians that the land might now be sold. Soon the *Georgia Journal* would be blaring from Milledgeville: "The party in opposition to the sale of the country found their greatest support and protection in these chiefs. Those who occupy their places are understood to be men of different dispositions and character. An intelligent Cherokee is said to have made the remark, when he heard of the death of Charles Hicks, that the Cherokees will sell their land now; those who are left have their price. Now, therefore, is a most suitable moment to urge the claims of Georgia in that quarter. And we believe our Chief Magistrate will not let it pass unimproved."[36] Indeed, President Adams appointed three generals—John Cocke, Alexander Gray, and George L. Davidson—as U.S. commissioners to seek a treaty of removal with the Cherokees. General Cocke appeared with his private secretary, Major Robert Hynds, at New Echota on July 3, 1827, when a special council was convened for the purpose of framing a written constitution for the Cherokee Nation.

Major Ridge met them in front of the council house and took the general by the hand as an old comrade-in-arms. Then he led the two up into the committee room, where he introduced the general as "a friend and old acquaintance who had served in the Creek War" and suggested that the chiefs give him "the hand of friendship." Everyone shook the general's hand, but if the chiefs expected him to divulge his mission at that particular moment, they were disappointed. Cocke evidently preferred to bide his time until he had the opportunity to sound out certain influential men. Thus, the commissioner withdrew with his secretary and the council adjourned, leaving the members chosen to frame the constitution—twenty-four in all—in possession of the council house. They named John Ross as president of the convention and Alexander McCoy as clerk.[37]

The next day Major Ridge and seven other chiefs waited on the general, who made his purpose clear, the wish to treat for land, but the chiefs were divided on whether to hear him in open council. He passed out "presents," and it was said that Major Ridge received one hundred dollars.[38] Cocke reported: ". . . we had reason to believe he was friendly to the object of the Government, and nothing but fear of losing his popularity and life prevented him from being with us."[39] The Ridge may have played on Cocke's credulity for the sake of a present, but it is unlikely that he wavered in his opposition to removal. In view of his adamant stand before

this incident and immediately afterward, it is more probable that
Cocke was under a misapprehension, owing to the language barrier
or a misinterpretation of The Ridge's professions of personal friendship. The general remained in the area for several days, trying
without visible effect "to prepare the Indians for a treaty."[40] He
then withdrew to the agency to await the arrival of his fellow commissioners, and the Cherokees were spared his importunities for
several weeks.

Meanwhile the constitution was drawn up, modeled after that
of the United States, and adopted on July 26, 1827. It was a document of which the more understanding Cherokees were proud.
However, a conservative minority under the leadership of an ancient
chief called Whitepath had fears as to what it might entail, and
for a while what was known as "Whitepath's Rebellion" seemed to
threaten opposition, but when the situation was explained, Whitepath's fears were allayed and the trouble subsided.[41] Boudinot would
soon begin to print the constitution, for all to see and read, in the
first issue of the *Phoenix*.

In the meantime the U.S. commissioners opened their campaign
again. On August 23 they issued an invitation for the chiefs to meet
them at the agency on September 18, when they would "fully explain, in general council, the views of the Government on subjects
calculated to promote [the Cherokees'] happiness and interest and
the welfare of the citizens of the United States." When the time
arrived, The Ridge and John Ross sent a joint letter stating that the
invitation was "too sudden and unexpected" for a council to be
convened. A few individuals appeared at the agency, but not enough
to serve the purposes of Cocke and his fellow commissioners. There
followed an interchange of letters, sometimes rather heated in tone,
between the three on the one hand and The Ridge and Ross on the
other. The two invited the commissioners to attend the October
council and there make their mission known, but at that time the
chiefs reiterated the old stand of the Cherokees that not one single
foot of soil would ever be sold.[42]

Cocke's failure and the publicizing of the Cherokee constitution
produced intense reaction in Georgia. The Cherokees considered
their constitution as a stride toward equal footing with the whites.
But if one purpose in adopting it had been to impress the outside
world, the move was only a qualified success. Hailed in the North,
praised even in Washington (though President Adams cautioned
that calling themselves "sovereign and independent" gave the Chero-

kees no leave to act independently in foreign relations), and discussed favorably as far away as England, the constitution yet failed to impress, indeed only exasperated, the one state the Cherokees needed most to mollify. Georgians were more convinced than ever that the time had come to push the Cherokees out of their state. In December, 1827, the Georgia legislature proclaimed that the Cherokee title to land in the commonwealth was only temporary, that the Indians were tenants at will, and that the state was empowered to take possession of the lands by any necessary means and extend over them the laws of Georgia. Governor John Forsyth notified the War Department that if the Indians had not begun their removal by the end of the coming year, Georgia would then take action to extend its laws over the Cherokee country.[43] Moreover, the combined pressure of Forsyth and Senator Wilson Lumpkin prevailed upon the president to send Colonel Hugh Montgomery as agent in 1828, charged to make a removal treaty if at all possible. Montgomery failed in that goal and succeeded only in so prejudicing the Indians against William Hicks, whom they had chosen at the fall council in 1827 to serve the remainder of Pathkiller's term, that all but Hicks himself could see he had no chance of reelection.

Under the old dispensation Major Ridge would have stood an excellent chance of becoming principal chief. But times had changed. He knew better than anyone else that only an educated man who could read and write English was suited now to hold the office, and he seems not even to have made himself available for it. As Speaker, however, he put what appeared to be a campaign statement into the July 2 issue of the *Phoenix,* addressing the young men of the nation: "Some time since," he said (no doubt John Ridge wrote at his dictation), "we have learnt that an appropriation of $50,000 had been made by Congress to defray the expense of holding a treaty with us for the purchase of land. Commissioners will probably be here at the time of the next Fall Council. But I have no fears respecting the conduct of you young men. I know you are decided friends of this our native country." He advised them to go to local meetings concerning candidates for the committee and the council. "You will do an excellent thing if you attend: for you shall have to elect those who will be the promoters of our national interests. It will be extremely well if good men are chosen and if they attend Council; for the negotiation will be with them. It is their part also to make laws for us." He cautioned moderation, then returned to the question of the land. "Let us hold fast to the country which we yet retain. Let us direct our efforts to agriculture, and to the increase of wealth, and to the promotion of knowledge." The statement was signed, "Your friend, THE SPEAKER."[44]

When the elections were held at the fall council of 1828, The Ridge was not returned to the speakership, but elevated to the new post of Counselor, of which there were three, corresponding somewhat in their advisory functions to the cabinet of the federal government. John Ross was the candidate against William Hicks for principal chief and won the election by an overwhelming majority, having proved himself in fourteen years of public life. George Lowrey gained the second post.[45] Seldom if ever had principal chiefs assumed office at a more critical time in Cherokee history. But John Ross, with Major Ridge as his main advisor, was a man equal to the responsibilities he had to face.*

Though only one-eighth Indian, he was thoroughly devoted to the Cherokee cause, with an educated understanding of the whites essential to the conduct of relations with them, now a paramount preoccupation of the tribe. He had recently moved to the Head of Coosa, conveniently near The Ridge's plantation, across the Oostanaula and about a mile downstream, where he had built a comfortable house, for he was well-to-do, even by white standards. In days ahead Major Ridge could often be found at Ross's house, discussing matters of state, some new perplexity that faced the Cherokees; or Ross would come to Ridge's ferry.

Known as Cooweescoowee to the Indians—the name of some mysterious white bird, perhaps the egret—Ross was thirty-eight years old when he became principal chief. As he was only five feet six inches tall, another Cherokee name for him was Tsan Usdi, or Little John. But Little John walked tall among the Cherokees. Everywhere he went in the nation, Indians of all descriptions—suave and prosperous mixed-bloods from the fertile valleys or poor and primitive full bloods of the mountain coves—turned out to take him by the hand. It was said that his popularity with the Indians had been cemented by his marriage to a nearly full-blood wife, a retiring woman known as Quatie.

*Grant Foreman was of the studied opinion that John Ross "did more for his tribe than any half dozen other Cherokees" (*A History of Oklahoma*, p. 143). Without question he was the foremost Cherokee of the nineteenth century. For his latest and best, biography see Gary Moulton, *John Ross: Cherokee Chief.*

"During the time of troubles of his people," wrote an acquaintance years later (the son of a lawyer Ross had retained in the interest of the nation), "he spent many days at my father's house. He appeared to center his mind and soul in the welfare of the Cherokees. I remember him well. . . . His complexion was a little florid. He had a dark brown, brilliant eye."[46]* There was nothing of the Indian in his appearance. He looked the complete white man, and strangers meeting him in Washington were surprised to learn that he was chief of the Cherokees.

He was the grandson of John McDonald, a Scots Tory agent among the Chickamaugas during the American Revolution. His father, another Scot of royalist sympathy whose name was Daniel Ross, had married Mary McDonald, a quarter-part Cherokee, and their children were raised like backwoods aristocrats. John Ross spoke English like a white man and was never fluent in Cherokee, yet in sympathy and spirit he was a thoroughgoing Indian, as devoted to the ancestral lands of the Cherokees as any full blood, and his people would have been hard pressed to find a more dedicated or able man to serve as chief. Ross had vigor, intelligence, character, integrity, and an iron will; and he would need every one of those qualities to defend the rights of his people, as one might suspect a month later when Andrew Jackson displaced John Quincy Adams as president of the United States.

The secretary of war—Jackson's boon companion Major John Eaton—again pressed the idea of emigration to the West on the delegation led by Ross to Washington in the winter of 1828 and 1829. The Cherokees dared hope that Jackson's administration would ease its pressure on that score, and The Ridge rode tirelessly about the nation, preaching against removal, to strengthen the spirit of resistance among the people. On February 9, 1829, he made "an eloquent speech" at a meeting in Turkey Town, and John Ridge recorded the sense of the company, which was signed by ten local citizens: "The sentiments we will . . . express will be simple and plain," the statement began. And after sketching the relationship

---

*Almost everyone who has written on Ross after Rachel Eaton's statement that he had blue eyes seems to have followed her lead. But the colored lithograph of Ross published by McKenney and Hall from the portrait by Charles Bird King substantiates the statement that Ross's eyes were brown. So also do the portraits of him by John Neagle in the Philbrook Art Center and the Museum of the Oklahoma Historical Society.

of the Cherokees with the American government since the days of
Washington, it continued:

We have noticed the ancient ground of complaint, founded on the
ignorance of our ancestors and their fondness for the chase, and for the
purpose of agriculture as having in possession too much land for their
numbers. What is the language of objection this time?
　　The case is reversed, and we are now assaulted with menaces of
expulsion, because we have unexpectedly become civilized, and because
we have formed and organized a constituted government. It is too
much for us now to be honest, and virtuous, and industrious, because
then are we capable to aspiring to the rank of Christians and Poli-
ticians, which renders our attachment to the soil more strong, and
therefore more difficult to defraud us of the possession. Disappointment inflicts on the mind of the avaricious white man, the mortification
of delay, or the probability of the intended victim's escape from the
snares laid for its destruction. It remains for us in this situation of the
question, to act as free agents in choosing for ourselves to walk in the
straight-forward path of the impartial recommendations of Washington,
Jefferson, Madison, and Monroe, as most congenial to our feelings and
knowledge of the means calculated to promote our happiness. We
hereby individually set our faces to the rising sun, and turn our backs
to its setting. As our ancestors revered the sepulchral monuments of
the noble dead, we cherish the sacred spots of their repose, . . . under
hillocks of clay that cover them from sight.
　　If the country, to which we are directed to go is desirable and well
watered, why is it so long a wilderness and a waste, and uninhabited
by respectable white people, whose enterprise ere this would have induced them to monopolize it from the poor and unfortunate of their
fellow citizens as they have hitherto done? From correct information
we have formed a bad opinion of the western country beyond the
Mississippi. But if report was favorable to the fertility of the soil, if
the running streams were as transparent as crystal, and silver fish
abounded in their element in profusion, we should still adhere to the
purpose of spending the remnant of our lives on the soil that gave us
birth, and is rendered dear from the nourishment we received from its
bosom.[47]

The sentiment of Turkey Town was in essence the sentiment of
Major Ridge and his son John. Both expressed the doctrine far and
wide.

　　Most Cherokees rallied behind them, and behind John Ross and
other leaders who opposed removal. But agents of the United States
moved among them and sought to stir up feeling in favor of emigration, and Colonel Montgomery pressed Jackson's line, when not

tending his plantation on the Chattahoochee. To find such men as William Hicks and Alexander McCoy succumbing to his blandishments was discouraging, even frightening. The fear that such individuals might, like McIntosh of the Creeks, take it upon themselves to sell Cherokee soil without consent from the general council began to haunt some of the more anti-emigration leaders. The eccentricities of Hicks, as time wore on, gave them no comfort. The check to his ambition had evidently been a blow from which he had never recovered. Nothing his friends could do—and he had many, Major Ridge included—could make him acceptable to himself. He was named a counselor, and Ross had taken him in his delegation to Washington.

But when he returned [wrote one who had the facts from Ross] he seemed estranged in his feelings, absent in his mind, bewildered, inconsistent and unaccountable in his conduct. On his approach to his home, within twenty miles of it, he would take short rides of twenty or five and twenty minutes and then stop. On the way, he evaded everyone's notice. When he approached his habitation, he went round about, making it appear as if he came from [the white part of Georgia], when in fact, he came from the opposite direction. He now remained at home. He was summoned to the Council at [New] Echota, but would not appear. He began to utter dark insinuations against the men who had been raised by his countrymen to power. Such a person would not be overlooked by the American agents.[48]

But more disconcerting still was the case of Alexander McCoy, who had asked that his holdings in New Echota be evaluated by an emigration agent. For his defection—or "disloyalty," as it was called —he was stripped of his post as clerk of the National Council, and John Ridge was chosen in his place. The leaders thought the time had come to adopt some drastic measure against possible betrayal of the nation. Major Ridge, it has been said, proposed the reenactment of an old law that prescribed death for anyone who "sold lands in treaty without authority of the nation," and perhaps he did in his capacity as counselor. It was the motion of a chief named Choonungkee, however, that placed the bill before the council, and John Ridge, as clerk, assumed the chore of reducing it to writing. Womankiller, more than eighty years old, spoke in favor of it, his speech transcribed by John Ridge and published in the *Phoenix*, and the bill was passed on October 24, 1829.[49]

The Blood Law read:

Whereas a Law has been in existence for many years, but not committed to writing, that if any citizen or citizens of this nation should treat and dispose of any lands belonging to this nation without special permission from the national authorities, he or they shall suffer death; —therefore, resolved, by the Committee and Council, in General Council convened, that any person or persons who shall, contrary to the will and consent of the legislative council of this nation in general council convened, enter into a treaty with any commissioner or commissioners of the United States, or any officers instructed for that purpose, and agree to sell or dispose of any part or portion of the national lands defined in the constitution of this nation, he or they so offending, upon conviction before any of the circuit judges of the Supreme Court, shall suffer death; and any of the circuit judges aforesaid are authorized to call a court for the trial of any such person or persons so transgressing. Be it further resolved, that any person or persons, who shall violate the provisions of this act, and shall refuse, by resistance, to appear at the place designated for trial, or abscond, are hereby declared to be outlaws; and any person or persons, citizens of this nation, may kill him or them so offending, in any manner most convenient, within the limits of this nation, and shall not be held accountable for the same.[50]

No doubt, when it was framed, Major Ridge and John Ridge and most of their close friends felt sure that the severity of this law would deter any disaffected chiefs from treating away Cherokee lands against the majority will.

Meanwhile the discovery of gold in the southeastern portion of the Cherokee Nation aggravated the Cherokee-Georgia controversy. For some time stray prospectors from the diggings in the mountains of North Carolina had searched for treasure in the Cherokee country, and by the summer of 1829 word had gone out that gold was there. An early discoverer would later testify that "within a few days it would seem as if the world must have heard of it, for men came from every state. . . . They came afoot, on horseback, and in wagons, acting more like crazy men than anything else."[51] Both the Cherokees and the people of Georgia put inordinate value on the discovery and on the mineral wealth believed to lie in the hills, and the rush gave the legislators of Georgia an excellent talking point —that the state was wrongfully deprived of properties of untold worth.

Encouraged by the attitude of Jackson, who in his first annual message to Congress had announced his intention of initiating an act that would remove all Indians to the West, Georgia put her threats into action and extended her laws over the Cherokee lands inside her bounds, to be effective by June 1, 1830. On December 19 the legislature passed a Cherokee code designed to strike at the heart of Indian resistance. By law large slices of Cherokee land were to be annexed to Hall, Habersham, Gwinnett, Carroll, and De Kalb counties. Cherokee laws were nullified within the area. Further meetings of the General Council and all other Cherokee assemblies were forbidden within the boundaries of Georgia. Arrest and imprisonment were decreed for all Cherokees who influenced their fellows to reject removal. Contracts between whites and Indians were declared null and void unless witnessed by two whites. Indians were prohibited from testifying against white men in Georgia courts. The law even forbade Cherokees to dig for gold in their own country.[52]

Soon Edward Everett, who would share the platform at Gettysburg with Abraham Lincoln years later, explained the meaning of the new legislation in the House of Representatives. White wrongdoers, he pointed out, "have but to cross the Cherokee line; they have but to choose the time and place, where the eye of no white man can rest upon them, and they may burn the dwelling, waste the farm, plunder the property, assault the person, murder the children of the Cherokee subject of Georgia, and though hundreds of the tribe may be looking on, there is not one of them that can be permitted to bear witness against the spoiler. When I am asked, then, what the Cherokee has to fear from the law of Georgia, I answer, that, by that law, he is left at the mercy of firebrand and dagger of every unprincipled wretch in the community."[53]

Everett's description of the situation in Cherokee country soon proved only too true to the actual facts. A combination of white men sought to victimize Major Ridge and other well-to-do Cherokees. They forged the signatures of the Indians on a number of notes and, trusting to the law that forbade Indians to testify against white men, instituted actions with the aim of securing possession of the Cherokees' property. The jury refused to sustain the rogues, however, and in reporting one of the cases, the *Georgia Journal* remarked: "We cannot omit to express ourselves decidedly hostile to the law excluding Indians from the privilege of testifying in our courts. It is unjust, and inexpedient and should be repealed."[54]

Georgia's action and the gold fever encouraged the presence of white intruders, many of them of the most disreputable character. Having failed to strike it rich in the mines, they looked about the Cherokee domain and found it inviting, with its fields of corn and cotton, its orchards, and its herds of hogs and cattle, flocks of sheep, and bands of horses. Some squatted down and started farming Cherokee land; others—thieves and cutthroats organized in bands known as "pony clubs"—roved about, running off poorly guarded livestock.

Some of these characters had moved into an area that had been in dispute for months—an area claimed by Georgia on the grounds that it had been Creek territory, settled by Cherokees only because the Creeks had let them "borrow" the land. In 1821 a delegation of Cherokee chiefs headed by The Ridge had gone to the town of General McIntosh and reached an agreement with the Creeks that recognized this territory as within the Cherokee domain, and this agreement had been accepted by the Treaty of Washington in 1826.[55] Yet Georgia now chose to deny it and to lay claim to the land.

Jackson's old friend, General Coffee, level-headed, slow-spoken, even-keeled, had been sent to take testimony on the controversy, much to the annoyance of certain Georgians, who had already shown their attitude toward Indians testifying. Governor George Gilmer angrily forwarded to Jackson an informer's report "that Major Ridge, a Cherokee, had some old drunken Indians, heretofore chiefs, drilling for a week, and then introduced them to Gen. Coffee as competent evidence." Gilmer then added to the report: "The constant and active efforts of Ridge to thwart the views of government renders this account highly probable."[56] Indeed, in the unanimity of details in the evidence given by the several ancient Cherokees Coffee felt a suggestion that their minds had been "warped" by hearing the same story repeated over and over. Nevertheless he reported, confidentially, to Secretary Eaton: "I cannot see any reasonable or plausible evidence on which [Georgia] rests her claim."[57]

When Coffee had finished his inquiry and was about to leave the nation, Major Ridge addressed him through his son John at Ross's house in the presence of some twenty chiefs, "in which talk he informed me," Coffee reported, "of many depredations committed in his nation by intruders and the frontier inhabitants of Georgia, and he requested me to represent them to our Govt. inasmuch as the agent . . . neglected to do his duty in that respect."[58] Coffee hesitated to interfere between the Cherokees and Colonel Montgomery, whose duty it was to oust intruders, but he agreed to inform the secretary of war of the situation. He gave further advice to the chiefs present—that in his opinion it was the duty of the principal chief to rid the nation of the intruders, and the General Council empowered Ross to do so.[59] He delegated the task to Major Ridge.

Wearing a horned buffalo headdress, The Ridge collected a force of some thirty Cherokees on January 4, 1830. Yelling and shouting, they bore down on the settlement of troublesome intruders at Beaver Dam and Cedar Creek near the Georgia-Alabama line. Ross had instructed The Ridge "to extend towards them all possible lenience and humanity." The warriors, though painted as in former times and dressed as for the warpath (no doubt for mere effect), "were prohibited from using ardent spirits whilst on duty."[60] They gave the intruders—some eighteen families—time to evacuate the houses, old homes of Cherokees who had emigrated west, then burned the buildings to the ground. They had no compunction about the burnings, for it was Cherokee property they destroyed. The Georgians published a version of the act which made it one of terrible inhumanity, Governor Gilmer protesting that the Indians, led by "the most active and malignant enemy of Georgia," had destroyed "all the houses occupied by the whites on a day when the earth was covered with snow and sleet. . . . A number of women, with infant children, were thus deprived of shelter from the severity of the coldest and most inclement weather." And the *Savannah Georgian* suggested that "a portrait of the enlightened leader of the Cherokee nation, Major Ridge, dressed in his Buffalo's head and horns, brandishing his tomahawk over suffering females and children, will form a valuable addition to the gallery of Indian portraits proposed by somebody at Washington."[61]

When the mission had been completed, Major Ridge's band returned home, except for four warriors. These had found a keg of whiskey at the house of one of the horse thieves and, disobeying orders, they lingered behind and got thoroughly drunk. The following morning some twenty-five whites returned to reconnoiter the scene and found the Cherokees too groggy to defend themselves. The intruders took them prisoners, bound them hand and foot, beat them unmercifully, and, loading them onto horses, set off for the Carroll County jail. One Indian, Chewoyee, kept falling off his horse till it was found that he was dead, whereupon they let the body lie where it fell. It was later discovered his skull had been fractured in two or three places. Near the jail two Cherokees, now sober, escaped from their captors.[62] The remaining prisoner was kept for several months behind bars.

Meanwhile whites were aroused throughout the state. "Such has been the excitement produced by the outrage," Gilmer wrote, "that it has been with the utmost difficulty that the people have been restrained from taking ample vengeance on the perpetrators." Bands of armed white men rode about the Cherokee country on the pretext that they were authorized to make arrests, and now and then they fired at Indians. They threatened to burn down the houses of Ross and The Ridge. Throngs of Indians collected with rifles to protect the property of their chiefs. Clashes with the armed bands and other serious trouble threatened.[63] Northern newspapers ran stories: "War in Georgia."

Both The Ridge and Ross could see that their one deed of active retaliation had accomplished little good. They could see that Boudinot was right when he editorialized in the *Phoenix:* "[This is] a circumstance . . . we have for a long time dreaded. . . . It has been the desire of our enemies that the Cherokees may be urged to some desperate act—thus far this desire has never been realized, and we hope, notwithstanding the great injury now sustained, their wonted forbearance will be continued. If our word will have any weight with our countrymen in this trying time, we would say, Forbear, forbear—revenge not, but leave vengeance to him 'to whom vengeance belongeth.'"[64] The Ridge and Ross were circumspect enough to know that warfare with the Georgians could lead only to disaster for the Cherokees. Above all they had no desire to give the Georgians an excuse for taking over the country by force. They decided to forbear—and henceforth, for better or worse, to trust for justice to the courts of the United States.

9 • AND THEN THE REVERSAL

ONE of the prominent Americans incensed at the president's insistence on the Indian Removal Bill was William Wirt, the attorney general under Monroe. The son of a Swiss-born tavern keeper, he had achieved renown as a lawyer and satisfaction as the author of a genial set of papers entitled *Letters of the British Spy*. The letters gave a picture of Virginia life, which Wirt had observed as a neighbor of Thomas Jefferson. The book became the most popular work of its sort in America, and had it not been published anonymously, it would have brought the author more acclaim than his prosecution of Aaron Burr. When Congress passed the Indian Removal Bill by a narrow margin on May 28, 1830, Wirt's annoyance at the president's policy became so keen that he accepted retention as counsel to the Cherokees.[1] He was only one of many distinguished lawyers interested in their condition.

Meanwhile Jackson decided to go to Tennessee that summer to meet with Indian delegations in an effort to implement the Removal Act. He called for the Cherokees to meet with him in Nashville, along with the Creeks, Chickasaws, and Choctaws, and to consider his proposal John Ross called a General Council in July.[2] Along with the opinions of Wirt the Cherokees received the advice of Jeremiah Evarts, who had championed the Indian cause during the Removal Bill debate in "Essays on the Present Crisis in the Condition of the American Indians." He had signed the twenty-four pieces with the pseudonym William Penn and published them in the *National Intelligencer*. Therein he had reminded the lawgivers of the Golden Rule and then continued: "Let the people of Georgia and the people of the United States reflect whether they would be willing to receive the same treatment with which the Cherokees are threatened. Would they be content to go into exile?"[3] Now Evarts advised the Cherokees to send Major Ridge with his son John and the principal chief to see Jackson "to learn his feeling and guard against the evil of [his] purchasing . . . individual Cherokees."[4]

The General Council convened in New Echota on the second Monday of July, 1830. Jackson's request was quickly disposed of; Evarts' advice notwithstanding, the chiefs voted against sending a deputation to Nashville that summer.* Three days were employed in reading and discussing Wirt's opinions on the legal problems facing the nation. Then, on Friday the sixteenth, following a speech by Major Ridge, the council passed a resolution authorizing Ross "to prosecute suits in behalf of the nation." Financing such a course would be a problem, for Jackson's administration had gone to a vital weakness in the Cherokee government—its lack of a financial system independent of the United States. To replenish its funds the Cherokee treasury looked to the periodic payment of the annuity—currently about six thousand dollars—due from the federal government. The secretary of war now decided that the annuity should be paid not as a lump sum into the Cherokee treasury but on a per capita basis to the Cherokee people.[5] Not only would such a procedure be a hardship for the people, some of whom would have to travel 180 miles for fifty cents, but it would all but hamstring the Cherokee government. Nevertheless the Indians determined to wage their fight in the courts of Georgia and the United States. Besides Wirt and Associates of Baltimore as chief counsel, Ross retained the Georgia firm of Underwood and Harris.

With no possibility of a federal loan, the Cherokees had to depend on northern sympathizers for their legal fees, or on individuals in their own midst. But even with payment so ill-assured, Wirt and his fellows rushed to the task.

They found an Indian case in the Georgia courts that could be carried to the U.S. Supreme Court by a writ of error. It involved a Cherokee, George Tassels, who had been convicted of murder and sentenced to hang. Wirt engineered an appeal, and on December 12, 1830, in an order signed by the Chief Justice, the Supreme

---

*Jackson attributed the decision of the Cherokees to Wirt. On August 25, 1830, he wrote: "The course of *Wirt* has been truly wicked. It has been wielded as an engine to prevent the Indians from moving X [across] the Mississippi and will lead to the destruction of the poor ignorant Indians" (*Correspondence*, IV, p. 177). Following the Cherokee council, John Ridge attended that called by the Creeks and, emphasizing Wirt's advice, prevailed upon the Creeks to likewise boycott the meeting with Jackson (*Cherokee Phoenix*, Sept. 4, 1830, p. 2, col. 2).

Court cited the state of Georgia to appear in Washington and show cause why a writ of error should not be issued in the case.[6] Georgia flouted the order, with fulminations from the new governor, Wilson Lumpkin. The Georgia legislature resolved that "the interference by the chief justice of the supreme court of the U. States, in the administration of the criminal laws of this state . . . is a flagrant violation of her rights." It directed the governor "and every other officer" to disregard the mandate of the Supreme Court and ordered the sheriff of Hall County to expedite the hanging of Tassels.[7] Abandoned by the administration, as well as scorned by Georgia, the Supreme Court was helpless to vindicate its authority, and thus the first move of Wirt came to nothing. He was undaunted, however. He had already raised another issue. The Cherokees, at his advice, had applied to the Supreme Court for an injunction to stop Georgia from executing her tyrannical Indian code.[8]

Meanwhile the Cherokees had convened their October council, again holding it in New Echota despite the decree that made it unlawful for them to meet on the soil of Georgia. It was the last time Tsalagi Tinilawigi would meet in the Cherokee capital. Indians came from every part of the nation, most of them dressed in white men's clothing, though a few mountain warriors wore various blends of Indian and white men's dress and a few patriarchs came in blankets and turbans. Many prosperous half bloods wore frock coats and beaver hats; most of the women were in skirts of printed calico, and children carried blowguns and bows and arrows. Some families came afoot, some on horseback, others in wagons and carriages; some brought dogs that barked and growled and scuffled and scratched. Council time provided the opportunity for a great social gathering, friend meeting friend, the members of divided families coming together after months or years.[9]

At last, on the eleventh, the council began. John Ridge took a seat on the National Committee and was elected president of that body. He had gone to Washington during the last session of Congress as the secretary of the Creek delegation, but the Indian Office had refused to receive him in that capacity, and so unable to serve the Creeks as in the past, he had disassociated himself once more from their affairs and returned to Cherokee politics. Going Snake, who had come to New Echota on a blooded mare and who was dressed in a frock coat and a cockade hat, was elected Speaker of the Council, while Alexander McCoy, restored to grace, became the clerk.[10]

Day after day John Lowrey, the white officer who had led the Cherokees in the Seminole War, appeared at the council house and listened intently to the proceedings. As he was said to represent the federal government, his presence aroused much speculation. On the twentieth he made his mission known, with John Ridge "linkstering" his address in Cherokee. He assured his audience—the committee and the council having assembled as a committee of the whole in front of the council house, the day too mild for them to remain indoors—that the American government desired to dispel "the evils and unhappy difficulties" that now existed between the Cherokees and the surrounding states. And "with a view to promote the future peace and happiness of all concerned," the United States proposed to enter a treaty with the Cherokees on terms that turned out to be the usual ones, involving an exchange of Cherokee land for "country west of the Mississippi." But there was a further disturbing detail in the document which John Ridge translated in the balmy sunshine—the confirmation of what had heretofore been rumor only: that whenever Georgia decided to enter Cherokee territory for the purpose of surveying it, the president would not interfere.[11]

Was it a threat from Jackson?

Major Ridge interrupted the proceedings and asked Colonel Lowrey to produce his credentials. They were read and found to be in order, and so it was known that the colonel was a personal emissary from Secretary Eaton, who had recently claimed that Indians were no more capable of being educated than wild turkeys: "The wild Turkey," Eaton had said, "though you shall take the egg and hatch it in your barnyard, will not forget his nature, but at maturity will seek the tallest forest tree, at nightfall, for his roosting place."[12] The secretary had betrayed the archaism of his knowledge of Cherokee advancement by inquiring how the tribe hoped to live whenever the game disappeared from the woods. To Colonel Lowrey's message the council gave its accustomed reply that the Cherokees had "long since come to the conclusion never again to cede *another foot* of land."[13] Moreover, it voted to send another delegation to protest in Washington against their continued harassment.

John Ridge was chosen as a delegate along with William Shorey Coodey, nephew of John Ross, and Richard Taylor, who was named to lead the deputation. Taylor was an older man, large and portly, "of a bland, open countenance, which seemed shaded with an expression so deeply pensive, if not sad, as to indicate that but little hope for the fortunes of his country linger[ed] around his heart."[14]

Often he smoked a silver pipe that had been presented to a Chero-kee chief by General Washington decades before. The delegates left for Washington in November, 1830, and on their arrival settled down at Brown's Hotel. There they met a correspondent of the *New York Observer* who described them as "well-dressed gentle-men of good manners—themselves good society for any sensible man—sitting at the publick tables throughout the City—undistin-guished from the common mass except it be in superior delicacy of feeling."[15] Ridge and Coodey struck this journalist as "men of liberal education, polished in their manners, and worthy of our society. The propriety and dignity of their demeanor are . . . commanding, prepossessing, and attractive. They enforce respect and esteem." In view of their youth the writer was amazed at their understanding of the affairs of state. "They actually know more of the institutions, laws, and government of the United States," he concluded, "than a large fraction of those who occupy seats in the House of Representa-tives; and this may be said without dishonoring that body."[16]

The Cherokees announced their presence to Secretary Eaton on December 9 and desired "the pleasure of taking their Great Father by the hand, when the President is at leisure to allow them . . . an interview."[17] Jackson granted them a courtesy appointment, and a few days later they waited on Eaton "for the purpose of ascertaining the views of the Government in relation to the withdrawal of troops from the Nation and [to] the progress Georgia was making in her legislature on the subject of our vacant lands, which it was [her] design to survey."[18]

John Ridge asked the secretary point-blank what the United States intended to do in the event that Georgia moved to force the Cherokee lands from the possession of the Indians. He insisted that his people had the right "to receive a direct and frank answer."

He wrote his father that he was surprised "to find the Secretary inclined to equivocate." Eaton replied that "the Government would decide on the matter when the crisis occurred," and sidestepped any further discussion by directing the Cherokees to address the War Department on the subject in writing. This William Coodey did on behalf of the deputation with a pen "of much ability, direct-ness and point."[19] But when the delegation attempted to draw against the Cherokee annuity for expense money, Eaton cut off inter-course with them, refusing to recognize them as a legally consti-tuted deputation, on the grounds that they had come without written authority to discuss a removal treaty.[20] This move, however, did not completely frustrate the Cherokees from pursuing their ends. John Ridge had written a five-page memorial for Congress in which he discussed the several developments that agitated his people. He expostulated on the Cherokee lands surrendered in effect by the general government to Georgia; on the president's winking at white intrusion on improvements abandoned by Arkansas emigrants; on the suffering of Cherokees at the gold mines from the hands of intruders, the Georgia guard, and troops of the United States; and on the subject generally of intruders on and about the Cherokee border, the rash of white squatters whom the agent neglected to remove after repeated complaints from the Cherokee chiefs. "I have . . . represented to Congress," he informed Major Ridge, "some of the aggravated cases of oppression our citizens have endured from the Georgians."[21]

However cold the administration, the Cherokee delegates were heartened by the encouragement of numerous well-wishers. "The kind condolence of acquaintances and friends of Indians throughout the U.S.," John Ridge wrote to Dr. Gold of Cornwall, "comes upon the ear like soft music of other days, when the administration of the general government observed a sacred regard for subsisting treaties with our Nation and maintained the faith and honor of united America, as handed down to them from their great revolutionary ancestors." Bluff, warmhearted David Crockett, with his homespun manner and his growing aversion for Andrew Jackson, took the delegation in tow and introduced them to many men in Congress, including several from Kentucky, who pledged support of Indian interests, and it soon became clear that the Cherokees had the backing of those who followed Henry Clay in his opposition to the president. With judgment swayed by wishful thinking, John Ridge attributed greater strength to the Whig forces than they actually enjoyed, and he optimistically advised Dr. Gold of his "conviction of the friendship of Henry Clay to the rights of the Cherokees. . . . It is to a change of this administration that we must now wait for relief."[22] And he wrote Major Ridge in a similar vein:

It would be unbecoming the frankness of a son to a father, did I withhold from your knowledge the views I entertain of political affairs and [on] what source we must rely for eventual success, in the struggles we maintain. This session of Congress is a short one, and will be closed little more than two months from this date. The policy of the President in regard to the Indians is deservedly unpopular and will meet with opposition in every stage where the action of Congress is requisite. . . .

We have strong, eloquent, and good men who feel for us, and are our friends. . . . There is no question of the Cherokees having a vast majority of the people of the United States in their favor, even of the Jackson party inclusive.[23]

And he advised Boudinot: "From private and public sources, we are induced to believe that Henry Clay is our friend, and will enforce the treaties. Bear up my friends for two years longer, and we are victorious—let the people understand that."[24]

Ridge added that New Jersey was on the Cherokees' side—Theodore Frelinghuysen was their champion in the Senate. A staunch supporter in the House was Edward Everett of Massachusetts, who worked to secure the Cherokees their annuity in the regular manner. The delegation had failed to see the matter up through the standing committee on Indian affairs, but in the face of vociferous opposition, Everett succeeded in bringing forward a motion on their behalf. He claimed the attention of the House and spoke for two whole days on Cherokee affairs, sometimes with effective irony:

Here, at the center of the nation, beneath the portals of the Capitol, let us solemnly auspicate the new era of violated promises, and tarnished faith. Let us kindle a grand council-fire, not of treaties made and ratified, but of treaties annulled and broken. Let us send to our archives for the worthless parchments, and burn them in the face of day. There will be some yearnings of humanity as we perform the solemn act. They were negotiated for valuable considerations; we keep the considerations, and break the bond. One gave peace to our afflicted frontier; another protected our infant settlements; nearly all were at our earnest request. Many of them were negotiated under the instructions of Washington, of Adams, and of Jefferson—the fathers of our liberty. They are gone, and will not witness the spectacle; but our present Chief Magistrate, as he lays them, one by one, on the fire, will see his own name subscribed to a goodly number of them. Sir, they ought to be destroyed, as a warning to the Indians to make them no more compacts with us.[25]

John Ridge and one of his colleagues sat in the gallery of the House and were deeply moved by Everett's sonorous words reverberating through the chamber. "I happened to be a spectator of this debate," wrote the correspondent of the *New York Observer.* On the second day, toward the close of the long speech, he found it hard to "shield the heart" against the "subduing power" of Everett's words. "Two of the Cherokees stood immediately behind me and over me. In the midst of Mr. Everett's peroration, I thought I heard some-

thing like a drop of rain fall upon . . . my cloak, near my ear.
I looked up, and the head of one of these Cherokees had fallen
upon his hand, and he was endeavoring to conceal his tears."[26]

Yet moving as Everett's speech was, his motion failed to carry
the House. That evening, February 21, 1831, the Cherokees joined
various other Indian deputations then in Washington—Iroquois,
Quapaw, Choctaw, and Creek—in agreeing to observe a day of fasting, humiliation, and prayer on account of their several disappoint-
ments. On the appointed morning—Sunday March 6—the delegations met in a room at Brown's and a native Oneida minister
preached a sermon in English, which most of those present understood. They fasted for the rest of the day and held another service
that evening, this time in a room at Gadsby's. They kept to themselves, and few white men knew of their observances. Thus, the
Indians of several tribes humiliated themselves for their respective
setbacks at the hands of the federal government.[27] Meanwhile John
Ridge and his colleagues, and to a lesser extent the other Indians
in the capital, were held in suspense concerning the suit the Cherokee Nation had lodged against the state of Georgia in the Supreme
Court.

The time came for Wirt and his associates to press the case. They
made their arguments before the Supreme Court on March 12 and
14, with Georgia disdaining to appear, refusing to admit the court's
jurisdiction. In his peroration Wirt declared:

We know that whatever can be properly done for this unfortunate
people will be done by this honorable court. Their cause is one that
must come home to every honest and feeling heart. They have been
true and faithful to us and have a right to expect a corresponding
fidelity on our part. Through a long course of years they have followed
our counsel with the docility of children. *Our* wish has been *their* law.
We asked them to become civilized, and they became so. They assumed
our dress, copied our names, pursued our course of education, adopted
our form of government, embraced our religion, and have been proud
to imitate us in every thing in their power. They have watched the
progress of our prosperity with the strongest interest, and have marked
the rising grandeur of our nation with as much pride as if they belonged to us. They have even adopted our resentments; and in our war
with the Seminole tribes, they voluntarily joined our arms, and gave
effectual aid in driving back those barbarians from the very state that
now oppresses them. They threw upon the field, in that war, a body
of men who descend from the noble race that were once the lords of

these extensive forests—men worthy to associate with the "lion," who, in their own language, "walks upon the mountain tops."* They fought side by side with our present chief magistrate, and received his personal thanks for their gallantry and bravery.[28]

On the morning of July 18, 1831, John Ridge and his friends joined the spectators who thronged the court to hear the decision. As the Chief Justice began to read in a faint, quavering voice, the crowd strained forward, toward the bench, the better to catch his feeble tones. It took the old man some twenty-five minutes to read the decision. At the outset Marshall plainly stated that his sympathies lay with the Indians. However, the Cherokees had sued as a foreign nation, a status the court found they did not have, even though they constituted a separate state. They were found rather to comprise "a domestic, dependent nation . . . in a state of pupilage." Therefore the court could not examine the merits or go into the moralities of their controversy with Georgia because, the Cherokees not constituting a "foreign nation," the court had no jurisdiction over the case.[29] Thus, John Ridge witnessed the circumvention of Wirt's second move, in spite of the sympathy that a majority of the Court professed for its motives.

Yet the delegation refused to accept the decision as a full defeat. They felt comfort in the Court's having found the Cherokees "a domestic dependent nation," and John Ridge wrote Boudinot that the president, when the deputation waited upon him after the decision, had no grounds, as reported, for making "inferences of desponding humiliation in the minds of the Delegation.—We felt none, and therefore could not exhibit any." To refute a Georgia news story that the delegation had asked if they had provoked the presidential anger, Ridge added: "Sooner than ask the President *if he was angry with me*, I would cut my tongue out. . . . I could not, unless the independence of my mind had been metamorphosed to the mentality of his 'palace slaves.'"

The conversation with the president proceeded for several minutes. Jackson, his face lined but relaxed in the satisfaction of victory, talked of friendship with the Cherokees. He mentioned his "disposition to do them good."

"I'm particularly glad to see you at this time," he said. "I knew that your claims before the Suprerme Court would not be supported. The court has sustained my views in regard to your nation." After

*A footnote in the original reads: "The Chieftain Ridge."

a pause the president resumed: "I blame you for suffering your lawyers to fleece you—they want your money, and will make you promises even after this." His voice, interrupted by a hacking cough, was confidential. "I have been a lawyer myself long enough to know how lawyers will talk to obtain their clients' money."

The delegates replied that, if the Cherokees had spent money in support of their national rights, it was agreeable to their own inclinations. "We don't believe you would blame the Cherokees for their efforts to maintain their rights before the proper tribunals."

"Oh no," Jackson answered. "I don't blame you for that. I only blame you for suffering the lawyers to fleece you.—I am a friend of the Cherokees, they fought with me in the war and freely shed their blood with the blood of my soldiers in defending the United States and how could I be otherwise than their friend?"

The delegation insisted on their "abstract rights of justice." But Jackson suddenly changed the subject; he began talking of the British treaty of 1783, then contrasted the condition of the Catawbas to their former state—to what they were when he was a young man. Then they had been warlike and had fought the Cherokees. "At one time," he reminded the delegation, "they took some of the Cherokee warriors prisoners, threw them in the fire, and when their intestines were barbecued, ate them. Now they were poor and miserable and reduced in numbers, and such will be the condition of the Cherokees," he prophesied, "if they remain surrounded by the white people."

At that moment a representative of Georgia was announced. The delegation, not wishing to share the president's drawing room with the Georgian, rose to depart. Each shook the old man's hand, Richard Taylor the last to do so, and Jackson held his fingers for some time, making the Georgian wait, while he repeated his professions of friendship. He asked the delegation to tell their people at their return what he had said. And he added: "You can live on your lands in Georgia if you choose, but I cannot interfere with the laws of that state to protect you."[30]

Jackson was sincere in what he said. He had a frontiersman's point of view, but it was that of an enlightened frontiersman. He believed he had the interest of the Cherokees at heart. He wished to see them neither debased nor destroyed. However, their only salvation, in his opinion, was removal beyond the reach of the whites.[31] Thus, the delegation should have seen that nothing had really changed, unless it was that Jackson was even more certain of having his own way. But they packed up and went home under the self-instilled illusion that the Supreme Court had really declared in the Cherokees' favor when it found them "a domestic dependent nation" and that the declaration somehow augured well for their condition.

Major Ridge accepted John's interpretation of Marshall's ruling, and Ross was also inclined to take an optimistic view of it, especially since the Cherokees had received a letter of sympathy from the Chief Justice. Several local councils were called in April, May, and June at places like Hickory Log, Pine Log, Taloney, and Setico—at towns in both Georgia and Tennessee—and Major Ridge and John Ross made the rounds, explaining the work of the delegation in Washington and assuring the common Indians of the positive aspect of the Supreme Court's position. They showed the letter in which John Marshall claimed to regret the decision the Court was bound to make in respect to the Cherokees' petition for an injunction.[32]

A Georgian reported his attendance at one of the meetings, "at which there were a great many Indians assembled, but they conversed," he wrote, "chiefly in their own language, in order no doubt to conceal from me their motives." He explained that Ross, Lowrey, and Major Ridge were present. They told the common Indians, who appeared to have no will of their own, to remain constant till Jackson's term of office expired. Then Henry Clay would become president, and Georgia's Indian code would be declared unconstitutional. They told the Indians, further, "that though they despaired of being looked upon as a foreign nation, they [would] be recognized as domestic dependents under the protection of the General Government alone, not subject to the laws of any state, and [would] be restored to all their ancient rights and privileges. They then read the decision of the Supreme Court, and the views of some Northern writers on the subject, and exhort[ed] them to submit to the laws of Georgia for the present, and patiently wait until Jackson shall have been removed."[33]* Major Ridge continued to ride during the summer and fall of 1831 "to persuade his countrymen" to refrain from removal and to remain fast in their ancient homelands.[34]

---

*Cf. Ira Dupree to Gov. Gilmer, June 3, 1831: "Ross and Ridge and others are determined at the expense of all truth and at the sacrifice of every honest principle, to deceive the nation and keep it in ignorance" (23rd Cong., 1st sess., S. Doc. 512, II, p. 488).

Meanwhile law and order had deteriorated throughout the Cherokee Nation. In June, 1830, when Georgia's laws were extended through the land, Major Ridge had made a circuit of the country with Ross and Lowrey to instruct the local sheriffs and the Cherokee courts to execute the Indian laws as usual.[35] But Georgia had reacted by declaring such enforcement a penitentiary crime; Cherokee law enforcement was thus paralyzed, and under such duress the nation lapsed into lawlessness.

At the same time, depredations of the pony clubs grew steadily worse. In the spring of 1831, Boudinot estimated that the thieves had made away with some five hundred head of cattle and horses.[36] They had evicted Cherokee families from their homes, burned down fences and houses, and occasionally they had not even stopped at murder. Increasing numbers of white families had squatted on Cherokee property, anticipating the Georgia survey and lottery that would parcel Cherokee lands among "fortunate drawers."

Multitudinous barrels of whiskey were carted into the nation, and confused and unhappy as they were, the Cherokee masses fell prey to drunkenness as never before. When drunk, the Cherokees were quarrelsome, frequently violent. Crimes of violence multiplied. Gambling too flourished on an unprecedented scale. Understanding the Georgia laws as little as they did, the Cherokees fell afoul of them in increasing numbers. There were wholesale arrests and confinements in unwholesome jails, a development that only demoralized the Indians further.

The missionaries looked on and saw the results of their long and arduous labors being rapidly undermined. They felt they could not watch the debasement of their charges without raising a protest, and this they had done as early as December 29, 1830, when the Moravians, Baptists, Congregationalists, and Presbyterians (the Methodists having already taken a similar stand) met in New Echota and drew up resolutions in defense of the Cherokees.

Much of their statement dwelt soberly on the advances the Cherokee people had made. It refrained from claiming all progress as a result of missionary activity, but gave credit to the benevolent influence of the federal government and its Indian policy. It attached value also to intermarriage as a force for improvement. When signed, the resolutions were sent to Boston, where they were published in the *Missionary Herald*.[37] In Georgia they provoked an immediate reaction in the legislature, which passed a law that no white man could remain in the Cherokee part of Georgia after March 1, 1831, unless he took an oath of allegiance to the state and secured a special permit from the governor. Violation of this law was made a prison offense.

Major Ridge was present at the mission house of Daniel Butrick and his brother-in-law Isaac Proctor at Taloney, which the missionaries preferred to call Carmel, when word of the new law arrived in a marked copy of the *Georgia Journal*. With some misgivings he listened to Proctor's opinion that the missionaries should leave the Georgia portion of the nation and to Butrick's sentiment that they should surrender to Georgia on all temporal matters. But before acting upon their feelings the missionaries wrote to the Prudential Committee in Boston for instructions. No doubt The Ridge was pleased on learning weeks later that advice had come from Boston for all missionaries sent out by the American Board to remain firm. It was a recommendation only, but they accepted it as an order and held to their posts, even while the Moravian brothers were moving out of Georgia, leaving their wives behind to manage their missions. Butrick, who had searched his Bible for guidance, was still of the opinion that his colleagues and he should submit to the will of Georgia, take the oath, and petition for a permit to remain with their flocks, but at New Echota, Worcester assumed a stiffer attitude and prepared to risk his freedom for the sake of his cause.[38]

The wait was short but nerve-racking, with the Georgia guard apprehending many Cherokees and holding them under wretched conditions, as if to foreshadow the handling of the missionaries. Not even Boudinot escaped harassment. He was twice hauled up before the guard to answer for "abusive and libelous articles," and on one occasion he was threatened with a flogging by the notorious Colonel C. H. Nelson, who had earned the disapproval of even Governor Gilmer.[39] On March 12 the first white arrests began. Though the guard had no warrants, it took Proctor, Worcester, and John Thompson, a blacksmith at Hightower, into custody along with John F. Wheeler and several other white men and marched them to the sound of fife and drum into headquarters at Lawrenceville, where they were consigned to the civil authorities. On this occasion the missionaries were allowed to retain their dignity. They received courteous treatment and found that many Georgians regarded their predicament with sympathy. When their case came to trial, the court released them on a writ of habeas corpus since, serving as postmasters at their respective posts and being licensed missionaries who spent federal funds appropriated for civilizing the Indians, they were considered agents of the United States.

If the missionaries rejoiced that their position had been vindicated by law, their cause for self-congratulation was short-lived. Governor Gilmer inquired of the president whether he considered the missionaries servants of the government. He did not, Jackson replied, and implemented his words by having the Postal Department relieve them as postmasters. The governor ordered the missionaries to leave the state, but they persisted at their posts, defiant. Soon, in late June and early July, came another series of arrests, the captives now including Butrick and Dr. Elizur Butler. The guard no longer handled the missionaries with its former forbearance. "These unoffending and guileless men," John Ridge declared, "were ignominiously received like felons—they were chained with horses' trace-chains around their necks and fastened, one to the neck of a horse, the other to the tail of a cart, and thus [were] dragged with bleeding feet, through the rough and tangled forest, over brake and bush and bog and fen, at the point of a bayonet, and even in sickness, with wounded feet, [they were] refused the privilege of riding their own horses."[40]

The hearing of the missionaries occurred in Lawrenceville on July 23. The authorities then released them pending their trial before the Supreme Court of Georgia. Of the eleven standing trial, nine relented, yielded to the will of Georgia, and were given their freedom. But Worcester and Butler sternly rejected the offer of clemency under such conditions and were convicted of felony offenses against the majesty of Georgia. The court sentenced both to four years' hard labor in the penitentiary at Milledgeville. Their fate aroused sympathy and anger in the North. Even in Georgia many citizens, though condoning the extension of state jurisdiction over the Cherokee country, were filled with revulsion at the treatment meted out to the missionaries. Their plight did much to swing a certain measure of public feeling in favor of the Cherokees, and their counsels— Underwood and Harris, Elisha W. Chester, and General Edward Harden—moved to carry their case before the Supreme Court of the United States. There Worcester and Butler had optimistic hopes of vindicating themselves and, at the same time, of proving the unconstitutionality of Georgia's Cherokee code. The Cherokees also, the Ridges included, attached enormous significance to the missionary case. With it they hoped to win a belated victory in their struggle against Georgia, the positive victory that William Wirt had failed to bring them.

As time for the October council of 1831 drew near, the question arose as to the advisability of convening it in New Echota in view of Georgia's ban against Cherokee assembly. Major Ridge received an invitation to meet with others of the executive council at Ross's house to determine the course to be followed. The assembled chiefs were of one mind as to the propriety of holding the council and after a sober discussion they decided to flout the Georgia guard and convene it in the Cherokee capital, according to the provisions of Cherokee law. Circulars were thus issued, calling for the General Council to meet as usual at New Echota.

Almost at once John Ridge and Boudinot convinced Major Ridge that such a course would be against the general interest, and the three hurried to Ross's house to advise a reconsideration of the resolution. Ross hesitated to reopen the matter. The three visitors pleaded that such a course might have unfortunate consequences.

Why did they think so? the principal chief asked.

Boudinot replied: "Because I've taken pains to ascertain the sentiments of the members of the General Council; and I've discovered that some of them, rather than attend at New Echota, will resign. Such an event will be most embarrassing to the public interest." It was most important, he added, that nothing interfere with the assembly because of the necessity of appointing a delegation to Washington. Major Ridge and John concurred in Boudinot's views, and raised a further objection. In New Echota the council would inevitably be interrupted by the Georgia guard; the people would not stand docilely by and see their chiefs and representatives made prisoners and dragged away to some filthy Georgia jail. There was sure to be serious trouble.

Ross disagreed, but admitted that further consideration was needed. "As mine is but a single opinion, and I am now only one against three, I'll do this, gentlemen. I'll ask the members here. We'll meet in my house as private citizens and discuss the expediency of assembling at New Echota or elsewhere in our public capacities. I know it's desirable to avoid excitement; and in the way I mention we shall best discover how it can be avoided."

Ross's plan was followed. Five days before the council was due to convene, the members met at his house. The two bodies preferred

John Ross, Principal Chief of the Cherokees. Courtesy of the Oklahoma Historical Society.

to discuss the question before them separately. The National Committee, with John Ridge at its head, withdrew and after deliberating voted against assembling at New Echota. Most of the members of the lower house took the other view, but when the two bodies came together to resolve their differences, the opinion of the committee prevailed. It was agreed that "the seat of government should be removed beyond the limits of Georgia."[41]

At last a spot at Chatooga, Alabama, was named as the new council site. It had served for a camp meeting, and there were "rude pulpits and platforms and sheds of rough boards on forked stakes canopied by the sky."[42] These served the Cherokees for their deliberations, and all in attendance were seated on rough logs in lieu of benches.

The council again appointed John Ridge and William S. Coodey to present the Cherokee grievances in Washington, and Richard Taylor was replaced by Judge John Martin, treasurer of the nation.[43] John Ross planned to travel with the delegation as far as Gainesville, Georgia. On the evening before their departure—November 30, 1831—considerable excitement was aroused by the attempt of a white ruffian to murder him and his brother Andrew on the road between The Ridge's house and Coodey's.

The Rosses had visited Lavender's Store and had then stopped at Major Ridge's house for a talk. While they sat before the fire, a loud knock sounded on the door, and a harsh voice called out, "Is John Ross there?" Ross went to the door and identified himself. A tall, gaunt stranger, who claimed that a horse of his had been stolen, wanted to know if anyone had recently crossed on Ross's ferry at the Head of Coosa, for he had trailed his horse to that point. He said, further, that he had hired a Cherokee at Lavender's Store to help him hunt the thief down. Later the stranger and the Indian he had hired, a dependable man named Onehutty, met the Ross brothers on the road. At the ferry they saw a horseman on the crown of a low hill, and the stranger and Onehutty set off in pursuit. When the Rosses overtook them, they had a third man in tow, "a chubb[y], grim-looking fellow, with a pair of large reddish mustaches which curled at the corners of his mouth."[44] The pretended thief turned out to be in league with the gaunt stranger, and on the road to Coodey's their real purpose became apparent—to kill and rob the Cherokee chief and his brother.

The tall stranger had lagged behind. Suddenly he dismounted

and aimed his rifle. "Ross," he shouted, "I've wanted to kill you for a long time, and I'll be damned if I don't do it now."

Ross wheeled his horse and galloped off. Over his shoulder he could see the stranger dash behind a tree and point his gun at Andrew, but Andrew galloped away too. "There can be no doubt that a premeditated plot of rapine and murder had been laid," Boudinot editorialized, "and that the Principal Chief was selected as a victim—but the design of these mercenary executors having failed, the next scheme suggested by their rapacity was to decoy Onehutty into their power for the purpose of robbing him of his horse."[45] The Cherokee, who had not been armed, appeared at the store the following morning with a vicious bruise on his cheek where he had been hit with a slab of rock. He had disarmed the gaunt stranger and stabbed him in the ribs with his own knife. There was no political significance to be attached to the incident, it was decided. Boudinot associated the ruffians with the pony clubs, and the matter illustrated as well as anything the disruption of order that Georgia's measures had caused in the Cherokee country. It was just such outrages, now occurring on a greater scale than ever, that John Ridge and his colleagues aimed to protest in the federal capital.

The delegation rode horseback as far as Athens, Georgia, from where they sent their horses home and took the stagecoach to Augusta. Along the route they found the white communities aboil with politics. The office hunters of Georgia had promised so much to the common people that they had grown "sick with the expectation of Indian land and gold. Their votes must get bought with a promise," wrote one of the delegates, probably Ridge, "and no candidate can succeed to any respectable appointment in their gift without it. This class is numerous, and all ignorant—they do not know anything about writs of error, the constitution of the United States, etc. They know they are poor and wish to be rich, and believe that, if they have luck, they will draw a gold mine, and most everyone expects to have his *luck in the lottery*."[46] Sailing from Augusta, the delegation arrived in Washington during the third week of December, 1831. They took quarters at the Indian Queen, where Jackson had recently made history by denouncing nullification in South Carolina.

The irony of the president's action was not lost on the Cherokees, acutely aware as they were of how the chief executive, while denouncing the doctrine in one state, had in effect allowed it to thrive in another. Only the year before John Ridge had scored the extinguishment of Indian rights in Georgia as "the twin brother of nullification, which has reared its head, and spoken the discordant sentiment of disunion in South Carolina." And he had taken the occasion to call the attention of sympathetic Americans "to the dangerous rock of state necessity."[47]

The delegation now prepared to continue exposing the disasters caused by Georgia's course. On December 29 they submitted a memorial to the secretary of war, Lewis Cass, who had succeeded Major Eaton since John Ridge's last sojourn in the city. The memorial inveighed against how Georgia had usurped the gold mines from Cherokee control; how Cherokees were arrested and driven from their homes in chains at bayonet point without legal process; and how the state had run preliminary surveys through the Indian country and proposed to divide it among Georgians by means of a gigantic lottery. It revealed how whiskey was sold by white traders contrary to both Cherokee and federal law, and how intruders were permitted to invade Cherokee land and despoil Cherokee improvements and harass the people. The tone was bitter.[48]

Cass, a ponderous, solemn man with a huge balding head, was honest and conscientious about the responsibilities of his office. He held several conversations with Jackson about the condition of Cherokees. "And I assure you," he wrote the delegation in a sober, carefully reasoned letter on January 10, 1832, "[the president] is exceedingly anxious for the termination of all your difficulties. Whatever you may have been told, or may be told, I know he is your friend, truly and sincerely so." What followed, as Cass continued, with telling forthrightness, was a realistic appraisal of the situation from the president's point of view:

He sees the embarrassments which surround you, and he is convinced that, for these, there is no remedy but in a removal beyond the immediate contact of the white people. As to coercion none will be applied. Such a measure is not in contemplation. You are free to remain with the privileges and disabilities of other citizens. If you and your people are prepared for this, any further observations from me are useless. But, if as the President believes, and as all experience has heretofore shewn, your people are not in a condition to resist the operation of those causes which have produced incalculable injury to the Indians, every dictate of prudence requires that you should abandon your residence, and establish yourselves in a country where abundance, peace and improvement are offered to you.

"I do not address you as I should the great body of your people,"

Cass added in closing. "You are well educated and intelligent, able to appreciate the value of our institutions, and fitted to enjoy them. Not so with your countrymen generally. As therefore you must judge for them, I trust you will view their situation as it is, and inquire what is best for them."[49] Thus, Cass not only revealed the administration as adamantly set in its course, but he also made a case that many thoughtful men deemed worthy of consideration.

Somewhere along the way in 1832—exactly when is not certain—John Ridge began to doubt the wisdom of the stand he and the Cherokees were taking. But if doubt assailed him as early as January, he showed no sign of it in his outward demeanor. To the world he was still the unyielding foe of Indian removal, and he was still calling Jackson by such epithets as "chicken snake" as late as April 6 and accusing him of having "time to crawl and hide in the luxuriant grass of his nefarious hypocrisy."[50] In January, finding the president and his secretary of war inflexible, and seeing that little progress could be made with Congress, Ridge decided that he could spend his energies better in a lecture tour of the North with Boudinot for the double purpose of arousing public sentiment in favor of the Cherokees and of raising funds for the *Phoenix*, stranded by the bankruptcy of the Cherokee treasury. He left Martin and Coodey to manage the business of the delegation, and the two cousins rode the stage to Philadelphia, where on the twelfth Ridge informed John Ross of his plan. It gave him pleasure to state "that the prospects of a great & vigorous expression of indignation from the city, against the cruelties of Georgia, and the policy of the U.S. is now flattering. It will be made either by public meeting or signatures obtained, from all parties at their residences, by men appointed for that purpose."[51] He referred to a memorial of protest to be signed by as many sympathizers as could be contacted by a volunteer canvass.

The well-wishers in Philadelphia included the venerable publisher Matthew Carey, who invited the travelers to dinner, subscribed ten dollars for Boudinot's fund, and offered a toast in an Irish accent: "Confusion to the Councils of Georgia and the administration in relation to the Cherokees." At the Atheneum they met Colonel McKenney, who had been forced from the Indian Office and who was sour now on Jackson's Indian policy. He seemed eager to regain John Ridge's friendship; through Boudinot he intimated "that he was willing to bury the Hatchet," and Ridge accepted the overture. "He is apparently as strong a friend as we have," John Ross was advised. "He designs to publish in this city short letters addressed to the

President which shall strike him as the lightning strikes the branch-
less pine." The colonel also had plans to publish lithographs of the
Indian portraits in Washington and with them short sketches of the
subjects. He asked John Ridge to intercede with Ross "to write a
sketch of the life of the Cherokee Cadmus, George Guess. . . . He
wishes to have the life of the inventor written by one of the Indians."52

From Philadelphia the cousins proceeded to New York City. Two
rallies, a week apart, were held at Clinton Hall. Theodore Dwight,
political satirist, chaired the first meeting and General James Tallmadge, antislavery politician, the second. Boudinot and John Ridge
spoke at both, and though Boudinot made an effective address, it
was Ridge's speech that the press played up. The *New York Commercial Advertiser* described "J. Ridge," as it chose to call him, as
"rather tall and slender in his person, erect, with a profusion of
black hair, a shade less swarthy, and with less prominence of cheekbones than our western Indians. His voice is full and melodious, his
elocution fluent, and without the least observable tincture of foreign
accent or Indian. Even his metaphors were rarely drawn from the
forest, and he had little or none of that vehement action that char-
acterizes the orators of uncivilized tribes."53 He began by outlining
the relations of the Cherokees with the federal government and the
advances which his people had made, the usual fare of his addresses.

"You asked us," he said, "to throw off the hunter and warrior
state: We did so—you asked us to form a republican government: We
did so—adopting your own as a model. You asked us to cultivate
the earth, and learn the mechanic arts: We did so. You asked us to
learn to read: We did so. You asked us to cast away our idols, and
worship your God: We did so."54

Ridge grew eloquent when touching on the abuses of his people,
and on the treaties violated, the promises broken, the federal laws
unexecuted; nor did his fervor diminish when he spoke upon the
treatment of the missionaries. "The simple story of their wrongs,"
ran the account in the *Commercial Advertiser*, "related in the un-
sophisticated language of nature, went home to the heart with irre-
sistible power. We only wish that we could adequately report the
feeling narrative and convey to the reader the unaffected manner of
the speaker. His narrative of the brutalities of the Georgia Guard
towards the Missionaries . . . was sufficient to fire the blood and rouse
the indignation of every American deserving the name of man."55

At the end of the second rally a standing committee was chosen,
including Chancellor James Kent of Columbia College; Philip Hone,

former mayor of the city; James Gore King, the merchant; Theodore Dwight; and General Tallmadge. Eight hundred dollars were collected for Boudinot's fund, and a memorial to Congress was put into circulation, to be signed eventually by six thousand people. With a feeling of success the Cherokees went on to New Haven, where they spoke on the same platform as Professor Benjamin Silliman and the Reverend Leonard Bacon and duplicated their triumph. They also spoke at Hartford, and money was collected and memorials circulated in both cities. Then late in February, Ridge and Boudinot went to Boston, where they spoke at the Old South Church at rallies led by Lyman Beecher and John Pickering, student of many Indian languages.[56]

Ridge and Boudinot were at the missionary rooms of the American Board in Pemberton Square when news arrived of the Supreme Court's decision in the case of *Worcester* v. *Georgia.* A friend who had just arrived from Washington inquired if they were prepared to hear the worst.

No, they were not, Ridge replied.

Then the friend revealed the decision—how the Supreme Court had ruled as unconstitutional the law which had imprisoned the missionaries and along with it the whole Indian code that Georgia had enacted. "The Cherokee Nation then," the decision had read, "is a distinct community, occupying its own territory . . . in which the laws of Georgia can have no right to enter but with the assent of the Cherokees. . . . The Act of the state of Georgia . . . is consequently void."[57] Ridge called the news "glorious."[58] Sympathizers rushed to congratulate him and Boudinot. Suddenly Dr. Beecher appeared. Boudinot asked him if he had heard the word from the capital.

"No, what is it?" When Boudinot explained, the old man jumped up and clapped his hands. "God be praised!" he exclaimed, then ran from the room to tell the news to his family.[59]

Any doubts John Ridge had felt about the Cherokee situation were dispelled in the jubilation he experienced. His sentiment agreed with Boudinot's—that the decision represented "a great triumph on the part of the Cherokees so far as the question of their rights were concerned. The question is for ever settled as to who is right and who is wrong, and the controversy is exactly where it ought to be, and where we have all along been desirous it should be. It is not now before the great state of Georgia and the poor Cherokees, but between the U.S. and the State of Georgia, or between the friends of the judiciary and the enemies of the judiciary. We can only look and see whoever prevails in this momentous crisis."[60] Boudinot and Ridge were both convinced, in their joy and excitement, that the Supreme Court and its friends would win in the showdown with Georgia, and that such a victory would mean an automatic triumph for the Cherokees in their struggle with the state. Neither knew that, on hearing of the ruling, Jackson had in effect remarked, "John Marshall has made his decision; let him enforce it now if he can."[61]

And in fact the governor of Georgia refused to release the prisoners, and soon rumors of the president's attitude were abroad. Newspapers learned from gentlemen who had received the news from "authentic sources in Washington" that Jackson had determined not to enforce the Court's decision.* Moreover, a series of releases were advertised for appearance in the *Washington Globe* to prepare the public for the stand the president would take.[62] After appearances at Salem and Newburyport, where Boudinot could not speak because of illness, the two cousins returned in alarm to Washington.

Ridge, whose exhilaration had been brief, at once secured an audience at the White House. When he asked point-blank "whether the power of the United States would be exerted to execute the decision and put down the legislation of Georgia," the president brusquely replied that it would not. Jackson then pleaded earnestly for him "to go home and advise his people that their only hope of relief was in abandoning their country and removing to the West."[63] Ridge must have reacted visibly in Jackson's presence, for on April 9 the president wrote his crony, General Coffee, "I believe Ridge has expressed despair, and that it is better for them"—the Cherokees—"to treat and move."[64]

But Ridge could not reveal his changing heart immediately to his fellow Cherokees. At this point he still maintained his old position in letters to Ross and Stand Watie, Boudinot's younger brother. Yet Amos Kendall, a member of Jackson's kitchen cabinet and later a counsel for the Western Cherokees, wrote in collaboration with

---

*Even if Jackson had wanted to enforce Marshall's decision, existing federal law gave him no power to act in the present crisis. See Ronald N. Satz, *American Indian Policy in the Jacksonian Era*, pp. 49–50: "Enforcement of the decision in *Worcester* v. *Georgia* was impossible under existing law. As President Jackson himself observed, 'the decision of the supreme court has fell still born.'" Anti-Jacksonians, Satz continues, knew that the president was powerless to act but saw in the situation a perfect opportunity to impugn the administration's integrity.

Samuel C. Stambaugh that this was the moment Ridge reversed his stand: "Ridge left the President with the melancholy feeling that he had [heard] the truth. From that moment he was convinced that the only alternative to save his people from moral and physical death was to make the best terms they could with the government, and remove out of the limits of the States."[65]

The reversal of John Ridge's stand had the pattern and much of the intensity of a religious conversion. First had come doubts, suppressed into the depths of his being, and then the temporary reintensification of his old beliefs. There had followed the shock of newly perceived reality, in this case the apprehension of what must surely be the fate of his people if they should remain in their old domain under existing conditions—the inevitable degradation, even destruction—and what a shock that realization was, for Judge Underwood, son of a lawyer for both the missionaries and the Cherokees, later declared: "Ridge loved his people as ardently as O'Connell loved the Irish."[66] In his childhood his parents had dedicated him to the service of the people, an understanding he had never evaded, no matter how strong his personal ambition. What mattered most was the Cherokee people, a consideration always at the back of his mind; they could not be allowed to perish. Suddenly, at the critical moment, came the shift of his whole mental organization, swift and total, forever changing his outlook. As soon as Ridge had renounced the cause of antiremoval, he espoused the cause of emigration with equal fervor, with what might even be called fanaticism. "This conviction," according to Stambaugh and Kendall, "he did not fail to make known to his friends."[67] To his comfort he found that Boudinot was reacting in a similar manner, but such were the circumstances that neither could at once announce his change of mind to the world. Such a disclosure, before the time was right, would have destroyed their entire influence with the Cherokee people.

The delegation publicly maintained their antiremoval stand, but even Martin and Coodey were privately impressed with the futility of their position. One after another, supporters in Congress, men who had given the Cherokees their warmest encouragement, now advised that they could no longer render aid and comfort to the antiremoval cause. The time had come, they said, when the Cherokees could no longer hope to regain their rights in the East. They should seek to make the best bargain possible with the government and remove to the West. At the same time, the delegation was put in touch with John McLean, a justice of the Supreme Court and a sympathetic Westerner to whom they were disposed to listen "as to a wise man and a friend."[68]

McLean frankly confessed that the Court was prostrate before Jackson's inaction and that the Cherokee cause in the East was lost. He not only recommended treating with the United States, but he also offered to serve as a commissioner at any treaty council to help ensure that the Cherokees should receive the best terms possible. John Ridge secured his promise to put his offer in a letter to Ross, an act that was to win a condemnation as "one of the most consummate acts of treachery toward [the] country that the annals of any nation affords."[69] McLean had to leave for Cincinnati before reaching a definite agreement with the delegation, but they intimated their willingness to advise their people to treat. The judge went home feeling certain that, if he were given full powers, he could secure a treaty from the Cherokees by early summer.

Meanwhile hints of the delegation's change of mind were seeping into the Washington papers. Ridge felt it necessary to send, over his Cherokee name of Skah-tle-loh-skee,* a disclaimer to the *National Intelligencer*, in which he reaffirmed an antiremoval stand. On the same date General Daniel Newnan, congressman from Georgia privy to the conference with McLean, announced to the press that "the Cherokee Delegation [at Washington] have at last consented to recommend to their people to make a treaty with the government upon the general basis that they shall acquire a patent for lands over the Mississippi, and, at a proper time, be allowed a delegate in Congress"—a letter which produced consternation among the Cherokees when reprinted in the *Phoenix* by Stand Watie, who was substituting for Boudinot as editor. Boudinot, who had been sending his brother careful instructions on what to print and what to ignore, may have allowed the letter as a kind of trial balloon. Coodey, on the other hand, found it expedient publicly to scotch Newnan's statement in a communication to the *National Intelligencer*.[70]

In the meantime the general received the true sentiment of the delegation when he met Martin and Coodey on the street and asked them about Ridge's disclaimer. He learned, "from both of them, that the door to future negotiations was still open." They assured

---

*The Indian name of John Ridge is thus printed in the contemporary newspapers, but the editor's preface of *The Life and Adventures of Joaquin Murieta* by Yellow Bird (John R. Ridge) spells it as Ska-lee-los-kee.

him that the Cherokees would meet any commissioners the president might send to the nation, but "that no man in the United States would be more acceptable to them, as a negotiator, than Judge McLean."[71] When Secretary Cass called the delegation to his office on April 16, he offered them a treaty on such liberal terms that they could not help but express themselves as favorable to it.

It represented that a "sufficiently extensive and fertile" country should be marked out for the Cherokees west of Arkansas, in the lands where their brethren were now located, and that this country would be conveyed by patents under provisions of the Removal Act. The Cherokees would be allowed to conduct their own government there, to appoint an agent to look after their affairs in Washington, and to send a delegate to Congress, preparatory to their transforming their country into a territory. White persons, unless specifically authorized by law, were to be excluded from the new lands. The treaty would authorize specific modes of emigration to the new domain, and the Cherokees would be allowed to choose the mode that suited them best, severally or individually; moreover, the United States would be bound to subsist them for one year after their arrival at their destination.

The Cherokees would receive an annuity in proportion to the value of the cession they would make; in addition they would receive all annuities due them from former treaties. All improvements in the ceded territory would be appraised and paid for. Schools would be fostered in the new land, blacksmiths supported, and supplies of iron and steel furnished for the building of schoolhouses, churches, council houses, and homes for a few of the more important chiefs. Each male adult would receive a rifle, and each family "a quantity of blankets . . . together with axes, ploughs, hoes, wheels, cards, and looms." Livestock in the East would be appraised and paid for, provisions would be made for Cherokee orphans, and the United States would guarantee protection from the hostilities of other Indians in the new land.

As a final principle the secretary's statement read: "It is the wish of the President that all of your people should remove, and he is therefore unwilling that reservations of land should be made in the ceded territory."[72] If any such reservations should be found necessary, Jackson insisted that the holders must understand that they had to become citizens of the state in which they lived, and that all relations between them and the United States, based on their former circumstances as Indians, must come to an end.

The Cherokee delegation declined to carry such proposals home in person, however receptive their attitude. Cass then told them that he would send the propositions by a special emissary. Elisha Chester, one of the attorneys for the missionaries, was chosen for the task.

Any confirmation the delegation needed of their disposition to treat came in early May when Ridge received a letter from David Greene of the American Board of Commissioners for Foreign Missions. Greene had just had a talk with Chester, and from the interview was convinced that all political groups in Washington thought it impossible to protect the Cherokees further in their rights and immunities where they now lived; he was prepared to advise Ridge to enter into a treaty. "It makes me weep to think of it," Greene added. "But if your friends in Congress think that all further effort in your behalf will be useless . . . then, for aught I can see, you must make the best terms you can, & go."[73] The last bulwark of American support for the antiremoval stand of the Cherokees had fallen. Who could blame the delegation for feeling it necessary to treat? No one except the majority of the Cherokees themselves, who loved their homes and passionately resented any act leading toward their loss.

When the delegation left for home on May 15, 1832, they were apprehensive of their reception, which was indeed cool, suspicious as the Cherokees were at rumors of a possible treaty. The prevailing mood of the Indians, however, was one of joy at what they perceived as success of their cause. Runners had informed the people of the Supreme Court decision even in the remotest mountain coves, and most Cherokees believed that their rights had been restored and that soon the nation would be living on the same footing as before. They held "frolics" to celebrate the imagined victory over Georgia, and many who had enrolled for the West now fled into the coves and hollows of the mountains to avoid the U.S. enrolling agent, reneging on their decision to emigrate now that the Cherokee Nation, as they believed, was once again secure.[74]

John Ridge found his own family "exulting in the decision of the Supreme Court," wrote Stambaugh and Kendall, "and [he] mournfully told them their hopes were utterly delusive . . . that their nationality in the East was forever extinguished."[75]

Major Ridge, while riding about the nation, had himself concluded that the plight of his countrymen was worse than ever. When he heard of Jackson's stand, he felt more apprehension for the Cherokee cause. He listened attentively to John's defense of his new-found creed—that there was no hope for the United States honoring its treaty obligations to protect the Cherokees from the encroachments of Georgia, no hope for the reinstatement of Cherokee law within the limits of the state, nor for the reinstallment of Cherokee government. The Cherokees, like many a tribe before them, could not expect to survive under state jurisdiction; they would be crushed by racial oppression if they stayed in the East, and if they would save themselves, they must emigrate west, under the terms of the federal government. Never would those terms be more generous than at the present time, ran the assurances of staunch friends in exalted places, assurances that John Ridge had accepted and for which he now argued eloquently. It would grieve him to leave the country of his birth, the country he loved so dearly, but his new stand placed the exile's lot before the ruin of his people.

It was not easy for Major Ridge to change his mind about removal, the course against which he had worked so long and hard, but the logic of John's arguments finally prevailed, and The Ridge was persuaded that the time had come for the Cherokees to treat and remove, to buy time as a separate and distinct community in the West,* where with ever more education they could meet the whites on an equal footing. Father and son were once again of a single mind as they turned their faces toward a worrisome future.

*In his remarkable letter to Albert Gallatin, in February–March, 1826, John Ridge predicted that in fifty years, "if not destroyed," the Cherokees would amalgamate with the whites of the United States. But as the Cherokee crisis intensified, the Ridges came like Boudinot to reject any early amalgamation and assimilation as the answer to the Cherokee dilemma. They became ardent Cherokee nationalists, believing that the salvation of their people and the progress of "civilization" among them could be retained only by their cohering in "a separate and distinct community." "As long as we continue as a people in a body, with our internal regulations," Boudinot summarized as a treaty spokesman, "we can [go on improving] in civilization and respectability." Only removal made it possible to so continue, the emigration leaders insisted: Only in the West could the Cherokees hope to retain their national identity—hence the necessity of their moving there, to remain as Cherokees indefinitely. For a cogent assessment of the spirit of nationalism that underlay the position of the treaty leaders, see Theda Perdue's introduction to *Cherokee Editor: The Writings of Elias Boudinot.*

10 • MANEUVERS OF DESPERATION

O N returning from Washington the Cherokee delegation had publicly favored calling a special council to consider the treaty proposals brought by Elisha Chester. Ross preferred to sidestep such proceedings. He told the emissary that he opposed the treaty and that most of the Cherokees supported his stand.[1] Only a small number of the more perceptive Indians, mostly mixed bloods, saw the handwriting on the wall. They favored giving Chester a hearing.

Their sentiment was recognized by the executive council, which voted in favor of a special council. It was decided to convene one on July 23, 1832, four days after a day of prayer and fasting that Ross had called. As Chatooga was not considered central enough for the people at large, they located the meeting place at Red Clay, just north of the Tennessee border out of the legal range of the Georgia guard. John Ridge stood in favor of returning the seat of government to New Echota, feeling that such a move might work in favor of a treaty. Major Ridge concurred in John's opinion and spoke in favor of New Echota. But his proposal was voted down, and the council was convened at Red Clay.[2]

The people collected at a large park between two lines of hills. It was watered by four springs and covered with woods, open beneath, since the undergrowth had been burned away in previous years. A rough shed served as a council house, to the east of which stood a grove of oaks where the chiefs often gathered to smoke their pipes.

No doubt the scene presented much the same appearance as that observed by a visitor to a later council. George William Featherstonhaugh, an Englishman, wrote:

Nothing more Arcadian could be conceived than the picture . . . presented, but the most impressive feature, and that which imparted life to the whole, was an increasing current of Cherokee Indians, men, women, youths, and children moving about in every direction, and in the greatest order; and all, except the younger ones, preserving a grave and thoughtful demeanor. . . . An observer could not but sympathize deeply with them; they were not to be confounded with the wild savages of the West, being decently dressed after the manner of white people, with shirts, trousers, shoes and stockings, whilst the half-breeds and their descendants conformed in everything to the custom of the whites, spoke as good English as [they], and differed from them only in a browner complexion, and in being less vicious and more sober. The pure bloods had red and blue cotton handkerchiefs on their heads in the manner of turbans, and some of these, who were mountaineers from the elevated districts of North Carolina, wore also deerskin leggings and embroidered hunting shirts; whilst their turbans, their dark coarse lank hair, their listless savage gait, and their swarthy Tarter countenances reminded me of the Arabs from Barbary. Many of these men were athletic and good-looking.[3]

Feeling ran high. The time had come to elect a new government, but in view of Georgia's threats against the Cherokees' exercise of government functions, the council decided against a national election. Instead, it passed a resolution continuing the same chiefs, legislative members and executive council in office. The measure was not generally popular. Numerous Cherokees believed passionately in national elections and thought that one should soon be held, whatever the risk. Many murmured in protest against the measure to continue Ross indefinitely as principal chief, and it did much to turn the Ridges against him, for they felt he had designed a subterfuge to deny them a hearing when they had urgent things to tell the people.[4] However strongly the Ridges had supported Ross in the past, a rivalry now sprang up between them, leading to much ill feeling, especially between Ross and John Ridge, who was full of confidence in himself and believed himself the ablest leader the Cherokees had produced. It was his firm opinion that his abilities and education gave him higher qualifications than Ross to serve as principal chief, and he resented being deprived of the chance to run for the office. Indeed, his opinion of Ross would in time approach that of Governor Lumpkin, who was to write in his memoirs that "Ross, when compared with such men as John Ridge and Elias Boudinot, [was] a mere pigmy."[5]

Futilely the Ridges and Boudinot and a few others raised their voices in favor of emigration; they were lonely figures surrounded by intense hostility. Ross used General Newnan's letter to whip sentiment against them and against other Washington delegates. A copy of it, clipped from a newspaper, was posted to a tree trunk for all to see. Cherokees clustered about it, and it was the object of bitter speculation. Chester wrote:

This was used to induce the populace to believe that [the delegation] had been bribed, and that they had entered into some arrangement with the Government, without any authority. Their influence, on which I calculated largely, was thus entirely prostrated, and the clamor raised upon the subject was well calculated to prevent all calm reflection upon the real situation and interest of their nation. It was in vain that they demanded an inquiry into their conduct; no opportunity was conceded them for making their defence. Thus circumstanced, they thought it would be worse than useless for them, at this time, to press the subject of a treaty upon the people who have long been accustomed to regard the advocating a sale of their country as the blackest crime.[6]

The acrimonious feelings produced by the report of the Washington delegates was so intense that Ross prevented a detailed account of it from running in the *Phoenix*. He was opposed to publicizing any divergence from the antiremoval point of view, insisting on what he called "*unity of sentiment and action* for the good of all."[7] With the Cherokee press thus muzzled, Boudinot did not hesitate to resign as editor. He took the action partly because he felt he had accomplished all he could in that position and partly in protest against the pressures brought against his speaking his mind in the present crisis.

"Were I to continue as editor," Boudinot informed Ross in his letter of resignation on August 1, "I should feel myself in a most peculiar and delicate position." He did not know whether he could, at one time, satisfy both his own views and the views of the Cherokee authorities. He believed it was the duty of every citizen to reflect upon the dangers which beset the nation, to weigh such matters, and come to a definite conclusion on what should be done in the last alternative. "I could not consent to be conductor of the paper without having the right and privilege of discussing these important matters; and from what I have seen and heard, were I to assume that privilege, my usefulness would be paralyzed by being considered, as I have already been, an enemy to the interests of my country and my people."[8]

Ross accepted the resignation, though Boudinot agreed to remain at the helm for another month while a search was made for someone to replace him. The talent hunt could not have been easy, for Ross needed not only an able editor but also one who shared his views, and already much of the brains and education of the Cherokees had gravitated into the thin and scattered ranks of the treaty advocates. Finally Ross's brother-in-law, Elijah Hicks, who constantly took his cue from Ross himself, was chosen to fill the vacancy.

Meanwhile the council proceeded in an atmosphere of bitterness. The seventeen-point proposal presented by Chester, of whom the Cherokees had grave doubts (had he not lived for years in Georgia?), was read and interpreted. With the Ridges and their sympathizers overwhelmed, the proposals were rejected, and the vote was carried to make the rejection unanimous. There was nothing the treaty advocates could do, if they hoped to retain enough influence to gain ground for their cause, but to accept the majority decision. Thus, Major Ridge and John were among the signers of the letter to the secretary of war on August 6, to call his attention to former decisions of the nation on the subject of a treaty "and to inform the President that the sentiments of the Cherokee people remain[ed] the same."[9]

Meanwhile, true to prediction, Jackson made no move to enforce the Supreme Court's decision, and Georgia proceeded with plans to finish the survey of Cherokee lands begun the year before. During the first campaign the surveyors had portioned the country into divisions of nine square miles. Now since April, 550 surveyors had overrun the land to carve it into plots of 160 acres apiece—except in the gold fields, where each plot comprised 40 acres—all to be distributed by lottery when the survey was completed. It was true that the surveyors, moving through woods with ax and chain, were improvements on whiskey peddlers and pony clubs. The rank and file of the Indians refused to take them seriously as they blazed trees and left strange numbers on the blazes, and jokes about such marks made their way into the *Phoenix;* but John Ridge and Boudinot, not to mention Major Ridge, knew that they spelled the coming defeat of the Cherokees, their certain expulsion from the lands of their fathers.[10]

If the reversal of John Ridge's attitude concerning removal bore a pattern similar to that of religious conversion, the upheavals of feeling in Major Ridge were associated with an actual conversion.

The Ridge had long been the object of Moravian prayers, and one day in 1830, in his concern, he had gone to Brother Clauder, who had filled the vacancy at Oothcaloga left by Father Gambold's death, and said, "My brother Watie and my friend William Hicks both belong to your church, but I am still a bad man." Later he added, "I was a young man when the first missionaries came into this country; they are gone now, yet I am still here. I am old now, and my head is turning gray and I cannot live many more years. . . . Many of my countrymen are now Christians; they no longer drink, and are better men than they were before; I too want to seek the good now!"[11] Brother Clauder had accepted him for "careful instruction," but after two years it was reported to Dr. Butler, still in prison, that The Ridge would enter the Presbyterian Church after the next communion, and not the Moravian. According to one historian, "Major Ridge was baptized in 1832."[12]

His new-found faith seemed to intensify his conviction of the necessity for removal. As the summer of 1832 slipped into autumn he worked sedulously with his small band of sympathizers to win more Cherokees in favor of a treaty, and in the midst of such endeavors he found the motives of the treaty advocates savagely impugned.[13] John Ross would soon be writing in transparent allusion: "A man who will forsake his country . . . in time of adversity . . . is no more than a traitor and should be viewed—and shunned as such."[14] In the *Phoenix*, Elijah Hicks issued a blast at Boudinot's patriotism, and Boudinot struck back in defense of both himself and his associates. He proclaimed that his patriotism—and by implication theirs—consisted in both "the love of country, and the *love of the people.*"

These are inseparable if the people are made the first victim, for in that case the country must go also, and there must be an end of the objects of patriotism. But if the country is lost, or is likely to be lost to all human appearance, and the people still exist, may I not, with a patriotism true and commendable, make a *question* for the safety of the remaining object of my affection?

In applying the above definition of patriotism to my conduct, I can but say that I have come to the unpleasant and most disagreeable conclusion . . . that our lands, or a large part of them are about to be seized and taken from us. Now, as a friend of my people, I cannot say *peace, peace*, when there is no peace. I cannot ease their minds with any expectation of a calm, when the vessel is already tossed to and fro, and threatened to be shattered to pieces by an approaching tempest. If I really believe there is danger, I must act consistently, and give alarm; tell our countrymen our true, or what I believe to be our true, situation.[15]

Well, there *was* danger, Boudinot maintained; it was "'immediate and appalling,' and it becomes the people of this country," he contended, "to weigh the matter rightly, act wisely, not rashly, and choose a course that will come nearest benefiting the nation."[16] That course in the final consideration must be removal, the object of Boudinot and the Ridges and the small faction coming into being about them. They were no traitors, this nascent treaty faction; their leaders acted, in the words of their defenders, "not for the injury of their nation, but to save it from further calamities, [perhaps even] from utter extinction."[17]

But their accomplishment was minimal that summer and autumn of 1832. Although the treaty leaders attracted a few additional men of talent and intelligence to their views, John Ross swayed the mass of the Cherokees, who accepted his word as gospel. What Ross told them—that the land could be, and would be, saved—coincided with their deepest desire, and the treaty advocates found themselves crushingly outnumbered when, on October 8, the regular council was convened at Red Clay. The incessant rains delayed Ross's arrival, but when on the second day he read his message to the assembled crowd, in a dry, matter-of-fact voice, his antiremoval line met with enthusiastic approval. Chester, more distrusted than ever by the Cherokee masses, was again present with the proposals from Washington, plus a letter from Secretary Cass. The unpopular emissary repeated the arguments he had used before. In addition, he explained how the imminent Georgia lottery would work. But the whole subject proved unwelcome to the Cherokees, fired as they were with Ross's address and their never-waning love of the land; and after a scant debate the council again rejected the American proposals.

Though Major Ridge was the most powerful orator in the nation, a kind of channel for the Cherokee folk spirit, he felt that now only educated leaders, with white men's skills, had the best right to govern his people, and so he was content to allow his son to step before him as leader of the treaty advocates. John's talents as an orator were no match for Major Ridge's; nevertheless he was a moving speaker, more fluent and emotional than John Ross, with the added advantage that he could address the people readily in their native tongue. Ross's speeches had to be turned into Cherokee by a native "linkster."

John Ross, painted by John Neagle circa 1848. Courtesy of Philbrook Art Center, Tulsa, Oklahoma.

John Ridge now begged the Cherokees to heed the voice of reason and go west before their plight became unendurable. With a skillful parliamentary maneuver he secured a reconsideration of the vote on Chester's proposals and offered a resolution to send a delegation to Washington with the authority to make a treaty of removal. Rejecting his resolution, the council voted instead to send a delegation composed of majority leaders—Richard Taylor, John F. Baldridge, and Joseph Vann, with Ross as chief counselor—to attend to the affairs of the nation before the federal government. Though ostensibly beaten, the treaty advocates yet considered the turn of events a sort of victory. As Chester informed Cass, they thought a treaty would be a "certain result" if matters were managed right by the War Department.[18]

On October 22, 1832, even before the council had adjourned, the wheels of the Georgia lottery began to roll, and "fortunate drawers" started to draw their prizes.[19] While the wheels turned, the Ridges went by invitation to a Creek council—one marked by bitterness and violence—in order to encourage the neighboring nation to emigrate before their situation deteriorated further (for the sooner the Creeks went west, they reasoned, the sooner the Cherokees would agree to follow: their advice to the Creeks on this occasion was conditioned, as it had usually been, by the exigencies of Cherokee politics).[20] They had hardly returned from the Creek country in November, 1832, when news arrived that the lottery wheels had ceased to spin while Georgia officials investigated charges of fraud hurled at Shadrach Bogan, the commissioner who supervised the lottery in Milledgeville.

It was found that Bogan had enjoyed ample opportunity for a sleight of hand in his own advantage. Boys at each wheel handed tickets bearing the drawn names and prizes to a manager, who gave them, in turn, to Bogan, who was seated in the center of the operation. It was his task to paste the names and prizes together, back to back, and then to file them. On investigation it was learned that to slips of five of the richest prizes drawn on a certain day he had pasted names in handwriting different from that of the clerk who had recorded the names on the rest of the tickets. It developed that the penmanship on the slips in question was Bogan's own and that the names were those of certain friends and relatives whose chances he had purchased. One of the prizes was the house and 160 acres of the John Ridge plantation.[21]

Bogan was tried and dismissed from office, his civil rights denied

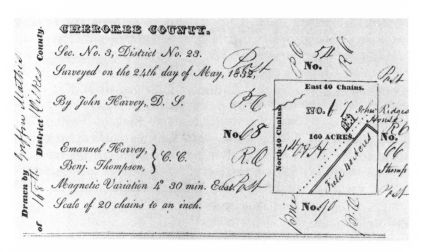

Georgia lottery record for John Ridge's home place. Courtesy of the Georgia Department of Archives and History.

him for twenty years. Concerning the crime, the *Phoenix* printed a comment from the *New York Spectator* that it was a mistake to denounce Bogan's offense, as a Georgia paper had done, as "one of the most stupendous frauds ever practiced on any community." The *Spectator* thought it trifling "compared with the *fraud* in which the Government of Ga. [was] engaged against the Cherokee community."[22] Meanwhile the five prizes appropriated by Bogan had been replaced in the lottery and drawn again. The plot containing John Ridge's house—plot No. 67, of the 23rd District of the 3rd Section —was finally granted to a Georgian named Griffin Mathis, whereas Major Ridge's house on plot No. 196 of the same district, was drawn by a Revolutionary War widow named Rachel Fergason.[23] Both of the Ridges were allowed to remain temporarily on their property. In fact, owing to their support of the emigration proposals, the governor of Georgia would soon guarantee them from eviction, along with Boudinot, until such time as they should move to the West. Governor Lumpkin requested the U.S. enrolling agent to "assure Boudinot, Ridge, and their friends of state protection under any circumstances." The governor felt that it was his "imperative duty" to "afford them every security which our laws will justify or authorize."[24] Specifically, the Georgia legislature ruled The Ridge's ferry immune from white encroachment. Only a few Cherokees received such special protection, and the favor shown the Ridges and

Boudinot was a factor that led many Cherokees vehemently to resent their behavior and think of them as traitors "bought" by the state of Georgia.*

As the lottery progressed, "fortunate drawers" descended over the nation like crows on a cornfield. They passed and repassed, according to the *Phoenix*, "single and in companies, not unlike John Gilpin's race to the country seat, in search of the splendid lots which the rolling wheel had pictured to their imaginations. Ho sir! Where is the nearest line to this place, what district, number, corner, lot, station, etc., are the impertinent questions forced upon us. When we see the palefaces again, they are closely viewing the marked trees and carved posts."[25] Some were not content merely to investigate, but came as intruders, ready to evict, for no Indian could testify against them in a Georgia court, and the evictions were legion, without reproof from the Georgia guard. Such intruders did not include the most prepossessing elements of the Georgia citizenry. An English observer would soon find them "tall, thin, cadaverous-looking animals, . . . as melancholy and lazy as boiled codfish, and when they dragged themselves about, [they] formed a striking contrast to some of the swarthy, athletic-looking Cherokees."[26] Another commentator speculated that they were victims of poor diet.

*In 1837, Boudinot claimed that Ross partisans had repeatedly accused the treaty leaders of being "interested persons," that is, of being "*bought* or *bribed*, and hence . . . subservien[t] to the Government." "And where is your proof?" he inquired of Ross in refuting the charges (Perdue, *Cherokee Editor*, pp. 201 ff.). Indeed there *is* no proof, in either "official records or other reputable authority." Grant Foreman claimed that "years of diligent search" had uncovered not "the slightest taint of dishonesty in the lives of Stand Watie, Boudinot, or the Ridges" (*A History of Oklahoma*, p. 143). More specifically, he claimed that there was "no evidence that the [treaty] signers [had] received financial rewards for their acts" (*The Five Civilized Tribes*, p. 423). My own efforts to pinpoint any corrupt practice by "Ridge & Co." have been equally unsuccessful. The only sensible conclusion is that accusations of bribery lodged by the Ross faction and their sympathizers were based on groundless suspicion.

Likewise, subsequent charges by the Treaty Party and others that Ross had "lined his pockets from the Removal" had no basis in fact. Foreman, finding no evidence of dishonesty on Ross's part, declared: "The intimation that Ross profited at the expense of the nation was a fiction growing out of the bitter feeling of the times" (*Chronicles of Oklahoma*, XII [1934]: 307). Nor could Moulton find any misappropriations by Ross in a careful review of his personal finances and those of the Cherokee nation. Doubtless Hitchcock (*A Traveler in Indian Territory*, p. 234) put his finger on a principal cause for questions when he noted: "It is unfortunate for [Ross's] reputation that several of his relatives, particularly his brother Lewis, have realized fortunes through his instrumentality, though it is fair to consider that this may have resulted from contracts properly made."

With such an invasion the lot of the Indians could only worsen. "The usual scenes which our afflicted people experience are dreadfully increased since your departure," John Ridge wrote to Ross in Washington in February, 1833: "they are robbed & whipped by the whites almost every day." Not even Ross himself would escape harassment, for before the crisis could run its course, he would ride home to the Head of Coosa to find his house and ferry and flocks of peacocks in the clutches of a stranger, who would even demand his horse. His sick wife, Quatie, and their children were crowded into two inadequate rooms, and his protests would be of no avail. All he could do was to take his family and move across the line into Tennessee and settle in a rough log cabin close to Red Clay.[27]

The invasion of the lottery winners distressed the Cherokees and disorganized their ways of life more than anything that had occurred before. Though the Indian farmers went on plowing and sowing, they were agonizingly aware that intruders, perhaps already on their way to the Cherokee Nation, might harvest what they had planted. What the Ridges saw in 1833 only confirmed their conviction that removal was the only solution to the Cherokee dilemma; yet though a treaty party was slowly growing, they put high value on national unity. Trusting that John Ross would change his stand and declare himself in favor of a treaty and that the masses could be won to their views, they rejected the divisive moves of John Walker, Jr., a malcontent chief whom the president had invited to Washington for manipulation as a foil against the official delegation.

In his letter to Ross of February, 1833, John Ridge mentioned certain Cherokees whom Walker had asked to accompany him thither. But the "aforesaid Gentlemen" were "too high-minded and patriotic" to acknowledge Walker as their leader. There was no doubt that Ross would see Walker there, Ridge added. "In this movement I attach no consequence so far as that individual is concerned, but it affords to my mind a clear view of the extent that Jackson will go to divide our nation." He then proceeded to give Ross earnest advice:

Let me urge it upon your consideration & that of every individual composing the Delegation to consult the best lights upon the Indian question at Washington. I have not room to say much, & it may be that the discussion of this subject may be disagreeable to you. But Sir, I have the right to address you as the Chief of the whole Cherokee nation upon whom rests, under Heaven, the highest responsibility — the well being of the whole people, and . . . I know you are capable of acting the part of a statesman in this trying crisis of our affairs. After we all know upon consultation in Council that we can't be a Nation here, I hope we shall attempt to establish [ourselves] somewhere else. *Where*, the wisdom of the nation must try to find.[28]

Nothing had changed when Ross returned, though the delegates had enjoyed two interviews with the president and frequent conferences with Secretary Cass and had seen much of Senator Theodore Frelinghuysen, who had informed them of the Mission Board's decision in Boston to accept a pardon for Worcester and Butler and to advise the Cherokees to emigrate. Frelinghuysen had also counseled removal, and conversations with Cass and the president had always returned to that alternative. Jackson had offered $2.5 million for the Cherokee domain in the East, in addition to an exchange of land in the West, and then had raised the offer to $3 million. Ross had declined, for as he had declared, the gold mines were alone worth more than such a sum. Besides, if the president could afford the Cherokees no protection in Georgia, how could he guarantee it to them in the West?[29]

The Ridges felt deep annoyance at learning of the thin results of Ross's negotiations, especially his refusal to consider the $3 million offered by the president for Cherokee lands. They were skeptical of the rumor spreading to the effect that a bribe of $50,000 had been offered Ross in Washington if he would conclude a treaty—a rumor that Ross himself or some of his close associates had apparently set in motion to fan the prejudice of the Cherokees against the federal government.[30] The Ridges were also skeptical of the construction that Ross now placed on a letter received from Elbert Herring, commissioner of Indian affairs, concerning the plague of white men in the nation. Herring had promised that a military force would forthwith "be sent to the assailed parts of your country for the purpose of expelling and keeping out intruders."[31] In jubilation Ross had interpreted the phrase "assailed parts of your country" to include Georgia, and owing to crossed wires in the War Department, such might well have been the original intent. At any rate Ross circulated the letter far and wide, with his broad construction; the Cherokees took hope in the promise of relief; and a rumor began to spread that Jackson had changed his mind, that he had instructed federal agents to purchase the claims of lottery winners, and that the Cherokees would be allowed to remain in their ancient homeland.[32]

John Ridge, however, refused to accept Herring's letter as Ross construed it. He acted on his skepticism and wrote to Secretary Cass to ask if Ross's sanguine interpretation could be correct.

According to the reading of that letter, it is considered by many that the views of the Executive may have undergone a change and that the action of this force will not be confined to any particular portion of our country, but that its blessings will be felt throughout. Under this view of the subject, considering the peculiar and unhappy condition of our people, it will not be a matter of surprise to you to learn that this favorable prospect has been hailed with feelings of much joy and gratulations. Aware, Sir, how much we trespass upon your time, we most respectfully enquire whether our "Great Father" has thus kindly thought of us, and will thus kindly exercise those paternal feelings which some of the undersigned have often heard him express toward the Cherokees.[33]

Major Ridge added his mark to his son's query, and William S. Coodey, William Hicks, and a relative of Susanna Ridge, named John Fields, added their signatures.

The reply that Cass directed Herring to make on May 1 was received by the younger Ridge at Red Clay, where the called council had met. He learned that "no change whatever [had] taken place in the opinions of the President" and that Jackson believed the immediate removal of the Cherokees, "in conformity with the very liberal terms held out to them," offered "the only prospect of their permanent and prosperous establishment."[34] And whatever Herring's original intent, it was now made clear that the promise applied only to intruders in states that had not extended their laws over the Indians. In other words the promise related only to intruders in Tennessee and North Carolina, where they were scarcely a problem. It did not cover the lottery winners of Georgia or even the citizens of Alabama and so was virtually useless to the Cherokees.

If John Ridge thought that by calling Ross's interpretation of Herring's letter into question he could discountenance the course of the principal chief, he was wrong. Ross had told the Cherokees what they wanted to hear, and they refused to find fault. Instead, it was Ridge who lost ground with them for going over the chief's head. No matter that his own construction of Herring's letter had proved correct. The *Phoenix* of Elijah Hicks branded his deed as "a consummate act of treachery" and accused "Mr. Ridge & Co." of influencing the secretary of war to modify a policy that would have worked for Cherokee good.[35]

The council at Red Clay, where John Ridge had read the reply from the Indian Office, proceeded with dramatic tensions. During the course of debate, according to Benjamin F. Currey, enrolling agent, Ridge "depicted, in an eloquent and impressive manner, the forlorn situation of the country."[36] According to another report, he "advocated a treaty, and with great force and effect urged the propriety of it, and was opposed to any long and unnecessary delay."[37] Ross's nephew Coodey presented a petition of protest against the course pursued by Ross and his associates. It was addressed to both houses of Tsalagi Tinilawigi and was signed by twenty-five treaty advocates, including Major Ridge, Boudinot, and Stand Watie. John Ridge and David Vann, as members of the National Committee, did not put their signatures to it, though both were present when it was framed, but they were pledged to support its measures when it came before the council. Among other matters, it demanded that Ross explain the reasons behind his perseverance in a devious course of delay—a course which promised, in the opinion of the signers, "everything but a speedy and favorable adjustment of existing difficulties."[38]

When the petition was discussed before the executive council, a division of opinion lasted for two days, with Ross and Lowrey taking one side and Coodey and The Ridge the other. "This discussion resulted in a compromise," Currey reported. Ross and Lowrey agreed that if the matter were not pressed before the present assembly, they would give the petition a full answer at the October council, where they expected "an immense concourse of people," and they promised to be governed afterward by their decision.[39]

A number of the treaty advocates, especially Walker, were opposed to granting Ross any "indulgences"—so much so that, when such was done, they could not be prevailed upon to remain on the council ground. The Ridge, however, thought it prudent to agree with Ross's request. For one thing, their supporters were growing in numbers, and they believed that the numbers would swell further as the country became more settled by whites. They could afford, then, to compromise with Ross for the sake of unity. But to circumvent any further pretext on Ross's part the treaty advocates requested that an exploring party be sent west to examine the country offered by the United States and make a report to the council.[40]

On May 20, as the council was preparing to adjourn, it adopted a set of resolutions that Ross had drafted complaining of the evasive answers of the secretary of war to a memorial submitted to him in Washington. Ross proposed that the memorial be forwarded to Congress as well, in hope that its reception there would be more favorable. The resolutions, which were highly critical of the U.S. government, "were not spread upon the Journals," according to Currey's report, whereupon John Ridge demanded they be made of record. He received Ross's consent, but his attention was diverted for a moment toward his father, who addressed a crowd in the adjoining grove. "Judge Taylor snatched the resolutions from the clerk's table." He joined John Ross, and they rode off, leaving no trace of the resolutions except in the memory of those present. Whatever else, the incident was a good example of the dissension between the factions.

"Old Major Ridge," Currey continued, "is the greatest orator in the nation; he dismissed the meeting, after giving it a concise and well arranged history of their present condition compared with what it had been; the probability of their being called upon in a few months, for the last time, to say whether they will submit always to the evils and difficulties every day increasing around them, or look for a new home, promising them freedom and national prosperity; advising them to bury party animosity, and in case they should conclude to seek a new home, to go in the character of true friends and brothers."[41]

No matter how emphatically Major Ridge might advocate the burial of factional tensions, they had mounted too high for conflicts to be avoided. Scarcely a month had gone by before violence erupted practically on his doorstep. It began at a nearby ball-play, where an antitreaty Indian picked a quarrel with John Fields, calling him a traitor and saying he ought to be killed. The argument reached a peak of intensity on the road, where a friend of Fields attacked the antitreaty man and knocked him senseless. Fields and his friend then went to Lavender's Store, where they were found by the associates of the wounded man. In the melee that followed, the ally of Fields was knocked unconscious with a ball stick, and Fields himself was carved "nearly into pieces." In trying to part the fighters Major Ridge's Negro, Peter, also received two slashes from the knife. In reporting the affair the *Western Herald,* at the gold town of Auraria, could infer that there existed such "hostile feeling between the two parties ... that they [were] disposed to manifest it, towards each other, upon every occasion." After the fray Major Currey had the antitreaty aggressors arrested and "bound over to appear at the Floyd circuit court to answer for their misconduct. This was considered necessary," he added in his report to the Indian Office, "to insure the future safety" of those who favored emigration.[42]

It saddened Major Ridge to see such rancor develop when the ultimate aims of both factions were identical—the well-being of the Cherokee people. General R. G. Dunlap of Tennessee recognized this truth as he traveled across the nation. He wrote to Jackson: "I have conversed freely with John Ridge, the leader of the treaty party, and with John Ross, who is on the opposite [and the] dominant side. I do sincerely believe that the ultimate views of both these men are the same in regard to the final destiny of their nation. They both have enlarged or enlightened views and their whole energies are bent on the establishment of their nation on certain immovable principles, such as will eventually redeem their countrymen from the savage to the civilized life." Yet however their ultimate goals might coincide, they seemed with each passing day to diverge more as regards the means. "Hence," as General Dunlap put the matter with firm insight and shaky grammar, "each are catching at everything to weaken the other, and gain or keep the ascendency, for the furtherance of their ends."[43]

John Ridge asked the general to pass a suggestion privately to Jackson: that a request from the president himself for the Cherokees to send an exploring party west might help to dispel some of the prejudice felt by the masses against the western lands. And another suggestion: Might not the United States ease its efforts for a while to enroll Cherokees for the West since it could be demonstrated that such emigration siphoned off the treaty party's main support? The general obliged; he even unsealed his letter so that John Ridge might read what he had written.

The immediate objective of the Ridges was to sway the October council to send a delegation to Washington empowered to treat, and with that purpose they journeyed to Red Clay, where the council convened on the fourteenth. It was a boisterous assembly. Ross read his address on the state of the nation, answering the May petition and admitting that the resolutions forwarded to Cass had received no satisfactory answer. But in the picture of gloom he painted was one bright ray—the fact that courts of Alabama had found the laws unconstitutional which the state had extended over the Indian lands. Though the division between the factions had only deepened, the Ridges were ready still to agree with Ross's plea that, when differences occurred, "the sentiments of the majority should prevail, and whatever measure is adopted by the majority for the public good . . . the duty of the minority [should be] to yield and unite in support of the measure."[44] Thus Ross erred in reacting so vehemently against the Ridges as a disloyal menace to Cherokee unity. Had he treated them more as "loyal opposition," he might have effectively neutralized the slow but tangible growth of their influence. But try as they might to make that influence felt at this time, they failed to induce the council to choose a delegation favorable to removal and clothe it with power to treat.

Instead, the council named a deputation from the antitreaty party—or National Party, as it was now called—with John Ross at its head. In spite of that defeat John Ridge sat as chairman of the select committee that drafted the report under whose terms the deputation was to proceed to Washington. The report said nothing of a treaty, but approved the appointment of "a Delegation in whose wisdom and integrity we can confide to carry the subject of our difficulties [before] the legislative branch of the General Government, and if possible to draw from it a favorable Resolution for the relief of our afflicted Nation."[45]

A close observer of the situation noted the difference in tone between the report and prior utterances of John Ridge and accounted for it on the grounds that he feared to speak out what he thought before the people, lest he should incur persecution from the stronger party. But there was a limit beyond which Ridge could not be pressed. He balked when Ross presented a power of attorney at the close of the council and requested that members of both houses sign it. Ridge objected that the instrument was intended to mislead U.S. officials into believing that the delegation was clothed with powers to treat, when in reality it was not. Ross acknowledged that such was his intention and justified it by saying that, after what had happened, the delegation would not be able to "elicit the views of the Executive in relation to their affairs" without such a show. All but Ridge signed the document. Major Currey at once reported Ross's breach of faith to Washington, and even before the delegation departed the Ridges registered their disgust at "Ross's duplicity" by enrolling for emigration along with Boudinot and David Watie.[46]

Meanwhile unrest increased throughout the nation, especially after a natural spectacle that filled many with fear and dread. At three o'clock in the morning on November 13, 1833, dazzling showers of meteors began to blaze across the sky. Later, when the morning star had risen, the showers increased to such intensity that, according to the *Phoenix*, "the world was literally striped with fire." The editor professed to leave to the astronomers "the causes of this profusion of lights."[47] Such sage advice, however, failed to allay the fears of the ignorant, persistent fears which lingered on for weeks and weeks; numerous Cherokees looked back upon the falling stars as a dire portent of the future, as well they might, had they known of certain facts: how in Washington the president gave Ross no encouragement in the struggle with Georgia, how most friends of the Cherokees thought a refusal to treat and a misguided attempt to remain in the ancient homeland would only result in "ruin inevitable" for the nation,[48] and how Ross was trying in every way to keep such knowledge from his people.

Soon a delegation went to Washington representing those Cherokees who had enrolled for emigration—a deputation of "Kitchen Chiefs," as they were labeled by the *Phoenix*.[49] They had no authority from the nation, and spoke only for the emigrating faction. Many who had enrolled for the West had met at the agency in December. They had elected William Hicks as their principal chief and John McIntosh as the assistant. Then an ad hoc committee had chosen eight delegates to proceed to Washington with instructions that Hicks and the assistant chief had signed on January 14, 1834. The delegation was thereby requested to unite with John Ross's deputation "for the purpose of effecting a general arrangement or treaty with the United States upon the basis proposed by the Secretary of War." If, however, no union could be formed with the national delegation, the emigration delegates were instructed "to effect a treaty for the present Emigrants & followers & those Emigrants who [had] preceded them." In doing so they were to secure as much land in the West as possible, "together with all the other advantages, privileges & annuities embraced in the propositions."[50] But before the eight could depart, the question of expenses had depleted their ranks so that only three actually went to Washington: T. J. Pack, John West, and Andrew Ross. John Ross thus found his brother an annoying thorn in his side.

The emigration delegates were received coldly by the national delegation, which rejected their plea for unity, but they were cordially welcomed by the War Department. In reporting their meeting with Jackson, however, the *Phoenix* could gloat that "they were found by the President to be destitute of the science of government."[51] The chief executive was not averse to reaching an agreement with a minority, but he wanted to deal with more knowing and sophisticated agents, ones who would hold more prestige with the Cherokee people. Andrew Ross agreed to return to the nation and bring back "a few of the chiefs or respectable individuals" that Jackson wished to deal with, and Elbert Herring made it clear that the U.S. government would pay their traveling expenses.[52]

Back in the nation Andrew Ross held a hushed conclave with the Ridges. Major Ridge agreed to go to Washington with him, along with Boudinot and James Starr. This move aroused much indignation among the people. Some fifty men of the Coosawatie district signed a protest against their going, denying The Ridge and Boudinot any authority whatsoever, and they had secretly to change their route in order to avoid an ambush laid to halt them.[53] But their presence in the capital added distinction to the emigration delegation. Among those they impressed was former Governor Gilmer, now a senator from Georgia. "Major Ridge," he wrote, "spoke English so badly that he conversed . . . through an interpreter. He was a very large man, with features indicative of clear perceptions. His conduct was dignified, and his whole demeanor distinguished for propriety. He was the noblest specimen I ever saw of an Indian uncrossed with the blood of the whites."[54]

While Major Ridge was thus available to sit to a portrait painter, it was decided that his likeness should help to dignify the gallery walls of the Indian Office. His portrait was painted, head and shoulders—the picture of an obvious gentleman, in a blue coat, a buff vest, and a high-collared, ruffled shirt. His eloquent eyes looked straight ahead, though his face, almost stern in expression, was turned somewhat to the side, in line with his broad shoulders. His hair, slightly waved and brushed back from his high forehead, was entirely gray. The strength of his face and the dignity of his bearing made him appear every inch a leader.[55]

The presence of the emigration faction at last stimulated Ross to discuss the possibility of a treaty with Secretary Cass. The question was raised: If the Cherokees should cede part of their lands, could or would the federal government guarantee them protection in what remained? The secretary answered no. Even on the understanding, Ross persisted, that in the end the Cherokees would accept American citizenship? Again the answer was no. Cass maintained that the president would negotiate only with the aim of removing the Indians west. But Ross had found a solution he considered the only possibility on which to treat. Let the Cherokees remain in the East on a part of their land, submit to the jurisdiction of the respective states, and eventually amalgamate with the whites.

Major Ridge conceded that such a course could be followed. But he believed that in such event the common Indian would, as Worcester wrote the board in Boston, "be perpetually made drunk by the whites, cheated, oppressed, reduced to beggary, become miserable outcasts, and as a body dwindle to nothing."[56] Such a prospect—the fate of the once powerful Catawbas—was unthinkable. It thus remained the moral crusade of the Ridges to "induce the Indians to abandon this land of whiskey kegs & bottles, the vile corruption of the whites, where . . . poor women [were] contaminated to become wretches."[57] As for John Ross's position, The Ridge maintained that not only was the principal chief not prepared to reveal his solution to the Cherokee people, but also he had no more authority to negotiate on such a basis than his brother Andrew had for taking the opposite extreme.

Andrew Ross seemed bent on signing a treaty at any cost. The War Department responded, and the president's crony, Major Eaton, was named a commissioner to carry on the negotiations. Major Ridge and Boudinot withdrew from the talks as soon as they foresaw the result—a treaty "made at loose ends, and containing no substance of national privileges, drawn just as ex-Secretary Eaton pleased." By its terms the Cherokee lands in the East would be ceded for a ridiculous consideration. Major Ridge was passionately protreaty, but he demanded terms that differed considerably from those espoused by either of the Rosses. "My father and Mr. Boudinot," wrote John Ridge, "acted in the middle path of those extremes, & desired to obtain new lands to be added to that of our country in the West, & to secure the means of reunion with our people there, & also funds for the support of schools & promotion of Christianity for our nation."[58] David Vann and John Walker, Jr., were also in Washington at that time, but they followed Major Ridge's lead and refrained from signing Andrew Ross's treaty. Still, Andrew Ross and three of his group put their signatures to it, to the consternation both of the national delegation and of Major Ridge and Boudinot.

The United States Senate would never ratify the treaty, and when it was brought before the council John Ross called in August, it goaded many Cherokees to a fury. In the face of their agitation Ross was less than candid about his own negotiations in Washington, and John Ridge believed he tried to misrepresent the concessions he had proposed to Cass, in particular the stipulation for merging the tribe with the United States in due course. Certainly he shied from clarifying that he had actually pressed such terms.[59] But because Major Ridge, the long-time bulwark against removal, had gone to Washington with Andrew Ross and worked tirelessly for emigration, it was he who bore the brunt of Cherokee wrath.

Tom Foreman, a turbulent character who had become a sheriff of the nation, spoke against him in vehement terms. He called The Ridge an enemy of the Cherokee people and claimed that but for him, and enemies like him, the Cherokees would have received relief from the United States government. He reminded those present that, though The Ridge was a member of the executive council, he had gone to Washington "to do something against his country." The gist of Foreman's words, as recorded by John Ridge, proclaimed that "Major Ridge had gone around the nation with the Chiefs & made speeches telling the people to love their land & in his earnestness [had] stamped the ground. The ground was yet sunk where he [had] stamped & now he was talking another way. If he, Foreman, had known that, he should not have voted for him. Yet these men had good clothes on—why could they not be satisfied with their property & not try to suck for more in the veins of their country?"[60]

While Foreman inveighed thus against The Ridge and his colleagues, an Indian in the audience was heard to whisper, "Let's kill them!"

John Ridge arose and expressed his surprise at such sentiments. He upheld his father: "Major Ridge had with distinguished zeal & ability served his country. He saw that it was on the precipice of ruin, ready to tumble down. He told [the people] of their danger. Did he tell the truth or not? Let every man look to our circumstances & judge for himself. Was a man to be denounced for his opinions? If a man saw a cloud charged with rain, thunder and storm . . . & urged the people to take care . . . , is that man to be hated or . . . respected?"[61]

Then Major Ridge defended himself in a dignified talk. He remarked that he "had not the vanity to hope for honors in his declining years. His sun of existence was going down. It was low. He had only a short time to live. 'It may be that Foreman has better expectations & that he should in slandering men establish his fame among you. But I have no expectation that he will enjoy it long, for we have no government. It is entirely suppressed. Where are your laws! The seats of your judges are overturned. When I look upon you all, I hear you laugh at me. When harsh words are uttered by men who know better . . . I feel on your account oppressed with sorrow. I mourn over your calamity.' "[62] Thus John Ridge recorded the substance of his father's words. But Foreman continued to agitate, and threats were made that if certain men did not take care they would be shot from their ponies.

Elijah Hicks chose this moment to present a petition signed by 144 Indians from six districts. It requested that the Ridges, along with David Vann, be impeached for "maintaining opinions and a policy to terminate the existence of the Cherokee community on the lands of [their] fathers." After deliberating, the council concluded that the accused were guilty as charged and voted that they be removed from office. In the committee, on receipt of the vote from the lower house, the documents were laid on the table and the clerk instructed to notify the accused to appear at the October council to answer the charges preferred against them.[63]

The Ridges and Vann would never be brought to trial, as matters worked out, but the incident illustrated the intensity of feeling rising against the advocates of removal. Before the council could adjourn, word came of an even more dramatic indication of that feeling. John Walker, Jr., who had left Red Clay prematurely, was waylaid for steps he had taken for a treaty—or so it was assumed—and dropped from his saddle by assassins hidden behind a log. To avoid a similar ambush the Ridges took a roundabout route home.[64] Though they had not abandoned hope that John Ross would change his policy, the lines between the factions seemed drawn fast. But the deadlock could not last. The Ridges vowed to make every effort to bring the futile maneuvers of desperation among the Cherokees to some decisive issue.

11 • THE TREATY OF NEW ECHOTA

A NDREW Jackson was resting at the Hermitage when he heard
of the shooting of John Walker, Jr. The news filled him with
rage, since Walker had received a promise of protection from
the general government. The president snatched a sheet of pea-
green stationery and slashed away at a letter to Major Currey. He
informed the agent of the report that "Ridge and other chiefs in
favor of immigration" had been threatened with death. "The Government of the U.S. has promised them protection," he wrote. "*It
will perform its obligation* to a tittle." And he instructed Currey to
inform John Ross and his council that they would be held responsible for any outrage committed by the National Party on members
of the emigration faction. He also charged Currey with investigat-
ing the facts of Walker's murder, a task the agent undertook without delay. Few agents were more conscientious about their duties
than Currey; Sam Houston considered him "as capable, faithful and
honest an agent as the Government ever had."[1]

Currey discovered that a fanatic named James Foreman and his
half brother, Anderson Springston, had perpetrated the ambush.
They were indicted in Tennessee, but after a full investigation the
Tennessee Supreme Court decided that the criminal laws of the state
did not extend over the affairs of the Cherokee Nation. Jackson's
guarantees thus lost many of their teeth. The assassins were allowed
to go free, and threats continued to circulate against the lives of
the Ridges and their associates. Major Ridge conferred with Ross
about the report that a certain Thomas Woodward had been engaged by the principal chief to take his life. Ross denied the allegation, claiming it was "high time [that] all such mischievous tales
should be silenced." They also discussed the rumor that Ridge sup-

porters were out to murder Ross. Ross was loath to heed such vicious stories and wrote to John Ridge that "partyism should be discarded. Our country and our people—should be our motto."[2] Death threats continued to weave about, however; even Major Currey's life was held to be in danger.

Meanwhile the Cherokees assembled at Red Clay for the annual October council. Ross and others who controlled proceedings declined to prosecute the impeachment charge against the Ridges and David Vann. They also declined to withdraw it, whereupon the three made "earnest solicitations" for a trial to clear their names, but the national committee refused to oblige them. The three therefore left the council before its adjournment and rode their horses homeward, satisfied that justice could no longer be expected from Ross. They decided to act independently—to call a council of their own at Running Waters on November 27, 1834. John Ridge sent out couriers to inform people of the meeting, while at the same time Ross employed runners to procure signatures (they entered the names of nearly every Cherokee, from infant babes to the old and decrepit) for a protest against the Andrew Ross treaty: they would ask the question "Do you love your land?" and subscribe the names of all who answered yes.[3]

The council at Running Waters lasted for three days, with Boudinot serving as chairman and Alexander McCoy as secretary. Only eighty-three Indians attended. Yet Boudinot predicted that the meeting would have a powerful effect. "It seems already," he added, "to have inspired a new energy in our people, who have determined to get out of the jurisdiction of the States." After a number of speeches the council named a panel of delegates to carry the Ridge party's case to Washington. John Ridge assumed leadership of the delegation, and his associates included Boudinot and McCoy, W. A. Davis, Archilla Smith, Samuel Bell, and John and Ezekiel West. On a motion of John Ridge the council then appointed a committee to draft resolutions expressing the views of the assembly "in regard to the present condition and future prospects of the Cherokee people" and to prepare a memorial for Congress.[4] John Ridge was largely responsible for accomplishing both tasks, with help from Boudinot and Archilla Smith. The resolutions, which were published in a number of newspapers, spelled out the stand which the Ridge party had taken in respect to emigration and a treaty, and Edward Everett announced the gist of the memorial when the delegates presented it to Congress the following January:

> [The emigration delegates] set forth in strong language the right of
> their people to the soil on which they live, and their sense of wrong
> done them in the measures taken to dispossess them. . . . They repre-
> sent the progress they have made in the arts of civilization—a progress,
> no doubt, well calculated to excite . . . the admiration of the friends
> of humanity, both here and in Europe. They express, however, the
> sorrowful conviction that it is impossible for them, in the present state
> of things, to retain their national existence, and to live in peace and
> comfort in their native region. They therefore have turned their eyes
> to the country west of the Mississippi, to which a considerable portion
> of their tribe have already emigrated; and they express the opinion
> that they are reduced to the alternative of following them to that
> region, or of sinking into a condition but little, if at all, better than
> slavery, in their present place of abode. They announce this conviction
> with the bitterness of language which might naturally be expected from
> men placed in their situation; and which I think will neither surprise
> nor offend any member of this House. In contemplating the subject
> of removal, they cast themselves on the liberality of Congress.[5]

Fifty-seven Cherokees signed the memorial, twenty by means of
handwriting, the rest by marks; and a certificate set forth that it
had been adopted in open council. John Ridge, who assumed responsibility for its composition, had handed it personally to Everett
and asked that he introduce it to the House.

Two weeks later, on February 4, 1835, Henry Clay presented the
same memorial to the Senate, with trenchant oratorical remarks:
"Sir," the senator from Kentucky rumbled in the direction of the
presiding officer, "it is impossible to conceive of a community more
miserable, more wretched. Even the lot of the African slave is preferable to the condition of this unhappy nation. The interest of the
master prompts him to protect the slave; but what mortal will care
for, [or] protect the suffering injured Indian, shut out from the
family of man?"[6] Like Everett, Clay now found it ironic to present,
so soon after he had argued against Jackson's Indian policy, a plea
for hastening the emigration of the Cherokees.

The Ridge delegation, ready to treat with the United States and
thus resolve a most perplexing situation, had the inside track in
Washington. They found themselves courted and flattered in contrast with the cool reception accorded Ross's deputation. Ross had
submitted his own memorial to Congress, requesting the U.S. government to purchase the land of the Cherokees in Georgia, to "grant
them a sufficient portion of it in fee simple," and at the same time

to extend to them the rights and privileges of Georgia citizenship.[7] All attempts to unite the two deputations failed, for the Ridge delegation strongly opposed Ross's proposition, believing that the common Indians would quickly squander such property secured to them in fee simple and thus be reduced to the most abject want and degradation. Nor did the terms prove more acceptable to the U.S. government. Jackson stubbornly felt that the only possible solution was removal, and on removal he insisted. At that point the Ridge delegation advised Lewis Cass that the best means of relieving the Cherokees would be "a preliminary treaty," signed by the delegation in Washington, to be sent to the nation for ratification.[8] The War Department decided to deal with the Ridge group, and the secretary appointed a commissioner for the purpose, a large man of flamboyant appearance, a former parson from Utica, New York, named John F. Schermerhorn. He was described by one observer as "a crafty and subtle individual."[9] A less flattering opinion was that of the missionary Isaac McCoy, who found him to be "full of zeal without much knowledge, and still less discretion."[10]

Schermerhorn reached a tentative agreement with Ridge that set the payment for Cherokee lands to be exchanged for country in the West at $3,250,000, a sum that was later raised to $4,500,000. But before the terms of a treaty could be drawn up, John Ross announced that he was ready to present another proposition. On February 11 the commissioner was thus ordered to suspend his negotiations with Ridge until it was known what Ross intended. Ten days dragged by. Then the National delegation proposed to sell the Cherokee lands outright for $20 million, a price that the United States immediately rejected, Jackson snorting, "Filibuster!" But Ross was ready with another offer—to let the amount be determined by the Senate.[11] "We are prepared, so far as we are concerned," he wrote in a letter signed by his delegation on February 28, "to abide by the award of the sense of the American Senate upon our proposition, and to recommend the same for the final determination of our nation."[12]

The proposition was transmitted to the Senate, and the senators recommended the payment of five million dollars. Such a sum Ross thought too small, and he at once showed a disposition to evade compliance with his promise. He was soon calling the Senate's resolution "a mere expression of opinion, [not] obligatory on the President."[13] On March 9, 1835, he forwarded a new plan—that "the whole matter should be referred to our nation" to be deliberated in a General Council. "And in order," he declared, "to insure harmony and good feeling among ourselves, it [is] greatly to be desired that the Cherokee people and their representatives should not be trammelled by any premature act on our part, and that the whole subject should be brought before them free from any suspicion or unjust imputations against ourselves or others."[14] It was clear to all that Ross was again pursuing stalling tactics, that his immediate objective was to hold the Cherokee question in suspension until the death of Jackson's administration, when, with a new government, his favorite scheme of naturalizing the tribe might be realized.

Schermerhorn had meanwhile received instructions to negotiate once more with the Ridge delegation, and a provisional agreement was reached on the basis of the Senate's determination. The terms were better than those achieved by Andrew Ross the year before—more what Major Ridge had advocated. The plan provided that the Indians would receive $4,500,000 for exchanging their lands in the East for thirteen million acres in the West. They would also receive an additional eight hundred thousand acres in the West, estimated to be worth $500,000, to make the sum total of the payment the equivalent of the Senate's specification. The plan also included a perpetual annuity to provide for a school fund, a feature on which the Ridges and Boudinot set great value.[15]

John Ridge wrote his father about the treaty on March 11:

It is very liberal in its terms—an equal measure is given to all. The poor Indian enjoys the same rights as the rich—there is no distinction. We are allowed to enjoy our own laws in the west. Subsistence for one, $25. for each soul for transportation, fair valuation, fair ferries & Improvements, $150 for each individual, more than forty thousand dollars perpetual annuity in the west, & a large sum of money to pay for the losses of the Cherokees against the white people. In fact—we get four millions & a half in money to meet all expenses & a large addition in land to that already possessed by our brethren in the west.[16]

Ross claimed that Schermerhorn's arrangement with the Ridge delegation would only increase disharmony among the Cherokees, and he insisted that the wishes of the whole nation be consulted in the application of the amount named by the Senate. Ridge realized that such an objection was a mere pretense on Ross's part, for the chief knew well that nothing was fixed hard and fast in the agreement except the total amount of five million dollars set by the Senate. The several stipulations were all subject to modifications, if the Cherokees should so request. As for Ridge, he thought his delegation had achieved an arrangement so fair and equitable that the mass of Cherokees could not possibly reject it, provided they were allowed to learn the truth. He suspected, however—indeed, he was convinced—that Ross would do everything in his power to keep them ignorant of the true situation, and his distrust of the chief sounded in his words to his father and friends: "Ross has failed," he wrote on March 10, "before the Senate, before the Secretary of War, & before the President. He tried hard to cheat you & his people, but he has been prevented. In a day or two he goes home no doubt to tell lies. But we will bring all his papers & the people shall see him as he is."[17]

The rivalry between Ross and Ridge had thus grown acute, and the bitterness increased with each day. "The issue is now fairly made up between us," Ridge had informed Stand Watie,[18] and he now girded himself for a strenuous duel to bring the provisions of the treaty before the people against the maneuvers of the chief. But before returning home to the struggle he suggested to the secretary of war that a friendly letter from Jackson, transmitted to the Cherokees through the commissioner and guaranteeing the gains of the treaty into the indefinite future, would make it easier for the Treaty Party to bring the truth to the people and to counteract the subterfuges of Ross and his minions.[19] Jackson responded to Ridge's satisfaction, providing Schermerhorn with an enthusiastic talk. The president's wisdom and forbearance during these negotiations inspired John Ridge's respect, and the young man's attitude toward Jackson changed completely. He came to regard the president as the staunchest friend the Cherokees had. Indeed, he named his new son Andrew Jackson Ridge.*

Soon after coming home that April, 1835, with books for Rollin and with shoes for Sarah and Miss Sophia Sawyer, the Ridges' school teacher, Ridge called a council at Running Waters to explain the occurrences at Washington. The attendance was small but spirited. "The proceedings at the City," Major Currey noted, "were read and supported by the eloquence of Major Ridge,"[20] who though sixty-four and ailing had lost none of his powers as an orator. It was then resolved that another council should be held on the first Monday in May. All who felt an interest in the unhappy condition of the Cherokees were invited to come, and at Currey's suggestion it was decided to combine the explanation of the treaty with the voting on how the next annuity payments would be made, in order to attract

*John Ridge had six other children: John Rollin, Clarinda, Susan, Flora, Herman, and Æneas.

more general attendance. In this way the people could be better prepared to give the treaty a proper hearing at the autumn council at Red Clay, where the U.S. commissioners would seek the will of the nation.[21]

In the meantime John Ross was active in stirring up resentment against the Ridge treaty. When Major Currey heard of certain remarks that he had made to a company at the house of George Lowrey, he accused him of lying and of trying to whip up "unmerited prejudice" against the Ridge delegation. Currey added that the president had directed him to warn Ross that he and his council would be held responsible if anything should happen to any member of the treaty delegation. It could be said in Ross's favor, however, that no matter how bitterly he opposed the Ridges' efforts to treat, he never at any time condoned the ideas of violence held by some of his followers. It was not his idea that the Ridges and their closest coadjutors live under constant threats of death—threats that could not be minimized after what had happened to Walker. On occasion Indians wrapped to the eyes in blankets haunted the edges of Running Waters; they merely loitered under the trees, but their presence filled the house with dread.[22] John Ridge could not help but feel uneasy. He felt chagrin, too, at the plummeting of his popularity among the general run of Cherokees. He kept hoping that more Indians would grasp the truth and flock to his banner, but there was no evidence of such a change by the first week of May.

The Ridges rationalized the unusual rains and the fact that it was planting time as the reasons for the poor attendance at their council. The fact was that Ross, having sent out many couriers, was entirely successful in boycotting the meeting, and only a hard core of Ridge followers attended, no more than a hundred, thus defeating the purpose of the assembly. But the Ridges hoped that more people would attend at a later time, so they petitioned Currey to defer the annuity vote to a later date when the streams would be more passable and when the people would be less concerned with planting crops. The new date was set for the third Monday in July, 1835.[23]*

*In the meantime the Cherokees met on May 11 at the council Ross had called at Red Clay to explain his lack of progress at Washington. His report excoriated the treaty delegates for "collusion" with the Jackson administration. In presenting the Ridge treaty to the assemblage he passed over cardinal portions of its terms, and John Ridge felt he meant to dupe the uninformed Indians, few of whom understood the course of action mapped out by the treaty delegates (Ross to the General Council, May 18, 1835, Payne Papers, Ayer Collection, Newberry Library; 25th Cong., 2d sess., S. Doc. 120 [Serial 315], pp. 368–71).

Ross thought twice about boycotting the Ridge council in July. He feared that the treaty faction might take advantage of the absence of Ross men to secure control of the year's annuity, as indeed they might have done if the election had taken place in May as planned. So now the chief about-faced and encouraged his followers to converge on Running Waters in a horde. In the time that intervened he sought to condition them against any lessons they might learn from the Ridges and their stalwarts by proclaiming that his party would doubtless gain better treaty terms at the Red Clay council in October. To counter such a line John Ridge secured a statement from the War Department that no propositions for a treaty would be made thereafter more favorable than those offered in the Ridge treaty.[24]

Moreover, as tension mounted and as threats of assassination continued to circulate, John Ridge felt it necessary to turn to the governor of Georgia for protection. The secret letter he wrote on May 18 called Lumpkin's attention to

the *banded outlaws* who are harbored by the Ross party for the purpose of intimidation or assassination. Richard the Third never had better instruments to promote tyranny. Have you not heard of the armed outlaws harbored by the Ross party . . . ? Here is a band, a well organized power against the lives of the friendly Indians, the lives of the whites, & their property which sets at defiance your constables & sheriffs & laughs at your Judges & Jurors. And to cap the climax of this league the ablest lawyers of your own state are retained to defend them if taken.

Now came the main point of Ridge's letter:

There is a remedy in your power, and it is to organize a guard of thirty men placed under the command of Col. Bishop to scour and range the fastnesses & to search for them in their caves,* and to suppress their secret meetings close to all-night dances where the leaders of the Ross party usually meet with them for consultation. I do earnestly hope that for the accomplishment of all the objects of mercy to the poor Indians, . . . you will give to these suggestions your serious consideration. These outlaws are fearfully increasing in the chartered limits of the State. . . . You must break up this incubus or nightmare which sets so heavily upon the breasts of the ignorant Indians. Depend upon it that it requires but this measure to dissipate the mists which now

---

*This word may be *coves*, the Southern term for gulches or canyons. However, there were many limestone caves in the Cherokee country, and they would have made appropriate hideouts for "outlaws" such as John Ridge described.

blind the eyes of some of our people. John Ross is unhorsed at Washington and you must unhorse him here.[25]

Thus circumstances drew the Ridges into an ever closer relationship with the authorities of Georgia, a development that only intensified the opinion of many Cherokees that they were traitors. At the same time, interested third parties informed Governor Lumpkin of the dangers to which the Ridges were personally exposed — the threats of assassination. In reply the governor promised that his friends could rest assured that the government of Georgia would "protect and defend them, in their persons and property, from the violence and outrage of their enemies." And to Colonel W. N. Bishop he sent instructions to be "vigilant and watchful" in guarding the Ridges from harm — even if it meant the arrest of John Ross.[26]

On July 18, 1835, the Cherokees arrived at Running Waters in bands that ranged from ten into the hundreds — men, women, and children — most of them collecting on the banks of a branch about two miles from the council grounds. It was a dismal and comfortless camp for them, with rain falling while they waited for the council. That same night, at the homes of John and Major Ridge, every bed and every bit of floor space were covered with the sprawling forms of Indians and mixed-bloods. Major Ridge accommodated Schermerhorn, who had arrived a few days earlier, full of zeal and resolution, while the commissioner's secretary, young Return J. Meigs, along with Major Currey and others, stayed at Running Waters. There the preparations had filled everyone with excitement, even the pupils in Miss Sawyer's school. Cattle had been slaughtered, and deep incursions were made into the contents of smokehouse and corncrib. John Ridge supported a house full of guests for four days, the expense of which was later repaid by the federal government. He charged each white man $1.10 for the keep of himself and a horse. He also invited John Ross to stay beneath his roof, perhaps only a polite gesture; at any rate the politic chief replied that he preferred to sleep with his people in the open, whatever the weather.

On the morning of the nineteenth, although Governor William Carroll, the second commissioner, had failed to come, the meeting was ready to begin. It opened with prayers by David Watie and a native preacher named John Huss. They were heard in silence by the crowd, perhaps the largest assemblage of Cherokees ever yet gathered in one place. There were present between twenty-five hundred and twenty-six hundred men, not to mention the women and children—in all at least four thousand souls, and they had come, according to Currey, "some starving, some half-clad, some armed, and scarcely any with provisions for more than one or two days."[27]

Fearing that disorder might break out in a crowd so large, Currey had requested that a detachment of the Georgia guard camp near the council ground, and the sound of fife and drums could be heard in the distance as the meeting got under way. But the Cherokees maintained exemplary order. The emigration agent explained the purpose of the council, then added some words of advice to the Ross faction. "I took occasion to say," he reported, ". . . that let them vote the money in what way they would, it could not save their country; that their party had been invited to express their views and wishes freely; instead of doing this they had withdrawn themselves from the ground and been counselled in the bushes. Why was this so? Were their chiefs still disposed to delude their people, when ruin demanded entrance at the red man's door, and the heavy hand of oppression already rested upon his head?"[28]

The atmosphere was electric. Ross responded to Currey's speech. He was sorry, he said, that the agent had been so personal in his remarks. He managed, however, to present a friendly appearance and claimed that he was "not disposed to quarrel with any man for an honest expression of opinion." John Ridge followed Ross to the speaker's box and proclaimed that he too wished to discard party bias "and sinister motives"; that insofar as he and his partisans had differed from Ross they had "done so from an honest conviction that it was the only way in which the integrity and political salvation of the Cherokee people could be preserved." He was ready to recognize Ross as principal chief as soon as Ross could—or would—advance a sounder plan than the Ridges had done. Until then he felt bound to act "on the suggestions arising out of the case," though it cost him his last drop of blood. He denied that Currey had indulged in personalities, while he affirmed that, if Ross's statements were sincere, it was hard to understand why such "large bodies of Indians had been withdrawn by their chiefs from the ground, and were not permitted to hear." For his own part, Ridge added, he wanted the whole nation to learn the truth, and to that end—to save his "bleeding and oppressed countrymen"—he was prepared to work with Ross, or with anyone else if necessary.[29]

At that point Schermerhorn, whom the Indians in the Ross faction had dubbed Skay-noo-yau-nah, or The Devil's Horn, addressed
the council. He requested that the factions name delegates to meet
with him and Governor Carroll on the thirtieth of the month at
the Cherokee agency to arrange preliminaries for a treaty convention. He also asked permission to address the council the following
morning concerning the treaty he was authorized to make with the
Cherokees. Ross answered that his people were short of provisions
and therefore not prepared for a prolonged meeting. Schermerhorn
answered that he would order rations for them if they would only
hear him. Ross conferred with his headmen; they agreed to listen to
The Devil's Horn, and so the commissioner directed Lavender to
furnish the stores without delay.

Archilla Smith, who had been a treaty delegate at Washington,
then introduced a resolution that the current annuity be equally
divided among the people. John Ridge seconded the motion, and he
and Smith and Major Ridge made enthusiastic speeches supporting
the resolution—speeches in which they seized the opportunity to
explain the treaty. And when they finished, it was too late to begin
the voting, and so the council was adjourned for the day.

It opened at nine o'clock the next morning, with Schermerhorn
ready to harangue the throng. He had ordered a high stand to be
erected during the night so that he could be better seen and more
generally heard, but as he prepared to mount it, Ross caught his
arm and requested that he delay his speech till after the voting. It
was a transparent dodge by Ross, who would doubtless encourage
his followers to dwindle away once the vote was taken. Schermerhorn reminded Ross of his promise and, insisting that he be heard
at once, pressed his claim with such persistence that the chief capitu-
lated. Schermerhorn explained the treaty at length, and the Cherokees listened with "great gravity and serious attention."[30]

Then the voting began. As every vote had to be recorded by
name, it was a tedious business which could not be finished that
day. It became evident, however, that Smith's resolution would be
defeated, and so a number of the Ridge faction refrained from voting,
and some even cast their votes against the resolution. Therefore the
114 ayes could hardly be considered an accurate index of the Ridge
party's strength. The nays numbered more than two thousand, an
overwhelming victory for Ross, though rather a Pyrrhic one in view
of all the treaty information that was disseminated. Such an airing
in public of the Cherokee condition was the last thing the chief

desired. The Ridges took full advantage of the situation, and when Edward Gunter introduced a resolution providing that the annuity be paid forthwith to the treasurer, Major Ridge offered an amendment that no part of the sum should be disbursed to lawyers.

John Ridge seconded the amendment, and both had a chance to speak again. "They went into a most pathetic description of national distress and individual oppression," Major Currey reported: "the necessity of seeking freedom in another clime; the importance of union and harmony, and the beauties of peace and friendship; but said if there were any who preferred to endure misery, and wed themselves to slavery, as for them and their friends, they craved not such company." The crowd had been drawn up to vote on Gunter's resolution. "But when the Ridges were speaking," Currey continued, "all the previous prejudices so manifestly shown by looks appeared to die away, and the benighted foresters involuntarily broke the line and pressed forward as if attracted by the power of magnetism to the stand, and when they could get no nearer they reached their heads forward in anxiety to hear the truth. After the Ridges had procured the desired attention, they withdrew their amendment."[31] It had been a mere maneuver to bring their point of view once more before the Cherokees.

Gunter's resolution, when brought to a vote, was carried by acclamation. The Indians had behaved with great decorum throughout the council. In spite of wet weather ball fields were laid off and ball-plays were staged, but with none of the violence that usually attended such contests. Seldom if ever, Currey reported, had "so great a number of persons of any color . . . met and preserved better order than was observed on this occasion." The concord was a tribute to the hold that Ross maintained on the rank and file of the Cherokees. Schermerhorn believed that Ross's sway over them was complete and reported to Washington that they were "drilled equal to a Swiss guard, *to do only what they were bidden.*"[32]

There was no question of Ross's influence on his countrymen or of his authority over them, but the secret of his control was that he led them according to their profoundest desires, their deepest bent, their instinctive will. Missionaries who understood Cherokee affairs denied the allegation that he ruled with an iron hand. They claimed he led by, in effect, following. As Worcester once remarked, "individuals may be overawed by *popular opinion*, but not by the *chiefs*. On the other hand, if there were a chief in favor of removal, *he* would be overawed by the *people*."[33] Ross never forswore his awe of the people—or his duty to them. The irony was that the Ridges and Boudinot, in acting for the people and their preservation, violated the people's fondest inclination, their desire to retain the land of their fathers, come whatever might. Such a violation would have its reckoning.

On July 29, John and Major Ridge, with twenty of their partisans, rode their horses to the Cherokee agency in response to Schermerhorn's bidding.[34] The purpose of the conference was to restore harmony between the factions and to agree upon some satisfactory modification of the treaty. It came to nothing, however, since Ross and his men failed to appear. The next day a messenger brought the Ridges a letter explaining that the chief was suffering from diarrhea. The tone was friendly, and Ross took the occasion to invite the Ridges to meet him elsewhere to settle all difficulties between the factions and unite to promote the common good of the Cherokees: "If you will signify to me your willingness to accept an invitation to hold such a conference, I will immediately advise with Mr. Lowery [sic] and fix on the time and place of the conference."[35]

Ross added that the meeting should comprise only Cherokees, a few chosen for their wisdom and moral worth. The Ridges approved, and the following day John Ridge wrote the chief a letter signed by both himself and his father. As their return route ran close to Ross's rude cabin near Red Clay, they took the liberty of delivering the reply in person.[36]

The party having left the agency at dawn, they drew their horses up at Ross's gate just as the chief sat down to breakfast. The Ridges accepted Ross's invitation to eat with him, along with as many of their men as could be crowded into the cabin. The rest were fed outside, and Ross's hospitality included feed for the horses. No one mentioned the proposed conference until the Ridges were ready to depart. Then John Ridge requested that its date should not conflict with a Green Corn Dance he had called for August 24. Ross hesitated to name a day. The convenience of the people would have to be consulted, he replied. It would be inconsiderate to call them at any time their crops required special attention. He promised to consult his associates, whereupon the Ridges and their cavalcade took a friendly leave.[37]

The Ridges might hope that Ross was ready to reverse his stand, but in reality nothing had changed. "Ross holds out the olive branch of peace to Ridge," wrote Major Currey to the commissioner of

Indian affairs, "while his confidential friends speak of slaying him, because they say he has forfeited his life by the laws of the nation."[38] Hardly a week went by that a Ridge adherent did not fall at the hands of Ross partisans. A treaty man named Hammer had received such a vicious beating that he had died on the spot.[39] Shortly afterward a treaty man named Crow was murdered at a frolic at which he had been chosen to preserve order. It was Cherokee custom to appoint someone respected for his virtues and venerable for his years to superintend such affairs. It was his responsibility to remain sober while others drank, so as to preserve order and decorum. Crow had successfully done his duty, and when the dancers were ready to disband, he was prompted by friends to speak about the sad condition of the nation. In a short talk he pleaded with all present to extricate themselves from all their difficulties by ratifying the Ridge treaty. No sooner had he concluded than he was assailed by a Ross man and stabbed in sixteen places.[40] On August 3 two followers of the Ridges, named Murphy and Duck, were knifed to death at another frolic.[41] Then two days later James Martin, formerly a Cherokee judge, threatened to take the life of John Ridge, or have it done. As soon as Major Currey heard of the threat, he had the old white-haired "judge" arrested, and Martin was released only after he had pleaded that he had been so beside himself with liquor that he was not responsible for anything he had said.[42] "The Ross Party," John Ridge wrote a little later, "tried hard to counteract the growth of our party by murders—it is dreadful to reflect on the amount of blood which has been shed by the savages on those who have only exercised the right of opinion."[43]

The time came for the Green Corn Dance at the council ground near Running Waters, and hundreds of people assembled, the dancers wearing mussel shells tied around their ankles and filled with gravel so as to rattle when they moved. Perhaps it was to this dance that Sally Ridge prepared to go in a new coach that Major Ridge was said to have ordered from New York City. As the story went, the coach "created a sensation. It was hung with leather swings attached to large 'C' springs, the driver's seat being on top. . . . The horses were harnessed to it, and the Negro driver stood ready. Chief Ridge inspected the outfit, even shaking the wheels to be sure they would stand up. Sarah came out in silks and feathers; her father assisted her to climb the folding steps, closed the steps and door, then walked around to the driver, took the reins, and ordered the driver to go back to his field work. Chief Ridge then mounted one of the horses, with the gathered reins in his hands, and galloped away to the 'Green Corn Dance.' "[44] The anecdote would survive in Rome to illustrate how Indian traits still clung to The Ridge after he had become a gentleman planter.

The frolic lasted for four or five days. Its real purpose was to stimulate sentiment in favor of the Ridge treaty. Both John and Major Ridge addressed the people. So too did Schermerhorn, who reported: "The ideas I suggested at Ridge's green corn dance of the possibility of an arrangement with the Indians of Georgia & Alabama on the crisis of the proposed treaty have spread through the country like wildfire."[45] Meanwhile John Ross, understanding the purpose of the Ridges, had encouraged other dances to be held elsewhere in order to rival and defeat the aims of the Ridge frolic. But Ross himself was defeated in his objective; the Georgia guard dispersed all the dances called by his supporters, leaving the Ridge dance alone unmolested, attended by an enormous crowd.[46]

The Ridges were slowly gaining new adherents now, and they were pleased to hear that certain of Ross's supporters had grown concerned about the head chief's stalling tactics. These partisans had called on Ross and told him plainly to settle the "treaty business" at the fall council or they would withdraw their support and throw it behind the Ridges. John Ridge wrote on September 22, 1835:

I feel pleasure now to say that our cause prospers, & I believe will result in the general cession of the Nation. . . . John Ross and his party will try to *outlive* the administration of Genl. Jackson if they are not forced into the treaty, & it now depends upon the treaty party to take a bold and decided stand. We have gained so much now in Georgia & Alabama that we shall soon organise chiefs & a regular Council for those two states and close the treaty—However this is conditioned upon the refusal of the Ross party to join in a general treaty—He has requested a Conference, and we have accepted it, & it is possible that we may agree to make a General Cession. This Conference will be held it is supposed on the 2nd Monday in Oct. next in the chartered limits of Tennessee—[47]

The time for the October council arrived, and the Ridges reached Red Clay as Indians streamed in from every quarter of the nation. "I cannot imagine a spectacle of more moral grandeur," wrote an eyewitness, "than the assembly of such a people under such circumstances." What the observer saw the first day he offered as the "first foretaste" of what the days that followed held in store: "The woods echoed with the trampling of many feet: a long and orderly procession emerged from among the trees, the gorgeous autumnal tints of whose departing foliage seemed in sad harmony with the noble spirit now beaming in this departing race. Most of the train was on foot. There were a few aged men, and some few women, on horseback. The train halted at the humble gate of the principal chief: he stood ready to receive them. Everything was noiseless." Warmed by their simple dignity, the witness described how they formed in double file to shake the chief's hand. "Their dress was neat and picturesque: all wore turbans, except four or five with hats; many of them, tunics with sashes; many, long robes, and nearly all some drapery: so that they had the oriental air of the old scripture pictures of patriarchal procession."

The account continued: "The salutation over, the old men remained near the chief, and the rest withdrew to various parts of the enclosure; some sitting Turk fashion against the trees, others upon logs, and others upon the fences, but with the eyes of all fixed upon their chief. They had walked sixty miles since yesterday, and had encamped last night in the woods."[48] The group was typical of those who arrived throughout the day, and who came for days thereafter. The general excitement was contagious.

The council opened with prayer. Schermerhorn was present, eager to press the matter of the treaty. But Ross, a master at delaying tactics, managed to postpone that business for several days. On October 19 he called for the conference specified by his letter of July 30—the conference between representatives of the two factions. Besides John Ridge the treaty panel included Boudinot, George Chambers, Charles Vann, and John Gunter, and they met with five men who represented the National Party. The two panels consulted for two days, and both produced resolutions. But the treaty panel found the statement of the Ross panel too general to accept, and the Ross men found the treaty panel's too particular. Three days later they arrived at a compromise, which John Ridge considered favorable to a treaty. To a well-connected Georgian he wrote from the council ground: "I consider that the Indian controversy is now closed. The Ross party and the Treaty party have united, and have agreed to close the Cherokee difficulties by a general treaty."[49]

As a next step Ross drew up a paper that granted full powers to a delegation of twenty persons either to treat with the federal commissioner at Red Clay or to go on to Washington for negotiations. To this document Ross added a clause protesting the acceptance of the $5 million set at his own request by the Senate. On the last evening of the council he read the instrument to the assembled people, and it was passed without the least deliberation. John Ridge wrote in a joint letter with other leaders:

The question was, Are you willing to take five millions of dollars for your country? No, no, was the cry of the people. Some few of the better informed were placed in different positions to lead the way, and the Indians, without knowing the difference between 5,000 and five millions, said No! They did not understand. Then the question was put, Are you willing to give full power to these twenty men to do your business? The answer was, Yes. They were dismissed, and they scattered that very night. There was no deliberation. . . . A vast majority . . . were of the opinion that they had rejected the propositions of the Government altogether, and had instructed their delegation to make no treaty, and consequently, *had saved the land.* This was the result of a manifest equivocation and double dealing with an ignorant people. None but the committee of negotiators remained with John Ross's council to reject [Schermerhorn's] propositions.[50]

John Ridge, Boudinot, and Charles Vann, who represented the Treaty Party on the delegation, went along with the rest, because of the "union," and put their names to the rejection of the Ridge treaty. They assumed that the delegates would accept a modified treaty in Washington. Besides, they were required to sign such papers, not as the sense of each delegate, but as the sense of the majority. "That was your decision," Boudinot later reminded Ross, "for I expressly made the question at the time. . . . I gave you sufficient intimation that I should sign . . . against my judgment."[51] No doubt John Ridge could have said the same.

Schermerhorn, his vanity piqued, remained determined to make a treaty in the Cherokee country. He announced that the commissioners would meet for that purpose with the Cherokees in a General Council at New Echota on December 21. He prophesied that the president would refuse to receive the delegation at Washington, for his instructions specified that the treaty must be made in Cherokee country. His words were confirmed by a dispatch that soon arrived from the secretary of war, but it failed to shake the determination of the delegates to go to Washington. John Ridge advised Schermerhorn frankly that few people, in his opinion, would assemble at New Echota. Boudinot joined him in counseling the commissioner to abandon his plan and return to Washington with the Cherokee delegation. The stubborn parson refused to listen. On November 3 he issued a formal invitation to the Cherokees to a council "after their ancient usages" to be held on their former council ground at New Echota on the third Monday "of the first winter month." The notice ended with a warning that all who failed to attend would be considered as giving assent and sanction to everything done there.[52] Schermerhorn asked Boudinot to translate the notice into Cherokee, and it was printed in Cassville, Georgia, presumably on the press of the *Cherokee Phoenix*, which Stand Watie, with help from the Georgia guard, had removed from the house of Elijah Hicks.*

About this time Boudinot decided not to accompany the delegation to Washington. Ross suggested that Major Ridge replace him. Apparently The Ridge was also disinclined to make the journey. John Ridge pressed for the selection of Stand Watie, and Ross agreed.

Meanwhile a stranger of considerable importance had come among the Cherokees. After twenty checkered years in Europe, where "Home, Sweet Home" had made him famous, John Howard Payne, actor, playwright, adventurer, had lately returned to America, poor in everything but reputation, plans, and energy. His supply of these seemed inexhaustible. Before long he had devised a scheme to change his fortunes—a weekly magazine, whose prospectus he had mailed to editors throughout the land. The new journal, he wrote, would bear a title in Old Persian, *Jam Jehan Nima*, or "The World from the Inside of a Bowl." It would issue from London, but its columns would advertise America, the wonders of the land and the ideals of the people. Soon Payne had launched an "experience jaunt," aiming to canvass every state in the union for literary materials and subscriptions. He had covered seven states before approaching Georgia in the summer of 1835. His intention of visiting the Cherokees had crystallized only after talks with several prominent Georgians. He arrived with letters of introduction to both the Ridges and to Ross.

Payne called on the Ridges first of all, and they found him a gentleman of grace and charm. "The *Ridge* party here, I knew already," he wrote. "The other day I had a very interesting interview with the principal chiefs of that party—the conversation was brief, but very characteristic. I have passed a couple of days & got very well acquainted with Boudinot, a Cherokee educated at the North, who married a Gold. . . . They are a very intelligent and

*Moulton (*John Ross*, p. 65) writes: "The seizure occurred only hours before wagons sent by Ross arrived to remove the press to the Red Clay area for its protection. Ostensibly, the Ridge faction intended to reinvigorate the moribund paper by making it an open forum." The final lot of the press is a mystery.

John Howard Payne, literary advisor to John Ross. Courtesy of Columbia University Library.

amiable couple. I was delighted with my reception from the family."[53]

Next Payne rode his horse to Red Clay, intending to spend only a day at the nearby cabin of John Ross. But he had now become so interested in Cherokee affairs that he thought of writing a history of the nation, and when Ross consented to let him transcribe official Cherokee records, he settled down for a protracted stay. The upshot was that he became a zealous partisan of Ross.

Payne was a fascinated visitor at the October council—the eye-witness quoted above—and he was surprised to find an old schoolfel-low there, a tall, craggy man, superior and insolent, whom the Cherokees called The Devil's Horn. He renewed his friendship with Schermerhorn, and soon their conversation touched upon the subject of the treaty. Payne's impression was that Schermerhorn would fail to achieve his objective at the council, and he stated as much. "I'll have a treaty within a week," Schermerhorn retorted testily, and thereafter the old schoolmates were at odds with one another. The commissioner's resentment was evident in a memoran-dum that he sent to the Office of Indian Affairs a few days later: "I find that the Indians, after their return from the Red Clay council, reported that they would now get their land back; that a great man (meaning J. H. Payne) had come from England, and now they would have everything righted; that he was very busy with the pen, and took down everything that passed. . . . I am sorry to find that not-withstanding Mr. Payne's pretensions to the contrary, he has been very busy meddling with Cherokee affairs, and done what he could to prevent an arrangement with the Government."[54]

Especially incensed was Major Currey when an officious letter by Payne appeared anonymously in the *Knoxville Register.* He prod-ded the Georgia guard to take action, even to the extent of tres-passing on Tennessee soil. About eleven o'clock on the evening of November 7, the cabin where Payne and Ross were engaged in writing was surrounded; "there was a loud barking of dogs, then the quick tramp of galloping horses, then the march of many feet," and suddenly armed men spilled into the room, "their bayonets fixed."[55] This platoon of Georgia guardsmen looked quite like "banditti," as Payne had called the guard in his letter. They arrested both men without deigning to give charges, took their papers into custody, and hurried them twenty-four miles on horseback, through a tor-rential rainstorm, to an improvised jail at Spring Place.

John Ridge was away from home when the arrest occurred, but on November 14, the day after his return, he hurried to Spring

Place. He went to the headquarters of Colonel Bishop and asked
for an interview with Ross. At first the request was denied, but
Ridge persisted, and finally Ross was sent for. Colonel Bishop remained in the room long enough to disclose the trumped-up reason
for the arrest. Ross and Payne were regarded as abolitionists, agents
of powerful men like Henry Clay, and worse still, it was believed—
or rather pretended—that they had plotted an insurrection among
the Negroes, who were to join the Indians in an uprising against the
whites. The charges were fantastic. Bishop left Ridge and Ross
together, and they agreed that a more plausible reason for the arrest
was to prevent Ross from leading the "union" delegation to Washington. As for Payne, it was clearly an attempt to intimidate him, to
discourage him from "meddling" further in Cherokee affairs. The
interview was short. Colonel Bishop returned, and Ross was taken
back to jail.

John Ridge was far from satisfied, and he remained to talk with
the colonel, with whom he was on good terms. The colonel allowed
him another interview with Ross that evening, and on Monday,
November 16, all three were closeted for several hours. What occupied the conversation does not seem to be of record, but at the end
of it Colonel Bishop returned Ross's papers. And after dinner he
exclaimed to a nearby sentinel, "Mr. Ross is discharged."[56] Payne
was retained in custody for another three and a half days, apparently
because his neat transcriptions were more legible and easier to copy
than Ross's original documents. It also seemed that the Georgia guard
suspected him of being a French spy, or pretended to, at a time
when U.S. relations with France were tense.

The Cherokee delegation departed for Washington shortly after
December 1, 1835. On reaching Athens, Tennessee, John Ridge read
in the *Knoxville Register* an account by Payne of his captivity at
Spring Place. Ridge also read with growing anger a so-called address
from the Cherokees to the American people: an effrontery that he
presumed was also of Payne's composition. Ross had approved the
statement and evidently intended to have it signed by the Cherokees
and circulate it. The words that Payne had put into their mouths—
that they did not want to relinquish their homeland and go to the
West, that they would prefer to remain as citizens of Tennessee and
Alabama, and that a small faction among the Indians had been
seduced by the United States into spreading lies about the Cherokee
officials and into favoring emigration—filled Ridge with dismay,
and on December 4 he dashed off a protest to the principal chief.

He declined going on with the delegation and cited Payne's paper as his reason. "That address," he wrote, "unfolds to me your views of policy diametrically opposed to mine [and those] of my friends, who will never consent to be citizens of the United States, or receive money to buy land in a foreign country."⁵⁷* It would seem that Ross had not taken his recent compromise seriously and had only shammed a readiness to conclude a treaty.

When Ross received the resignation, he implored John Ridge to travel on to Washington and preserve at least a semblance of unity. This at last Ridge consented to do, he and Stand Watie reaching the city late in December along with the rest of the union delegates. They took quarters in what they called "Mrs. Arguelles' Boarding House," Ridge fanning a slender hope that Ross might yet find it expedient to accept a removal treaty. As Boudinot later informed the principal chief, "It was not until that hope was eradicated by your continued evasive and non-committal policy, and the refusal of the Government to negotiate with you at Washington, that [John Ridge] broke his connexion with you, to do the best the times and circumstances presented." Boudinot further declared: "He stuck with you as long as there was a bare probability of your doing what the compromise called for, and he left you as soon as he was satisfied that even that bare probability did not exist."⁵⁸

Meanwhile Schermerhorn, despised though he was by most of the Cherokees, had gone ahead with his scheme to conclude a treaty at New Echota. "I am happy to find," he wrote on December 19, "that we have lost none of our old friends in consequence of Ridge's compromise with Ross. His father, Major Ridge, will be here today. He and his family take an active part in preparing for the Council."⁵⁹ The Ridge justified his intentions on the grounds that an intelligent minority had a moral right, indeed a moral duty, to save a blind and ignorant majority from inevitable ruin and destruction.

Between three and four hundred people, many of them mixed-bloods or white men who had married Indian women, trekked into the former capital of the Cherokees. It was a smaller number than the organizers of the council had hoped for; for one thing, the large throng of Indians expected from the Valley Towns and the mountains

*Ross had, in fact, approached the Mexican chargé d'affaires, J. M. de Castillo y Lanzas, about the possibility of the Cherokees settling in Mexico, an overture that came to nothing, as did a similar proposition to emigrate to the Oregon country.

of North Carolina failed to appear. People from various parts of the Cherokee country explained that the "constituted authorities" had sent runners into the different districts to warn the Cherokees from the council.

A sixteen-year-old white onlooker would later recall the scene as the Indians waited for the talks to begin. "I mixed freely with the assemblage," he wrote, "smoked pipes and ate connahany, a kind of hominy, and laughed and chatted with the young folks. . . . The Indian men of the crowd sat around and smoked for hours, plunged into deep meditation and reflection. Occasionally one would say something in the Indian language, very little of which I understood, in reply to which a number would give a gutteral grunt. That would be followed by another long silence. So the time wore on, nothing being done, and if the affairs of Europe had been under settlement, they could not have been more deliberate."[60]

In spite of the absence of one of the commissioners—for Governor Carroll was still ailing with rheumatism—the council convened in the council house on December 22. John Gunter was appointed presiding officer, with Alexander McCoy as secretary. The next morning Schermerhorn addressed the assembly—"in his usual style," commented a bystander, "only a little more so." On the twenty-fourth Major Currey read the proposed treaty, and its various clauses as well as a brief comment by the commissioner were "linkstered" into Cherokee. Before the session was finished there sounded a cry of fire, fire! The roof of the council house was ablaze, and a pro-Ross observer deemed the flames "emblematic of the indignation of Heaven at the unlawful proceedings."[61] Everyone scuffled out, the fire was extinguished, the people reassembled inside, and listened attentively, smoked their pipes, and said not a word. Only occasional grunts could be heard as indications of their feelings. It may have been at this point that Major Ridge rose to speak. In substance he said:

I am one of the native sons of these wild woods. I have hunted the deer and turkey here, more than fifty years. I have fought your battles, have defended your truth and honesty, and fair trading. I have always been the friend of honest white men. The Georgians have shown a grasping spirit lately; they have extended their laws, to which we are unaccustomed, which harass our braves and make the children suffer and cry; but I can do them justice in my heart. They think the Great Father, the President, is bound by the compact of 1802 to purchase this country for them, and they justify their conduct by the end in view. They are willing to buy these lands on which to build houses and clear fields. I know the Indians have an older title than theirs. We obtained the land from the living God above. They got their title from the British. Yet they are strong and we are weak. We are few, they are many. We cannot remain here in safety and comfort. I know we love the graves of our fathers. . . . We can never forget these homes, I know, but an unbending, iron necessity tells us we must leave them. I would willingly die to preserve them, but any forcible effort to keep them will cost us our lands, our lives and the lives of our children. There is but one path of safety, one road to future existence as a Nation. That path is open before you. Make a treaty of cession. Give up these lands and go over beyond the great Father of Waters.[62]

Deep feeling in The Ridge's words moved the people, and they grunted approval. Several old men, with tears in their eyes, gathered around, grasped his hand with affection and respect, and promised to follow him to the strange land in the West.

Later Boudinot addressed the council, saying in substance that he desired to make the treaty, but he did not forget the natural feelings of Tom Foreman and others, who with fierce words and bitter feelings had opposed and defeated the treaty at Red Clay:

No, these braves are not here. Their places are vacant. Ross has induced them not to come. They are at their homes, with the loud thunder. Ah! They will come again. I know I take my life in my hand, as our fathers have also done. We will make and sign this treaty. Our friends can then cross the great river, but Tom Foreman and his people will put us across the dread river of death! We can die, but the great Cherokee Nation will be saved. They will not be annihilated; they can live. Oh, what is a man worth who will not dare to die for his people? Who is there here that would not perish, if this great nation may be saved?[63]

The next day a committee of twenty, including Major Ridge, Boudinot, Andrew Ross, John Gunter, and James Starr, was appointed to negotiate provisionally with Schermerhorn and to report to the people on Saturday night. It was a move that would be criticized by opponents as a ruse to conceal the paucity of attendance at the council. The committee was not prepared to give their report at the time appointed, but even if they had been ready, the people were in no condition to hear it, since many were drunk from their celebration of Christmas. On Monday evening, the twenty-eighth, the committee reported to the council that they had agreed with the commissioner and recommended that the treaty—substantially the same that had been offered to the Cherokees at Red Clay—be closed. The same committee was authorized to do so. Then the

purpose as soon after the ratification of this Trea
ty as an appropriation for the same shall be made
It is however not intended in this article to interfere
with that part of the annuities due the Cherokees west
by the Treaty of 1819

Article 19 This treaty after the same shall be
ratified by the President & Senate of the United States
shall be obligatory on the contracting parties.

In testimony whereof the Commissioners and
the Chiefs head men & people whose names are
hereunto annexed being duly authorized by
the people in general Council assembled have
affixed their hands & seals for themselves
& in behalf of the Cherokee Nation.

Cue te hee his mark   (Seal)   Wm Carroll (Seal)

Te gah e ske his mark (Seal)   J. F. Schermerhorn (Seal)

Robert Rogers   (Seal)   Major his X Ridge (Seal)
John Gunter   mark
                       (Seal)   James his X Foster (Seal)
                                        mark
John A. Bell   (Seal)   Tesa Ta esky his X mark (Seal)

Charles F. Foreman (Seal)   Charles his X moore (Seal)
                                        mark
William Rogers   (Seal)   George his X Chambers (Seal)
                                        mark
George W Adair   (Seal)   Tah yeske his X mark (Seal)

Elias Boudinot   (Seal)   Archilla his X Smith (Seal)
                                        mark
James Starr   (Seal)   Andrew Ross (Seal)

Jesse Halfbreed his mark (Seal)   William Lasley (Seal)

First signature page, Treaty of New Echota. Courtesy of the
National Archives.

commissioner suggested that a delegation of thirteen should accompany him to Washington, whereupon a committee of three was appointed to nominate the delegation. But as some fifty men applied for the honor of a mission to Washington, the nominating committee reportd to the commissioner that the selection of a panel was "a matter of great delicacy" and requested that he name the delegates himself. To this the people objected, and after several speeches on the subject Schermerhorn declined the chore, and it was held over for a later time.[64]

On Tuesday evening, December 29, 1835, the committee of twenty, along with several witnesses, met with Schermerhorn in the parlor of Boudinot's house. A fire burned on the hearth and lit the room with its flicker, along with candlelight. The treaty was read once more, while the Indians smoked their pipes in silence. When it came time to sign the document, which had been freshly transcribed that day, there was some hesitation, no one volunteering at once to be the first to sign. The mark of an Indian named Cae-te-hee was the first to appear in the final order of names on the signature page. But John Gunter may actually have been the first to sign—so at least it would be remembered by one who was there. Nine of those representing the Cherokees were literate in English and could write their names; eleven signed by means of their marks.[65]

The Ridge was reported to have said as he made his mark, "I have signed my death warrant."[66] That may well have been so, for it agrees with his statement to Colonel McKenney at Philadelphia five months later. When the colonel remarked on the peril in which he had placed himself, Major Ridge replied: "I expect to die for it."[67]*

On the next morning the committee of twenty reported to the council that the treaty was signed, and the council approved the act unanimously. Then it appointed the delegation to go with Schermerhorn to Washington, with Major Ridge as its chief, and instructed

*Cf. Schermerhorn's statement: "These men before they entered upon their business, knew they were running a dreadful risk; for it was death by their laws for any person to enter [an unauthorized] treaty with the United States.... But Ridge, Boudinot, Bell, Rogers and others, their associates who finally united in making the New Echota treaty, had counted the cost, and had deliberately made up their minds, if need be, to offer up their lives as a sacrifice, to save ... their nation from inevitable extermination and ruin.... I consider Ridge, Boudinot, and Bell and their associates as having acted on the purest principles of patriotism" (Little Rock *Arkansas Gazette*, Oct. 2, 1839, p. 2; copied from *Utica Observer*, July 17, 1839).

the members "to use their best influence with the Red Clay delegation to sign [the] treaty, and to do what might be necessary to
secure its ratification by the Senate of the United States."[68] The
blankets that had been brought to the council ground for the comfort of the Cherokees during the cold winter nights were given to
them, one to each person. Then the council adjourned, having trans-
acted one of the most fateful bits of business in all of Cherokee
history. The consequences of it were to dominate Cherokee life for
decades to come.

12 • HONEY CREEK

THE first contingent of the New Echota delegation arrived in Washington on January 27, 1836. Schermerhorn, Major Ridge, and Boudinot did not appear, however, until February 3.[1] They at once wrote Ross of the proceedings at New Echota and sent a copy of the treaty, with an appeal for the Red Clay delegation to sign it. It was suddenly observed that the conduct of John Ridge "became mysterious toward [that] delegation," and shortly thereafter he and Stand Watie left Mrs. Arguelles' boarding house and took quarters at the hotel where the removal delegates had stopped.[2] The two lost no time in signing the Treaty of New Echota, an action which, on Ridge's part, Ross characterized as a "fourth entire revolution in politics within as many months: varying as often as the moon, without the excuse of lunacy for his changes."[3] Whatever hopes the treaty leaders had that Ross would come to terms and find the treaty acceptable were soon dashed. He remained so bitterly opposed to its terms that he did not even answer the pro-treaty appeal.

Boudinot later wrote of the intransigence of Ross's course from that time on:

In this state of things, utterly unable himself to consummate a treaty which he may think preferable, Mr. Ross is using his influence to defeat the only measure that can give relief to his suffering people. . . . He says he is doing the *will* of the people, and he holds their authority; they are opposed, and it is enough. The will of the people! The opposition of the people! This has been the cry for the last five years, until that people have become but a mere wreck of what they once were; all their institutions and improvements utterly destroyed; their energy enervated; their moral character debased, corrupted and ruined. The whole of that catastrophe . . . might have been averted, if Mr. Ross . . .

291

had met the crisis manfully as it became him to do, and unfolded to his confiding people the sure termination of these things; they might now have been a happy and prosperous community, a monument to his forecast and wise administration as an Indian chief. But, no sir, he has dragged an ignorant train, wrought upon by near-sighted prejudice and stupid obstinacy, to the last brink of destruction.[4]

The Ridges and their friends signed several supplementary articles, and on February 11 they approved a "statement of consent," which allowed the treaty to go to the Senate for action.[5] There it aroused storms of protest. A widespread perception was that it was a fraud. Strong speeches were delivered against it, and in the House, John Quincy Adams called it an "eternal disgrace upon the country."[6] Dissenting memorials arrived from multitudes of American citizens and from numerous organizations. And to a protest written by John Howard Payne, who remained in touch with Ross, the Cherokees affixed nearly sixteen thousand signatures, many duplicated and many fraudulent—even suckling babies were found to have "signed" the petition. With all the questionable names, however, the protest represented a formidable opposition among the Cherokee people.[7] Had Adams still been president, the treaty would have doubtless been set aside, as McIntosh's treaty had been scrapped in 1825. But Jackson pressed it with unyielding determination, and it was approved in the Senate on May 17 by a margin of one vote. "The ratification of this treaty for the removal of the Cherokees," wrote Senator Benton of Missouri, "was one of the most difficult and delicate questions which we ever had to manage, and [one] in which success seemed to be impossible up to the last moment."[8] Had a particular senator not been absent, or had another not switched his vote at the last moment, the treaty would have failed to carry. Jackson proclaimed it law on May 23.

John Ridge was nettled by insinuations that he had signed the treaty out of ambition to become principal chief after the removal. In brushing the charge aside, he spoke in third person: "You say John Ridge was prompted by a selfish ambition when he signed the treaty. It is not so. John Ridge signed his death warrant when he signed that treaty, and no one knows it better than he. . . . John Ridge may not die tomorrow . . . ; but sooner or later he will have to yield his life as the penalty for signing. John Ridge has not acted blindly, for he sees plainly that his people cannot hope to stand against the white man in their present situation. By removing to the west they may in time learn to hold their own with the white man. Let it not be said that John Ridge acted from motives of ambition, for he acted for what he believed to be the best interests of his people."⁹ Abundant evidence exists that he and his fellow treaty leaders all acted from the purest of motives, and with the love of true patriots.

The Red Clay delegation called them traitors, however, and hurled more threats against their lives. In writing home, John Ridge declared: "The Ross party here already count my death as certain." It was something he was ready for, he explained: "If I can relieve my bleeding countrymen . . . I am even prepared to be immolated to gratify the ambitions of my enemies."¹⁰ And in a joint letter with Boudinot and Stand Watie he informed Schermerhorn that some Cherokees

may be secretly induced to assassinate, by John Ross & his friends, but it will be done so secretly that only one or two may fall. What will that be to the joy which the treaty will ultimately give to the Indians? the thousands who will emigrate and be happy? the thousands who will be relieved from the lowest state of wretchedness and who, now reduced almost to nakedness and starvation; buffeted and lacerated by the settlers among them; driven, with their women and little ones, from their cabins and their fields, to the woods and mountains, stripped of the little property they once possessed, [are now] wandering outcasts . . . dependent on the cold charity of their new oppressors?¹¹

The treaty delegation remained in Washington long enough to finish their business with the government. On May 21, Major Ridge and seven of his friends wrote the commissioner of Indian affairs to suggest that it was "of the utmost importance" that they leave the capital as soon as possible. They wondered if the commissioner could make a decision on the estimates that they had had the honor of presenting to him the day before. "The disturbances among the Creek Indians," they explained, "and the possibility of the contagion extending to our people, together with the probability of an excitement . . . caused, perhaps, by some of the other Delegation, require our presence at home. Our duties, as friends of peace, and the preservation of our people, demand our return."¹² The Indian Office paid their expenses, and they left for home on May 26.

On coming into the Cherokee country they received several warnings of threats against their lives, and a friend wrote Boudinot: "We recommend for your safety [that] you and your family . . . leave the country until the excitement is over."¹³ They found many Cherokees in want, having been turned from their homes, wandering destitute, without money for provisions, and fed by those who had little subsistence themselves. The season for planting had been bad, owing to excessive rain, and the price of corn had risen. But in the midst of such sad conditions John Ridge found that his own fields were thriving, and The Ridge was pleased to see that Susanna had made a good crop, directing the blacks with firmness and efficiency.[14] But good crops would be necessary to feed the myriad hungry Cherokees who would stop at their doors, for Cherokee hospitality dictated that no one, not even a stranger, should be turned away. Indeed, a few months later Ridge would state: "My father . . . is nearly eat out of his stock and corn—a bare supply for the time he remains is hardly at his command. My own condition is even worse— I have only 3 shoats left, and I have been purchasing beef. I yet keep an open house for Cherokees."[15]

In the meantime, two weeks after reaching home, he wrote to the president, and both he and Major Ridge signed the letter. It reported the home situation as they saw it:

There was a strong warlike excitement in the minds of the whites, and rumor, with her thousand tongues, filled the land with Cherokee hostility or intentions of war. We have examined into the truth, and find the reverse of all these stories. A great many of the Cherokees have been disarmed of their rifles by the Georgians. . . , greatly to the injury of the Indians, as they are in a wretched condition for food. The appropriations demanded by the treaty have been so long delayed that we have, on our own responsibility, issued provisions, as far as our individual means allowed.

Then after painting an overly optimistic picture of the people's reception of the treaty, the letter continued:

. . . now we come to address you on the subject of our griefs & afflictions from the acts of the white people. They have got our lands and now they are preparing to fleece us of the money accruing from the treaty. We found our plantations taken in whole or in part by the Georgians— suits instituted against us for back rents for our own farms. These suits are commenced in the inferior courts, with the evident design that, when we are ready to remove, to arrest our people, and on these vile claims to induce us to compromise for our own release, to travel with our families. Thus our funds will be filched from our people, and we shall be compelled to leave our country as beggars and in want.

Even the Georgia laws, which deny our oaths, are thrown aside, and notwithstanding the cries of our people, and protestation of our innocence and peace, the lowest classes of the white people are flogging the Cherokees with cowhides, hickories, and clubs. We are not safe in our houses—our people are assailed by day and night by the rabble. Even justices of the peace and constables are concerned in this business. This barbarous treatment is not confined to men, but the women are stripped also and whipped without law or mercy.... Send regular troops to protect us from these lawless assaults, and to protect our people as they depart for the West. If it is not done, we shall carry off nothing but the scars of the lash on our backs, and our oppressors will get all the money. We talk plainly, as chiefs having property and life in danger, and we appeal to you for protection.[16]

While Major Ridge had been in Washington, a Georgian named Cox had usurped a long piece of cleared field across the Oostanaula from the Ridge house and Lavender's Store,[17] and there was nothing The Ridge could do about it—he had neither recourse to justice in the courts nor protection from law. Most of such dispossessions took place in Georgia, but sometimes they happened also in other states. John Ridge, for example, had trouble about his farm and ferry in Alabama.

The trouble had begun the year before while Ridge was in Washington. A swaggering white man named John H. Garrett, who had been elected a major general in the Alabama militia and who liked to talk of dueling and "the code," forcibly ejected William Childers, Ridge's tenant and ferryman, and seized possession of the farm and ferry. In Ridge's absence Sarah, his wife, appealed to Major Currey, who ordered Garrett off and in turn appealed for justice to the governor of Alabama. Garrett was still in possession of the property in the summer of 1836, having put up structures on the opposite side of the Coosa from Ridge's buildings. Ridge now took the matter to General John E. Wool, who had just been sent with American troops to police the Cherokee Nation and disarm the Indians while they prepared to remove under the New Echota Treaty. The general sent troops to oust Garrett, and Childers was reinstalled as tenant and ferryman. Garrett soon returned, however, with a large force of men; he had, moreover, secured a writ of possession and an injunction from the chancery court of Cherokee County, Alabama, forbidding Ridge and Childers further use of the ferry and farm. Childers was ejected a second time, and when Ridge appealed once more to General Wool, the general advised that Garrett could not be removed without bloodshed and that it would be sensible to submit to force and look to the United States for spoliation under the Treaty of New Echota.[18] That was the course which Ridge elected to follow.

The treaty had named a committee authorized to transact all business on the part of the Cherokees that might arise in connection with executing the treaty. Both factions were represented on the panel. The name of Ross led the list, but he and his men chose not to serve. As the committee was empowered to fill any vacancy caused by death or refusal to serve, it came to be packed with treaty men.[19] John Ridge was chosen president. The Indians declined to serve without compensation, so it was agreed that Ridge would receive six dollars a day while the committee sat, and the rest four dollars each.

The treaty also provided for two U.S. commissioners to transact business on behalf of the federal government, and Governor Carroll and Governor Lumpkin were chosen to fill the posts. Lumpkin had ended his final term as governor of Georgia in November, 1835. He had intended to settle down as a gentleman planter in Athens, Georgia, near the state college, of which he was a trustee. But when the treaty was ratified, Jackson commissioned him to help execute it: no one, after all, had agitated for it more loudly than he. He would have declined the vexing and laborious task except that Jackson had enclosed the commission in a private letter that left the governor no graceful way out.

Lumpkin opened correspondence with Ridge in June, sending a handful of lawyers' bills in which certain services were charged for two or three times. The committee scaled the fees down drastically, but their real work could not begin until the commissioners arrived in New Echota.[20] Ridge waited restlessly at Running Waters for a call to duty, but before it came, he brought his family to New Echota; Sarah was feeling sickly, and he did not wish to leave her behind. He settled her and the children in Boudinot's house, which he rented. Boudinot was glad to let the house. Harriet had died in childbirth on a hot day in August and was buried in a lonely grave at the edge of the almost deserted town. Memories of her so saddened Boudinot that he had broken up his household and was ready to take his children elsewhere. The rent money would help in their support.

Before plunging into the work of the committee, Ridge felt it necessary to call a general council of the nation to meet in New Echota on September 12 to explain the treaty to the rank and file and deliberate certain affairs of the nation. Not only he but also Major Ridge and then other prominent members of the Treaty Party signed the announcement to John Ross. The upshot was that Ross himself called a council to meet at Red Clay on September 15. It would be futile, Ridge knew, to hold a council at about the same time that Ross did, so he postponed his call for a meeting.

General Wool, who had felt immediate sympathy for the Cherokees in their plight, but who was staunch in his support of the treaty, wondered about the wisdom of permitting Ross to hold a council. "One thing is certain," he wrote the War Department, "no good will come of it, and much evil may be anticipated. Major Currey & John Ridge have both been here; they both predict much evil from the meeting."[21]

In the absence of clear-cut instructions from Washington, Wool allowed the council to convene, and as predicted, Ross used the occasion to harden his followers' resistance to the treaty. Some three thousand Cherokees attended, and General Wool was present with troops at an encampment a quarter of a mile from the council ground. He had two interviews with Ross. "I told him the destinies of these people were in his hands. It was in his power to do them much good or much evil."[22] And it was clear to Wool that the latter alternative would occur if Ross went ahead with his present intentions.

The Treaty Party called its own council in October. On the eleventh Wool reported to the commanding general of the U.S. Army: "I leave this morning for New Echota, where I have a camp of two companies of volunteers, to watch the movements of a council of Cherokees now sitting at that place, and to prevent disturbances which might arise between the parties of Ross and Ridge."[23] No serious trouble occurred, however; the treaty was explained, and certain matters, notably the debts of the nation, were debated. But the shadow of John Ross fell across the council, and its effectiveness was less than Ridge desired. For some time Major Ridge had been ailing; he was now silent, and his eloquence was sorely missed.

Meanwhile Governor Lumpkin had arrived in the old Cherokee capital. The public buildings were in such ruin and disrepair that he could find no suitable place for his quarters and his office. His problem was solved, however, when the Cherokees built two cabins for the commissioners—one to live in and one in which to do their work. As yet no word had come from Carroll. On September 24, Lumpkin complained to the president: "No claim whatever under the Treaty can be adjudicated by a single Commissioner. And not a single Indian or family will emigrate until their claims are adjusted and settled." Without any word from Carroll, Lumpkin nevertheless gave public notice that the commissioners would be "in attendance at New Echota, on the 10th of October next," and he invited claimants to appear before them.[24] The tenth arrived, and Carroll was still immobilized by rheumatism. On the twentieth Lumpkin reported to the commissioner of Indian affairs: "I assure you, sir, I have not been idle while here alone. I have received and examined a great mass of papers and claims arising under the treaty. I have made my notes on many of these papers, registered, arranged, and filed them. I have had the Indian Committee here in session for ten or twelve days past, and have a great portion of the business in which they were expected to render aid in a state of preparation and forwardness."[25]

One of the first requests that the committee made of Lumpkin was for rations to feed indigent Cherokees. General Wool had issued food to them on his own responsibility, but declined to do so any longer. Lumpkin assumed responsibility for the rations, and the Indians were fed. But the absence of his colleague prevented the transaction of other urgent business. Those Indians who were eager to start for the West had sold their grain and provisions, had bought horses and wagons to emigrate themselves, and had been waiting for weeks to have their affairs adjusted.[26] There was nothing to do but wait, however exasperating it became. Finally the president appointed Colonel John Kennedy to take Carroll's place, and at last some cases could be completed, some Indians readied for the march west.

The Indian committee met at the call of the commissioners and in many respects were subject to the commissioners' authority. The committee turned to their tedious routine with enthusiasm, and John Ridge wrote: "We will carry out the treaty triumphantly notwithstanding John Ross's efforts to delude the ignorant class."[27] Their largest duty was the audit of individual Cherokee claims on which the commissioners had to act, work that involved the evaluations made by appraisers whom Major Currey had sent to every part of the nation. But other duties fell to their lot. They certified who among the Cherokees were capable of removing themselves, and they had the responsibility of selecting the missionaries and teachers who would go west with the tribe. Boudinot served as clerk for all such transactions.

"The Indian Committee," Lumpkin wrote, "needed much instruction to prepare them for an enlightened discharge of their duty." But they learned readily, and Lumpkin was patient, "urging them to a faithful discharge of their official duty." He continued:

... while I shall never cease to bear witness to the honor and fidelity of Ridge and his party, ... it cost me great care, watchfulness and labor to prevent [them] from running into gross improprieties and extravagance. He and many of his friends had often been lobby members of Congress, and had acquired some taste for extravagance, especially when exercised at the expense of the Government. In a word, the Committee, instead of continuing to view themselves as a business committee, appointed to procure and investigate facts and report thereon to the Commissioners, aspired to the dignity of what they had witnessed in Congressmen. They wished the sessions of this Committee to be interminable. They admired the compensation of four dollars per day. They wished to get rid of the tests of the Commissioners on their proceedings. They became pleasantly and gentlemanly assuming. It became necessary to correct their high notions and set them right.[28]

The commissioners held a conference with the committee for that purpose on December 16, and on the next day sent John Ridge a corrective letter. The letter, Lumpkin noted, had the desired effect. "A few days only for reflection was all that was necessary. . . . They laid aside their extravagant assumptions, returned to their sober duty, and no further difficulty occurred."[29]

In the course of their work they examined hundreds of Cherokee claims and interviewed the claimants who flocked into New Echota. These came from every part of the nation, in every conceivable manner, some in aristocratic carriages, some in wagons, some in carts, some on horseback, and many on foot. Many brought blankets and small pots and wooden spoons. But there was inadequate shelter for them, and the weather was often cold. The commissioners had requisitioned blankets from General Wool, and these were distributed, along with army rations. Although some of the Indians had brought salt and hominy, others had come empty-handed and would have gone hungry but for the issue of food. They would build fires and smoke pipes while they waited, an encouraging number of Ross men in their midst.

General Wool had stationed troops in New Echota to keep order, but there was little trouble except when the Indians secured whiskey. Then they became quarrelsome, prone to scuffle and fight. For the most part, however, the scene was one of peace and good order. "About fifteen hundred or two thousand Indians would be off this fall," wrote Major Currey to the commissary general. ". . . Major Ridge, Judge Martin, and Joseph Vann are of this number."[30] Unfortunately the disbursing agent was late in arriving to authorize their collection of dues for departure. Hence delays of weeks, even months, in their starting out for what they still called Arkansas, though in truth their lands lay past the western boundary of that state.

The number who were actually ready to emigrate by the new year was only six hundred, most of them comfortably fixed members of the Treaty Party. They had taken advantage of the treaty provisions to move themselves, and had been certified by the committee as capable of doing so. Having at last drawn their money, they set out with carriages and wagons, accompanied by slaves, saddle horses and droves of oxen. Their route lay through Tennessee, Kentucky, the southern tip of Illinois, Missouri, and the northwest corner of Arkansas into the lands of "the Cherokees West," or the northeast part of present-day Oklahoma. Major Ridge had planned to leave at that time with his family. His house, his ferry, his total improvements were evaluated at $24,127, a figure which made him the third richest man in the Cherokee Nation, only the valuations of Lewis Ross and "rich Joe Vann" exceeding his.[31] He drew additional sums for spoliations and had been certified by the committee as "capable." He had, all ready for travel, a family coach, carriages for his Negroes, and a wagon for such personal effects as he had retained. But owing to his failing health he had to postpone his departure.

About that time Sally left his household—Sally, who had become a charming Cherokee belle, though her coloring, like that of Major Ridge himself, was dark, much darker than John's. "A full dark Cherokee," observed Miss Sawyer, the schoolteacher, ". . . a young lady of superior talent . . . very interesting in her person & appearance."[32] She was graceful in form and movements. She dressed well, mostly in blue calico, then considered a fine fabric, and more than one white man wanted to marry her. According to the legend that grew up about her:

She was a most accomplished rider. . . . Once her lover, the man she at last married, "bought from a Tennessee drover a nag for Miss Sally to ride on." He presented it to her, saddled and bridled, and begged the pleasure of riding with her. She mounted on the pony gaily, but something about the bridle needed adjusting, the lover slipped it off the pony's head to fix it. No sooner loose than the pony bounded off unfettered, and he and Miss Sally, for thirteen miles, tried for the mastery of the situation. "Miss Sally rode him down," it is said, and ever afterward the pony seemed a dispirited animal.[33]

The man she married was a young Georgian named George W. Paschal. He was small in stature, with dark eyes and hair; his face was sallow; by temperament he was quick, nervous, energetic. A lawyer by training, he had turned his eyes toward the Cherokee country during the gold rush. "With his diploma well mounted, with two law books in his mails, the young master of contingent remainders bade adieu to his mother and rode toward the land of gold."[34] After the Treaty of New Echota he had joined the volunteers, was made a lieutenant, and became the aide-de-camp of General Wool. For a while he was in command of troops stationed in New Echota, and that may well be where he had met the Ridges. At any rate he sued for Sally's hand, and she accepted his proposal.

"In February A.D. 1837," he wrote, "Miss Ridge was enrolled as one of her father's family. He took transportation in kind for his family & commuted for subsistence for himself & family. But before they left the Eastern country I married his daughter & she consequently did not accompany her father. In the summer following I enrolled & under an order of Genl. Nathaniel Smith transported my own family."[35] Before the Paschals could get under way, however, with George still wearing his uniform, though now a civilian, they were detained by the sheriff of Cass County, who arrested Paschal on charges preferred by a whiskey peddler named Robert Kirkham. While still in the army, and with the approval of the commissioners, he had destroyed some whiskey that Kirkham was selling in New Echota. The sheriff held Paschal until he deposited $300 with Lavender, who put up his bail. Also his carriage horses were attached. When the suit was tried, the court handed down a judgment of $230 against him, plus court costs, for which Paschal would later file a successful claim against the government.[36] At last he and Sally began their journey, with a commission from John Ridge to purchase improvements in the vicinity of a stream called Honey Creek.

In the meantime, owing to his frail health, The Ridge had decided to accept transportation from the government instead of emigrating independently. Besides himself, his party consisted of Susanna; Watty; Clarinda, the feebleminded child of John Ridge; one of Boudinot's children; and eighteen slaves. David Watie and his family were also ready to go. The detachment they joined numbered 466 individuals, half of them children. General Nathaniel Smith, who had replaced Major Currey as emigration agent at the latter's death in December, made preparations to move these Indians to Ross's Landing, where provisions could be had at lower cost. But a large majority of the Indians refused to leave New Echota until

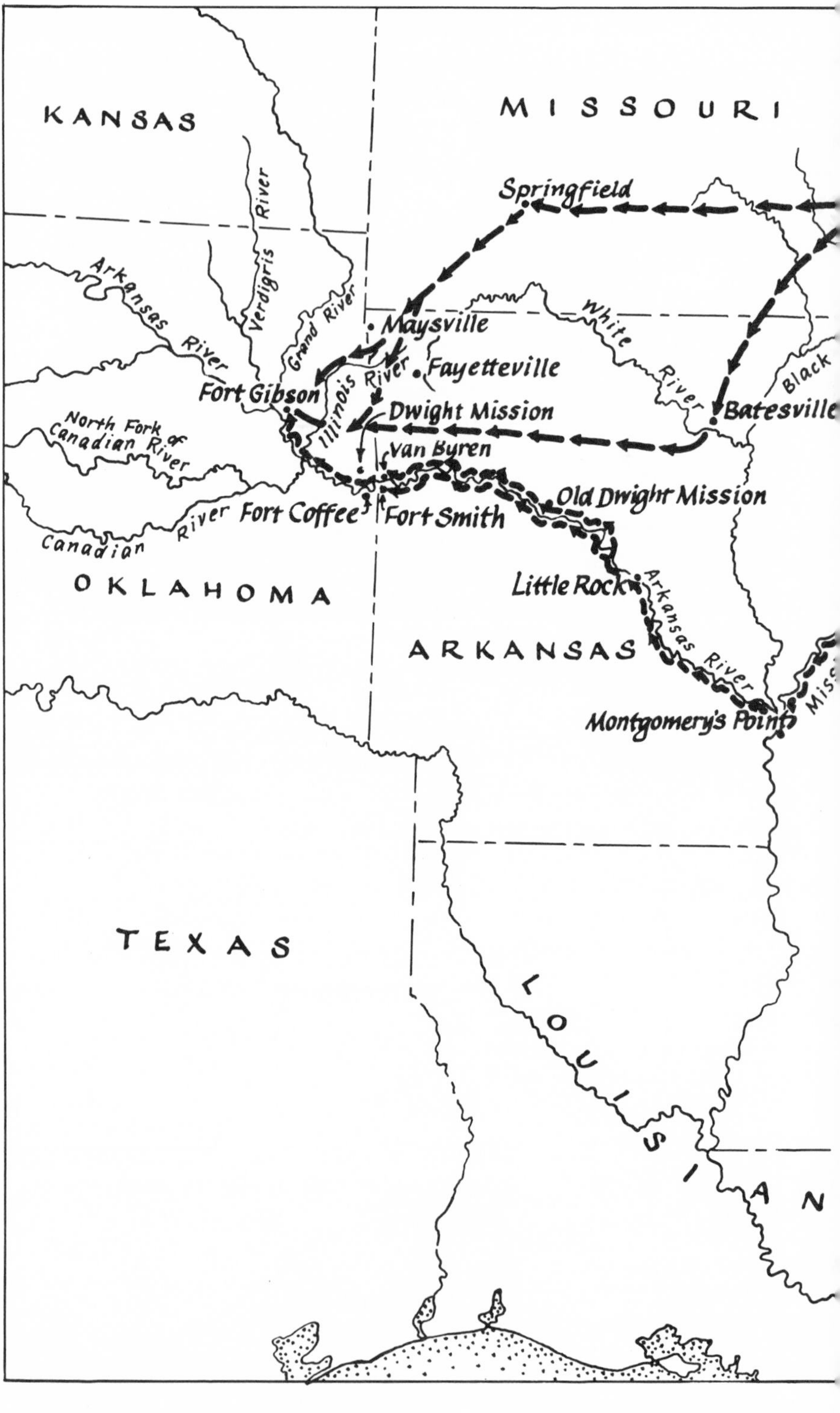

KANSAS
MISSOURI
Springfield
Verdigris River
Arkansas River
Grand River
Maysville
White River
Fayetteville
Illinois River
Black
Fort Gibson
Dwight Mission
Batesville
North Fork of Canadian River
Van Buren
Old Dwight Mission
Fort Coffee
Fort Smith
Canadian River
Little Rock
Arkansas River
OKLAHOMA
ARKANSAS
Montgomery's Point
TEXAS
LOUISIAN

K E N T U C K Y

Ohio River

ackson
Jonesboro · Golconda
rdeau Paducah · Hopkinsville

· Nashville
· McMinnville
Rattle Snake · Cherokee Agency
Springs ᷒ Ross' Landing (Chattanooga)
· Red Clay
TENNESSEE · Springplace
Tennessee Huntsville · New Echota
Muscle Shoals River
· Creek Path
Guntersville

MISSISSIPPI

GEORGIA

ALABAMA

← Land Route
←-- Water Route

The Trail *of* Tears

0   50   100 MILES

FLORIDA

the year's subsistence to which they were entitled on arriving in the West was commuted and they received the value of it in cash. Major Ridge urged this course to the people, and John Ridge pressed it "clamorously." The request was endorsed by Governor Lumpkin and supported by General Wool, so General Smith agreed to comply.[37] The Cherokees went docilely then to Ross's Landing, where many of them got drunk and disorderly.

On March 3, 1837, the whole band was herded onto a flotilla of flatboats, eleven in all, divided into three groups. Dr. John S. Young, who took charge of the movement, ordered about 150 bushels of cornmeal, seventy-eight barrels of flour, and twelve thousand pounds of bacon stowed on the boats to feed the travelers along the way. "It is mournful to see how reluctantly these people go away," wrote a missionary, "—even the stoutest hearts melt into tears when they turn their faces toward the setting sun—& I am sure that this land will be bedewed with a Nation's tears—if not with their blood. . . . Major Ridge," the missionary added, "is . . . said to be in a declining state, & it is doubted whether he will reach Arkansas."[38]

The Ridge and his family had no special accommodations during the first days of the trip. In the open boats they were exposed to the wind, and the wind was cold. The little fleet made five miles downriver the first afternoon, then landed so that the Indians might camp for the night. On the sixth the boats reached Gunter's Landing, a collection of crude wooden stores upon a high sandy bank. Dr. Young refused to put in to the landing, but ordered the boats tied to an island to prevent the Indians from going ashore and getting drunk. Waiting for them here was the steamer *Knoxville*, captained by George Washington Harris, not yet the author of uproarious tales about Sut Lovingood. A number of passengers were given deck passage on the steamer, but Major Ridge received preferential treatment. While twenty dollars was the cost of transporting the ordinary Cherokee, General Smith had allocated three hundred dollars for cabin passage for The Ridge and his family, and they made the rest of the trip in comfort.[39] At 9:00 A.M. on March 7 the *Knoxville* paddled forth with the flatboats tied to her stern. On reaching Decatur, Alabama, they found the river too low to permit navigation of Muscle Shoals, so the Indians were herded off the boats and placed on the open cars of the Tuscumbia, Courtland, and Decatur Railroad—said to be the first railway west of the Appalachians. The cars hauled them to Tuscumbia, where they camped to wait for the boats that would take them down the river.

On the morning of the thirteenth the steamboat *Newark* arrived
with two sixty-ton keelboats in tow and moored at the landing near
where the Indians had camped. "Immediately the whole posse of
them," wrote Dr. Clarke Lillybridge, the physician for the journey,
"were in motion bringing their effects to the boats. The day was
spent in getting things arranged on board. At night the emigrants
laid themselves down as they could, cheerful in the expectation of
being under way in the morning."[40] Their departure, however, was
delayed till four in the afternoon, with the Cherokees cross and
restless at the wait. They steamed down the river all that night
and all the next day, reaching Paducah, Kentucky, at ten in the
evening. The keelboats proved more satisfactory than the flatboats;
indeed, Dr. Young attributed much of the trip's success to the
former, which he described as "spacious, well covered, painted,
[and] dry. They were kept constantly clean and well ventilated,
by means of side doors, which [allowed] the Indians [to sleep] without being exposed to the night air or inclement weather. On the top
of each keel were three hearths, which added to the one on the deck
of the steamboat, made fireplaces which enabled the Indians to cook
and eat at regular periods without it being necessary for the boats
to stop."[41]

About dawn of the eighteenth the boats ran afoul of a snag, and
there was some apprehension among the Indians; "one wheel was
considerably damaged and the top of the keels burst in." But the
boats continued their progress, striking down the Ohio and into the
Mississippi. It rained frequently, and high winds blew from the
south. "The wind," wrote Dr. Lillybridge, "makes it difficult for
the Indians to cook, as their fires are on top of the Boats."[42]

About dawn of the eighteenth the boats arrived at Montgomery
Point, Arkansas, and there a pilot came on board to take the *Newark*
up the muddy Arkansas River. Progress was much slower upstream,
and the boats did not reach Little Rock until the evening of the
twenty-first. To prevent a whiskey frolic there, the passengers were
landed on the shore opposite the town, whose lights across the
water were soon dimmed in the glare of the Cherokees' crackling
fires. The next day the *Newark* could proceed no further, but a
steamboat of lighter draft, the *Revenue,* took the keelboats in tow.
The weather turned mild and clear, but the further the boats
ascended the river, the greater the danger of running aground. Once
as the *Revenue* strained to get free of a yellow sandbar, her guard
passed over the guard of a keelboat and stove in the top of the

smaller craft, to the consternation of the Cherokees.[43] The river, however, was placid, the current rather sluggish, the water yellow-brown in hue. There was a dank, muddy smell in the air. The banks were festooned with vines, bushes, and trees, all intensely green.

On the twenty-fifth Major Ridge and Susanna, both troubled with a severe cough, asked for Dr. Lillybridge, and he prescribed for their difficulties. Apparently the medicine helped, for the doctor's journal makes no further mention of attendance upon them. The Ridge's name next occurred in the entry for March 27, the day they reached Fort Smith, a stop beyond Van Buren. There a friend advised Major Ridge to go no farther by boat but "turn back to Van Buren, as that was the most eligible route to the lands he had selected. About 2 miles above Fort Smith," the doctor wrote, "the Boats landed to set Major Ridge and his friends on shore. Immediately the larger proportion of the Detachment were in motion, and in spite of the advice of the Agents and those who were acquainted with the country, they landed their effects & considered themselves at home."[44] The boats took the rest of the detachment to Fort Coffee, which they reached at noon the following day—the end of a journey unusual in the history of Indian removal: no one had died en route.

Major Ridge had already decided to settle in the vicinity of Honey Creek in the northeast corner of the Cherokee lands, not far from the cornerstone (on the Cherokee line) that marked the border between Missouri and Arkansas. The country was, as Susanna later remembered, "an entire wilderness."[45] To get there The Ridge led his friends, including the Fields, up the old military highway known as the Line Road because it ran roughly parallel to the western boundary of Arkansas. It turned out to be a rough course; "the trees were razed close to the ground," according to a traveler who had gone that way the year before—a statement not intended to imply that any of the stumps had been uprooted.[46] The road crossed numerous unbridged streams, and the lack of ferry facilities was by no means its chief hazard. The border country was infested wth desperadoes who had squatted in abandoned cabins and sold whiskey to the Indians and were not averse to relieving a traveler of his money in some lonely ambush. No doubt Major Ridge and his friends had procured some means of conveyance at either Fort Smith or Van Buren, and luck was on their side: they traveled the Line Road without mishap. Honey Creek, their destination, rose in Arkansas, flowed for a brief stretch through the corner of Missouri, and turned into the Indian country at Southwest City on the Missouri-Cherokee line. It finally flowed, cool and clear, into the Neosho or Grand River.

The Ridge's party arrived in time to see the bottomlands aflame with redbud that ranged from pink through crimson on to purple. Dogwood, too, bloomed in cascades of gleaming white, and fragrant wild plum blossoms glowed along the courses of small streams. Honey Creek, they found, was aptly named. As Washington Irving had lately said of the Indian country, "the wild honey-bee swarms in myriads, in the noble groves and forests which skirt and intersect the prairies, and extend along the alluvial bottoms of the rivers. It seems to me as if these beautiful regions answer literally to the description of the land of promise, 'a land flowing with milk and honey'; for the rich pasturage of the prairies is calculated to sustain herds of cattle as countless as the sands upon the seashore, while the flowers with which they are enamelled render them a very paradise for the nectar-seeking bee."[47] Irving, on his tour of the prairies, had accompanied a commissioner sent by the War Department to examine the lands set aside for Indian migration.

The Ridge purchased improvements at the mouth of Honey Creek, where the land was rich and fertile, and started laying plans to clear large fields. "We had to undergo many privations in [the] new Country," Susanna later recalled. "But we bore [them] all under the belief that we had found a comfortable home for our children and grandchildren. We expended much money and labor on building houses and clearing land."[48] Some of it was prairie land, less of a problem to turn into fields than the wooded ground, thick with oak, hickory, ash, persimmon, pine, and cedar—or, along the bottoms, with cottonwood, maple, sycamore, willow, and sweet gum, as well as long lianas of wild grape. The Ridge put his blacks to work, bought stock and farming equipment, and soon had the beginnings of a splendid farm. His nearest neighbors were some of the Fields, who settled on the north side of Honey Creek.*

---

*Meanwhile a rumor had spread through the Cherokee Nation East that Major Ridge had died on reaching his destination. "From Arkansas," wrote a missionary, "we have the intelligence, upon good authority, that the celebrated & well known Major Ridge departed this life since his arrival in his new home. He had been in a low state of health long before he left here & doubts were entertained whether he would live to see his new home; he survived however for a few weeks after his arrival" (H. G. Clauder to Theodore Shultz, June 27, 1837, Cherokee Mission, Moravian Archives, Winston-Salem, N.C.).

The U.S. commissioners called the Cherokee committee back into session in New Echota during June, 1837, and they remained at their task throughout the summer. Late in the season Governor Lumpkin wrote the commissioner of Indian affairs: "We are now busily engaged in settling up all the affairs of such Cherokees as have determined to emigrate this fall, and if you were here to witness the bustle and business now going on, you would be ready to conclude that the spirit of emigration among the Cherokees was such as to remove all doubts of their yielding . . . without further trouble."[49] In September, John Ridge resigned from the committee in order to prepare for his own removal. On the twenty-seventh he sent a farewell letter to Lumpkin and Kennedy, expressing his appreciation for the humanity they had shown the Cherokees. He did not know, he confessed, what history would have to say about the Ridge name, for their motives had been misrepresented by opponents and their reputations blackened by the "awakened prejudices" of the ignorant part of the Cherokee people. The Ridges' merits he left to the consideration of God and "an enlightened world."[50]

The commissioners replied:

Under no circumstances can a reflecting man bid a final adieu to the beloved land of his birth, and that of his fathers for generations past, without exciting the strongest emotions of the human mind. But to command a sufficient stock of reason, fortitude, and energy to overcome not only the prepossessions of our minds in favor of our native land, but to be the leader and guide of a whole nation, in making a similar sacrifice . . . requires the most lofty efforts of man. Sir, you have made this sacrifice. You have made this effort, in the face of death and the most determined opposition from high sources, to save your people from certain impending ruin and destruction. We trust—we hope—we think—success will crown your efforts. May the God of our fathers prosper your way! May you long live to be useful to your people![51]

The evaluation of John Ridge's improvements had come to $19,741.67. The value of his crops amounted to $1,745, a sum paid to him by the new owner, and he had commuted the transportation and subsistence for himself and family. He had another claim outstanding, for the income from his ferry during the period General Garrett had held it, but he had no hopes that it would be adjudicated before he left for the West. He and his wife went to Creek Path, at the mouth of Wills Valley, where for several months their children had studied at the school of the missionary William Potter. Boudinot, who had recently remarried, was also there with his family, and together they made final arrangements for the journey west. Ridge had sent most of his Negroes and horses ahead to "Arkansas" in the charge of William Childers, his former ferryman. He had kept back three of the blacks—a woman called Maria to do the cooking, a man named Henry to drive the carriage, and a woman named Mary to take care of the children. He also kept back three horses—two to draw the carriage and one, a pony named Dick, "which Rollin [would] not allow to leave him."[52]

Their party was small: besides Ridge and Boudinot and their respective families there were William Lassley and his family and a lone woman, Polly Gilbreath, whom the Ridges had invited to accompany them. Their route lay north from Creek Path for about thirty miles through northern Alabama, then through Tennessee to Nashville, the backwoods capital of a backwoods state. While waiting in the town for their horses to be reshod, Ridge and his friends rode some twelve miles to the Hermitage and called on Jackson,[53] who was still charged with vital force, though his hearing was failing and his right eye was nearly useless. His home was open to all, and he graciously received the Cherokees. Though retired from office, he still followed developments in Indian affairs.

In all probability Ridge's party followed the route recommended by the superintendent of emigration as the best, though it was somewhat longer than other possibilities. If so, they drove north through Kentucky, reaching the Ohio River at Berry's Ferry. They presumably crossed the river at that point, coming into Golconda, an insignificant village on the opposite shore. On a Sunday, when not camped near a church, they would spend the day at rest in their tents. On one such occasion Mrs. Boudinot, whose name had been Delight Sargent before her marriage, was reading to Boudinot and the children from the biography of William Carey, an English missionary to India. Ridge, whose family tent was close by, approached the flap of the Boudinot tent and said: "Please tell what you're reading." Mrs. Boudinot sketched the main lines of Carey's life, how he had left a shoemaker's bench and gone to India with his family and how eventually after many trials he became a distinguished Oriental scholar. Then she added, "And since the days of the Apostle Paul, who has equaled him?"

Ridge exclaimed that she was describing the missionary Worcester, and he hoped to see the day, he added, when Worcester's work should be appreciated, with him at the head of a college among the Cherokees. "Our school fund is ample, as you know."[54] No doubt Boudinot agreed, for he was planning to work with Worcester again on reaching the Cherokee Nation West.

The party rode west across the tip of southern Illinois, "the land of Egypt," as it was sometimes called. The road threaded through low, rich alluvial tracts that bordered the Mississippi, or across marshlands that reeked of stagnant water and rotting vegetation. The party crossed deeper swamps over miserable bridges, and soon they reached the river proper. In all probability they ferried to Cape Girardeau, then headed through the lower reaches of Missouri. In a few days the road traversed the Ozark plateau, an undulating country of green hills and fertile valleys, well watered with brooks full of fish, where one traveler described the way as "a good road through a rocky and romantic country."[55] Soon beautiful little prairies appeared, and in two or three more days the region grew wilder, abounding in elk, deer, hares, pheasants, turkeys, and prairie fowl. There were also bears, panthers, wolves, wildcats, foxes, and opossums, so the journey impressed Rollin as "a zestful voyage of discovery among new flora and fauna."[56] The trek came to an end in late November, 1837, after about seven weeks of travel.

"I . . . found my father and mother and all my friends . . . in good health," Ridge wrote. He claimed to like the upper northeastern part of the Nation better than any other land on which the Cherokees had settled. "The country there is best adapted for agriculture & water privileges. It is superior to any country I ever saw in the U.S. Missouri or that part next to the Cherokees is populating very fast and in a few years it will be the garden spot of the United States. The Cherokees have settled here almost altogether in consequence of their being introduced in this quarter by the agents. . . . Honey Creek, near the Senecas, is unsettled, & all the region about there is large enough for the whole Nation." John Ridge was genuinely enthusiastic about his new home. "Perfect friendship and contentedness," he said, "prevail over this land."[57]

Ridge's brother-in-law, George Paschal, had bought for him a small improvement for $125 from David Jones, a Western Cherokee. It would seem that the price was right and that Ridge had not been "gouged," as some of the immigrants were. As he said, "The 'new comers' who are ignorant of the country are subjected to the speculations of the old settlers—places have been purchased here for $500—$1000 to $2000."[58]

Evidently John Ridge moved his family into temporary quar-

ters, one of the buildings included among the improvements he had
bought. But at once he began thinking of a new dwelling place and
in December bought 4,716 feet of plank from a man named Shears
at a cost of $117.90. For some reason, however, the house was not
raised until the following March, perhaps the interval necessary to
secure the logs for its construction. It contained four rooms and had
a separate kitchen. The carpenter, George Starnes, charged $32 for
eight squares of flooring and $36 for six squares of ceiling. Two
finished doors cost $5.50 apiece, and five window frames and shut-
ters the same amount each. The house was later called "a good
double log house."[59] In all probability the logs had come from the
40 acres of timbered land that Ridge had directed his field hands to
clear. In addition he ordered 150 acres of prairie land fenced and
broken, some of which were sown in timothy and clover and some
planted in corn. He bought an adequate amount of farming equipment, including a wagon. Further improvements comprised a
smokehouse, outhouses, cribs, stables, lots, and pastures.

On coming west Ridge decided to disengage himself from Cherokee affairs and in addition to farming apply his talents to "a mer-
cantile business." Late in 1837 he entered a partnership with Major
Ridge, and they opened a general store on Honey Creek in what
seems to have been an impressive building for the time, costing
them $1,500. William Childers acted as their agent, going about
the country to buy corn and hogs, important items in the Cherokee
diet. Corn cost fifty cents a bushel, and hogs five cents a pound.
On January 5, 1838, forty-one hogs were butchered, producing 5,631
pounds of pork, which brought a handsome profit from the hungry
Cherokees, except that more than a wise amount was sold on credit.
On March 5, Ridge and Childers signed a contract, according to
which the latter would receive $450 a year for attending the business
"and keeping a store . . . to date from 1st Dec. 1837."[60] For a while
George Paschal also worked as a clerk in the store.

Left free from the confinement of trade, John Ridge seized the
opportunity to wander about the Cherokee land and examine it at
his leisure. "I have traveled extensively in that country," he later
wrote, " — once from my residence, near the corner of Missouri and
Arkansas, to Fort Smith, through Flint District, where I had the
pleasure of beholding fine springs of water, excellent farms and comfortable houses, and mills, and mission schools, belonging to the
Cherokees; and every evidence of prosperity and happiness was to be
seen among the Cherokees as a people."[61] He saw persons who had

arrived before him and persons who had come since, but he heard but one sentiment, or so he claimed: how happy and contented they were in their new home. He joked with some and inquired whether they wanted to return to Georgia, even if they could have their old rights back. In almost every case they answered no, nothing could make them return. Ridge estimated that on this trip he had traveled over eighty-eight miles in a straight line.

Next he went to that part of the nation called the Neutral Lands, which had been added by the Treaty of New Echota and which extended north into present-day Kansas.

I rode over it, about two days, and I there found Mr. Joseph Rogers, our Cherokee friend, from the Chattahoochee, pleasantly situated in the finest region... I ever beheld in any part of the United States. The streams of all sizes, from the rivers to the brooks, run swiftly over clean stones and pebbles, and water is clear as crystal, in which excellent fish abound.... The soil [ranges] from the best prairie lands to the best bottom lands, in vast tracts. Never did I see a better location for settlements [with] better springs.... God has thrown His favors here with a broad cast. In this region are numerous mills, and it is of itself capable of supporting a larger population than the whole Cherokee Nation, East.[62]

On returning he made a second trip, one of seventy-five miles to Fort Gibson, finding rich soil and superior natural advantages. On the way he stopped at the straggling town of Park Hill, where Boudinot had settled near Worcester. They had resumed collaboration in translating useful books into Cherokee, and Worcester had issued a Christian almanac, in Cherokee and English, calculated for the meridian of Fort Gibson. Ridge wrote:

I found this extensively in circulation amongst the Cherokees, and, in fact, I was pleased to find that religious tracts, in the Indian language, were on the shelves of full-blooded Cherokees, and everyone knew and seemed to love the Messenger, as they called Mr. Worcester. I very often met with new emigrants from the Eastern Nation, either arriving or settling the country, or on their way to Fort Gibson, to draw the balance of their dues for their lands and improvements. These newcomers were formerly of opposite portions of the old nation. There was no disposition to quarrel, but every [inclination] to cultivate friendship and rejoice together in possession of this fine country.... Many of the Cherokees have turned their attention to merchandising, and some have supplied themselves with goods from New Orleans and New York, besides other places more convenient to the nation.[63]

For his own firm John Ridge purchased merchandise in New Orleans, Pittsburgh, and New York. He was ready to journey east with Sarah sometime in March, 1838. They had invited Miss Sawyer to come to their new home and teach their children as before, and she had arrived in December at the new Dwight Mission, where Ridge had sent a servant to bring her on to Honey Creek.* They now left the children in her care, intending to be gone for only three months.

In New York City, where Ridge made numerous wholesale purchases, he found the religious community receptive to the skillful propaganda circulated by John Ross. Since the ratification of the treaty, Ross had published two long letters on Cherokee affairs, both in pamphlet form, for which he had received literary advice from John Howard Payne. The second pamphlet had effectively challenged the right of the government to treat with a splinter faction of the tribe and had presented a telling array of precedents for nullifying treaties that had been unjustly negotiated. Ross's arguments had won widespread appreciation for his point of view. "Instead of receiving the late Treaty as a blessing to the Cherokees," Ridge noted, "and as a measure of relief to them, [the people of New York City] considered it the source of all [Cherokee] afflictions.

---

*Ridge had a small double-story schoolhouse raised, the lower floor for instruction, the upper story for living quarters for Miss Sawyer and a few young girls. The building was located only an eight-minute walk from the Ridge house, close enough for Miss Sawyer and her charges to take meals with the family. "These [young girls]," the teacher wrote to Boston, "with Mr. R's children & what Cherokee pupils can be gathered from families who we hope will settle around us will constitute my field of labor." Before long she had twenty-two pupils, of such a variety of age, character, and improvement that she had to teach them almost individually. Miss Sawyer's relations with the Ridge family were happy. She was pleased that Ridge had taken a stand on morals, "and in favor of the Christian religion," though she feared it was a stand "that will be difficult for a man of his habits & temperament to retain. He cannot hear truth without uneasiness," she reported. "He cannot escape it in the position in which he has placed himself. He has tampered with the cause of temperance, by selling wine, until he has become disgusted with wine drunkards, & says he will sell no more. He has a most interesting family of sons, who, if they follow the instructions he is causing them daily to receive, will shun the path of the destroyer, & loathe the vices of their people. The only daughter who is capable, & of sufficient age to receive instruction, is almost constantly with me—a sprightly, lovely child, full of budding promise, & if we are faithful, this gem of character will open into full-grown flower & finished beauty" (Sophia Sawyer to David Greene, Dec. 27, 1838, Houghton Library, ABC, 18.3.1, X: 319).

I attempted to explain John Ross's position* in the papers; and many of them are now convinced that the Treaty [is] in the right."[64]

The Ridges proceeded to the home of Sarah's family in South Lee, Massachusetts, a picturesque town in the Berkshire Hills. There Ridge fell ill, and while he convalesced during the summer, Sarah went home alone, to be with the children. By September he was able to travel. As he reached Kentucky, the news broke (to be relayed from paper to paper) of a large intertribal council that the Cherokees had called, at which ten tribes or so would be represented. John Looney, second principal chief of the Western Cherokees, had invited Major Ridge to address the assembly. The object of the meeting was to revive the memory of ancient alliances between the tribes, to review the belts of wampum in their archives, and in Indian phraseology, to polish the chain of friendship and make it bright, and to clear all stones from the pathway so that one nation might visit another without bruising its feet.[65] On hearing of it, General "Granny" Gaines had panicked and spread alarm about a possible uprising along the frontier. The newspapers gave credence to the Gaines fairy tale, and many white families along the border became alarmed. Ridge went at once to the office of the *Louisville Journal* "to remonstrate to us," the editor wrote, "and through us to the country, against this extraordinary proceeding on the part of General Gaines."[66] Ridge emphasized that the "meeting [was] entirely pacific—entirely deliberative—and by no means of a hostile character."[67]

Then he hurried home.

The deadline set by the Treaty of New Echota for forced removal—May 23—had come and gone. Soon masses of Indians would be pouring into the Cherokee Nation West. Many would

---

*Ross's original aim had been to prevent the ratification of the treaty. This failing, he worked tirelessly to have the treaty quashed, then to have its terms modified so that the Cherokees might receive greater benefits. Five million dollars, he insisted, was too little money, considering the character and extent of the Cherokee cession, with its mines and forests, its quarries and farms, and at one point he fruitlessly proposed $13 million as a juster payment. His intransigence in the interest of greater amounts of money appalled the treaty leaders, who deplored his insensitivity to the moral condition of the Cherokee people and his evident willingness to sacrifice them on the altar of Mammon. See Boudinot's excoriation of his materialism in "Documents in Relation to the Validity of the Cherokee Treaty of 1835 [*Letters and Other Papers Relating to Cherokee Affairs*]," 25th Cong., 2d sess., S. Doc. 121 (Serial 315), pp. 41–43.

have money in their pockets, received for spoliations or from the sale of property in the East. They would be wanting to buy supplies and materials of all sorts, and the Ridges were prepared to sell them a wide variety of goods—foodstuffs, hats, clothing, shoes and leather-ware, tools, agricultural implements, and all kinds of hardware, including firearms—in short, all that one might expect to find in a frontier general store. Out of feelings of human kindness the Ridges proposed to sell on credit to Indians who were out of pocket, to the extent of nine or ten thousand dollars. They were prepared to make these sales in the expectation of collecting the money as soon as the Cherokees had received their per capita allowance from the United States as promised under the treaty.[68] They readied their wares and waited for the exodus from the East.

13 • THE TRAIL OF TEARS

THE condition of the Cherokees before their final displacement from the East had so roused the sympathies of General Wool that he claimed he would remove "every Indian tomorrow"—if he could—"beyond the reach of the white men." He likened the whites to vultures waiting to strip the Cherokees of everything they had and everything they expected from the government.[1] But Wool had appealed to the Cherokees in vain: the bulk of them made no moves to prepare for the westward trek. At no time since the ratification of the treaty had the masses shown any inclination to budge, and in the fall of 1837, emigration fell below the superintendent's expectations.

Only 325 Cherokees transported themselves that year, and the detachment General Smith sent west about the time of Ridge and Boudinot's removal numbered only 365 persons, mostly of the Treaty Party. Dysentery and diarrhea had raged in the emigration depots while they waited to leave. Conducted by B. B. Cannon, this detachment took the route through Kentucky, Illinois, and Missouri and reached the Indian country late in December after losing fifteen persons along the way. On crossing the Cherokee line, exhausted and travel-worn, they went into camp to care more properly for the sick.[2]

General Smith planned to send another party west in early 1838. On April 5, with Lieutenant Edward Deas in charge, 250 Cherokees embarked on the steamboat *Smelter*, with one keelboat in tow. They reached Little Rock six days later, then transferred to a steamboat of lighter draft. There followed ten days of tedious warping over successions of sandbars, after which Lieutenant Deas placed the company on a train of sixteen wagons, which brought them to the Indian country by the twenty-eighth, with only two lives lost.[3]

Experience indicated that water travel was less exhausting, less hazardous to life, than the overland route; and many Cherokees who had gone by boat wrote back to their friends to select that means of removing if they had any choice. Most Cherokees felt a prejudice against water travel, however, and requested the overland route, if they made any choice at all. The truth was that the majority still clung to their land and to their faith in John Ross, and instead of preparing for emigration they waited to see what the chief would do. Ross was still in Washington, resisting the treaty, as spring approached.

"The spring of 1838 opened most beautifully," one Georgia settler later reminisced:

There was no cold weather after the first of March. Vegetation advanced without any backsets from cold. The buds burst into leaves and blossoms; the woods were green and gay and merry with the singing birds. The Indians started to work in their fields earlier than before. Usually they were lazy and late in starting with their crops, working around logs in their fields and letting bushes and briers grow in the fence corners. That spring you could see the smoke of their log heaps or piles of ashes where the logs had been. Fence corners and hedgerows were cleaned out. The ground was well plowed and the corn planted better than ever before. Soon it was knee-high and growing nicely. . . . After all the warning and with the soldiers in their midst, the inevitable day appointed found the Indians at work in their houses and in the fields.[4]

On May 8, General Winfield Scott, a dominating man of six feet three inches, arrived at the agency to replace the interim successor of General Wool. Scott had spent his last ten days in Washington perfecting his plans for the roundup, and while, like Wool, he felt deep sympathy for the Cherokees, he resolved to spare no pains in executing the treaty. Two days after his arrival he gave a carefully prepared speech to sixty chiefs and headmen assembled at the agency.

The president, he explained, had sent him with soldiers to enforce the treaty. "The emigration must be commenced in haste, but, I hope, without disorder. . . . The full moon of May is already on the wane, and before another shall have passed away, every Cherokee man, woman and child must be in motion to join their brethren in the far West. . . . I come to carry out that determination. My troops already occupy many positions in the country that you are to abandon; thousands and thousands are approaching from every quarter, to render residence and escape alike hopeless. . . . The desire of every one of us is to execute our painful duty in mercy. . . ."

The Cherokees listened in stony silence.

General Winfield Scott, who commanded the roundup of the Cherokees before their removal west. Courtesy of Columbia University Library.

General Scott continued: "Will you then, by resistance, compel us to resort to arms? God forbid! Or will you, by flight, seek to hide yourselves in mountains and forests, and thus oblige us to hunt you down? . . . I am an old warrior, and have been present at many a scene of slaughter; but spare me, I beseech you, the horror of witnessing the destruction of the Cherokees."[5]

In order to reach more Indians, the general ordered his address printed in Athens, Tennessee, and distributed as handbills throughout the Cherokee Nation. He put copies in the hands of his soldiers and sent copies to various newspapers, which published it in their columns, where it created a favorable impression. In response to the talk a few families came to the agency, where Scott had made his headquarters, and offered themselves for voluntary removal. At the same time, the general hastened preparations to collect the mass of the Cherokees. He divided the country to be scoured into three separate districts: the eastern, which comprised the Cherokee country in North Carolina and eastern Tennessee; the western, which included Cherokee lands in Alabama, the rest of Tennessee, and Dade County, Georgia; and the middle, which embraced the bulk of the Cherokee lands in Georgia.

On May 17, 1838, Scott issued a general order to his troops. It was a fatherly kind of lecture which sought to impress upon the men the necessity of executing the treaty in a humane and merciful manner. The soldiers were ordered to show all possible kindness and avoid all acts of oppression, insult, or brutality. No indecent language was to be used in the roundup. Indians fleeing to the forests or the mountains should be pursued and invited to give themselves up, but in no case would they be fired upon unless they made a stand to resist. Horses should be used to carry Indians found too sick or feeble to march. "Infants, superannuated persons, lunatics and women in a helpless condition, will all, in the removal, require peculiar attention, which the brave and the humane will seek to adopt to the necessities of the several cases."[6]

Scott found that preliminary steps had been taken by his predecessor, stores of rations collected, and twenty-three military posts established in various parts of the Cherokee Nation. They consisted of stockades built of split logs, sharpened and set in the ground picketwise, and were manned by militia. Scott planned for the troops to go forth daily, in squads, to capture and bring in all Indians living in the environs and to forward them at regular intervals to the four main emigration depots. Three of these camps were located in Tennessee: one at the agency at Calhoun, one near Cleveland, and one at Ross's Landing. The fourth was in Alabama, at Gunter's Landing. May 23, 1838, the deadline set by the treaty, arrived; and three days later the grim roundup work began. Seven thousand soldiers took part in the operation.

James Mooney, a pioneer ethnologist who later interrogated many actors of that hapless drama, wrote: "Squads of troops were sent to search out with rifle and bayonet every small cabin hidden away in the coves or by the sides of mountain streams, to seize and bring in as prisoners all the occupants."[7] The roundup concentrated first on the Indians in Georgia, some eight thousand souls, and the soldiers took them pretty much where—and as—they found them. In the opinion of the missionary Butrick, the humane orders of General Scott were either obeyed or flouted according to the disposition of individual officers and their men. "Families at dinner," according to Mooney, "were startled by the sudden gleam of bayonets in the doorway and rose up to be driven with blows and oaths along the trail that led to the stockade. Men were seized in their fields or going along the road, women were taken from their wheels and children from their play."[8]

In one instance two youngsters fled to the woods in fear of the approaching soldiers. Their mother begged permission to go and find them, or at least to wait until they reappeared. She gave her word that, if granted her plea, she would follow the soldiers to the stockade, but her tearful entreaties were refused. The soldiers drove her away with other prisoners, and it was not till later that the lost children were recovered through the help of friends. In other instances children, on being found away from home, were herded to the stockades along with strangers, and women on visits to friends were not allowed to rejoin their families before being marched away; nor were men, separated from their families by the demands of the day, allowed to return to their houses. One Indian was bringing home a freshly killed deer to his hungry brood, but was hurried off to a fort instead with empty hands.[9]

Niles' National Register ran an eyewitness report that the soldiers sometimes drove their captives with whoops and halloos as though they were cattle; they sometimes drove the Indians through rivers without giving them time to remove their shoes and stockings. "The scenes of distress exhibited at Ross's Landing," the correspondent wrote, "defy all description. On the arrival there of the Indians, the horses brought by some of them were demanded by the commissioners of Indian property . . . for the purpose of being sold. The owners refused to give them up, — men, women, children *and horses* were driven permiscuously into one large pen, and the horses taken out by force, and cried off to the highest bidder, *and sold for almost nothing.* "10

More often than not, the Indians lost all personal property except the clothes on their backs — their cattle, hogs, horses, and all of their household effects.* "In many cases," Mooney wrote, "on turning for one last look as they crossed the ridge, [the captives] saw their homes in flames, fired by the lawless rabble that followed on the heels of the soldiers to loot and pillage. So keen were these outlaws on the scene that in some instances they were driving off the cattle and other stock of the Indians almost before the soldiers had fairly started the owners in the opposite direction."11 This white riffraff even desecrated graves, rifling them of silver pendants and other objects of value the Cherokees had left with their dead.

Mooney continued:

To prevent escape the soldiers had been ordered to approach and sur-round each house, as far as possible, so as to come upon the occupants without warning. One old patriarch when thus surprised calmly called his children and grandchildren around him, and kneeling down, bid them pray with him in their own language, while the astonished sol-diers looked on in silence. Then rising he led the way into exile. A woman, on finding the house surrounded, went to the door and called up the chickens to be fed for the last time, after which taking her infant on her back and her other children by the hand, she followed her husband with the soldiers.12

The operation by its very nature was cruel. A deaf-mute who in bewilderment turned right when ordered to go left was shot and killed. A man who struck a soldier goading his wife with a bayonet received a hundred lashes, but such incidents were unusual and did not represent the common experience. The wonder is that more cases of wanton brutality did not occur. Certainly the outraged accusation that ran in *Niles' National Register*—that "in most cases the humane injunctions of the commanding general were disregarded"—was a distortion of fact.13 On the other hand General Scott's conviction that his orders were for the most part executed as humanely as the circumstances permitted was open to question. The truth seems to have lain somewhere between the two extremes.

*Many claims to cover such losses were later pressed successfully against the federal government.

But there was justice in the general's claim that a great deal of the Cherokees' trouble was their own fault for having placed too much faith in John Ross. Many of their hardships might have been avoided if they had put their affairs in order and prepared themselves for the exodus. "If Ross had told them the truth in time," John Ridge complained bitterly, "they would have sold off their furniture, their horses, their cattle, hogs, and sheep, and their growing corn."[14] The soldiers had no time to let the Cherokees do what they should have done beforehand. It was for that reason that so much of their stock and personal property was lost.

General Scott had planned for the roundup to take no more than twenty days. In actuality it required twenty-five. The only real difficulty occurred in the Smoky Mountains, where three hundred Cherokees had hidden out. The resistance eventually led to bloodshed by the Indians and, in retaliation, to the execution of a fifty-year-old man named Tsali, or Charley,[15] who later became an idealized legend among the descendants of those who remained untaken in the Smokies.

Meanwhile, forcible emigration began on June 6, 1838, when some 800 Cherokees, conducted by Lieutenant Deas, left Ross's Landing by boat. The Indians managed to secure whiskey early on the trip and became disorderly. So many escaped that Deas found he had only 480 emigrants left on arriving at Paducah. The much-diminished party reached its destination on the nineteenth. A second detachment numbering 875 had left Tennessee four days before, and on the seventeenth a third group, 1,070 strong, was gotten under way. The last was the most unmanageable of all, owing to a rumor that the emigration was going to be postponed.

The rumor was true. By the middle of June the Tennessee River had ceased to be navigable. The next detachments would have to be sent by land. But a terrible drought had settled over the country, drying up wells and springs and watercourses so thoroughly that good drinking water was not to be found on portions of the route. Besides, the season of fever had set in, making illness inevitable. Several chiefs petitioned General Scott to suspend further emigration until the return of the cool season. This he agreed to do, setting September 1 as the date to resume the evacuation. "By the conditions then obtained," he wrote, "the great body of the Cherokees remaining east for the first time consented to emigrate, or to do any act tending to their emigration."[16]

For the land at large the drought was unfortunate; for the Cherokees it was a calamity. In the camps, subsisting on food they were not accustomed to, they fell sick in multitudes. There were epidemics of "putrid dysentery," measles, whooping cough, pleurisy, and bilious fever, and reports went out that the Cherokees were dying like flies. General Scott contradicted such rumors. "There is no more sickness amongst the Indians," he contended, "than might ordinarily take place amongst any other people under the same circumstances. The Indians are encamped over a space of about forty square miles; are well provided for, with wholesome provisions, good physicians and medicine, and conduct themselves very discreetly."[17] But the truth, when all reports were in, seems to have been more dismal than General Scott had apprehended. Dr. Butler, the missionary, probably hit the mark when he reported some two thousand deaths in the camps that broiling summer.[18]

In anticipation of needs in September the general ordered the surrounding country to be scoured for wagons that might be bought for the coming trek. On July 13, John Ross returned from Washington, where he had succeeded in having payment under the treaty raised to $6,647,067, the extent to which he could get terms of the treaty modified; and Scott received directions from the War Department to place further movements in the chief's hands.[19] Then followed a conference between Scott and the Cherokee council, at which a working agreement was reached. General Scott approved an allowance of $65 per head for removal and promised to furnish one-half of the amount in advance. From this fund it was agreed that the Cherokees would provide their own subsistence and means of travel, to begin the first of September. Thirteen detachments, numbering about 1,000 souls apiece, would start for the West, one after another at intervals of three or four days. The migration thus became a national movement on the part of the Indians, and for the first time occurred "a unanimity of feeling and concurrence of the whole tribe." On October 15, Scott would report that "among the party of 12,500 [to be transported] there has prevailed an almost universal cheerfulness since the date of the new arrangement."[20]

Without salary, John Ross assumed the title of Superintendent of Removal and Subsistence, and Lewis Ross took the contract to furnish transportation and supplies. The secretary of war criticized the contract as exorbitant—indeed "more than double the amount on which the appropriation of Congress for that object was based."[21] General Scott defended his arrangements, attributing most of his embarrassments and difficulties to the drought that had "nearly desolated so many states." He claimed that during the last eight weeks of its duration not even a detachment as small as one hundred Indians, with their horses, could have located sufficient water for many marches together on the road. "But for the drought," he wrote, "I would have quashed the contract with Lewis Ross as extravagant, and the renewed movement, beginning with September, would have escaped ice, snow, and bad roads."[22] As the matter developed, no rain came until late in September, and the emigration had to be delayed another month, making it impossible to avoid the discomforts of winter. On September 23 a short, light drizzle partially laid the dust, and on the twenty-eighth came a heavier, more refreshing rain to break the dry season at last.[23]

A contingent of Cherokees who belonged to the Treaty faction refused to emigrate under the management of Ross and were allowed to move separately, conducted by Lieutenant Deas. They numbered nearly seven hundred persons, some of them among the most educated members of the tribe. Starting from near the agency on October 11, they traveled the length of Tennessee, reaching Memphis late in November. There they crossed the Mississippi and continued their journey through Arkansas. They passed through Little Rock in the middle of December and reached the Cherokee country on January 7, 1839.[24]

Meanwhile the Indians of the Ross faction assembled for a final council at Rattlesnake Springs, near present-day Charleston, Tennessee. The council resolved to retain the old laws and constitution of the eastern nation on arriving in the West. The people then started to move, and as they followed along the north bank of Hiwassee River, their 645 wagons, five thousand horses, and large number of oxen looked like "the march of an army, regiment after regiment, the wagons in the center, the officers along the line and the horsemen on the flanks and at the rear."[25]

The first detachment, led by John Benge, started toward Nashville on October 1. William S. Coodey, its contractor, described the beginning of the trek. He told of the caravan stretched along the road through a thick forest. Knots of people clustered around certain wagons and lingered with sick friends or relatives who must be left behind. The temporary huts covered with boards and bark that had been their only shelter during the long, hot summer were afire, sending up smoke, crackling and falling into heaps of embers. "The day was bright and beautiful, but a gloomy thoughtfulness was strongly depicted in the lineaments of every face. In all the bustle of preparation there was a silence and stillness of the voice that betrayed the sadness of the heart. At length the word was given to *move on.*" Coodey peered along the train and saw the venerable form of Going Snake, whose head was whitened by eighty winters and who sat astride his favorite pony. The old chief forged ahead and led the way, followed by a company of young men on horseback. "At this very moment a low sound of distant thunder fell on my ear. . . . It was [noticed] by several persons near me and [regarded] as ominous of some future event in the West."[26]

The second detachment started three days later. By the early part of November twelve parties were on the road—a road churned by thousands of hooves and hundreds of wheels, until with the excessive autumn rains it became an endless quagmire. The thirteenth party, accompanied by Ross and his family, traveled by water. Lt. H. S. Scott, who was sent by the commanding general to observe the progress of the earliest detachments, reported that "the greatest harmony & cheerfulness" prevailed and that the Indians had encountered no mishaps, except for the death of four children. "In both [of the first] parties they have established among themselves a species of police guard whose duties are to seize & promptly punish any offences against good order. The interior management is therefore excellent."[27] The outlook of a later caravan was not so promising, however. Its physician complained to Ross that this party included a large number of sick, aged, and infirm persons who had of necessity to be hauled in the wagons, of which there were only forty. There was also the need to haul forage from place to place to suit the convenience of the contractors. Also, they had to take on six barrels of sugar and four of coffee as well as salt and soap to last the emigrants for the next lap of the trek. "The fact is the detachment cannot progress under such circumstances. We have had to double many of the teams ascending the mountains."[28]

A traveler from Maine who passed several contingents on the highway described one

detachment of the poor Cherokee Indians . . . about eleven hundred Indians—sixty wagons—six hundred horses, and perhaps forty pairs of oxen. We found them in the forest camped for the night by the road side . . . under a severe fall of rain accompanied by heavy wind. With their canvas for a shield from the inclemency of the weather, and the cold wet ground for a resting place, after the fatigue of the day, they spent the night. . . . Many of the aged Indians were suffering extremely from the fatigue of the journey, and the ill health consequent upon it. . . .

The Trail of Tears, *by Robert Lindneux.* Courtesy of Woolaroc Museum, Bartlesville, Oklahoma.

Several were then quite ill, and an aged man, we were informed, was then in the last struggles of death. . . .

We met several detachments in the southern part of Kentucky on the 4th, 5th, and 6th of December. . . . The last detachment which we passed on the 7th [comprised nearly] two thousand Indians with horses and mules in proportion. The forward part of the train we found just pitching their tents for the night, and notwithstanding some thirty or forty waggons were already stationed, we found the road literally filled with the procession for about three miles in length. The sick and feeble were carried in waggons—about as comfortable for traveling as a New England ox cart with a covering over it—a great many ride on horseback and multitudes go on foot—even aged females, apparently nearly ready to drop into the grave, were traveling with heavy burdens attached to the back—on sometimes frozen ground, and sometimes muddy streets, with no covering for the feet except what nature had given them. . . . We learned from the inhabitants on the road where the Indians passed that they buried fourteen or fifteen at every stopping place, and they make a journey of ten miles per day only on an average.[29]

The winter, with its ice and sleet and snow, was as fiercely freezing as the summer had been dry and torrid, and the Cherokees on the road suffered acutely from the cold. Fatigue, overexertion, insufficient clothes and bedding left them prone to illness. They suffered not only the same diseases they had contracted in the detention camps, but from others as well: pneumonia, tuberculosis, and a sickness not yet named by medical science—pellagra. One of the casualties was Quatie Ross, wife of the chief, who gave her blanket to a sick child. The child survived, but Quatie's cold became pneumonia, and she died at Little Rock.[30]

A full blood later recalled his experience on the road: "Long time we travel on way to new land. People feel bad when they leave Old Nation. Womens cry and make sad wails. Children cry and many men cry, and all look sad like when friends die, but they say nothing and just put heads down and keep on go towards West. Many days pass and people die very much." The full blood would further recall that his father, an old man, suddenly collapsed in the snow and could not struggle to his feet again. Space was made for him in a covered wagon, but all the old man's strength was gone, and he lingered for only another day. "We bury him close by trail," the full blood said; and then the company toiled on. In another week the full blood's mother cried out, then sank in the trail. "She speak no more," the full blood said; "we bury her and go on." The contingent struggled on for three more weeks. Then the full blood's brothers and sisters, five in all, sickened and died. "One each day," he remembered, "and all are gone." They were buried beside the trail, and the company moved forward through the wind and snow; days passed, and there were still more bodies to bury; yet the company always pressed on. "Looks like maybe all be dead before we get to new Indian country," the full blood said, "but always we keep marching on"; and while they marched, their ears were filled with crying and moaning from the wagons that carried the children, the aged, the sick, and the dying. The moaning through days and nights so impressed itself on the Indian's mind that he still seemed to hear it after years had passed, and he would declare: "People sometimes say I look like I never smile, never laugh in lifetime."[31]

Several of the caravans halted at the edge of the frozen Mississippi, prevented by ice from crossing, "with hundreds of sick and dying penned up in wagons or stretched upon the ground, with only a blanket overhead to keep out the January blast."[32] The ice was too thin to support the wagons and too thick to allow the boats to shove through. When at last they had managed to ferry the river, the later contingents had to cross Missouri by way of Springfield in order to ensure themselves a supply of game, the earlier parties having killed off all the game en route through northern Arkansas.

A party conducted by Elijah Hicks reached Indian territory on January 4, 1839, the first contingent under Ross's management to conclude the journey. All the detachments were on the road longer than the eighty days planned for. Their travel time ranged from 93 to 139 days, for an average of 116.[33] The last to arrive, on March 25, was a party led by Peter Hilderbrand.

No one knew exactly how many Cherokees had perished in the ordeal, beginning with the detention camps in the old nation. The trail was especially hard on babies, children, and the aged. Four thousand deaths, nearly one-fifth of the entire Cherokee population, is the estimate usually cited, one made by Dr. Butler the missionary, who said: "From the first of June I felt I have been in the midst of death."[34]* The road the Cherokees had followed was truly a "trail where they cried." "The history of this Cherokee removal . . . ," Mooney concluded, "may well exceed in weight of grief and pathos any other passage in American history. Even the much-sung exile of the Acadians falls far behind it in its sum of death and misery."[35] The shock of the roundup, the tedium of the detention camps, the distresses of the march to the West had generated a hatred so terrible it could hardly be contained. It needed objects to smite, and the objects were at hand. Butler put the matter in a sentence: "*All* the suffering and *all* the difficulties of the Cherokee people [were] charge[d] to the accounts of Messrs. Ridge and Boudinot."[36]

In the spring of 1839, on a trip to the East to purchase additional merchandise, John Ridge spent five days in Washington and there encountered Schermerhorn, over whose handclasp he declared:

My brother, we have been laboring long together in a good cause—the salvation and happiness of the Cherokees. You for what you have done, have been abused, misrepresented and slandered by your countrymen: and I might yet someday die by the hand of some poor infatuated Indian, deluded by the counsels of Ross and his minions; but we have this to console us, we shall have suffered and died in a good cause. My people are now free and happy in their new homes, and I am resigned to my fate, whatever it might be.[37]

*Later Butler upped his estimate to 4,600 deaths.

14 • THE RECKONING

O N arriving in the West, the Treaty Party had accepted the government of the Western Cherokees as their own, with no questions about its simple and primitive workings. There was no written constitution, and only a few written laws. Twice a year the Old Settlers met in council at Tahlonteskee, their capital, where in a rude council house not far from the Illinois River they elected their chiefs and other national officers—councilmen, judges, and sheriffs to keep the peace. The Cherokee Nation West was divided into four districts, and they were governed in a loose manner, in much the same way the old nation had been governed twenty years before. To this system the Treaty Party made no objection, and they caused no friction in integrating themselves into the society of their western brothers.

The Old Settlers might feel reservations about the Treaty of New Echota, but they did not regard the signers of it as criminals who had forfeited their lives. Not long after the arrival of the Ridges, however, a rumor began to circulate that John Ridge had laid plans to sell a part of the western domain, and when he went east with his wife in 1838; it was whispered about that the trip was made for the purpose of striking a bargain with the United States. Some of the Old Settlers declared that if he should do such a thing, he would die for it. But on his return in the autumn, with the lands still intact, the matter was dropped.[1]

Neither John Ridge nor the major had any intention of returning to politics, at least for the present.* They planned to devote their

---

*Ridge family tradition would later hold, quite erroneously, that in 1839, John Ridge was deeply involved in Cherokee politics. During the Civil War, for instance, John Rollin Ridge declared in the *Red Bluff* (Calif.) *Beacon* that not only had his full attention to agriculture, stock raising, and operating their store. It was gratifying, however, to find that all the while their influence with the Old Settlers was steadily growing. As for Boudinot, the first tentative objection of the western council to his teaming again with Worcester to translate the Bible into Cherokee was effectively countered by the missionary's determined defense.[2] As time went on, Boudinot was also accepted as a valuable addition to the establishment of the Old Settlers. As for the Treaty Party in general, they had gone at once about the task of finding locations, building houses, and opening up farms. They felt themselves almost as much at home as the Old Settlers themselves.

The coming of the Ross faction, who became known as the Late Immigrants, created an integration problem, owing to the resolution they had adopted at Rattlesnake Springs. The Late Immigrants were not prepared to accept the government of the Old Settlers; they had resolved to bring their own government with its laws and constitution with them. Report of this resolve disturbed many of the Old Settlers. "The critical situation of the Nation," wrote Miss Sawyer in May, "I cannot communicate. It is such a time of excitement. . . . The atmosphere of the old nation in its most disturbed state, compared to this, was like the peaceful lake to the boisterous ocean."[3]

"When Ross himself arrived," wrote the missionary Cephas Washburn, "he was visited by some intelligent individuals of the 'old settlers,' who mentioned this report to him & told him that such a course would occasion great commotion. He denied the truth of the report & said that he & his people were ready to come under the government and laws already existing here. This quieted the people, & the newcomers were everywhere welcomed by the old settlers & aided in finding suitable places for residence. All supposed that the Cherokees were reunited as one people, henceforth to live in harmony."[4]

Then at Ross's suggestion a council was called to effect a formal union between the Old Settlers and the Late Immigrants. The council convened on June 3, 1839, at Takatoka, or Double Springs, not far from the present site of Tahlequah, Oklahoma, and within a week six thousand Cherokees had gathered, mostly Late Immigrants

father been available for principal chief, but also his election to that office had been assumed by many Cherokees as a matter of course. Nothing could be further from the truth, unless it was the treaty leaders' claim that John Ross was behind the frequent threats against their lives.

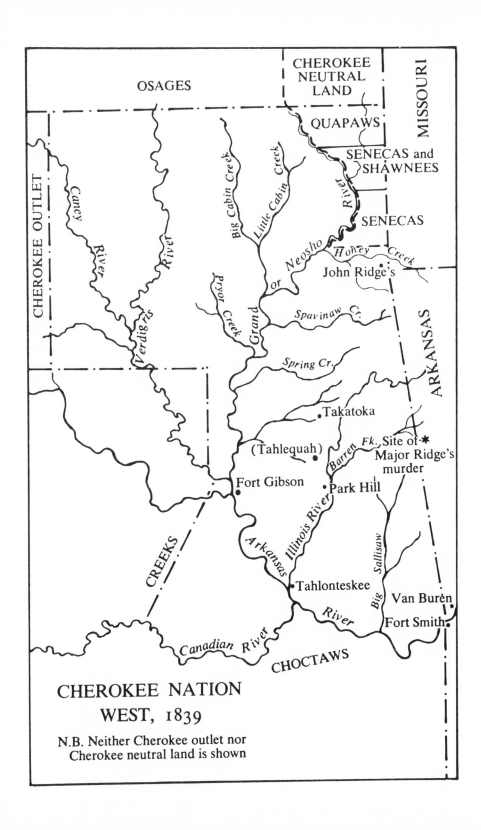

OSAGES

CHEROKEE
NEUTRAL
LAND

MISSOURI

CHEROKEE OUTLET

QUAPAWS

SENECAS and
SHAWNEES

SENECAS

Caney River

Verdigris River

Big Cabin Creek

Little Cabin Creek

Neosho River

Honey Creek

John Ridge's

Pryor Creek

Grand or

Spavinaw Cr.

Spring Cr.

ARKANSAS

Takatoka

(Tahlequah)

Barren Fk.

Site of ✱
Major Ridge's
murder

Fort Gibson

Park Hill

Illinois River

CREEKS

Arkansas

Sallisaw

Big

Van Buren

Tahlonteskee

Fort Smith

River

Canadian River

CHOCTAWS

CHEROKEE NATION
WEST, 1839

N.B. Neither Cherokee outlet nor
Cherokee neutral land is shown

and Old Settlers, with a few of the Treaty Party appearing as on-lookers. The Ridges, Boudinot, and Stand Watie arrived on the fourteenth, with the intention of merely watching the proceedings. They found, however, that their presence was arousing resentment among the Late Immigrants, and so they left the same day rather than become a cause of disturbance and invite assassination.[5]

The business at last got under way. "Speeches were made on both sides," wrote Washburn, "congratulating each other that they were now reunited as one nation, after having been separated for so long."[6] John Brown, the son of Colonel Richard Brown and now first chief of the Old Settlers, was about to announce that the object of the meeting had been accomplished, but before he could speak John Ross inquired upon what terms the immigrants would be received. Brown replied that he considered the immigrants had been received already and that they had "expressed full satisfaction at their reception." Ross indicated his strong feeling that the immigrants should be given a more explicit, a more formal reception, and that the Old Settlers should spell out "the privileges to which they were entitled." To this Brown agreed, and he made another speech to the new arrivals.

"We cordially receive you as brothers," he said:

We joyfully welcome you to our country. The whole land is before you. You may freely go wherever you choose & select any places for settlement which may please you, with this restriction, that you do not interfere with the private rights of individuals. You are fully entitled to the elective franchise; are lawful voters in any of the districts in which you reside, & eligible to any of the offices within the gift of the people. Next October, according to law the term of service of the chiefs will expire & any of you are eligible to those seats. Next July will be an election in our districts for members of both houses of our legis-lature, for judges, sheriffs, etc. At those elections you will be voters & you are eligible to any of those offices. A government was, many years since, organized in this country, & a code of laws was established, suited to our condition & under which our people have lived in peace and prosperity. It is expected that you will all be subject to our govern-ment & laws until they shall be constitutionally altered or repealed & that in all this you will demean yourselves as good & peaceable citizens.[7]

The common people among the newcomers responded cheerfully to Brown's address, but Ross announced how important he deemed it for his faction to remain "as an organized body politic, for the purpose of settling their accounts with the United States, & for securing certain claims for spoliations."[8]

Brown rose and said: "For the settlement of all matters growing out of your removal from the old nation & for your subsistence for one year, & for the adjustment of all claims against the United States, you are freely allowed your own Chiefs & Committee & Council, & Judges & Sheriff, with the name and style of the Eastern Cherokee Nation."[9] Liberal as such an overture was, Ross found it unsatisfactory and made then his most galling objection, a disapproval of the Old Settlers' code and government.

"The government is modeled after your own," Brown replied, "& the laws are the same."[10] He suggested further that at the October council steps could be taken toward revising and enlarging the code and drawing up a constitution, which could be laid before the whole people for adoption.

Since the Ross faction outnumbered the Old Settlers together with the Treaty Party more than two to one, it was evident that Ross would soon be in control of the government under the procedure proposed by Brown. Still he refused to accept the overtures of the Old Settlers; whereupon, thoroughly frustrated, Brown announced the council was adjourned. Ross wished a convention called at once to make a new constitution to govern the entire nation. Brown rejected that proposal in turn, and the council broke up on June 19. The Old Settlers left the council ground immediately, but Ross requested his followers to remain. Two more days passed in the transaction of business concerning the removal, and Ross dismissed the people on June 21. At that time he wrote to Montfort Stokes, the U.S. agent to the Cherokees: "The reasonable propositions submitted to the consideration of the representatives of our western brethren have not been received by them in a manner compatible with the wishes of the whole people." He added that such behavior on the part of the Old Settlers could not "fail to disturb the peace of the community, and to operate injuriously to the best interests of the nation."[11]

The failure of the council to effect a union of factions created a great consternation among Ross's followers. Some of them recalled that the Ridges and Boudinot had talked privately with the officers of the Old Settlers, and in their excited frame of mind, suspicions grew that the treaty leaders had counseled the Old Settlers to take the course they did. Such thoughts were the fuse that exploded all the precariously pent emotions aroused by the shock of the roundup and the miseries of the journey west. Men who had lost wives and children or other relatives in the expulsion could no longer honor

Ross's plea for forbearance toward the signers of the treaty. And even as the council was breaking up, a band of them held a secret conclave, carefully guarded from Ross's knowledge, in which they invoked the Blood Law. The cause of this action, according to a suppressed report of John Bell, a representative from Tennessee, "was the sudden breaking forth of long-smouldering resentment — an ebullition of rage and disappointment occasioned by [the Ridges'] supposed intrigue and management in defeating the object of the general council which had broken up without settling on a plan of government for the whole nation."[12]

That such was the case emerged from the testimony of Thomas Hindman, a white man who had attended the council. "We were in the entry between two cabins," he said, "and as we were standing [there], the two Ridges passed us coming from the council ground. They left that same evening. I never heard either of the Ridges or Boudinot say anything about the council, but I saw them frequently holding private conversations with the western chiefs. I know that the general belief and declaration of the western and eastern people was that the Ridges and Boudinot had influenced the western chiefs to break up the council."[13]

A leader of the secret meeting read the law against the unsanctioned sale of land — the law which John Ridge had put into writing in 1829.* Major Ridge, John Ridge, Boudinot, Stand Watie, John A. Bell, James Starr, George W. Adair, and possibly others were named as the accused. Three men from the clan of each defendant were called to sit in judgment, the authority of each judge extending only to the cases of fellow clansmen. Thus three men from the Deer clan weighed the fate of Major Ridge and condemned him to die. The same verdict occurred in the case of everyone else accused. Then, according to Allen Ross, a son of the chief, "A committee was appointed to arrange details and in response to that committee report numbers were placed in a hat for each person present; twelve of these numbers had an X mark after the number which indicated the Executioners. All present were asked to draw. When I came to draw the chairman stopped me and told me that I could not draw as the committee had another job for me on that day." After the lots had been cast, young Ross asked what he was supposed to do. The chairman replied that he was to go to his father's house that evening and stay the night with him, and the next day too, "and if

*See Chapter 8 above.

possible to keep him from finding out what was being done."[14]

The violence was well planned and executed. The murder parties mounted their horses and set forth in the early hours of morning, Saturday, June 22. The first, a company of some twenty-five men, said to include some who had been fed and clothed by the Ridges, reached the house of John Ridge at daybreak. With rifles ready they surrounded the house. Three dismounted, went to the door, and forced it open. In addition to Ridge and his family, Sarah's sister and brother-in-law were asleep in the house. Neither they nor the family were harmed; John Ridge was the only intended victim at this particular place. The three "executioners" stole quietly through the house, and finding Ridge asleep, they snapped a pistol at his head. The pistol failed to fire.[15] They grabbed Ridge and dragged him from bed, and though he was a light, slender man, he fought back vigorously. No match for his assailants, he was dragged from the room and into the yard, while his awakened wife and children wailed in alarm. Shouts of the adversaries drowned Ridge's own cries, "for they were instructed not to listen to him lest they would be persuaded not to kill him."[16] Sarah rushed to the door, but several rifles pushed her back. Two men held Ridge securely by the arms, others by the body. Still another raised a knife and stabbed deliberately again and again, until twenty-five wounds pierced the body. Then a swipe of the knife severed the jugular vein, the twenty-sixth wound. They threw Ridge into the air as high as they could, and when the bleeding body struck the earth, each assassin stamped on it "as they marched over it by single file."[17]

Ridge did not die immediately. Sarah ran to him as the assailants galloped away. He struggled to raise himself on his elbow and made a desperate effort to speak, but blood flowing from his mouth prevented him. Instead of speech he made unintelligible gurgles. "In a few moments more he died," wrote his son Rollin, who had watched through the indistinct light.

Then succeeded a scene of agony . . . which might make one regret that the human race had ever been created. It has darkened my mind with an eternal shadow. In a room prepared for the purpose lay pale in death the man whose voice had been listened to with awe and admiration in the councils of his Nation, and whose fame had passed to the remotest of the United States, the blood oozing through his winding sheet and falling drop by drop on the floor. By his side sat my mother, with hands clasped and in speechless agony—she who had given him her heart in the days of her youth and beauty, left the home of her parents and followed the husband of her choice to a wild and distant land. And bending over him was his own afflicted mother, with her long, white hair flung loose over her shoulders, crying to the Great Spirit to sustain her in that dreadful hour. And in addition to all these, the wife, the mother, and the little children, who scarcely knew their loss, were the dark faces of those who had been the murdered man's friends, and possibly some who had been privy to the assassination, who had come to smile over the scene.[18]

The murderers had meanwhile ridden south to Beattie's Prairie, where they stopped at the house of Joseph Lynch, a cohort of Ross. Lynch had slaughtered a beef for them, and they ate their fill and boasted of the morning's work. Their number included Daniel Colston, John Vann, a man named Hunter, and three brothers—Archibald, James, and Joseph Spear. The last named later bragged of having wielded the knife that found John Ridge's heart.[19]

The second band, some thirty strong, was not so quick to strike. On arriving at Park Hill early in the morning, they hid in a thick stand of trees near the house that Boudinot was building. They waited till nine in the morning, when Boudinot left Worcester's home, where he was staying with his family, and came to the unfinished building, on which several carpenters were at work. While Boudinot talked to them, four Cherokees approached and asked for medicine to treat some sick ones in their families. As Boudinot was in charge of the public medicines, it was correct for them to come to him with such a request. He started toward the mission with two of the men. One dropped behind, and when they had walked about half the distance, he plunged a knife into Boudinot's back. Boudinot shrieked and collapsed in the dewy grass. The other Cherokee swung a tomahawk and split Boudinot's head, and swung again and again until Boudinot's skull was cloven in six or seven places.[20]

On hearing the shriek the carpenters left their shingling and ran to the spot, too late to help or to apprehend the murderers, who ran from the scene in furious haste, joined the armed horsemen in the woods, and made their escape. Boudinot's wife, Delight, came at a run in time to see her husband die. She called his name. His eyes opened. Then they were glazed in death. And when Worcester saw the body a moment later, he exclaimed: "They have cut off my right hand!"[21]

A Choctaw, who was clearing a projected burial ground within view of the tragedy, was sent to warn Stand Watie. He rode Worces-

Stand Watie, brother of Elias Boudinot. Courtesy of the Western History Collections, University of Oklahoma Library.

ter's horse, Comet, so named because of its speed, and after a mile or so he arrived at the store that Watie was keeping. He called Watie aside near a sugar barrel, as though sugar were the object of his visit, and since several antitreaty men were present, he bargained in a loud voice while telling the news in a whisper. Stand Watie left through a back door, mounted Comet, and made his escape.[22] Later in the day, according to a story that may be legend, he rode back to Park Hill and up to Worcester's door. He stepped inside where Boudinot's body lay in the midst of a throng, including some recognized as partisans of Ross. He drew back the sheet that covered his brother's gashed face and looked down at it long and earnestly. Then he turned to the crowd and said he would give ten thousand dollars for the names of those who had done the deed.* No one answered, but it was later known that the assassination party included men named Johnston, Soft-shelled Turtle, Money Taker, Car-soo-taw-dy, Joseph Beanstalk, and Duck-wa. It was claimed that a man named Sanders had led the band, and that Edward Gunter had been seen in the woods nearby after Boudinot had fallen.[23]

The third band struck at Major Ridge on the same morning. Having learned that he had left the previous day for Van Buren, where one of his slaves lay ill, they had followed him down the Line Road. They discovered where he had spent the night, beneath the roof of Ambrose Harnage, at Cincinnati, Arkansas, and they rode ahead to form an ambush. They hid in brush and trees on a series of benches overlooking an unobstructed spot where the road crossed White Rock Creek (later known as Little Branch), just a mile inside of Arkansas and seven miles from Cane Hill. At ten o'clock Major Ridge came riding down the highway with a colored boy in attendance. Several rifles cracked. The Ridge slumped in his saddle, his head and body pierced by five bullets. He toppled from his horse as it reared and then plunged, its freshly shod hooves grating against a sandstone bank, leaving creases in the soft rock. The boy galloped away, to carry the news of his master's death to a nearby settlement, then known as Dutchtown (later Dutch Mills), Arkansas. Some of the settlers hurried to the ambush scene and recovered Major Ridge's body. They buried it in a small cemetery

*Morris J. Wardell, in *A Political History of the Cherokee Nation* (p. 19*n*), cites $1,000 as the sum offered. Kenny A. Franks, biographer of Watie, accepts the larger figure.

at Piney, a brief distance inside the Cherokee Nation. And a runner
sent by Sarah Ridge to warn her father-in-law of danger rode back
to Honey Creek with the mournful tidings of his death.[24]*

*At word of Major Ridge's fate John Ross was heard to say: "Once I saved
Ridge at Red Clay, and would have done so again had I known of the plot"
(Edmund Schwarze, *History of the Moravian Missions among Southern Indian Tribes
of the United States*, p. 191).

EPILOGUE

THE Reverend Cephas Washburn preached the funeral service for John Ridge, and the slain leader was buried about 150 yards from his house on Honey Creek in a clearing that was later known as Polson cemetery, the burial place to which the remains of Major Ridge would come to rest in 1856.[1] At nearly the same hour in Park Hill, Worcester delivered the sermon over Boudinot's coffin, praising "the loveliness, integrity and Christian worth" of his murdered friend and maintaining that death had come because of "his desire for the good of his people" and that signing the Treaty of New Echota was the only act of his life that could be called into question. The grave had been dug outside the flinty ground that became the Park Hill cemetery, and when the hole was filled, an unmarked slab of stone, rough and hastily hewed, was placed above it.[2]

News of the murders had spread like fire through parched brush, stirring the nation into an uproar. As soon as John Ross had learned of Boudinot's assassination, he had sent a brother-in-law to verify the tragedy. And when the emissary returned, he brought a warning for Ross to be on guard against reprisals from Stand Watie, who held the chief responsible for the triple murder. Watie had gathered a band of fifteen treaty men, and heavily armed, they prowled the countryside in search of assassins, while the danger that threatened the principal chief caused antitreaty men to gather about the Ross house as a self-appointed guard. Ross immediately dispatched a letter to General Matthew Arbuckle at Fort Gibson, appealing for federal troops to prevent more bloodshed. In reply the general invited the chief to the fort for military protection. But the men who had rallied around Ross refused to let him go unless they also went as his bodyguard. Their numbers mounted daily until they totaled five hundred warriors. Indeed, the Ross forces so outnumbered the treaty band that not Ross but Stand Watie, John A. Bell, and other leaders of the Ridge party sought security at Fort Gibson.[3]

Fearful of another attack, Sarah Ridge fled with her children to Arkansas for safety, leaving property and improvements behind, except for merchandise in the store, which was hauled across the line at excessive expense. John Ridge's share of the stock was eventually sold at auction at only a fraction of its retail value, whereas after her first terror had subsided, Susanna Ridge had her husband's portion returned to the Cherokee Nation, where it would be retailed from the Ridge store at normal prices.[4]

Meanwhile the convention called to reach a compromise between the factions began to assemble on July 1 at Illinois Camp Ground near the present site of Tahlequah. Almost all those present were Ross supporters, for members of the Treaty Party were afraid to come, and most Old Settlers had responded to the entreaties of their principal chiefs to boycott the meeting, though the few Old Settlers who did attend included such influential men as Sequoyah and John Looney. One of the earliest acts of the council was to proclaim an amnesty for all crimes committed since the arrival of the Late Immigrants, thus extending pardon to the assassins of Boudinot and the Ridges. Not that most Cherokees thought of the triple bloodbath as a crime. In popular estimation the killings were "executions" under the law forbidding sale of land without authority from the nation.* The murdered men were declared outlaws by the convention, and so were all the treaty signers still alive, unless they came forward and publicly confessed to have been in error. Seven did so, more from fear than from conviction, but all the rest persisted stubbornly in defending the moral necessity of their deed. Watie and Bell later published an open letter in the *Arkansas Gazette* which stated that they would die, unyielding and defiant, before accepting amnesty on such humiliating terms.[5]

Before adjournment the convention framed an Act of Union for

---

*In a letter to George W. Paschal, Daniel Butrick argued against the notion popular with Ross supporters that the Ridges and Boudinot had forfeited their lives under a written law that was operative in the West. The crux of his argument was that the authority of the Blood Law of 1829 was limited to former Cherokee territory in the East. Thus, he did not recognize the validity of the Rattlesnake Springs resolution, a view that won approval from the Treaty Party (Butrick to Paschal, March 30, 1840, National Archives, RG 75, Letters received by the Office of Indian Affairs, M-234, Ross 84, frames 0498-99).

the entire nation, the first of three such acts within the year. Ross sent the document by messenger to the joint council of Old Settlers and Treaty men that John Brown had called for July 22, 1839, near the mouth of the Illinois River. But the messenger and his paper were both spurned. Each side earnestly desired a settlement, but neither could tolerate the idea of surrendering authority to the other. Ross acted as if the two governments had been consolidated into one, even though his "usurpation of power" brought protests from Old Settlers and Treaty Party alike.

For that purpose a group of treaty leaders met at Price's Prairie on August 21, 1839, with George W. Adair presiding. The meeting appealed to the federal government to aid in the punishment of the assassins of Boudinot and the Ridges. And it resolved to send two delegates to Washington—Watie and Bell—to petition the secretary of war and make arrangements, if at all possible, for protection and relief from Ross's rule. This was a tacit admission that Ross had won the struggle for power, and indeed John Brown, who had no relish for a martyr's fate, soon fled to Mexico for refuge.[6] In September, Ross supervised the framing of a new constitution for the nation, a work that only when redone the next year became acceptable to the Old Settlers.

The commissioner of Indian affairs requested General Arbuckle to "adopt the most prompt and energetic measures to discover, arrest and bring to condign punishment the murderers of the Ridges and Boudinot." Public opinion in Arkansas was clamoring for the assassins of Major Ridge to stand trial in a state court for having committed their crime on Arkansas soil. But when the alleged killers were demanded of Ross, he claimed to have no knowledge of their identities. General Arbuckle had his list of accused men, and he was doubly determined to bring to justice those implicated in the death of Major Ridge: James Foreman, Isaac and Anderson Springston, Bird Doublehead, and James and Jefferson Hair. The general sent companies of dragoons to scour the Cherokee Nation, accompanied by treaty men who served as interpreters and guides. But the search, with its legality open to question, proved to be fruitless and was finally abandoned. None of the killers was ever brought to justice, though as time passed, some of them came to violent ends. James Foreman was a case in point. In 1842 he picked a fight with Stand Watie and fell at Watie's hands. At a trial in Benton County, Arkansas, Watie was acquitted on the grounds of self-defense.[7]

Unification of the Cherokee Nation proved illusory. Disorder continued for years, something like a Corsican vendetta raging between the Ross and Ridge adherents, with a mournful succession of murders. The Ridge faction killed their oppressors without warrant of law, the Ross supporters committing "similar excesses, sometimes in the name of the law. Life and property were not safe and a state almost of civil war existed."[8] With differences so wide and deep dividing the parties, and with feelings growing ever more intense, President Polk suggested a solution to the problem—a problem that baffled his Indian Office and kept the southwestern frontier in a constant state of alarm: he would separate the Cherokees into autonomous groups, each with its own territory and its own government. That proposal, coming from one with ample might to implement it, caused John Ross such dismay that he offered concessions to the Treaty Party sufficient to make a reconciliation possible under a new treaty. This was signed at Washington in 1846 by delegates from all three parties. It was said that even Ross and Watie shook hands on that occasion and promised to bury their personal animosities.[9]

Three years later, in September, 1849, Susanna Ridge died at nearly eighty years of age. Her daughter Sally would soon divorce George Paschal, later to marry a Texas pioneer named Pix. The children of John Ridge had meanwhile reached maturity in Fayetteville and Osage Prairie, Arkansas. Susan married J. Woodward Washbourne, a son of Cephas Washburn, to whose family name he restored an earlier spelling. Flora married Dr. William D. Polson and went to live in the Cherokee Nation. Æneas practiced medicine briefly in Washington County, Arkansas, before his death in 1859. Herman was killed by Union Cherokees at Honey Creek in an early stage of the Civil War. And the youngest brother, Andrew J., pursued a successful legal career, first in Texas, then in California.[10]

No doubt the most interesting of John Ridge's children was the eldest son, John Rollin, who spent two years at a highly respected school in Great Barrington, Massachusetts. Memories of his father's violent death left him obsessed with fantasies of revenge as he grew to maturity; he followed as if in a fascination the notoriety of the "Starr boys," desperado sons of James Starr, who was himself cut down by Ross adherents; and John Rollin Ridge's marriage to Elizabeth Wilson, a young white woman of Fayetteville, could not divert such a vengeful romantic from involving himself in the Ross-Ridge feud. In self-defense he was forced to kill Judge David Kell and then flee from the Cherokee Nation to escape trial, which he feared would scarcely be impartial. In 1850 he crossed the plains to California. There he toiled as a placer miner before acquiring fugitive recognition as "Yellow Bird," the frontier poet—"biographer" of Joaquin Murieta, the daring bandit chieftain from Sonora around whose crimes he cast a legendary glamour much like Robin Hood's. The span of his career as John R. Ridge, outspoken editor of several newspapers in California, included the years of the Civil War, when his twilight actions as a Knight of the Golden Circle counterpointed the fearless exploits of Stand Watie as a brigade commander in the Confederate Army.[11]

The quiet established by the Treaty of 1846 had reflected only a surface healing of the profound cleavage between the Ross and Ridge parties. With the coming of the Civil War, the fissure reopened with catastrophic violence, the Ross Cherokees siding eventually with the Union and the treaty partisans following Watie in allegiance to the Confederacy. The war devastated the Cherokee Nation. But before it was over, Watie rose to the rank of brigadier general, and it was said that he was the last Confederate general to lay down his sword. His adherents proudly called themselves the Southern Cherokees.[12]

With peace, both Watie and Ross sent delegations to Washington. Watie summoned John R. Ridge from California to head the Southern deputation, and on his arrival in the capital, with his stint as an active Copperhead unknown there, Yellow Bird was "recognized by the Government as the *loyal* chief of the Ridge Party."[13] The Southern delegates labored to secure federal recognition of a Southern Cherokee Nation, separate and distinct from the Cherokees under Ross. They nearly achieved their purpose, but someone, it was claimed, had worked adroitly behind the scenes to block their aims. When at last a treaty was made, it was not with the Southern delegation that the Indian Office concluded final negotiations but with its Union counterpart. It looked as if the Ross-Ridge feud would be perpetuated. Ross died on August 1, 1866, however, and his passing encouraged the realignment of forces. Warring factions were pacified to a great extent under the chieftaincy of a shrewd and circumspect fullblood named Louis Downing, and the reunification brought the Cherokees long-sought peace and prosperity.[14] Not that factionalism was entirely contained. A legacy of hatred smoldered on for generations, coloring Cherokee history even after tribal government was superseded in 1907 by formation of the State of Oklahoma.

NOTES

THE National Archives microfilm program was in progress when
I examined federal records in Washington pertaining to the
Cherokee Indians. For some series I was allowed to examine the
original documents; for others microfilm substitutes were made available in the search room. Hence the citation of government files in the
following notes involves a mixed style. For records examined on microfilm, the pertinent roll numbers and (when available) the frame numbers
of individual documents are listed. For the originals that were examined, however, the original file numbers are cited, by which the respective documents can be found on microfilm readily enough, whenever
its use is required.

At the Newberry Library, in Chicago, my examination of the John
Howard Payne papers, in the Ayer Collection, involved a series of
typed duplicates in place of the original papers. Hence citations of
documents from that series of Payne papers refer, in most instances,
to the aforesaid typescripts and not to the original manuscripts.

Lyman Draper manuscripts relative to the southern Indians were
examined in transcript form and on microfilm in the Western History
Collections of the University of Oklahoma Library. Some were also
seen in transcript form in the Grant Foreman Collection.

The Jackson papers in the Library of Congress were examined
on microfilm at Columbia University. All mention of Jackson manuscripts in the notes, unless otherwise specified, refer to that collection.

CHAPTER 1: BORDER WARRIOR

1. Stand Watie Papers, Western History Collections, University of Oklahoma Library, Series IV, Vol. 9, p. 8. For published source see 29th Cong.
1st sess., House Doc. 185 (Serial 485), p. 104.
2. *Writings of Sam Houston*, V, p. 520.
3. *New York Tribune*, May 28, 1866, p. 6, col. 1.
4. Thomas L. McKenney and James Hall, *History of the Indian Tribes of*

345

North America, ed. F. W. Hodge, II, p. 326.

5. The *Dictionary of American Biography* accepts ca. 1771 for The Ridge's birth, following McKenney and Hall; so also does Emmet Starr, *History of the Cherokee Indians,* p. 112. Mabel Washbourne Anderson (a descendant) in *The Life of General Stand Watie,* p. 9, states "about 1770."

6. See the report of missionaries Steiner and Schweinitz (1799) in Samuel Cole Williams, ed., *Early Travels in the Tennessee Country,* pp. 480–85, for descriptions of the town and environs a generation after The Ridge's birth.

7. "Major Ridge" in McKenney and Hall, *Indian Tribes,* I, pp. 368–69. This biographical essay constitutes the principal source of data about The Ridge's youth. John Howard Payne describes it as an "account supplied by [The Ridge's] son for . . . 'The Indian Tribes of North America' " (Payne Papers, Ayer Collection, Newberry Library, VI, p. 194). McKenney and Hall took full responsibility for the volume in which the sketch appears, and internal evidence suggests they revised whatever account John Ridge had submitted.

8. McKenney and Hall, *Indian Tribes,* I, pp. 368, 369; Emmet Starr Papers, Oklahoma Historical Society.

9. Starr, *Cherokee Indians,* p. 381; see also genealogical chart in Edward Everett Dale and Gaston Litton, eds., *Cherokee Cavaliers;* Mary Brinsmade Church, "Elias Boudinot: An Account of His Life Written by his Granddaughter . . . Oct. 1, 1913," in the Fred S. Barde Collection, No. 2011, Oklahoma Historical Society; E. C. Starr, *History of Cornwall, Connecticut,* p. 276; Emmet Starr Papers, Oklahoma Historical Society.

10. David H. Corkran, *The Cherokee Frontier,* p. 61.

11. McKenney and Hall, *Indian Tribes,* I, p. 369.

12. Sketch of E. C. Boudinot, *The Encyclopedia of the New West,* s.v. "Indian Territory," p. 9. On occasion John Rollin Ridge used an almost identical expression.

13. Quoted in John P. Brown, *Old Frontiers: The Story of the Cherokee Indians from Earliest Times to . . . 1838,* p. 8.

14. Emmet Starr Papers, Oklahoma Historical Society; Church, "Elias Boudinot."

15. Brown, *Old Frontiers,* pp. 67, 478.

16. "Remarkable Fulfillment of Indian Prophecy," *Cherokee Phoenix,* June 23, 1832, p. 2, col. 4; James Mooney, *Myths of the Cherokee,* Bureau of American Ethnology 19th Annual Report, Part I, p. 239.

17. David H. Corkran, "A Cherokee Migration Fragment," *Southern Indian Studies,* IV (1952): 27; Henry Rowe Schoolcraft, *Notes on the Iroquois,* pp. 163, 358–59. See Leander Leitner, ed., *The Walum Olum,* Part 4, for reference to traditional conflicts between the Delawares and the Cherokees, that is, the Tallegwis.

18. Schoolcraft, *Iroquois,* p. 157; C— —, "Indian Traditions," *Cherokee Advocate,* July 20, 1853, p. 2, cols. 3–4.

19. "Remarkable Fulfillment."

20. William Fyffe to Brother John, February 1, 1761, quoted in Grace Steele Woodward, *The Cherokees,* p. 33.

21. Archibald Henderson, *Conquest of the Old Southwest,* pp. 265–68; E. F. Rockwell, "Parallel and Combined Expeditions against the Cherokee Indians . . . in 1776," *Historical Magazine,* XII (Oct., 1867): 219–20; Statement of James Martin, *North Carolina State Records,* XXII, pp. 146–47; Deposition of Robert

F. Dews . . . January 21, 1777, ibid., pp. 995–1005; McKenney and Hall, *Indian Tribes*, I, p. 369.

22. J. G. M. Ramsey, *Annals of Tennessee*, p. 266.
23. John Haywood, *The Natural and Aboriginal History of Tennessee*, p. 254.
24. McKenney and Hall, *Indian Tribes*, I, p. 369.
25. Francis R. Goulding, *Sal-o-quah*, pp. 97–98, gives a description of dazing fish with buckeye juice.
26. James Mooney, "Sacred Formulas of the Cherokees," in *Bureau of American Ethnology 7th Annual Report*, pp. 369–70.
27. McKenney and Hall, *Indian Tribes*, I, p. 368.
28. Judge J. W. H. Underwood, "Reminiscences of the Cherokees,"*Cartersville* (Ga.) *Courant*, April 2, 1885, p. 1, col. 4.
29. McKenney and Hall, *Indian Tribes*, I, pp. 370–71.
30. Ibid., p. 371..
31. James Sevier to Lyman C. Draper, August 19, 1839, in *American Historical Magazine*, VI: 43.
32. McKenney and Hall, *Indian Tribes*, I, p. 371. The authors cite The Ridge's age as fourteen when he first went on the warpath, but the events described are those of 1788.
33. Lyman Draper Papers, 32-S, 140–80; *Maryland Journal*, September 16, 1788; Ramsey, *Annals*, pp. 421–22.
34. McKenney and Hall, *Indian Tribes*, I, pp. 371–72.
35. Brown, *Old Frontiers*, p. 279; James Adair, *Adair's History of the American Indians*, ed. S. C. Williams, pp. 415–16.
36. Draper Papers, 32-S, 140–80; Brown, *Old Frontiers*, p. 280; Ramsey, *Annals*, p. 422.
37. McKenney and Hall, *Indian Tribes*, I, p. 372.
38. Col. Jos. Brown's notes, Draper Papers, Series XX, Vol. 5, 52–1.
39. Draper Papers, 30-S, 320–21.
40. McKenney and Hall, *Indian Tribes*, I, pp. 372–73; Draper Papers, Series XX, Vol. 5, 52–1; Vol. 7, 26; *American State Papers, Indian Affairs*, I, p. 47; Brown, *Old Frontiers*, pp. 293–94; Ramsey, *Annals*, pp. 518–19.
41. Brown, *Old Frontiers*, p. 294.
42. *American State Papers, Indian Affairs*, I, pp. 28, 46; *Journals of the American Congress*, IV, p. 860; Randolph C. Downes, "Cherokee-American Relations in the Upper Tennessee Valley, 1776–1791," *East Tennessee Historical Society's Publications*, No. 8 (1936): 49–50.
43. Ramsey, *Annals*, p. 518.
44. Sevier's report in S. C. Williams, *History of the Lost State of Franklin*, p. 218. See also Brown, *Old Frontiers*, pp. 297–98.
45. McKenney and Hall, *Indian Tribes*, I, pp. 373, 374.
46. John L. McCoy to Col. J. A. Bell, Aug. 3, 1882, Bell Papers, Western History Collections, University of Oklahoma Library, Series IV, Vol. III, p. 8.
47. McKenney and Hall, *Indian Tribes*, I, p. 373.
48. Gov. Blount to Gen. James Robertson, May 20, 1792, in Thomas E. Matthews, *General James Robertson, Father of Tennessee*, p. 100.
49. Ramsey, *Annals*, p. 567; John P. Brown, "Eastern Cherokee Chiefs," *Chronicles of Oklahoma*, XVI (1938): 26.
50. McKenney and Hall, *Indian Tribes*, I, p. 374; *American State Papers*,

Indian Affairs, I, p. 455.
    51. *American State Papers, Indian Affairs*, I, p. 457; McKenney and Hall, *Indian Tribes*, I, p. 374.
    52. *Calendar of Virginia State Papers*, VI, pp. 409–10; *American State Papers, Indian Affairs*, I, pp. 455, 457, 459; Ramsey, *Annals*, p. 577.
    53. McKenney and Hall, *Indian Tribes*, I, pp. 374–75.
    54. Ibid., p. 375.
    55. *American State Papers, Indian Affairs*, I, p. 468; Ramsey, *Annals*, p. 580.
    56. Ramsey, *Annals*, pp. 580–81.
    57. McKenney and Hall, *Indian Tribes*, I, p. 375.
    58. Ramsey, *Annals*, p. 581; *American State Papers, Indian Affairs*, I, p. 468.
    59. *Calendar of Virginia State Papers*, VI, p. 586.
    60. Sevier's report, *American State Papers, Indian Affairs*, I, pp. 469–70.
    61. Ibid., pp. 536–38.
    62. Silas Dinsmoor to Col. David Henley, Eustinali, March 18, 1795, Ayer N. A. 243, Ayer Collection, Newberry Library.
    63. Quoted in Brown, *Old Frontiers*, p. 445.

CHAPTER 2:   YOUNG CHIEF

    1. McKenney and Hall, *Indian Tribes*, I, p. 377.
    2. Ibid.
    3. Descriptions of the characteristics of Cherokee councils are to be found in the Payne Papers, Ayer Collection, Newberry Library, VI, pp. 204–205; in *Adair's History of the American Indians*, ed. S. C. Williams, p. 460; and in Haywood, *Natural and Aboriginal History of Tennessee*, pp. 255–58.
    4. Jedidiah Morse, *Report to the Secretary of War on Indian Affairs, p.* 71.
    5. McKenney and Hall, *Indian Tribes*, I, p. 379.
    6. Benjamin Hawkins to James McHenry, Secretary of War, May 4, 1797, "Letters of Benjamin Hawkins," *Georgia Historical Society Collections*, IX, p. 136.
    7. McKenney and Hall, *Indian Tribes*, I, p. 379.
    8. E. E. Dale and Gaston Litton, in *Cherokee Cavaliers*, p. 12n, date the wedding as 1792 but cite no authority for the statement. So also does Mabel Washbourne Anderson, *General Stand Watie*, p. 9.
    9. John R. Ridge, according to Carolyn T. Foreman in *Chronicles of Oklahoma*, XIV (Sept. 1936): 308, described himself as "the grandson of Chief Ka-nun-ta-cla-ge and Princess Se-hoya." Cf. Anderson, *General Stand Watie*, p. 9.
    10. McKenney and Hall, *Indian Tribes*, I, p. 380.
    11. Descriptions of the old Cherokee marriage ceremony appear in *Cherokee Advocate*, May 9, 1874; in Goulding, *Sal-o-quah*, pp. 230–31; and in the *Atlanta Constitution*, Nov. 10, 1889, p. 6, cols. 2–3. See also Cephas Washburn, *Reminiscences of the Indians*.
    12. "Letters of Benjamin Hawkins," *Georgia Historical Society Collections*, IX, p. 20.
    13. John Ridge to Albert Gallatin, Feb. 27, 1826, Payne Papers, Ayer Collection, Newberry Library, VIII.
    14. McKenney and Hall, *Indian Tribes*, II, p. 326.
    15. Extract from a letter of Anna Gambold, July 29, 1819, in *The Weekly*

Recorder (Chillicothe, Ohio), Oct. 13, 1819, p. 66, cols. 2–3.

16. Daniel S. Butrick, "A brief review of the history of the Cherokee nation for a few years back," Payne Papers, Ayer Collection, Newberry Library.

17. Quoted in Morse, *Report to the Secretary of War*, Appendix, p. 155.

18. McKenney and Hall, *Indian Tribes*, I, p. 380.

19. Unidentified talk, National Archives, RG 75, Records of the Cherokee Agency in Tennessee, M-208, Roll 3.

20. George White, *Historical Collections of Georgia*, p. 476.

21. John R. Ridge, *Poems*, p. 4.

22. John Ridge to Albert Gallatin, Feb. 27, 1826, Payne Papers, Ayer Collection, Newberry Library, VIII, pp. 109–10. For revised version, see William C. Sturtevant, ed., "John Ridge on Cherokee Civilization in 1826," *Journal of Cherokee Studies*, VI (Fall, 1981): 84.

23. Ridge to Gallatin, Feb. 27, 1826, Payne Papers, Ayer Collection, Newberry Library, VIII, p. 110.

24. McKenney and Hall, *Indian Tribes*, I, pp. 380–81.

25. Ibid., p. 381.

26. Meigs to Gov. McMinn of Tennessee, Jan. 17, 1817, in National Archives, RG 75, Records of the Cherokee Agency in Tennessee, M-208, Roll 7.

27. Spring Place Diary, 1803, entry for Aug. 18, trans. Carl Mauelshagen, Georgia Department of Natural Resources.

28. Henry Dearborn to R. J. Meigs, April 23, 1804, in National Archives, RG 75, Letters sent by the Office of the Secretary of War relating to Indian affairs, Letter Book B, p. 1.

29. Payne Papers, Ayer Collection, Newberry Library, II, p. 28; VI, p. 194.

30. *East Tennessee Historical Society's Publications*, No. 1, p. 131.

31. The classic study of Cherokee land cessions is found in Charles C. Royce, *The Cherokee Nation of Indians*, Bureau of American Ethnology 5th Annual Report. See pp. 174–93.

32. Doublehead's venality is revealed in Nicholas Byers (U.S. factor) to R. J. Meigs, Aug. 4, 1805, in National Archives, RG 75, Records of the Cherokee Agency in Tennessee, M-208, Roll 3; Byers to Meigs, Aug. 16, 1805, ibid.; Dearborn to Meigs, June 25, 1804, in National Archives, RG 75, Letters sent by the Office of the Secretary of War relating to Indian affairs, Letter Book B, p. 6; Secretary of War to Meigs, Jan. 8, 1806, ibid, p. 153; Secretary of War to Meigs, Jan. 10, 1806, ibid., p. 150; Payne Papers, Ayer Collection, Newberry Library, II, pp. 26–27.

33. National Archives, RG 75, Letters sent by the Office of the Secretary of War in relation to Indian affairs, Letter Book B, p. 142; Royce, *Cherokee Nation*, pp. 183, 193; Payne Papers, Ayer Collection, Newberry Library, II, pp. 26–27; Black Fox and twenty-two other chiefs to Meigs in National Archives, RG 75, Records of the Cherokee Agency in Tennessee, M-208, Roll 3.

34. *American State Papers, Indian Affairs*, I, p. 754; Secretary of War to Meigs, April 1, 1807, in National Archives, RG 75, Letters sent by the Office of the Secretary of War in relation to Indian affairs, Letter Book B, p. 300.

35. McKenney and Hall, *Indian Tribes*, I, p. 385.

36. Payne Papers, Ayer Collection, Newberry Library, II, p. 26.

37. Ibid., p. 28.

38. A. V. Goodpasture, "Indian Wars and Warriors in the Old Southwest,"

Tennessee Historical Magazine, IV (1918): 272; Starr, *History of the Cherokee Indians,* pp. 40–41.

39. Payne Papers, Ayer Collection, Newberry Library, II, p. 28.

40. Payne's account gives the name as Bone Cracker; others give Dry Bones.

41. Deposition of Caleb Starr concerning the death of Doublehead, dated Aug. 11, 1838, in National Archives, RG 75, Office of Indian Affairs, Removal Records (Cherokee), First Board of Cherokee Commissioners files, Heirs of Doublehead for spoliations.

42. Ibid.

43. In addition to authorities cited above, this account of Doublehead's death rests on "Col. Phillip's testimony relating to the death of Doublehead . . . Highwassee, Aug. 15, 1807," in National Archives, RG 75, Records of the Cherokee Agency in Tennessee, M-208, Roll 3; J. F. H. Claiborne, *Life and Times of General Sam. Dale, the Mississippi Partisan,* pp. 45–49; Brown, *Old Frontiers,* pp. 451–53.

44. McKenney and Hall, *Indian Tribes,* I, p. 385.

45. Rev. Gideon Blackburn to Jedidiah Morse, in *Missionary Herald (The Panoplist),* IV (Dec., 1808): 325ff.

46. Ibid.; Starr, *History of the Cherokee Indians,* p. 41.

47. McKenney and Hall, *Indian Tribes,* I, p. 382.

48. *Cartersville* (Ga.) *Courant,* Apr. 2, 1885, quoted in George M. Battey, *A History of Rome and Floyd County,* I, pp. 216–17.

49. Meigs to Secretary Eustis, July 31, 1811, in National Archives, RG 75, Records of the Cherokee Agency in Tennessee, M-208, Roll 4.

50. *American State Papers, Indian Affairs,* I, p. 754.

51. Ka-ti-hee to Black Fox, Feb. 15, 1808, in National Archives, RG 75, Records of the Cherokee Agency in Tennessee, M-208, Roll 4.

52. Royce, *Cherokee Nation,* pp. 199ff; *American State Papers, Indian Affairs,* I, p. 722; Elias Earle to Gen. Armstrong, July 19, 1813, in National Archives, RG 107, Office of the Secretary of War, Letters received, registered series, 1801–60, M-221, Roll 52: D-F 1812–14.

53. "Spring Frog's account of Colonel Earle's people," Mar. 15, 1814, in National Archives, RG 107, Office of the Secretary of War, Letters received, registered series, 1801–60, M-221, Roll 55: M-231(7).

54. The Ridge's talk duplicated the sense of the message of Chulioa et al. in "Remonstrance of the Cherokees against Colonel Elias Earle's entering on land at the Chicamauga [*sic*] Creek," undated (Jan., 1808?), ibid.

55. Ka-ti-hee to Black Fox, Feb. 15, 1808; William Brown's affidavit, dated 15 Feb. 1808, in National Archives, RG 75, Records of the Cherokee Agency in Tennessee, M-208, Roll 4.

56. Meigs to Gen. Armstrong, March 27, 1814 (with enclosures), in National Archives, RG 107, Office of the Secretary of War, Letters received, registered series, 1801–60, M-221, Roll 55: M-310(7); Meigs to Armstrong, April 15, 1814, ibid., M-316(7); Armstrong to Meigs, March 24, 1814, in National Archives, RG 75, Letters sent by the Office of the Secretary of War in relation to Indian affairs, Letter Book C, p. 166.

57. Gen. Dearborn to Meigs, May 5, 1808, in National Archives, RG 75, Letters sent by the Office of the Secretary of War in relation to Indian affairs, Letter Book B, pp. 376–77.

58. Ibid.; *Cherokee Phoenix,* June 25, 1831, p. 1.

59. McKenney and Hall, *Indian Tribes,* I, p. 383.

60. Ibid., p. 384.
61. *Cherokee Phoenix*, Dec. 3, 1831, p. 2, col. 3: Cherokee Council to Joseph McMinn, June 30, 1818, in National Archives, RG 75, Documents relating to the negotiation of ratified and unratified treaties with various Indian tribes, T-494, Roll 1, frames 0362-63.
62. Cherokee Council to Joseph McMinn, June 30, 1818.
63. John Stuart, *A Sketch of the Cherokee and Choctaw Indians*, p. 15.
64. Statement of Col. Meigs respecting the object of the deputation to Washington in 1808-1809, in National Archives, RG 75, Office of Indian Affairs, Miscellaneous Files.
65. Cherokee Delegation to Thomas Jefferson, Dec. 21, 1808, in National Archives, RG 75, Records of the Cherokee Agency in Tennessee, M-208, Roll 4.
66. *Cherokee Phoenix*, Feb. 21, 1828, p. 1, cols. 1-2.
67. Ibid., col. 2. Talks to both can also be found in National Archives, RG 75, Letters sent by the Office of the Secretary of War in relation to Indian affairs, Letter Book B, pp. 416-17; Richard Peters, *Case of the Cherokee Nation against the State of Georgia*, pp. 57-58n.
68. McKenney and Hall, *Indian Tribes*, I, pp. 384-85.
69. Payne Papers, Ayer Collection, Newberry Library, II, p. 46.
70. Cherokee Council to Meigs, Sept. 27, 1809, in National Archives, RG 75, Records of the Cherokee Agency in Tennessee, M-208, Roll 4.

CHAPTER 3: THE CREEK WAR

1. A brief but informed discussion of Tecumseh's visit to the Creeks in 1811 can be found in R. S. Cotterill, *The Southern Indians*, pp. 172-73.
2. Col. Hawkins to the Secretary of War, Sept. 21, 1811, in National Archives, RG 107, Office of the Secretary of War, letters received, registered series, M-221, Roll 37.
3. A Choctaw tradition. See H. S. Halbert and T. H. Ball, *The Creek War of 1813 and 1814*, pp. 42-43.
4. Cotterill, *Southern Indians*, pp. 172-73; Henry Adams, *History of the United States of America during the Administrations of Thomas Jefferson and James Madison*, VIII, pp. 220-21.
5. Quoted in Glen Tucker, *Tecumseh: Vision of Glory*, pp. 82-83.
6. Halbert and Ball, *Creek War*, p. 73.
7. Col. Hawkins to The Big Warrior and others, June 16, 1814, in *American State Papers, Indian Affairs*, I, p. 845.
8. Thomas S. Woodward, *Woodward's Reminiscences of the Creek or Muscogee Indians*, p. 116.
9. Col. Hawkins to the Secretary of War, Jan. 13, 1812, in National Archives, RG 107, Office of the Secretary of War, letters received, registered series, M-221, Roll 37.
10. James Mooney, *The Ghost Dance Religion*, Bureau of American Ethnology 14th Annual Report, p. 687. Mooney stated that Thomas L. McKenney was the best authority for Tecumseh's prophetic boast to The Big Warrior (McKenney and Hall, *Indian Tribes*, I, p. 94), having "derived [the] information from Indians at the same town a few years later."
11. *American State Papers, Indian Affairs*, I, p. 845.
12. Cherokee Delegation to President Madison [1816], in National Archives,

RG 75, Records of the Cherokee Agency in Tennessee, M-208, Roll 6.
    13. Choctaw tradition; George W. Campbell to Lyman C. Draper, Draper
Collection, Western History Collections, University of Oklahoma Library, X,
p. 62.
    14. Meigs to Secretary Eustis, Dec. 4, 1811, in National Archives, RG
75, Records of the Cherokee Agency in Tennessee, M-208, Roll 5; descriptions
of the earthquakes appear in Haywood, *Natural and Aboriginal History of Tennessee*, pp. 28–31; *The American Historical Magazine*, V: 235–37.
    15. Spring Place Diary, entry for Feb. 11, 1812, Mauelshagen translation,
Georgia Department of Natural Resources, Atlanta.
    16. *American State Papers, Indian Affairs*, I, p. 846.
    17. Cotterill, *Southern Indians*, p. 178.
    18. John Parris, *The Cherokee Story*, p. 39.
    19. Col. Hawkins, Creek Agency, May 11, 1812, in *American State Papers,
Indian Affairs*, I, p. 809.
    20. Letter dated June 12, 1812, Andrew Jackson Papers, Roll 5.
    21. McKenney and Hall, *Indian Tribes*, I, p. 386.
    22. "The North American Indian," *The Hesperian*, VIII (May, 1862): 100.
    23. McKenney and Hall, *Indian Tribes*, I, pp. 387–88.
    24. Spring Place Diary, Feb. 10, 1811, Moravian Archives, Winston-Salem,
N.C. (extract translated by Sophie Wilkins).
    25. McKenney and Hall, *Indian Tribes*, I, p. 388.
    26. Ibid.; Spring Place Diary, Feb. 10, 1811.
    27. *Cherokee Advocate*, Nov. 16, 1844; Mooney, *The Ghost Dance Religion*,
pp. 676–77, and Mooney, *Myths of the Cherokee*, Bureau of American Ethnology
19th Annual Report, Part I (1900), p. 88.
    28. Meigs to Secretary Eustis, May 8, 1812, in National Archives, RG 75,
Records of the Cherokee Agency in Tennessee, M-208, Roll 5; *American State
Papers, Indian Affairs*, I, p. 809. The document in question offering Cherokee
service makes no mention of The Ridge's name, but the wrapper covering
the record copy in the Cherokee agency files bears the following label: "A
proposition of Walker, Lowry [*sic*] & Ridge to offer their services in the
expected war with the English."
    29. Secretary of War to Meigs, May 29, 1812, in National Archives, RG 75,
Letters sent by the Office of the Secretary of War in relation to Indian affairs,
Letter Book C, p. 133.
    30. Andrew Jackson, *Correspondence of Andrew Jackson*, ed. John Spencer
Bassett, I, p. 228.
    31. Jackson, *Correspondence*, I, p. 232.
    32. Gov. Willie Blount to Jackson, July 21, 1812, in Jackson Papers, Roll 5.
    33. Secretary of War to Col. Meigs, April 28, 1812, and Aug. 11, 1812, in
National Archives, RG 75, Letters sent by the Office of the Secretary of War
in relation to Indian affairs, Letter Book C, pp. 127, 145.
    34. Charles Hicks to Meigs, Feb. 5, 1821, in National Archives, RG 75,
Records of the Cherokee Agency in Tennessee, M-208, Roll 9.
    35. Merritt B. Pound, *Benjamin Hawkins, Indian Agent*, p. 220; *American
State Papers, Indian Affairs*, I, p. 813.
    36. Adams, *History of the United States*, VII, p. 232; Halbert and Ball,
Creek War, pp. 129ff; Woodward, *Woodward's Reminiscences*, pp. 97–98.
    37. Mooney, *Myths of the Cherokee*, p. 216; Angie Debo, *The Road to Dis-
appearance*, p. 79.

38. Robert J. Walton to [?], Alcofee, July 26, 1813, Georgia Department of Archives and History. "Finding on our return here that hostile Indians were waylaying all the paths leading to Tuckabatchee with intention to kill McIntosh he determined to write the chiefs and go himself to expedite the succours which he expected to obtain from the Cherokees."

39. McKenney and Hall, *Indian Tribes*, I, p. 390.

40. Ibid., pp. 390-91.

41. Ibid., p. 391.

42. Extract of letter to Meigs from the War Department, Aug. 26, 1813, in Return J. Meigs folder, Georgia Department of Archives and History.

43. Meigs to Gov. Mitchell, Sept. 17, 1813, Georgia Department of Archives and History.

44. Strother to Jackson, Oct. 9, 1813, Jackson Papers, Roll 61, frame 21; Meigs to Gen. Armstrong, Dec., 1813, in National Archives, RG 75, Records of the Cherokee Agency in Tennessee, M-208, Roll 6; Pathkiller to Jackson, Oct. 29, 1813, Jackson Papers, Roll 7.

45. McKenney and Hall's representation of The Ridge as chiefly responsible for Cherokee enlistment, energetic as his efforts were (*Indian Tribes*, I, p. 391), is an exaggeration.

46. John Walker to Col. Meigs, Oct. 15, 1813, in National Archives, RG 75, Records of the Cherokee Agency in Tennessee, M-208, Roll 6; Walker to Meigs, Nov. 5, 1813, ibid.

47. Meigs to Cherokee warriors, Oct. 30, 1813, miscellaneous manuscripts, Western History Collections, University of Oklahoma Library.

48. Muster rolls and payrolls of Captain Saunders's company, Nov. 7, 1813, to Jan. 6, 1814, in National Archives, RG 94, Records of the Adjutant General's Office, Volunteer organizations and state militia, War of 1812, Box 331.

49. Meigs to Cherokee warriors, Oct. 30, 1813, miscellaneous manuscripts, Western History Collections, University of Oklahoma Library.

50. John Walker to Col. Meigs, Nov. 5, 1813, in National Archives, RG 75, Records of the Cherokee Agency in Tennessee, M-208, Roll 6; John Lowrey to Jackson, Nov. 7, 1813, Jackson papers, Roll 7 (also Roll 61). Henry Adams (*History of the United States*, VII, 237) puts the matter dryly: "In every attack on an Indian village a certain number of women and children were necessarily victims, but the proportion at Taleshatchee seemed large." John Walker reported (to Meigs, Nov. 5, 1813): "The situation looked dismal, to see women and children slaughtered with their fathers."

51. *Davy Crockett's Own Story*, pp. 70, 71.

52. Gideon Morgan, Jr., to Jackson, Nov. 4, 1813, Jackson Papers, Roll 61.

53. Gen. White to Jackson, Nov. 5, 1813, Jackson Papers, Roll 61; Jackson to White, Nov. 7, 1813, ibid.; Jackson to Col. Lowrey, Nov. 7, 1813, ibid.; Jackson, *Correspondence*, I, p. 343.

54. Jackson, *Correspondence*, p. 352n; White to Jackson, Nov. 7, 1813, Jackson papers, Roll 61; Col. Lowrey to Jackson, Nov. 7, 1813, ibid.

55. Jackson to Gov. Blount, Nov. 15, 1813, Jackson Papers, Roll 61.

56. Gen. Cocke to Jackson, Nov. 14, 1813, Jackson Papers, Roll 61; Gen. Cocke to Col. Meigs, Nov. 22, 1813, in National Archives, RG 107, Letters received by the Office of the Secretary of War, registered series, 1801-60, M-221, Roll 55.

57. Morgan to Meigs, Nov. 23, 1813, ibid.

58. Ibid.

59. Bassett in Jackson, *Correspondence,* I, p. 361*n*.
60. Meigs to Secretary of War, Dec. 5, 1813, in National Archives, RG 107, Letters received by the Office of the Secretary of War, registered series, 1801–60, M-221, Roll 55.
61. Brainerd Journal, entry for July 6, 1817, in Houghton Library, Archives of the American Board of Commissioners for Foreign Missions (hereafter cited as ABC), 18.3.1, II: 2; Robert Grayson to Jackson, Feb. 11, 1814, Jackson Papers, Roll 8; Jackson to The Pathkiller, Feb. 18, 1814, ibid., Roll 61.
62. Gen. Cocke to Gen. Armstrong, Nov. 30, 1813, in National Archives, RG 107, Letters received by the Office of the Secretary of War, registered series, 1801–60, M-221, Roll 51.
63. Jackson, *Correspondence,* I, pp. 387ff; *American State Papers, Military Affairs,* III, p. 786; Jackson to Gov. Blount, Dec. 18, 1813, Jackson Papers, Roll 61. Gen. Cocke's version of his troubled relations with Jackson is quoted in Parton, *Life of Andrew Jackson,* I, pp. 449–54.
64. Gideon Morgan to his Cherokee regiment, Dec. 15, 1813 (forwarded to Jackson and filed under date of Jan. 16, 1814), Jackson Papers, Roll 8. Muster rolls in National Archives, RG 94, Records of the Adjutant General's Office, continue The Ridge's first term of service until Jan. 6, 1814.
65. McKenney and Hall, *Indian Tribes,* I, p. 391. Again the authors assign Major Ridge exaggerated credit for the Cherokee recruitment.
66. Cherokee chiefs in the vicinity of Hightower to Col. Meigs, Jan. 16, 1814, in National Archives, RG 75, Records of the Cherokee Agency in Tennessee, M-208, Roll 6.
67. Col. Meigs to Secretary of War, May 5, 1814, Jackson Papers, Roll 10.
68. Jackson to Morgan, Feb. 26, 1814, Jackson Papers, Roll 61; Morgan to Jackson, Feb. 22, 1814, ibid., Roll 9; Morgan to Jackson, Feb. 9, 1814, ibid., Roll 8.
69. Muster rolls and payrolls of Col. Morgan's Cherokee regiment, Jan. 27, 1814, to April 11, 1814, National Archives, RG 94, AGO, Volunteer Organizations and State militia, War of 1812, Box 331.
70. Jackson to W. B. Lewis, Feb. 21, 1814, in Parton, *Life of Andrew Jackson,* I, p. 502.
71. Gen. Johnston to Jackson, March 23, 1814, Jackson Papers, Roll 9; Jackson to Gen. Pinckney, March 23, 1814, ibid.
72. "Memorandum by Capt. Read, from which the communications to Gen. Pinckney, Blount and Sec. of War [were] made of the affair of the Horseshoe," Jackson Papers, Roll 9.
73. Jackson to Pinckney, March 28, 1814, *Correspondence,* I, p. 489; Jackson to Gov. Blount, March 31, 1814, ibid., p. 490; Gen. Coffee's report, April 1, 1814, in S. G. Heiskell, *Andrew Jackson and Early Tennessee History,* I, p. 503; Col. Morgan to Gov. Blount, April 1, 1814, in Heiskell, *Andrew Jackson,* pp. 504–505; *Niles' Weekly Register,* XII (April 19, 1817): 121–22; Statement of the Whale, Feb. 18, 1843, in National Archives, RG 75, Letters received by the Office of Indian Affairs, M-234, Roll 87, frames 0270–71.
74. McKenney and Hall, *Indian Tribes,* I, p. 392.
75. Jackson to Pinckney, March 28, 1814; Coffee's report, April 1, 1814; Morgan to Blount, April 1, 1814.
76. McKenney and Hall, *Indian Tribes,* I, p. 393.
77. Gen. Carroll quoted in Philo Goodwin, *Biography of Andrew Jackson,* pp. 87–88; Jackson, *Correspondence,* I, p. 492.

78. Halbert and Ball, *Creek War*, p. 277.
79. Woodward, *Woodward's Reminiscences*, p. 117.
80. Col. Meigs to the Secretary of War, May 5, 1814, Jackson Papers, Roll 10; *Cherokee Phoenix*, Mar. 19, 1831, p. 2, cols. 2–3, reprinting from *National Intelligencer* (letter of John Ridge to the editor).
81. "Claims by Cherokees for losses due to spoliation of U.S. troops during Creek War," National Archives, RG 75, Records of the Office of Indian Affairs.

CHAPTER 4: CHEROKEE DIPLOMACY

1. Col. Meigs to the Secretary of War, May 15, 1814, in National Archives, RG 107, Letters received by the Office of the Secretary of War, M-221, Roll 55; Secretary of War to Jackson, May 31, 1814, *American State Papers, Indian Affairs*, II, p. 594.
2. Memo of Jackson's itinerary to Fort Jackson, June–July, 1814, Jackson Papers, Roll 11.
3. Meigs to Jackson, July 6, 1814, Jackson Papers, Roll 11.
4. Meigs and Cherokee chiefs to Jackson, Aug. 4, 1814, Jackson Papers, Roll 11.
5. Extract, Deposition of Walter Adair, Dec. 14, 1829, in National Archives, RG 75, Letters received by the Office of Indian Affairs, M-234, Roll 73, frames 0519-20.
6. Ibid.; Cherokee Delegation to the War Department, March 4, 1816, John Ross Papers, Gilcrease Institute, 16-5.
7. Documents in re Creek-Cherokee boundary, No. 5, Meigs to the Secretary of War, Feb. 27, 1816, *Cherokee Phoenix*, April 14, 1830, p. 2, cols. 1–2.
8. Creek-Cherokee agreement, Aug. 9, 1814, Jackson Papers, Roll 11.
9. Pound, *Benjamin Hawkins*, p. 238; Cherokee Delegation to the War Department, March 4, 1816, Ross Papers, Gilcrease Institute, 16-5.
10. The Big Warrior to Jackson, April 16, 1816, in Jackson, *Correspondence*, II, p. 239.
11. Jackson to Rachel Jackson, Aug. 5, 1814, HM 22990, Huntington Library.
12. Col. Robert Butler to Col. Meigs, Sept. 11, 1814, in National Archives, RG 75, Records of the Cherokee Agency in Tennessee, M-208, Roll 6.
13. Jackson, *Correspondence*, II, p. 41.
14. Meigs to the Cherokee council, Sept. 20, 1814, in National Archives, RG 75, Records of the Cherokee Agency in Tennessee, M-208, Roll 6.
15. The Pathkiller and Chulioa to Meigs, Sept. 24, 1814, ibid.
16. Major Walker to Meigs, Nov. 25, 1814, ibid.
17. Meigs to the Secretary of War, May 5, 1814, Jackson Papers, Roll 10.
18. Jackson to Col. Lillard's command, Jan. 8, 1814, Jackson Papers, Rolls 61 and 62.
19. Jackson, *Correspondence*, II, 255, 256.
20. Meigs to Jackson, Aug. 7, 1816, in National Archives, RG 75, Records of the Cherokee Agency in Tennessee, M-208, Roll 7.
21. War Department to Col. Hawkins, July 12, 1815, in National Archives, RG 75, Letters sent by the Office of the Secretary of War relating to Indian affairs, Letter Book C, pp. 237-38; War Department to Gen. Sevier, Sept. 2, 1815, ibid., Letter Book C, p. 263; Meigs to Hawkins, Sept. 17, 1815, in

National Archives, RG 75, Letters received by the Office of the Secretary of War relating to Indian affairs, M-271, Roll 1, frames 1234–38.

22. Journal of occurrences of the convention of the Creeks at Tuckabatchee, Sept., 1815, in National Archives, RG 75, Documents regarding negotiations of ratified and unratified treaties with various Indian tribes, T-494, Roll 1, frames 0200–0207.

23. Ibid.

24. Pound, *Benjamin Hawkins*, p. 238.

25. Receipt of the Cherokee officers who distinguished themselves, Oct. 31, 1815, in National Archives, RG 75, Records of the Cherokee Agency in Tennessee, M-208, Roll 6.

26. Meigs to the Secretary of War, Nov. 4, 1815, ibid.

27. Meigs to Charles Hicks, Dec. 19, 1815, Ross Papers, Gilcrease Institute, 15-1; The Pathkiller to Cherokee Delegation [1816], ibid., 16-2.

28. Meigs to the Secretary of War, Jan. 10, 1816, in National Archives, RG 75, Letters received by the Office of the Secretary of War relating to Indian affairs, M-271, Roll 1, frame 1232.

29. *Niles' Weekly Register*, X (March 2, 1816): 16.

30. Payne Papers, Ayer Collection, Newberry Library, II, pp. 2–3.

31. Parton, *Life of Andrew Jackson*, II, pp. 355–56.

32. Col. John Lowrey to President Madison, Feb. 16, 1816, in National Archives, RG 75, Records of the Cherokee Agency in Tennessee, M-208, Roll 7.

33. Cherokee Delegation to President Madison [1816], ibid., Roll 6.

34. Cherokee Delegation to President Madison, Feb. 19, 1816, in Ross Papers, Gilcrease Institute, 16-3.

35. *Religious Intelligencer*, IV (Feb., 1820): 617–18.

36. "Copy of a conversation between President Madison and Col. John Lowry [*sic*]," Ross Papers, Gilcrease Institute, 16-1.

37. Meigs to Cherokee Deputation, Feb. 28, 1816, in Miscellaneous manuscripts, Western History Collections, University of Oklahoma Library; Cherokee Delegation to the War Department, March 4, 1816, Ross Papers, Gilcrease Institute, 16-5.

38. Cherokee Delegation to the Secretary of War, March 12, 1816, in National Archives, RG 75, Letters received by the Office of the Secretary of War relating to Indian affairs, M-271, Roll 1, frames 0935–39; Secretary Crawford to Commissioners Barnett, Hawkins, and Gaines, Mar. 14, 1816, in National Archives, RG 75, Letters sent by the Secretary of War relating to Indian affairs, Letter Book C, p. 309; *Cherokee Phoenix*, April 14, 1830, p. 2, col. 2.

39. Royce, *Cherokee Nation*, pp. 197–209; Charles J. Kappler, ed., *Indian Affairs: Laws and Treaties*, II, pp. 124–26; Secretary Crawford to Meigs, May 4, 1816, in National Archives, RG 75, Letters sent by the Office of the Secretary of War relating to Indian affairs, Letter Book C, pp. 310, 340.

40. Receipt for expenses of Richard Taylor, Major Ridge, and servant, signed by Addison Garrick, Knoxville, April 12, 1816, in National Archives, RG 75, Records of the Cherokee Agency in Tennessee, M-208, Roll 7.

41. *Cherokee Phoenix*, April 14, 1830, p. 2, col. 3, extract No. 8; Secretary Crawford to Commissioners Barnett, Hawkins, and Gaines, Apr. 16, 1816, in National Archives, RG 75, Letters sent by the Secretary of War relating to Indian affairs, Letter Book C, p. 328.

42. Deposition of Major Ridge, Dec. 21, 1829, *Cherokee Phoenix*, June 12, 1830, p. 4, cols. 1–2; *Niles' Weekly Register*, X (Aug. 17, 1816): 415.

43. Ibid., X (July 20, 1816): 352.

44. Parton, *Life of Andrew Jackson*, II, p. 356; Jackson, *Correspondence*, II, p. 246; *American State Papers, Indian Affairs*, II, pp. 113–14.

45. Jackson, *Correspondence*, II, pp. 243, 254.

46. Ibid., p. 254.

47. *American State Papers, Indian Affairs*, II, p. 113.

48. Cotterill, *Southern Indians*, pp. 199–200; Jackson, *Correspondence*, II, p. 261.

49. Cherokee Delegation to the War Department, March 20, 1816, Cherokee Nation Papers, Western History Collections, University of Oklahoma Library; Secretary Crawford to Meigs, Sept. 18, 1816, in National Archives, RG 75, Records of the Cherokee Agency in Tennessee, M-208, Roll 7.

50. Meigs to Gov. McMinn, Jan. 17, 1817, ibid., Roll 7; "Toochalar: Observation to Col. Meigs . . . 9 Jan. 1817," ibid.

51. Jackson, *Correspondence*, II, pp. 298, 307.

52. *American State Papers, Indian Affairs*, II, p. 142; Jackson, *Correspondence*, II, p. 301*n*.

53. *Niles' Weekly Register*, XII (Aug. 2, 1817): 368; Cotterill, *Southern Indians*, p. 204.

54. Resolution of the Cherokee Committee, Sept. 3, 1817, Payne Papers, Ayer Collection, Newberry Library, VII [1], p. 34; *American State Papers, Indian Affairs*, II, p. 143.

CHAPTER 5: THE TORCHLIGHT

1. Quoted in Linton Collins, "The Activities of the Missionaries among the Cherokees," *Georgia Historical Quarterly*, VI (Dec., 1922): 298.

2. Secretary Crawford to Rev. Cyrus Kingsbury, May 14, 1816, in National Archives, RG 75, Letters sent by the Office of the Secretary of War relating to Indian affairs, Letter Book C, pp. 349–50.

3. Quoted in Collins, "Missionaries among the Cherokees," p. 298.

4. [Sarah Tuttle], *Letters and Conversations of the Cherokee Mission*, I, pp. 15–16; Mooney, *Myths of the Cherokee*, pp. 104–105.

5. Brainerd Journal, May 14, 1817, Houghton Library, ABC, 18.3.1, II: 1; "A Catalogue of Cherokee Scholars that have belonged to the School at Brainerd," Houghton Library, ABC, 18.3.1, II: 159; Kingsbury to S. A. Worcester, June 30, 1817, Houghton Library, ABC, 18.3.1, III: 9.

6. Spring Place Diary, Jan. 10, 1810, Mauelshagen translation, Georgia Department of Natural Resources.

7. Ibid., June 15 and 25, 1810; Col. Meigs to the children at the Spring Place school, Aug. 5, 1810, Moravian Archives, Winston-Salem, N.C.

8. Isabel Brown et al. to Col. Meigs, July 30, 1810, Moravian Archives, Winston-Salem, N.C.

9. Herman Daggett to Jeremiah Evarts, Dec. 16, 1820, Houghton Library, ABC, 12.1, II (2d series): 120.

10. John Gambold to J. van Vleck, Jan. 11, 1819, Moravian Archives, Winston-Salem, N.C.

11. Spring Place Diary, Dec. [?], 1810; Adelaide Fries, ed., *Records of the Moravians in North Carolina*, VII, p. 3143; VIII, p. 3791; the Gambolds to C. L. Benzien, Dec. 19, 1810, Moravian Archives, Winston-Salem (trans. Sophie Wilkins).

12. The Gambolds to Charles Gottlieb Reichel, Nov. 18, 1810, Moravian Archives, Winston-Salem (trans. Sophie Wilkins).

13. Mooney, *Myths of the Cherokee,* p. 84; Edmund Schwarze, *History of the Moravian Missions among Southern Indian Tribes of the United States,* p. 178.

14. John Ridge to Albert Gallatin, Feb. 27, 1826, Payne Papers, typescript, Ayer Collection, Newberry Library, VIII, p. 114. For a revised version, see William C. Sturtevant, ed., "John Ridge on Cherokee Civilization in 1826," *Journal of Cherokee Studies,* VI (Fall, 1981): 87.

15. Schwarze, *Moravian Missions,* pp. 114–15; "Books in possession of John and Anna R. Gambold at Spring Place, Cherokee Country," Miscellaneous manuscripts, American Philosophical Society Archives, Philadelphia.

16. John R. Ridge, *Poems,* Preface, p. 5.

17. John Ridge to Albert Gallatin, Feb. 27, 1826, Payne Papers.

18. Anderson, *General Stand Watie,* rev. ed., p. 11.

19. Spring Place Diary, Moravian Archives, Winston-Salem, N.C., Jan. 18, 1811. Where not otherwise indicated, quotations from the Spring Place Diary, as well as from most of the letters of the Gambolds, were translated by Sophie Wilkins.

20. Spring Place Diary, Moravian Archives, Winston-Salem, N.C., Aug. 12, 1811.

21. Quoted in Schwarze, *Moravian Missions,* p. 114.

22. Spring Place Diary, Moravian Archives, Winston-Salem, N.C., Jan. 13, Feb. 13, and Apr. 4, 1814.

23. Ibid., Nov. 25, 1814.

24. Ibid., Feb. 9, 1815.

25. The Gambolds to J. van Vleck, Mar. 7, 1815, Moravian Archives, Winston-Salem, N.C.

26. Spring Place Diary, Moravian Archives, Winston-Salem, N.C., Jan. 26, 1815.

27. The Gambolds to J. van Vleck, April 17, 1815, Moravian Archives, Winston-Salem, N.C.

28. Spring Place Diary, Moravian Archives, Winston-Salem, N.C., Apr. 10, 1815.

29. The Gambolds to J. van Vleck, Apr. 17, 1815, Moravian Archives, Winston-Salem, N.C.

30. Spring Place Diary, Moravian Archives, Winston-Salem, N.C., Aug. 12, 1815.

31. Ibid., Oct. 16, 1815.

32. Ibid., Oct. 17, 1815.

33. "A Catalogue of Cherokee Scholars . . . at Brainerd," Houghton Library, ABC, 18.3.1, II: 159; Kingsbury to Worcester, June 30, 1817, ibid., III: 9.

34. See Report of Jeremiah Evarts, May 23, 1818, in *Missionary Herald,* XIV (1818): 342, for an account of operations at Brainerd.

35. Brainerd Journal, July 4 [1817]; retold in Marion Starkey, *The Cherokee Nation,* pp. 53–54.

36. B. B. Edwards, *Memoir of the Rev. Elias Cornelius,* p. 77.

37. Instructions to the Cherokee Deputation, Sept. 19, 1817, Houghton Library, ABC, 18.3.1, II: 97.

38. Quoted in Robert Sparks Walker, *Torchlights to the Cherokees: Brainerd Mission,* p. 66.

39. Ibid., p. 67.

40. For convenience I have quoted from Walker, *Torchlights*, pp. 67–68; Edwards, *Elias Cornelius*, pp. 73–74, and the *Religious Intelligencer*, II (1818): 713–14, also give the speech in substantially the same words.

41. Edwards, *Elias Cornelius*, p. 74.

42. Brainerd faculty to S. Worcester, Sept. 25, 1818, Houghton Library, ABC, 18.3.1, II: 116.

43. Ibid.; the Gambolds to J. van Vleck, Sept. 26, 1818, Moravian Archives, Winston-Salem, N.C.

44. Secretary Calhoun to Jackson, Dec. 30, 1817, Jackson Papers, Vol. 43, #6996; Morgan to Jackson, Feb. 20, 1836, in National Archives, RG 75, Letters received by the Office of Indian Affairs, M-234, Roll 80, frames 0449–50; The Pathkiller to Jackson, Feb. 17, 1818, Jackson Papers, Vol. 47, #7227.

45. Payroll of the "Company of Cherokee Warriors Commanded by Captain Ridge in the Service of the United States Marching against the Seminole Indians" in National Archives, RG 75, Indian Accounts, Account No. 3875; affidavit of John Lowrey, Dec. 30, 1821, enclosed with Meigs to Calhoun, Jan. 3, 1822, in National Archives, RG 107, Letters received by the Office of the Secretary of War, M-221, Roll 96: M-85 (16); *American State Papers, Military Affairs*, I, pp. 697–98. Short accounts of the Seminole campaign occur in Marquis James, *Andrew Jackson, Border Captain*, pp. 309–14, and in Edwin C. McReynolds, *The Seminoles*, pp. 82–87.

46. Report of Jeremiah Evarts, May 23, 1818, *Missionary Herald*, XIV (1818): 344–45; Schwarze, *Moravian Missions*, p. 109.

47. Schwarze, *Moravian Missions*, p. 110; Edwards, *Elias Cornelius*, pp. 119–21.

48. Secretary Calhoun to Cornelius, July 18, 1818, in National Archives, RG 75, Letters sent by the Secretary of War relating to Indian affairs, Letter Book D, pp. 185–86; *Missionary Herald*, XIV (1818): 257, 400.

49. The Gambolds to J. van Vleck, Sept. 26, 1818, Moravian Archives, Winston-Salem, N.C.

50. Starkey, *Cherokee Nation*, pp. 55–56.

51. Susanna Ridge to John Ridge, n.d. (transcript), Moravian Archives.

52. Journal of Daniel S. Butrick, 1818, Houghton Library, ABC, 18.3.1, III: 140–42; Brainerd missionaries to S. Worcester, Sept. 25, 1818, Houghton Library, ABC, 18.3.1, II: 116; Brainerd Journal, ibid., ABC, 18.3.1, II: 12.

53. *Missionary Herald*, XVII (Mar., 1821): 73.

54. John R. Ridge, *Poems*, Preface, p. 5.

CHAPTER 6: CORNWALL

1. Susanna Ridge to John Ridge, July 21, 1820 (transcript), Moravian Archives, Winston-Salem, N.C.

2. The Gambolds to J. van Vleck, Oct. 2, 1818, Moravian Archives, Winston-Salem, N.C.; Brainerd missionaries to S. Worcester (?), Oct. 6, 1818, Houghton Library, ABC, 18.3.1, II: 118.

3. The Gambolds to J. van Vleck, Sept. 26, 1818, Moravian Archives, Winston-Salem, N.C.

4. John Ridge to the Gambolds, Oct. 24, 1818; Darcheechee to the Gambolds, Oct. 24, 1818, ibid.

5. Fries, ed., *Moravians in North Carolina*, VII, pp. 3363, 3371.

6. John Ridge to the Gambolds, Oct. 24, 1818; Dr. Dempsey to the Gambolds, Oct. 26, 1818, Moravian Archives, Winston-Salem, N.C.

7. Fries, ed., *Moravians in North Carolina*, VII, pp. 3371, 3379.

8. Herman Daggett to S. Worcester, Dec. 18, 1818, Houghton Library, ABC, 12.1, II (2d series): 101.

9. Adam Hodgson, *Letters from North America*, II, p. 300.

10. T. S. Gold, *Historical Records of the Town of Cornwall, Litchfield County, Connecticut*, p. 37.

11. E. C. Starr, *History of Cornwall, Connecticut*, p. 140; Daggett to J. Evarts, Nov. 4, 1818, Houghton Library, ABC, 12.1, II (2d series): 100.

12. George White, *Historical Collections of Georgia*, p. 671.

13. Daggett to Worcester, Dec. 18, 1818, Houghton Library, ABC.

14. Daggett to Worcester, Feb. 6, 1819, Houghton Library, ABC, 12.1, II (2d series): 102; John Ridge to the Gambolds, Feb. 15, 1819, Moravian Archives, Winston-Salem, N.C.

15. Payne Papers, Ayer Collection, Newberry Library, VIII, p. 63.

16. Ibid., p. 82.

17. John Ridge to the Gambolds, Feb. 15, 1819, Moravian Archives, Winston-Salem, N.C.

18. Daggett to Worcester, Aug. 6, 1819, Houghton Library, ABC, 12.1, II (2d series): 106; Daggett to Worcester, Feb. 6, 1820, ibid., 114.

19. The schedule is reconstructed from remarks in Gold, *Cornwall*, pp. 341, 343; Starr, *Cornwall*, pp. 153–54; Ralph H. Gabriel, *Elias Boudinot, Cherokee, and His America*, chap. 6; Morse, *Report to the Secretary of War*, Appendix, pp. 272–73.

20. Starr, *Cornwall*, p. 382.

21. Ibid., pp. 141, 155; Daggett to Evarts, May 18, 1821, Houghton Library. ABC, 12.1, II (2d series): 125.

22. Edwin Welles Dwight, *Memoirs of Henry Obookiah;* Gabriel retells the story in *Elias Boudinot*, Chap. 4.

23. Hodgson, *Letters*, II, pp. 288–300; Starr, *Cornwall*, p. 142.

24. *Religious Intelligencer*, IV: 166; *Missionary Herald*, XVII (Aug., 1821): 257; XVIII (May, 1822): 161; Morse, *Report to the Secretary of War*, Appendix, p. 272.

25. John Ridge to President Monroe, Ayer Collection, 761, Newberry Library.

26. Morse, *Report*, Appendix, p. 272.

27. Daggett to Evarts, May 7, 1821, Houghton Library, ABC, 12.1, II (2d series): 124.

28. Daggett to Evarts, Dec. 16, 1820, Houghton Library, ABC, 12.1, II (2d series): 120; Daggett to S. Worcester, Feb. 6 and May 18, 1820, ibid., 114 and 115; Daggett to Evarts, July 11, 1821, ibid., 128; Daggett to Evarts, Aug. 6, 1821, ibid., 129.

29. Spring Place Diary, Jan. 10, 1821, Moravian Archives, Winston-Salem, N.C.

30. J. R. Schmidt to Jacob van Vleck, Sept. 6, 1821, Moravian Archives, Winston-Salem, N.C.; Butrick's Journal, Aug. 31, 1821, Houghton Library, ABC, 18.3.1, III: 129; Wm. Chamberlin to Elias Cornelius, Aug. 27, 1821, ibid., 19. Chamberlin's name is sometimes spelled Chamberlain.

31. Ellen M. Gibbs, quoted in Starr, *Cornwall*, p. 155.

32. Starr, *Cornwall*, pp. 147, 155.

33. C. E. B. in *Boston Courier*, Mar. 15, 1832, p. 2, col. 2.

34. Chamberlin's Journal, July 8, 1822, Houghton Library, ABC, 18.3.1, III: 27.

35. Gold, *Cornwall*, p. 351.

36. Starr, *Cornwall*, p. 155.

37. *Savannah Georgian*, Oct. 23, 1821, p. 3, col. 4.

38. *Cartersville* (Ga.) *Courant*, Mar. 19, 1885, p. 1, col. 2.

39. McKenney and Hall, *Indian Tribes*, II, p. 328.

40. The paragraphs concerning John Ridge's courtship are based largely on the statement of Ellen M. Gibbs, as quoted in Starr, *Cornwall*, pp. 154-57, as well as in Walker, *Torchlights*, pp. 159-63.

41. *Religious Intelligencer*, X (Oct., 1825): 280.

42. John R. Ridge, *Poems*, Preface, p. 5.

43. Daggett to Evarts, Sept. 18, 1822, Houghton Library, ABC, 12.1, II (2d series): 141.

44. Daggett to Evarts, May 18, 1822, Houghton Library, ABC, 12.1, II (2d series): 134; Evart's memo regarding Brainerd Mission, No. 3, dated May, 1822, ABC, 18.3.1, II: 156; Daggett to Evarts, July 20, 1822, ABC, 12.1, II (2d series): 136; Daggett to Evarts, Sept. [?], 1822, ABC, 12.1, II (2d series): 141.

45. Daggett to Evarts, Sept. 18, 1822, Houghton Library, ABC, 12.1, II (2d series): 140.

46. Boudinot to Evarts, Nov. 12, 1822, Houghton Library, ABC, 12.1, II (2d series): 164.

47. *Missionary Herald*, XIX (Jan., 1823): 29; *Report of the American Board of Commissioners for Foreign Missions . . . 1823*, pp. 76-77.

48. Reported in *Religious Intelligencer*, VII (Dec., 1822): 446.

49. *Missionary Herald*, XIX (Jan., 1823): 30.

50. Ibid.

51. *United Brethren's Missionary Intelligencer*, I (1824): 448; *Christian Mirror*, Feb. 21, 1823, p. 2, col. 2; *Missionary Herald*, XIX (June, 1823): 22, 170.

52. Walker, *Torchlights*, p. 193.

53. *Cartersville* (Ga.) *Courant*, March 19, 1885, p. 1, col. 2.

54. *United Brethren's Missionary Intelligencer*, I (1822): 19; Schwarze, *Moravian Missions*, p. 131.

55. *Boston Recorder*, IV (Oct. 2, 1819): 162, col. 2.

56. *Report of the American Board . . . 1822*, p. 49.

57. *United Brethren's Missionary Intelligencer*, I (1822): 24.

58. *Report of the American Board . . . 1822*, p. 53.

59. George Battey, *History of Rome and Floyd County*, I, p. 27.

60. Quoted in Peter Jones, *History of the Ojebway Indians*, pp. 187-88.

61. *New York Mirror*, June 17, 1826.

62. Butrick's Journal, 1819-45, undated entry, Houghton Library, ABC, 18.3.3, IV.

63. Abraham Steiner to John Heckwelder, Mar. 6, 1820, Vaux Papers, Pennsylvania Historical Society.

64. *United Brethren's Missionary Intelligencer*, I (1823): 349.

65. 16th Cong., 1st sess., S. Doc. 103 (Serial 27), p. 1.

66. *Boston Recorder*, IX (Feb. 21, 1824): 30, col. 2.

67. Ibid.; *American State Papers, Indian Affairs*, II, pp. 468-69.

68. Butrick's Journal, Houghton Library, ABC, 18.3.3, IV.

69. Quoted in Gaston Litton, *History of Oklahoma*, I, pp. 76-77.

70. McIntosh to Ross, Oct. 21, 1823, in National Archives, RG 75, Letters received by the Office of the Secretary of War relating to Indian affairs, M-271.

71. Payne Papers, Ayer Collection, Newberry Library, II, pp. 159–60.

72. Ibid.; Butrick to Treat, Feb. 23, 1847, Houghton Library, ABC, 18.3.1, XI: 220.

73. *Boston Recorder*, IX (Feb. 21, 1824): 30.

74. National Archives, RG 75, Letters received by the Office of Indian Affairs: Creek Agency 1824-25, M-234, Roll 219, frames 1082-85.

75. U.S. Commissioners to McMinn, Oct. 27, 1823, in National Archives, RG 75, Records of the Cherokee Agency in Tennessee, M-208, Roll 9.

76. "Then and Now," *Fort Smith Herald*, May 21, 1870, p. 2, col. 1.

77. Marriage Certificate of John Ridge, at Cornwall Free Library; "Then and Now"; Anderson, *Stand Watie*, p. 81; *Niles' Weekly Register*, XXVIII (July 9, 1825): 298.

78. *Christian Herald*, X (Dec. 20, 1823): 468.

79. "Then and Now."

80. Quoted in Gold, *Cornwall*, pp. 31–32.

81. T. O. Mabbott and F. L. Pleadwell, eds., *The Life and Works of Edward Coote Pinkney*, pp. 96–99.

82. Vol. VIII (1824): 715.

83. Litchfield *American Eagle*, Mar. 22, 1824; quoted in Gabriel, *Elias Boudinot*, pp. 61–62.

84. Aug. 10, 1824.

85. Gabriel, *Elias Boudinot*, pp. 76–77; *Niles' Weekly Register*, XXVIII (July 9, 1825): 298.

86. Mary B. Church, "Elias Boudinot," *Magazine of History*, XVII (Dec., 1913): 212.

87. Ibid.

88. Ibid., p. 214.

89. David Brown to Evarts, Sept. 29, 1825, Houghton Library, ABC, 18.3.1, V: 289.

90. Chamberlin's Journal, Aug. 24, 1825, Houghton Library, ABC, 18.3.1, IV: 43.

91. *Niles' Weekly Register*, XXVIII (July 9, 1825): 298.

92. Gabriel, *Elias Boudinot*, p. 91. This work contains the most complete account available of the marriage of Boudinot and Harriet Gold, pp. 65–92.

93. Starr, *Cornwall*, p. 155.

CHAPTER 7: AGENTS FOR THE CREEKS

1. Nathan Sargent, *Public Men and Events*, I, pp. 54–55.

2. John C. Calhoun to Cherokee delegation, Jan. 5, 1824, in National Archives, RG 75, Letters sent by the Secretary of War in relation to Indian affairs, Letter Book F, p. 28; Calhoun to Cherokee delegation, Jan. 8, 1824, ibid., p. 29.

3. *Memoirs of John Quincy Adams*, ed. Charles Francis Adams (Philadelphia, 1874), VI, p. 229.

4. *American State Papers, Indian Affairs*, II, p. 473.

5. Ibid., p. 474.

6. John Quincy Adams, *Memoirs*, VI, p. 272.

7. *National Intelligencer,* Apr. 10, 1824, p. 2, col. 3.
8. Adams, *Memoirs,* VI, pp. 255–56.
9. *National Intelligencer,* Apr. 10, 1824, p. 2, col. 1.
10. 18th Cong. 1st sess., House Doc. 133 (Serial 102), pp. 3–4.
11. Adams, *Memoirs,* VI, p. 272.
12. Cherokee delegation to Messrs. Gales and Seaton, Apr., 1824, in John Ross Papers, Gilcrease Institute, 24-2.
13. Adams, *Memoirs,* VI, pp. 272, 373.
14. Starr, *Cornwall,* p. 352.
15. Quoted in Rufus Rockwell Wilson, *Washington: The Capital City,* I, p. 178.
16. Mrs. W. P. Ross, *The Life and Times of Honorable W. P. Ross,* in Sketch, "Major George Lowry," no pp.
17. Quoted in *The Illinois Intelligencer* (Vandalia), Aug. 20, 1824, p. 2, col. 5.
18. Adams, *Memoirs,* VI, p. 373.
19. Cotterill, *Southern Indians,* p. 218.
20. McKenney to the Cherokee delegation, Mar. 30, 1824, in National Archives, RG 75, Letters sent by the Office of Indian Affairs, Letter Book I.
21. Charles Hicks to McKenney, Jan. 14, 1825, in National Archives, RG 75, Letters received by the Office of Indian Affairs: Cherokees (East) 1825; J. R. Schmidt to A. Benade, Feb. 16, 1824, Moravian Archives, Winston-Salem, N.C.
22. Adams, *Memoirs,* VI, p. 373.
23. Elijah Hicks to McKenney, July 1, 1824, in National Archives, RG 75, Letters received by the Office of Indian Affairs: Cherokees (East) 1824.
24. Schwarze, *Moravian Missions,* pp. 174–75.
25. "Extracts from a diary kept by J. C. [and Frederic] Ellsworth at Haweis Cherokee Mission," transcript, Indian Archives Division, Oklahoma Historical Society; *Report of the American Board . . . 1823,* pp. 68–69.
26. Wm. C. Chamberlin's diary, Oct. 24, 1824, Houghton Library, ABC, 18.3.1, IV: 39.
27. Ibid., Oct. 25–26, 1824.
28. *Boston Recorder,* X (Mar. 12, 1825): 44.
29. Ibid.
30. Ibid., X (July 20, 1825): 124.
31. Ibid., X (Mar. 12, 1825): 44.
32. *Niles' Weekly Register,* XXVIII (July 9, 1825): 296.
33. *Red Bluff* (Calif.) *Beacon,* Sept. 4, 1862, p. 2, col. 3.
34. *Niles' Weekly Register,* XXVIII (Mar. 19, 1825): 48.
35. U.S. Commissioners to Creek chiefs, Dec. 9, 1824, in *American State Papers, Indian Affairs,* II, p. 570.
36. Dec. 14, 1824, ibid., p. 572.
37. Report of T. P. Andrews, Special Agent, Aug. 1, 1825, in National Archives, RG 75, Letters received by the Office of Indian Affairs: Creek Agency 1824-25 (O), M-234, Roll 219, frame 0502.
38. A. J. Pickett in White, *Historical Collections of Georgia,* pp. 170–73. See also the Cherokee wife of McIntosh to the U.S. Commissioners, May 3, 1825, in National Archives, RG 75, Letters received by the Office of Indian Affairs: Creek Agency 1824-25 (O), M-234, Roll 219, frames 0636-38; Alex. Ware to Gov. Troup, May 1, 1825, ibid., 1825-26 (P), Roll 220, frame 1682; Payne Papers, Ayer Collection, Newberry Library, VI, pp. 192–93, and VIII, p. 119.

39. See David Brown's remarks in *Niles' Weekly Register,* XXIX (Oct. 15, 1825): 106–107: "The news of McIntosh's death gave universal satisfaction in the Nation. I say *satisfaction,* the same that is felt when a dangerous rattle-snake is killed."

40. *Savannah Georgian,* Oct. 4, 1825, p. 2, col. 6.

41. Payne Papers, Ayer Collection, Newberry Library, VI, p. 193.

42. *Savannah Republican,* Aug. 2, 1825, p. 2, col. 4.

43. Gen. Gaines to Secretary Barbour, Nov. 28, 1825, in National Archives, RG 107, Letters received by the Office of the Secretary of War, registered series 1801–60, M-221, Roll 101 (G-157 [19]).

44. *Savannah Republican,* Dec. 8, 1825, p. 2, col. 5; *Boston Recorder,* X (Dec. 30, 1825): 211; Report of Gen. Gaines of attendance at Creek Council, fall, 1825, in National Archives, RG 75, Letters received by the Office of Indian Affairs: Creek Agency 1824–25 (O), M-234, Roll 219, frame 0592.

45. The Pathkiller and Charles Hicks to Col. Montgomery, Oct. 24, 1825, in National Archives, RG 75, Letters of the Cherokee Agency in Tennessee, M-208, Roll 10, frame 213; *Savannah Georgian,* Nov. 19, 1825, p. 2, col. 2; Dec. 7, 1825, p. 2, col. 3; Dec. 19, 1825, p. 2, col. 4.

46. *Religious Intelligencer,* X (Oct., 1825): 280–81. See also *Georgia Journal* (Milledgeville), June 5, 1830, p. 3, col. 3; *Cartersville* (Ga.) *Courant,* Mar. 19, 1885, p. 1, col. 2.

47. Quoted in J. Orin Oliphant (ed.), *Through the South and the West with Jeremiah Evarts in 1826* (Lewisburg, Pa., 1956), p. 115.

48. *Savannah Georgian,* Nov. 12, 1825, p. 2. col. 2.

49. *Niles' Weekly Register,* XXIX (Nov. 26, 1825): 194.

50. Quoted in Wilson, *Washington,* I, p. 204.

51. Outline of an interview between the Secretary of War and the Creek Delegation, Nov. 30, 1825, in National Archives, RG 75, Letters sent by the Office of Indian Affairs, Letter Book II, pp. 269–74.

52. National Archives, RG 75, Documents relating to the negotiation of ratified and unratified treaties with various Indian tribes, T-494, Roll 1, frames 0777–81.

53. Creek Delegation, Dec. 16, 1825, ibid., Roll 1, frames 0798–99.

54. Adams, *Memoirs,* VII, p. 106; John Ridge to McKenney, Jan. 18, 1826, in National Archives, RG 75, Documents relating to the negotiation of ratified and unratified treaties with various Indian tribes, T-494, Roll 1, frames 0817–20.

55. Kappler, ed., *Indian Affairs: Laws and Treaties,* II, p. 188.

56. Apr. 12, 1826, in National Archives, RG 75, Letters sent by the Office of Indian Affairs, Letter Book III, p. 27.

57. *Niles' Weekly Register,* XXX (June 10, 1826): 257–58.

58. McKenney, note attached to "List of division of funds," Apr. 25, 1826, in National Archives, RG 75, Letters received by the Office of Indian Affairs: Creek Agency 1825 (P)-26, M-234, Roll 220, frames 0223–24.

59. *Niles' Weekly Register,* XXX (June 10, 1826): 257–58.

60. Ibid., pp. 277–80; Thomas Hart Benton, *Thirty Years' View,* chap. 24.

61. *Register of Debates in Congress,* II¹ (May 19, 1826), p. 774.

62. To Opothle Yoholo and others, May 20, 1826, in National Archives, RG 75, Letters sent by the Office of Indian Affairs, Letter Book III, pp. 78–80.

63. Receipt for eighteen medals, Mar. 31, 1826, in National Archives, RG 75, Letters received by the Office of Indian Affairs: Creek Agency 1825 (P)-26,

M-234, Roll 220, frame 0217.

64. McKenney to John Ridge, Dec. 14, 1825, in National Archives, RG 75, Letters sent by the Office of Indian Affairs, Letter Book II, p. 309.

65. Frances Trollope, *Domestic Manners of the Americans*, pp. 220-21.

66. Letter of James Barbour, Jan. 26, 1832, in [Thomas L. McKenney], *Catalogue of One Hundred and Fifteen Indian Portraits.*

67. Mar. 4, 1826, in National Archives, RG 75, Office of Indian Affairs— Miscellaneous letters received.

68. A draft dated Feb. 27, 1826, exists in the Payne Papers, Ayer Collection, Newberry Library, VIII; the finished version, dated Mar. 10, 1826, is held in Box 64-3, Gallatin Papers, New-York Historical Society. A rough collation of the two versions appears in William C. Sturtevant, ed., "John Ridge on Cherokee Civilization in 1826," *Journal of Cherokee Studies*, VI (Fall, 1981): 79-91.

69. American Antiquarian Society, *Transactions*, II, p. 97.

70. *Savannah Georgian*, Sept. 19, 1826, p. 3, col. 4.

71. Crowell to Sec. Barbour, Sept. 30, 1826, in National Archives, RG 75, Letters received by the Office of Indian Affairs: Creek Agency 1825 (P)-26, M-234, Roll 220, frames 0274-77.

72. Ridge to Boudinot, June 14, 1831, *Cherokee Phoenix*, July 9, 1831, p. 2, col. 4.

73. Debo, *The Road to Disappearance*, p. 92.

74. The *Savannah Georgian*, Sept. 19, 1826, p. 3, col. 4, specified the amount as $3,500, but Col. Benjamin Gold, during a visit to the Cherokee Nation in 1829 (*Magazine of History*, XVII [Dec., 1913]: 218), suggested that Ridge received five or ten thousand dollars. As Ridge continued to demand ten thousand, it may be inferred that he received five thousand.

75. John B. Hogan to Gen. George Gibson, June 18, 1835, transcript in Foreman Collection, Gilcrease Institute, Box 37, Binder 79.

76. *Red Bluff* (Calif.) *Beacon*, Sept. 4, 1862, p. 2, col. 3.

77. McKenney and Hall, *Indian Tribes*, II, p. 21.

78. 20th Cong. 1st sess., House Doc. 238 (Serial 174), p. 9.

79. To the Chiefs and Headmen of the Cherokee Nation, June 25, 1827, in National Archives, RG 75, Letters sent by the Office of Indian Affairs, Letter Book IV, p. 83.

80. Act of the chiefs and headmen of the Upper Towns in General Council, Feb. 17, 1827, in National Archives, RG 75, Letters received by the Office of Indian Affairs: Creek Agency, 1827-28, M-234, Roll 221, frames 0176-78.

81. *Cherokee Phoenix*, June 25, 1828, p. 2, col. 3.

82. McKenney and Hall, *Indian Tribes*, II, pp. 24-25.

83. *Cherokee Phoenix*, June 25, 1828, p. 2, col. 3.

84. McKenney and Hall, *Indian Tribes*, II, pp. 25-26.

85. *Cherokee Phoenix*, June 25, 1828, p. 2, col. 4.

86. Ibid.

87. Ibid.

88. McKenney and Hall, *Indian Tribes*, II, pp. 26, 27.

89. Lt. J. N. Vinton (special agent) to Sec. Barbour, Mar. 7, 1827, in National Archives, RG 75, Letters received by the Office of Indian Affairs: Creek Agency 1827-28, M-234, Roll 221, frames 0606-7.

90. McKenney and Hall, *Indian Tribes*, II, p. 28.

91. Ibid., pp. 28, 29.

366 CHEROKEE TRAGEDY

92. *Cherokee Phoenix,* Apr. 3, 1828, p. 3, col. 1.
93. See 20th Cong., 1st sess., House Doc. 219 (Serial 173).
94. Debo, *The Road to Disappearance,* p. 94.

CHAPTER 8: "NOT ONE MORE FOOT OF LAND"

1. Philip Hemphill and James Liddell, Cherokee Valuations for Floyd and Walker Counties, Ga., in National Archives, RG 75, Records of the First Board of Cherokee Commissioners, Property Valuations (hereafter cited as Hemphill and Liddell), pp. 12–13.
2. Quoted in Willie Stewart White, "The Cherokee Indians of North Georgia," manuscript, p. 55, in W. S. White Papers, Southern Historical Collections, University of North Carolina Library.
3. Quoted in Gold, *Cornwall,* p. 350.
4. McKenney and Hall, *Indian Tribes,* I, p. 395.
5. Hemphill and Liddell, pp. 12–13.
6. Susan Prather, *Talonika, the Cherokee,* p. 7.
7. Hemphill and Liddell, pp. 12–13.
8. Quoted in Gold, *Cornwall,* p. 350.
9. Hemphill and Liddell, pp. 12–13.
10. McKenny and Hall, *Indian Tribes,* I, p. 382.
11. "The Lavender Family," manuscript, Georgia Department of Archives and History. See also Battey, *History of Rome and Floyd County,* I, pp. 26–27, 39–40, 261.
12. To Albert Gallatin, Feb. 27, 1826, Payne Papers, Ayer Collection, Newberry Library, VIII, p. 105.
13. Hemphill and Liddell, pp. 12–13.
14. John R. Ridge, *Poems,* Preface, p. 5.
15. Gold, *Cornwall,* p. 350.
16. John R. Ridge, *Poems,* Preface, p. 6.
17. Hemphill and Liddell, pp. 14–15.
18. John Rice, Henry McCoy, Rezin Rawlings, and George Massey, Cherokee Valuations in Alabama, 1836, Records of the First Board of Cherokee Commissioners, Property Valuations, in National Archives, RG 75, pp. 69–70.
19. National Archives, RG 75, Letters sent by the Office of Indian Affairs, Letter Book II, pp. 300–301.
20. *Niles' Weekly Register,* XXIX (Oct. 15, 1825): 105–107.
21. Starr, *Cherokee Indians,* p. 49.
22. Woodward, *The Cherokees,* p. 144.
23. Moody Hall, Diary entry for Aug. 9, 1825, Houghton Library, ABC, 18.3.1, V: 338.
24. Starkey, *Cherokee Nation,* pp. 92–93.
25. *An Address to the Whites, Delivered in the First Presbyterian Church on the 26th of May, 1826,* pp. 3–4. All other quotations from Boudinot on his lecture tour are from this pamphlet. For notice of the Charleston stop, see *Christian Spectator,* VIII (1826): 162–63; *New York Observer,* III (Feb. 25, 1826): 31.
26. *New York Observer,* III (March 4, 1826): 35, col. 5; III (March 25, 1826): 46, col. 3; *Boston Recorder,* XI (April 21, 1826): 63, col. 3; XI (April 28, 1826): 67, col. 1; Gabriel, *Elias Boudinot,* p. 116.
27. S. A. Worcester to J. Evarts, Jan. 8, 1827, Houghton Library, ABC,

18.3.1, V: 234; quoted in Gabriel, *Elias Boudinot*, p. 99.
28. *Atlanta Constitution*, Dec. 1, 1889, p. 5, col. 1.
29. Woodward, *The Cherokees*, p. 152.
30. P. 15.
31. *Cherokee Advocate*, Jan. 24, 1874.
32. A copy of the Prospectus, said to have been printed in Tennessee, is on file in the miscellaneous Cherokee papers at the Gilcrease Institute, Tulsa. The note on it by William Chamberlin was dated Dec. 10, 1827.
33. *Cherokee Phoenix*, June 25, 1828, pp. 2–3; July 2, 1828, p. 2.
34. See Gabriel, *Elias Boudinot*, pp. 113–14.
35. *United Brethren's Missionary Intelligencer*, II (1827): 402, 479; Schwarze, *Moravian Missions*, p. 181.
36. *Georgia Journal*, May 22, 1827, p. 3, col. 4.
37. John Ross and Major Ridge to U.S. Commissioners, Sept. 27, 1827, *Cherokee Phoenix*, May 21, 1828, p. 2; 20th Cong., 1st sess., House Doc. 106 (Serial 171), pp. 8–9.
38. Maj. Robert Hynds to Gen. John Cocke, Jan. 5, 1843, Miscellaneous Cherokee Documents, Gilcrease Institute.
39. 20th Cong., 1st sess., House Doc. 106 (Serial 171), p. 7.
40. Gen. Cocke to the Secretary of War, in National Archives, RG 75, Letters received by the Office of Indian Affairs: Cherokee Agency (East), 1826–28, M-234, Roll 72, frames 0248–49.
41. Payne Papers, Ayer Collection, Newberry Library, II, p. 97; Starkey, *Cherokee Nation*, pp. 104–105.
42. 20th Cong., 1st sess., House Doc. 106 (Serial 171), pp. 11, 15ff.
43. Gabriel, *Elias Boudinot*, p. 123.
44. Statement dated The Ridge's Ferry, June 24, 1828, *Cherokee Phoenix*, July 2, 1828, p. 3, cols. 1–2.
45. *Cherokee Phoenix*, Oct. 22, 1828, p. 2, col. 1.
46. *Cartersville Courant*, Mar. 5, 1885.
47. *Cherokee Phoenix*, Mar. 4, 1829, p. 2, col. 5; p. 3, col. 1.
48. Payne Papers, Ayer Collection, Newberry Library, II, pp. 86–87.
49. *Savannah Georgian*, Oct. 31, 1829, p. 2, col. 1; *Cherokee Phoenix*, Oct. 28, 1829, p. 3, col. 2; Payne Papers, Ayer Collection, Newberry Library, VI, pp. 197–98; Butrick, "A brief review of the history of the Cherokee nation for a few years back," ibid.
50. Quoted, Payne Papers, Ayer Collection, Newberry Library, VI, p. 199.
51. Quoted in Fletcher Green, "Georgia's Forgotten Industry: Gold Mining," *Georgia Historical Quarterly*, XIX (June, 1935): 100.
52. See Woodward, *The Cherokees*, pp. 158–59.
53. [Jeremiah Evarts, ed.], *Speeches on the Passage of the Bill for the Removal of the Indians, Delivered in the Congress of the United States, April and May, 1830*, p. 262.
54. *Cherokee Phoenix*, May 22, 1830, p. 2, col. 1; June 5, 1830, p. 3, col. 2; July 31, 1830; Allan G. Fambrough to Gov. Gilmer, July 12, 1830, in Georgia Department of Archives and History; *Savannah Georgian*, Nov. 18, 1830, p. 2, col. 4; see also *Niles' Weekly Register*, XXXIX (Nov. 27, 1830): 219.
55. *Cherokee Phoenix*, Mar. 4, 1829, p. 2, col. 5.
56. Gilmer to Jackson, Dec. 29, 1829, in 23rd Cong., 1st sess., S. Doc. 512, II (Serial 246), p. 216; George R. Gilmer, *Sketches of Some of the First Settlers of Upper Georgia*, p. 260.

57. Dated Jan. 15, 1830, in National Archives, RG 75, Letters received by the Office of Indian Affairs: Cherokee Agency (East), 1830–31, M-234, Roll 74, frame 0043.
58. Gen. Coffee to Sec. Eaton, Jan. 21, 1830, ibid., frames 0053–54.
59. Elizur Butler to J. Evarts, Feb. 12, 1830, Houghton Library, ABC, 18.3.1, IV: 81; Letter of John Ross, Feb. 13, 1830, *Cherokee Phoenix*, Feb. 17, 1830, p. 2, col. 5.
60. Letter of John Ross, Feb. 13, 1830, *Cherokee Phoenix*, Feb. 17, 1830, p. 2, col. 5.
61. Gilmer, *Sketches*, pp. 263–64; *Savannah Georgian*, Apr. 17, 1830, p. 2, col. 3.
62. Butler to Evarts, Feb. 12, 1830; S. A. Worcester to Evarts, Feb. 10, 1830, Houghton Library, ABC, 18.3.1, V: 265.
63. Gilmer, *Sketches*, p. 264; Worcester to Evarts, Feb. 10, 1830, Houghton Library, ABC, 18.3.1, V: 265; Butler to Evarts, Feb. 12, 1830, ibid., IV: 81.
64. *Cherokee Phoenix*, Feb. 10, 1830, p. 2, col. 5.

CHAPTER 9: AND THEN THE REVERSAL

1. John Pendleton Kennedy, *Memoirs of the Life of William Wirt*, II, pp. 240, 252–59.
2. S. A. Worcester to Evarts, July 16, 1830, Houghton Library, ABC, 18.3.1, V: 279.
3. See the volume of the essays in gathered form under the same title, p. 95.
4. Evarts to John Ross, July, 20, 1830, Ross Papers, Gilcrease Institute, 30–2.
5. Worcester to Evarts, July 16, 1830, Houghton Library, ABC, 18.3.1, V: 279.
6. Woodward, *The Cherokees*, p. 164.
7. *Niles' Weekly Register*, XXXIX (Jan. 8, 15, 1831): 338, 353.
8. Albert J. Beveridge, *Life of John Marshall*, IV, 541.
9. Starkey, *Cherokee Nation*, pp. 147–48, describes preparations for the council.
10. *Cherokee Phoenix*, Oct. 16, 1830, p. 1, col. 5.
11. 23rd Cong., 1st sess., S. Doc. 512, II (Serial 246), pp. 179–80; *Cherokee Phoenix*, Oct. 23, 1830, p. 3, cols. 1–3.
12. *Cherokee Phoenix*, Oct. 23, 1830, p. 2, col. 2.
13. 23rd Cong., 1st sess., S. Doc. 512, II (Serial 246), pp. 180–81.
14. *Religious Intelligencer*, XV (Jan. 15, 1831), p. 520, quoting an account from the *New York Observer*.
15. *Cherokee Phoenix*, Mar. 12, 1831, p. 1, col. 1, quoting the *New York Observer*. The correspondent was Calvin Colton.
16. Calvin Colton, *Tour of the American Lakes and Among the Indians of the Northwest Territory, in 1830*, II, pp. 171–72.
17. Cherokee Delegation to Hon. John H. Eaton, Dec. 9, 1830, in National Archives, RG 75, Letters received by the Office of Indian Affairs: Cherokee Agency (East), 1830–31, M-234, Roll 74, frame 0112.
18. [John Ridge to Major Ridge, Dec. 25, 1830], *Cherokee Phoenix*, Feb. 12, 1831, p. 2, cols. 4–5.
19. Ibid.
20. 23rd Cong., 1st sess., S. Doc. 512, II (Serial 246), p. 265.

21. *Cherokee Phoenix*, Feb. 12, 1831, p. 2, cols. 4–5.
22. Gold, *Cornwall*, p. 350.
23. *Cherokee Phoenix*, Feb. 12, 1831, p. 2, cols. 4–5.
24. Athens, Ga., *Athenian*, April 19, 1831, p. 2, col. 3.
25. *Register of Debates in Congress*, VII (1831), pp. 715–16. Everett's speech was carried between pp. 685 and 717.
26. *Cherokee Phoenix*, Mar. 26, 1831, p. 2, col. 3, quoting from the *New York Observer*.
27. Colton, *Tour of the American Lakes and Among the Indians*, II, pp. 204–205, 208–10.
28. Richard Peters, ed., *The Case of the Cherokee Nation Against the State of Georgia*, pp. 157–58.
29. Beveridge, *John Marshall*, IV, pp. 544–45; *Cherokee Phoenix*, Apr. 16, 1831, p. 2, col. 4, quoting the *New York Observer*.
30. John Ridge to Elias Boudinot, May 17, 1831, *Cherokee Phoenix*, May 21, 1831, p. 2, col. 5; p. 3, cols. 1–2.
31. For a clarification of Jackson's seemingly contradictory attitude toward Indians, see Francis P. Prucha, "Andrew Jackson's Indian Policy: A Reassessment," *Journal of American History*, LVI (Dec., 1969): 527–39.
32. John Ross to Thomas W. Harris, Apr. 27, 1831, Ross Papers, Gilcrease Institute, 31–4; 23rd Cong., 1st sess., S. Doc. 512, II (Serial 246), pp. 486–87.
33. *Augusta Constitutionalist*, June 10, 1831, p. 2, col. 3, quoting the *Macon Telegraph*.
34. Benjamin Currey to Lewis Cass, Dec. 21, 1831, in National Archives, RG 75, Letters received by the Office of Indian Affairs: Cherokee Emigration, 1828–36.
35. Starkey, *Cherokee Nation*, pp. 206–207.
36. Editorial, *Cherokee Phoenix*, Mar. 26, 1831, p. 3, cols. 1–2.
37. See Vol. XXVII (1831): 79–82.
38. Butrick, [Statement concerning the Cherokee Mission], Feb. 23, 1847, Houghton Library, ABC, 18.3.1, XI: 220; the Proctor-Butler inquiry, ibid., VII: 1. For an account of the missionary stand written from the papers of the American Board, see Starkey, *Cherokee Nation*, Chap. IX.
39. Starkey, *Cherokee Nation*, p. 159.
40. *Cherokee Phoenix*, Feb. 18, 1832, p. 1, col. 4.
41. Payne Papers, Ayer Collection, Newberry Library, II, pp. 109–13.
42. Ibid., p. 113.
43. Curry to Elbert Herring, Nov. 7, 1831, in 23rd Cong., 1st sess., S. Doc. 512, II (Serial 246), p. 649.
44. *Cherokee Phoenix*, Jan. 21, 1832, p. 1, cols. 3–5.
45. Ibid., col. 5.
46. Ibid., Dec. 24, 1831, p. 3, cols. 3–5.
47. Ibid., Apr. 16, 1831, p. 2, cols. 1–2.
48. 23rd Cong. 1st sess., S. Doc. 512, II (Serial 246), p. 731.
49. National Archives, RG 75, Letters sent by the Office of Indian Affairs, Letter Book VIII, p. 6.
50. John Ridge to Stand Watie, Apr. 6, 1832, in Dale and Litton, eds., *Cherokee Cavaliers*, p. 8.
51. John Ridge to John Ross, Jan. 12–13, 1832, Ross Papers, Gilcrease Institute, 32–1.
52. Ibid.

53. Reprinted, *Cherokee Phoenix*, Mar. 3, 1832, p. 1, cols, 4–5.
54. Ibid., Feb. 18, 1832, p. 2, cols. 3–4, quoting the *New York Commercial Advertiser*.
55. Ibid.
56. *Cherokee Phoenix*, Mar. 24, 1832, p. 2, cols. 2–4; *Boston Recorder*, XVII (Mar. 7, 1832): 38, col. 3; (Mar. 14, 1832): 42, col. 4.
57. *Niles' Weekly Register*, XLII (Mar. 17, 1832): 48; Beveridge, *John Marshall*, IV, pp. 550–51.
58. *Cherokee Cavaliers*, p. 8.
59. Boudinot to Stand Watie, Mar. 7, 1832, ibid., p. 6.
60. Ibid., p. 5.
61. Remark reported by Horace Greeley, *The American Conflict* (Hartford, Conn., 1865–67), I, p. 106.
62. *New York Observer*, X (Mar. 24, 1832): 3, col. 3.
63. 29th Cong., 1st sess., House Doc. 185 (Serial 485), p. 50.
64. Jackson, *Correspondence*, IV, p. 430.
65. 29th Cong., 1st sess., House Doc. 185 (Serial 485), p. 50.
66. *Cartersville* (Ga.) *Courant*, Mar. 26, 1885, p. 1, col. 1.
67. 29th Cong., 1st sess., House Doc. 185 (Serial 485), p. 50.
68. Journal of Isaac McCoy, Kansas State Historical Society, entry for Apr. 15 [1832].
69. *Cherokee Phoenix*, July 20, 1833, p. 3, col. 3. McLean's letter to Ross, dated May 23, 1832, is filed in the Ross Papers, Gilcrease Institute, 32–4.
70. *Cherokee Phoenix*, May 12, 1832, p. 2, col. 5; May 26, 1832, p. 2, col. 4.
71. 23rd Cong., 1st sess., S. Doc. 512, III (Serial 247), pp. 203–204.
72. Ibid., pp. 816–17.
73. David Greene to John Ridge, May 3, 1832, Houghton Library, ABC, 1.3.1, I: 1.
74. Hugh Montgomery to Cass, April 23, 1832, in National Archives, RG 75, Records of the Cherokee Agency in Tennessee, M-208, Roll 10, frame 31.
75. 29th Cong., 1st sess., House Doc. 185 (Serial 485), p. 50.

CHAPTER 10: MANEUVERS OF DESPERATION

1. 23rd Cong., 1st sess., S. Doc. 512, III (Serial 247), p. 372.
2. Ibid., p. 391; Payne Papers, Ayer Collection, Newberry Library, II, pp. 113–15.
3. George William Featherstonhaugh, *A Canoe Voyage up the Minnay Sotor*, II, pp. 231–32.
4. Ibid.; Starkey, *Cherokee Nation*, p. 190; Payne Papers, Ayer Collection, Newberry Library, II, p. 115.
5. Wilson Lumpkin, *The Removal of the Cherokee Indians from Georgia*, II, p. 187.
6. 23rd Cong., 1st sess., S. Doc. 512, III (Serial 247), pp. 421–22.
7. Quoted in Moulton, *John Ross*, p. 51.
8. 25th Cong., 2d sess., S. Doc. 121 (Serial 315), pp. 3–4; *Cherokee Phoenix*, Aug. 11, 1832.
9. 23rd Cong., 1st sess., S. Doc. 512, III (Serial 247), pp. 418–19; *American State Papers, Military Affairs*, V, pp. 28–29.
10. *Cherokee Phoenix*, Apr. 21, 1832, p. 3, col. 1; May 26, 1832, p. 2, col. 5.

11. Oochgelogy [i.e., Oothcaloga] Diary, Moravian Archives, Winston-Salem, N.C., Mar. 4, 7, 1830.
12. Schwarze, *Moravian Missions*, p. 193; Payne Papers, Ayer Collection, Newberry Library, VII, p. 139; Starr, *Cornwall*, p. 353.
13. 25th Cong., 2d sess., S. Doc. 121 (Serial 315), p. 7.
14. Ross to "My Friends," Aug. 9, 1833, Georgia Department of Archives and History.
15. 25th Cong., 2d sess., S. Doc. 121 (Serial 315), p. 9.
16. Ibid.
17. 29th Cong., 1st sess., House Doc. 185 (Serial 485), p. 50.
18. *Cherokee Phoenix*, Oct. 27, 1832, p. 2, col. 5; 23rd Cong., 1st sess., S. Doc. 512, III (Serial 247), pp. 511, 513.
19. *Niles' Weekly Register*, XLIII (Oct. 27, 1832): 131.
20. Woodward, *Woodward's Reminiscences*, p. 124.
21. *Savannah Georgian*, Dec. 3, 4, 5, 10, 18, 25, 1832.
22. *Cherokee Phoenix*, Feb. 2, 1833, p. 2, col. 4.
23. Original Plat Book, District 23, Section 3, Surveyor General's records, Georgia Department of Archives and History.
24. Gov. Lumpkin to B. Currey, Dec. 13, 1834, Georgia Department of Archives and History.
25. *Niles' Weekly Register*, XLIII (Jan. 26, 1833): 363–64.
26. Featherstonhaugh, *Canoe Voyage*, II, p. 226.
27. Ross Papers, Gilcrease Institute, 33–2; Starkey, *Cherokee Nation*, p. 217; Moulton, *John Ross*, p. 62.
28. Ridge to Ross, Feb. 2, 1833, Ross Papers, Gilcrease Institute, 33–2.
29. *Cherokee Phoenix*, Aug. 10, 17, and Sept. 21, 1833; Starkey, *Cherokee Nation*, pp. 225–26.
30. 23rd Cong., 1st sess., S. Doc. 512, IV (Serial 248), pp. 168–69, 200.
31. *Cherokee Phoenix*, July 20, 1833, p. 2, col. 1.
32. 23rd Cong., 1st sess., S. Doc. 512, IV (Serial 248), p. 169.
33. Ibid., p. 170.
34. 23rd Cong., 1st sess., S. Doc. 512, III (Serial 247), p. 681.
35. *Cherokee Phoenix*, July 20, 1833, p. 2, cols. 2–3; Aug. 17, 1833, p. 3, col. 3.
36. 23rd Cong., 1st sess., S. Doc. 512, IV (Serial 248), p. 413.
37. Thomas Glascock to Gov. Lumpkin, May 24, 1833, Georgia Department of Archives and History.
38. 23rd Cong., 1st sess., S. Doc. 512, IV (Serial 248), pp. 415–16.
39. Ibid., p. 412.
40. Glascock to Lumpkin, May 24, 1833.
41. 23rd Cong., 1st sess., S. Doc. 512, IV (Serial 248), p. 413; quoted in Grant Foreman, *Indian Removal: The Emigration of the Five Civilized Tribes of Indians*, p. 248.
42. Auraria, Ga., *Western Herald*, July 30, 1833, p. 2, col. 5; p. 3, col. 1; Currey to Elbert Herring, June 28, 1833, in National Archives, RG 75, Letters received by the Office of Indian Affairs: Cherokee Emigration, 1832–33, M-234, Roll 75, frame 0538.
43. Dunlap to Jackson, Aug. 25, 1833, in National Archives, RG 75, Letters received by the Office of Indian Affairs: Cherokee Emigration, 1832–33, M-234, Roll 75, frames 0583–93.
44. *Cherokee Phoenix*, Nov. 23, 1833, p. 1, col. 3.
45. Ibid.

46. Clay to Cass, Dec. 18, 1833, in National Archives, RG 75, Letters received by the Office of Indian Affairs: Cherokee Emigration, 1832-33, M-234, Roll 75, frame 0575; Currey to Herring, Nov. 4, 1833, in 23rd Cong., 1st sess., S. Doc. 512, IV (Serial 248), p. 644; Lumpkin to Cass, Nov. 18, 1833, ibid., p. 718.

47. *Cherokee Phoenix*, Dec. 7, 1833, p. 3, col. 3.

48. David Greene to Dr. Butler, March 11, 1834, Houghton Library, ABC, 1.3.1, I: 371.

49. April 5, 1834, p. 3, col. 3.

50. Instructions, dated Jan. 14, 1834, in National Archives, RG 75, Letters received by the Office of Indian Affairs: Cherokee Emigrations, 1834-36, M-234, Roll 76, frames 0096-97.

51. April 5, 1834, p. 3, col. 3.

52. Elbert Herring to Andrew Ross, Mar. 9, 1834, in National Archives, RG 75, Letters sent by the Office of Indian Affairs, Letter Book XII, p. 332.

53. To Cass, May 3, 1834, in National Archives, RG 75, Letters received by the Office of Indian Affairs: Cherokee Emigration 1834-36, M-234, Roll 76, frames 0093-95; Montgomery to Herring, Apr. 1, 1834, ibid., frame 0241; Currey to Lumpkin, Nov. 18, 1834, Georgia Department of Archives and History.

54. Gilmer, *Sketches of Some of the First Settlers of Upper Georgia*, p. 373.

55. A request that Major Ridge's portrait be painted—dated May 30, 1834, signed by eleven prominent Cherokees, and addressed to the commissioner of Indian affairs—is found in the Indian Office files, M-234, Roll 76, frame 0086. The artist was probably Charles Bird King.

56. Quoted in Starkey, *Cherokee Nation*, p. 241.

57. John Ridge to D. Greene, July 24, 1834, Houghton Library, ABC, 18.3.1, VIII: 213.

58. Ibid.

59. Moulton, *John Ross*, p. 57.

60. Currey to Cass, Sept. 15, 1834, in National Archives, RG 75, Letters received by the Office of Indian Affairs: Cherokee Agency (East) 1834-36, M-234, Roll 76, frames 0135-45. Currey's letter embodies an account by John Ridge of the August, 1834, council.

61. Ibid.

62. Ibid.

63. Ibid.; 25th Cong., 2d sess., S. Doc. 121 (Serial 315), p. 11.

64. Currey to Cass, Sept. 15, 1834; Payne Papers, Ayer Collection, Newberry Library, II, p. 141.

CHAPTER 11: THE TREATY OF NEW ECHOTA

1. Jackson, *Correspondence*, V, p. 288. The original, dated Sept. 3, 1834, is filed in National Archives, RG 75, Field Papers (Cherokees), Box III; Sam Houston to Andrew Ross, Apr. 29, 1834, in Luquer-Payne Collection, Special Collections, Columbia University Library.

2. Currey to Lumpkin, Sept. 13, 1830, in National Archives, RG 75, Records of the Cherokee Agency in Tennessee, M-208, Roll 10, frame 244; John M. Lea, "Indian Treaties of Tennessee," *American Historical Magazine*, VI (Oct., 1901): 378; Ross to Ridge, Sept. 12, 1834, in Ross Papers, Gilcrease Institute, 34-33.

3. John Ridge et al. to B. Currey, Nov., 1834, in National Archives, RG 75, Letters received by the Office of Indian Affairs: Cherokee Agency (East), 1834–36, M-234, Roll 76, frame 0206; Currey to Lumpkin, Nov. 18, 1834, Georgia Department of Archives and History.

4. Milledgeville *Southern Recorder,* Dec. 30, 1834, p. 3, cols. 3–4; *Augusta Georgia Constitutionalist,* Dec. 30, 1834, p. 2, col. 4.

5. *Niles' Weekly Register,* XLVII (Jan. 24, 1835): 362.

6. *Congressional Globe,* II, pp. 195–96.

7. *Augusta Georgia Constitutionalist,* Jan. 29, 1835, p. 2, col. 3.

8. 25th Cong., 2d sess., S. Doc. 120 (Serial 315), pp. 351–52.

9. Quoted in *Tulsa Daily World,* Jan. 5, 1936, Sec. 4, p. 9; 25th Cong., 2d sess. S. Doc. 120 (Serial 315), p. 95.

10. Journal of Isaac McCoy, Apr. 15, 1832, Kansas State Historical Society.

11. 25th Cong., 2d sess., S. Doc. 120 (Serial 315), pp. 97–98.

12. Quoted, *Augusta Georgia Constitutionalist,* July 21, 1835, p. 2, cols. 2–3.

13. Quoted in Moulton, *John Ross,* p. 67.

14. Quoted, *Augusta Georgia Constitutionalist,* July 21, 1835, p. 2.

15. 25th Cong., 2d sess. S. Doc. 120 (Serial 315) p. 98.

16. Dale and Litton, eds., *Cherokee Cavaliers,* pp. 12–13.

17. Ibid., p. 13.

18. Undated letter, Ridge to Stand Watie, 1835, Watie Papers, Western History Collections, University of Oklahoma Library.

19. 25th Cong., 2d sess., S. Doc. 120 (Serial 315), pp. 359–60.

20. Ibid., p. 362.

21. Currey to Herring, Apr. 16, 1835, in National Archives, RG 75, Letters received by the Office of Indian Affairs: Cherokee Agency (East), 1834–36, M-234, Roll 76, frame 0498.

22. Currey to Ross, April 19, 1835, ibid., frames 0507–508; Starkey, *Cherokee Nation,* p. 253.

23. 25th Cong., 2d sess., S. Doc. 120 (Serial 315), pp. 368, 371–72.

24. C. A. Harris to W. H. Underwood and John Ridge, May 25, 1835, in National Archives, RG 75, Letters sent by the Office of Indian Affairs, Letter Book XVI, pp. 317–18.

25. John Ridge to Lumpkin, May 18, 1835, Georgia Department of Archives and History.

26. Lumpkin to Col. Z. B. Hargrove and Col. Wm. Hardin, May 28, 1835, Georgia Department of Archives and History, Governor's Letter Book (Lumpkin), 1833–35, p. 370; Lumpkin to Col. Bishop, June 17, 1835, ibid., Governor's Letter Book, 1835–40, Part I, p. 31.

27. 25th Cong., 2d sess., S. Doc. 120 (Serial 315), p. 390.

28. Ibid.

29. Ibid., p. 396.

30. Journal of Return J. Meigs, the younger, microfilm of typescript M2972, Southern Historical Collections, University of North Carolina Library; Payne Papers, Ayer Collection, Newberry Library, II, pp 131–40; White, *Historical Collections of Georgia,* pp. 144ff.

31. 25th Cong., 2d sess., S. Doc. 120 (Serial 315), p. 392.

32. Ibid., pp. 393, 461.

33. *Missionary Herald,* May, 1830, p. 155.

34. 25th Cong., 2d sess., S. Doc. 120 (Serial 315), pp. 449, 533.

35. 24th Cong., 1st sess., House Doc. 286 (Serial 292), p. 60 (annexed

item #26).
　36. Ibid., pp. 60–61 (annexed item #27).
　37. Payne Papers, Ayer Collection, Newberry Library, VII (2), pp. 284–85.
　38. 25th Cong., 2d sess., S. Doc. 120 (Serial 315), p. 474.
　39. Hargrove to Lumpkin, June 19, 1835, Georgia Department of Archives and History.
　40. Milledgeville *Federal Union*, Aug. 1, 1835, p. 3, cols. 3–4.
　41. Battey, *History of Rome and Floyd County*, I, p. 211.
　42. 25th Cong., 2d sess., S. Doc. 120 (Serial 315), p. 468; John Ross Papers, Gilcrease Institute, 35–14.
　43. Clemens de Baillou, ed., *John Howard Payne to His Countrymen* (Athens, Ga., 1961), p. 8.
　44. Battey, *History of Rome and Floyd County*, I, pp. 261–62.
　45. Schermerhorn to Lumpkin, Sept. 8, 1835, Georgia Department of Archives and History.
　46. Currey to Lumpkin, Aug. 26, 1835, ibid.; *Augusta Georgia Constitutionalist*, Sept. 4, 1835, p. 3, col. 2.
　47. De Baillou, *John Howard Payne to His Countrymen*, p. 7.
　48. 25th Cong., 2d sess., S. Doc. 120 (Serial 315), p. 578.
　49. Milledgeville *Federal Union*, Nov. 20, 1835, p. 2, col. 6.
　50. 24th Cong., 1st sess., House Doc. 286 (Serial 292), p. 160.
　51. 25th Cong., 2d sess., S. Doc. 121 (Serial 315), p. 30.
　52. 25th Cong., 2d sess., S. Doc. 120 (Serial 315), pp. 533–34; 25th Cong., 2d sess., S. Doc. 121 (Serial 315), p. 29; 25th Cong., 2d sess., S. Doc. 120 (Serial 315), p. 518.
　53. J. H. Payne to Thatcher T. Payne, Sept. 26, 1835, Luquer-Payne Collection, Special Collections, Columbia University Library.
　54. 25th Cong., 2d sess., S. Doc. 120 (Serial 315), pp. 494–95.
　55. Payne's account, quoted in Battey, *Rome and Floyd County*, I, p. 58.
　56. Ibid., p. 65.
　57. 25th Cong., 2d sess., S. Doc. 121 (Serial 315), p. 32.
　58. Ibid., pp. 30, 32.
　59. 25th Cong., 2d sess., S. Doc. 120 (Serial 315), p. 494.
　60. *Cartersville* (Ga.) *Courant*, Mar. 26, 1885, p. 1, col. 3.
　61. 24th Cong., 1st sess., House Doc. 286 (Serial 292), p. 120.
　62. *Cartersville* (Ga.) *Courant*, Mar. 26, 1885, p. 1, col. 3.
　63. Ibid.
　64. 24th Cong., 1st sess., House Doc. 286 (Serial 292), p. 121.
　65. *Cartersville* (Ga.) *Courant*, Mar. 26, 1885, p. 1, col. 3; Signature page, Treaty of New Echota (Ratified Indian Treaty No. 199), National Archives.
　66. Starkey, *Cherokee Nation*, p. 267, 312.
　67. Thomas L. McKenney, *Memoirs Official and Personal, with Sketches of Travels among the Northern and Southern Indians*, I, p. 265.
　68. 25th Cong., 2d sess., S. Doc. 120 (Serial 315), p. 517.

CHAPTER 12: HONEY CREEK

　1. National Archives, RG 75, Letters received by the Office of Indian Affairs: Cherokee Agency, 1836, M-234, Roll 80, frame 0224.
　2. 24th Cong., 1st sess., House Doc. 286 (Serial 292), p. 31.

3. John Ross, *Letter . . . in Answer to Inquiries of a Friend*, p. 13.
4. 25th Cong., 2d sess., S. Doc. 121 (Serial 315), p. 26.
5. 25th Cong., 2d sess., S. Doc. 120 (Serial 315), p. 519.
6. Woodward, *The Cherokees*, p. 193.
7. 29th Cong., 1st sess., House Doc. 185 (Serial 485), p. 53; Royce, *Cherokee Nation of Indians*, p. 283.
8. Benton, *Thirty Years' View*, pp. 624–26.
9. Quoted in Anderson, *Stand Watie*, p. 18*n*; from Joseph Thoburn, ed., *A Standard History of Oklahoma*, I, p. 104*n*.
10. 29th Cong., 1st sess., House Doc. 185 (Serial 485), p. 53.
11. 24th Cong., 1st sess., House Doc. 286 (Serial 292), p. 161.
12. National Archives, RG 75, Letters received by the Office of Indian Affairs: Cherokee Agency, 1836, M-234, Roll 80, frame 0219.
13. George Kellog to Boudinot, ibid., frame 0040.
14. Battey, *Rome and Floyd County*, I, p. 212.
15. John Ridge to Lumpkin, Nov. 2, 1836, in National Archives, RG 75, Removal Records, First Board of Cherokee Commissioners, Letters of the Cherokee Committee.
16. The Ridges to President Jackson, June 30, 1836, in National Archives, RG 75, Letters received by the Office of Indian Affairs, M-234, Roll 80, frames 0488–89.
17. Battey, *Rome and Floyd County*, I, p. 212.
18. Ibid., pp. 216–17; National Archives, RG 75, Letters received by the Office of Indian Affairs: Cherokee Agency (East), 1834–36, M-234, Roll 76, frames 0465–68, 0723–24; Removal Records, Fourth Board of Cherokee Commissioners, Cherokee Minute Docket, Vol. I, pp. 56ff.
19. Wilson Lumpkin, *The Removal of the Cherokee Indians from Georgia*, II, pp. 23–24.
20. Ibid., pp. 122–23, 156–57.
21. John Ridge et al. to John Ross, Aug. 17, 1836, in National Archives, RG 75, Removal Records, First Board of Cherokee Commissioners, Letters of the Cherokee Committee; *American State Papers, Military Affairs*, VII, p. 555; 25th Cong., 1st sess., House Doc. 46 (Serial 311), p. 62.
22. *American State Papers, Military Affairs*, VII, p. 557.
23. 25th Cong., 2d sess., S. Doc. 120 (Serial 315), p. 50.
24. Lumpkin, *Removal*, II, p. 44.
25. Ibid., pp. 57–58.
26. Ibid., p. 57.
27. Ridge to Lumpkin, Nov. 2, 1836, in National Archives, RG 75, Removal Records, First Board of Cherokee Commissioners, Letters of the Cherokee Committee.
28. Lumpkin, *Removal*, II, pp. 85–86.
29. Ibid., p. 86.
30. 25th Cong., 2d sess., S. Doc. 120 (Serial 315), p. 709.
31. 25th Cong., 3rd sess., S. Doc. 277 (Serial 342), passim.
32. Sophia Sawyer to D. Greene, Dec. 24, 1833, Houghton Library, ABC, 18.3.1, VIII: 179.
33. *Atlanta Constitution*, Oct. 27, 1889, p. 5, col. 3.
34. *In Memoriam—Hon. George W. Paschal*, p. 4.
35. George W. Paschal Letter Book No. 1, Eno Collection, Arkansas Historical Commission, p. 12.

36. Clara B. Eno, *History of Crawford County, Arkansas*, p. 181.

37. 25th Cong., 2d sess., S. Doc. 120 (Serial 315), p. 877.

38. H. G. Clauder to Theodore Schultz, Mar. 17, 1837, Cherokee Mission, Moravian Archives, Winston-Salem, N.C.

39. 25th Cong., 2d sess., S. Doc. 120 (Serial 315), p. 1049.

40. Grant Foreman, ed., "Journey of a Party of Cherokee Emigrants," *Mississippi Valley Historical Review*, XVIII (Sept., 1931): 238.

41. 25th Cong., 2d sess., S. Doc. 120 (Serial 315), p. 898.

42. Foreman, "Journey . . . ," p. 245.

43. Ibid., pp. 241–44.

44. Foreman, "Journey . . . ," p. 245.

45. Susanna Ridge to the Hon. John C. Spencer, June 7, 1842, in National Archives, RG 75, Letters received by the Office of Indian Affairs: Cherokee Agency, 1842, M-234.

46. John Gould Fletcher, *Arkansas*, p. 79.

47. Washington Irving, *A Tour of the Prairies*, pp. 50–51.

48. Susanna Ridge to the Hon. John C. Spencer, June 7, 1842.

49. Lumpkin to C. A. Harris, Sept. 8, 1817, in National Archives, RG 75, Removal Records (Cherokee), First Board of Cherokee Commissioners, "Cher. Letter Book, Lumpkin & Kennedy, 1836–39," p. 50.

50. John Ridge to Lumpkin and Kennedy, Sept. 22, 1837, in National Archives, RG 75, Removal Records, First Board of Cherokee Commissioners, Letters of the Cherokee Committee.

51. Lumpkin, *Removal*, II, p. 141.

52. John Ridge to Eliza Northrup, Nov. 1, 1836, transcript courtesy E. E. Dale, original at the Cornwall Free Library, Cornwall, Conn.

53. John Golden Ross to John Ross, Oct. 29, 1837, Ross Papers, Gilcrease Institute, 37–49; Wm. P. Ross to John Ross, Nov. 28, 1837, ibid., 37–66; Starkey, *Cherokee Nation*, p. 282, makes it Major Ridge who visited the former president.

54. Nevada Couch, *Pages from Cherokee Indian History*, pp. 24–25.

55. *United Brethren's Missionary Intelligencer*, VII (1842): 411.

56. Starkey, *Cherokee Nation*, p. 311.

57. John Ridge to John Kennedy, Jan. 16, 1838, in National Archives, RG 75, Removal Records, First Board of Cherokee Commissioners, Letters of the Cherokee Committee.

58. Ibid.

59. Ridge accounts, HM1730, Henry E. Huntington Library; Indian-Pioneer Historical Project, Oklahoma Historical Society, LXXV, p. 388.

60. Ridge accounts, HM1730, Huntington Library.

61. Lumpkin, *Removal*, II, p. 202.

62. Ibid., pp. 202–203.

63. Ibid., pp. 203–204.

64. Ibid., p. 205.

65. *United Brethren's Missionary Intelligencer*, VII (1842): 414–15.

66. Grant Foreman, *Advancing the Frontier, 1830–1860*, p. 200.

67. Henry R. Schoolcraft, *Personal Memoirs of a Residence of Thirty Years with the Indian Tribes on the American Frontiers*, p. 606.

68. Statement of H. A. Anderson et al. dated Sept. 13, 1839, in National Archives, RG 75, Special File 53, Cherokee File A686.

CHAPTER 13:   THE TRAIL OF TEARS

1. Gen. Wool, quoted in Mooney, *Myths of the Cherokee*, p. 127.
2. Nathaniel Smith to C. A. Harris, Oct. 15, 1837, in National Archives, RG 75, Indian Office Special File 31 (Gen. Nathaniel Smith); Smith to Harris, Sept. 22, 1837, ibid.; Journal of B. B. Cannon, National Archives, RG 75, Indian Office Special File 249, C553.
3. Journal of Edward Deas, ibid., D209-17.
4. William J. Cotter, *My Autobiography*, pp. 38-39.
5. *Niles' National Register*, LIV (June 2, 1838): 210.
6. Order No. 25, May 17, 1838, in 25th Cong., 2d sess., House Exec. Doc. 453 (Serial 331).
7. Mooney, *Myths of the Cherokee*, p. 130.
8. D. S. Butrick to J. H. Payne, June 6, 1839, Payne Papers, Ayer Collection, Newberry Library, XI, p. 67; Mooney, *Myths of the Cherokee*, p. 130.
9. Butrick to Payne, June 6, 1839.
10. *Niles' National Register*, LIV (Aug. 18, 1838): 385.
11. Mooney, *Myths of the Cherokee*, p. 130.
12. Ibid., p. 131.
13. Butrick to Payne, June 6, 1839; *Niles' National Register*, LIV (Aug. 18, 1838): 385.
14. Little Rock *Arkansas Gazette*, Oct. 2, 1839, p. 2, col. 4.
15. *Niles' National Register*, LV (Jan. 5, 1839): 290; Mooney, *Myths of the Cherokee*, p. 131.
16. 27th Cong., 3rd sess., House Rep. 288 (Serial 429), p. 36.
17. *Niles' National Register*, LIV (Aug. 18, 1838): 387.
18. Starkey, *Cherokee Nation*, p. 295.
19. 27th Cong., 3rd sess., House Rep. 288 (Serial 429), p. 37.
20. *Niles' National Register*, LIV (Aug. 25, 1838): 407; LV (Nov. 24, 1838): 204.
21. National Archives, RG 75, Letters sent by the Office of Indian Affairs, Letter Book XXV, p. 83.
22. 27th Cong., 3rd sess., House Rep. 288 (Serial 429), p. 37.
23. Gen. Scott to Joel Poinsett, Sept. 28, 1838, in National Archives, RG 75, Indian Office Special File 31 (Gen. Smith).
24. Foreman, *Indian Removal*, p. 301.
25. Quoted, ibid., p. 302.
26. Payne Papers, Ayer Collection, Newberry Library, VI, pp. 179-80.
27. Lt. H. S. Scott to Gen. Scott, Oct. 11, 1838 in National Archives RG 75, Letters received by the Office of Indian Affairs: Cherokee Emigration, M-234, Roll 115, frame 0860.
28. Dr. Powell to John Ross, Oct. 21, 1838, Foreman Transcripts, Oklahoma Historical Society, Archives Division, "Letters and Documents: Cherokee 1826-1884," pp. 195-96.
29. Quoted, Foreman, *Indian Removal*, pp. 305-307, from *New York Observer*, Jan. 26, 1839, p. 4.
30. Woodward, *The Cherokees*, pp. 217-18.
31. *Sunday Oklahoman*, Apr. 7, 1929, section F, p. 6.
32. Mooney, *Myths of the Cherokee*, p. 133.
33. 27th Cong., 3rd sess., House Rep. 288 (Serial 429), p. 70.

34. Butler to Greene, Jan. 25, 1839, Houghton Library, ABC, 18.3.1, X: 73.
35. Mooney, *Myths of the Cherokee*, p. 130.
36. Butler to Greene, Aug. 2, 1838, Houghton Library, ABC, 18.3.1, X: 70a.
37. Little Rock *Arkansas Gazette*, Oct. 2, 1839, p. 2, cols. 3-4.

CHAPTER 14:   THE RECKONING

1. Grant Foreman, *The Five Civilized Tribes*, pp. 288-89.
2. Little Rock *Arkansas Gazette*, Oct. 2, 1839, p. 2, col. 3; Gabriel, *Elias Boudinot*, p. 175.
3. Quoted in Starkey, *Cherokee Nation*, p. 305.
4. Cephas Washburn to D. Greene, Aug. 12, 1839, Houghton Library, ABC, 18.3.1, X: 55.
5. Morris J. Wardell, *A Political History of the Cherokee Nation*, pp. 14-15.
6. Washburn to Greene, Aug. 12, 1839.
7. Ibid.
8. Ibid.
9. Ibid.
10. Ibid.
11. *Report of the Commissioner of Indian Affairs, 1839*, p. 357.
12. Evan Jones to J. H. Payne, July 22, 1839, Payne Papers, Ayer Collection, Newberry Library; 26th Cong., 1st sess., House Exec. Doc. 2 (Serial 363), p. 340; "Mr. Bell's Suppressed Report in Relation to the Difficulties between the Eastern and Western Cherokees," *Cherokee Advocate*, Mar. 5, 1846, p. 1, col. 2.
13. Thomas Hindman's Testimony (1840?), Ross Papers, Gilcrease Institute, 40-57.
14. 29th Cong., 1st sess., House Doc. 185 (Serial 485), p. 55; Butrick, "A brief review of the history of the Cherokee nation for a few years back," Payne Papers, Newberry Library; Deposition of Allen Ross, in Grant Foreman, ed., "The Murder of Elias Boudinot," *Chronicles of Oklahoma*, XII (Mar., 1934): 23.
15. Anderson, *Stand Watie*, p. 20n; *New York Observer*, Aug. 17, 1839, p. 131, col. 3; *Niles' National Register*, LVI (Aug. 3, 1839): 362; Ethan Allen Hitchcock, *A Traveler in Indian Territory*, ed. Grant Foreman, p. 82.
16. John R. Ridge, *Poems*, Preface, p. 7.
17. Letter of John A. Bell and Stand Watie, Little Rock *Arkansas Gazette*, Aug. 21, 1839, p. 2, col. 4, reprinted in *Niles' National Register*, LVII (Oct. 5, 1839): 85; Starr, *History of the Cherokee Indians*, p. 113; *Niles' National Register*, LVI (Aug. 3, 1839): 362.
18. John R. Ridge, *Poems*, Preface, pp. 7-8.
19. 29th Cong., 1st sess., House Doc. 185 (Serial 485), p. 54; 26th Cong., 1st sess., S. Doc. 347 (Serial 359), pp. 16, 27, 50; Hitchcock, *Traveler*, p. 82; Speech of A. W. Arrington in [George W. Paschal], "The Trial of Stand Watie," *Chronicles of Oklahoma*, XII, no. 3, (Sept., 1934), pp. 317-18.
20. *Niles' National Register*, LVII (Oct. 5, 1839): 85; 29th Cong., 1st sess., House Doc. 185 (Serial 485), p. 54. See also Carolyn Foreman, *Park Hill*, p. 36.
21. Worcester to Greene, June 26, 1839, Houghton Library, ABC, 18.3.1, X: 136; Gabriel, *Elias Boudinot*, p. 177; Rachel C. Eaton, *John Ross and the*

Cherokee Indians, p. 97; Althea Bass, *Cherokee Messenger*, p. 255.

22. [Reminiscences of Mary Worcester Williams], *Lewiston Journal,* Magazine Section, Nov. 17, 1917, pp. I-A, 7. According to a marginal note on this item (Foreman Collection, Gilcrease Institute, Box 16, Vol. 11, p. 29), Mrs. Williams claims that the reporter, in saying her brother had warned Stand Watie, had misquoted her; she added that the man who had warned Watie was the Choctaw Indian mentioned in the text. Gen. Arbuckle (26th Cong., 1st sess., S. Doc. 347 [Serial 359], p. 22) states that one of Boudinot's carpenters had warned Watie.

23. Anderson, *Stand Watie*, p. 21; 26th Cong., 1st sess., S. Doc. 347 (Serial 359), pp. 16, 27; Arrington in [George W. Paschal], "The Trial of Stand Watie," *Chronicles of Oklahoma*, XII, No. 3 (Sept., 1934), pp. 317–18.

24. 29th Cong., 1st sess., House Doc. 185 (Serial 485), pp. 54–55; *Niles' National Register,* LVII (Oct. 5, 1839): 85; Statement of Zeke Proctor, Sept. 30, 1937, Indian-Pioneer History Project for Oklahoma, Oklahoma Historical Society, LX, p. 485; John R. Ridge, *Poems,* Preface, p. 8.

1. Anderson, *Stand Watie*, p. 77n; interview with Professor T. L. Ballenger, Tahlequah, Okla., Sept. 16, 1961; Gen. Lee B. Washbourne to the writer, July 16, 1966, reporting an affidavit in his possession to the effect that Major Ridge's remains had been removed to the Polson cemetery in 1856.

2. Couch, *Pages from Cherokee Indian History*, p. 18n; Carolyn T. Foreman, *Park Hill,* p. 36.

3. Worcester to Greene, July 17, 1839, Houghton Library, ABC, 18.3.1, X: 137; 26th Cong., 1st sess., House Doc. 222 (Serial 368), p. 3; 26th Cong., 1st sess., House Doc. 129 (Serial 365), pp. 54–56; Thomas Hindman's Testimony (1840?), Ross Papers, Gilcrease Institute, 40–57; 26th Cong., 1st sess., House Doc. 2 (Serial 363), p. 362; Statement of Lt. Jay Robinson, July 7, 1840, Ross Papers, Gilcrease Institute, 40–38.

4. Sawyer to Greene, Oct. 11, 1839, Houghton Library, ABC, 18.3.1, X: 322; John R. Ridge, *Poems,* Preface, p. 8; Ridge claims in National Archives, RG 75, Indian Office Special File No. 53, M-574, Roll 6.

5. 26th Cong., 1st sess., House Doc. 129 (Serial 365), p. 5; Washburn to Greene, Aug. 12, 1839, Houghton Library, ABC, 18.3.1, X: 55; Worcester to Greene, July 17, 1839, ibid., 137; *Arkansas Gazette,* Aug. 21, 1839, p. 2, cols. 4–5, reprinted in *Niles' National Register,* LVII (Oct. 5, 1839): 85. See also 26th Cong., 1st sess., House Doc. 2 (Serial 363), p. 376.

6. 28th Cong., 1st sess., House Doc. 234 (Serial 443), pp. 28–29; Butrick's Journal, Jan. 1, 1840, Houghton Library, ABC, 18.3.3, IV.

7. Commissioner of Indian Affairs to Capt. Wm. Armstrong, Aug. 20, 1838, in National Archives, RG 75, Letters sent by the Office of Indian Affairs, Letter Book XXVII, pp. 186–87; S. G. Simmons to Lt. Col. R. B. Mason, Oct. 24, 1839, in Grant Foreman Notebook, FNO-6, Foreman Collection, Oklahoma Historical Society (transcribed from Fort Gibson Letter Book No. VI, p. 154); 26th Cong., 1st sess., S. Doc. 347 (Serial 359), pp. 16, 62; Worcester to Greene, Jan. 21, 1840, Houghton Library, ABC, 18.3.1, X: 141; Statement of Lt. Jay Robinson, July 7, 1840, Ross Papers, Gilcrease Institute, 40–38; [G. W. Paschal], "The Trial of Stand Watie," *Chronicles of Oklahoma,* XII

(1934): 305-39.
  8. Grant Foreman, ed. *Indian Justice* (Oklahoma City, 1934), p. 59*n.*
  9. Wardell, *A Political History of the Cherokee Nation*, chap. IV.
  10. *Cherokee Advocate*, Sept. 3, 1849, p. 3, col. 4; genealogical data from Gen.
Lee B. Washbourne; see also genealogical chart in Dale and Litton, eds.,
Cherokee Cavaliers; Fayetteville *Arkansian*, Mar. 5, 1859, p. 2, col. 2; Apr. 2,
1859, p. 2, col. 2; Sarah (Ridge Paschal) Pix to Stand Watie, May 1, 1864,
Watie Papers, Western History Collections, University of Oklahoma Library,
Series IV, Vol. 9, p. 153; Dale and Litton, eds., *Cherokee Cavaliers*, pp. 198*n*, 199*n*.
  11. John R. Ridge, *Poems*, Preface, pp. 8-9; Franklin Walker, *San Francisco's
Literary Frontier*, pp. 46-54, 111, 227-28.
  12. For Watie's war experience, see Franks, *Stand Watie*, chaps. VII-X.
  13. *Cherokee Cavaliers*, pp. 243-44.
  14. Wardell, *A Political History of the Cherokee Nation*, pp. 105-203, 212ff.

SELECTED BIBLIOGRAPHY

RECORD AND MANUSCRIPT COLLECTIONS

The purpose of this list is to indicate the locations of manuscript materials that contributed either direct quotations or background information for the foregoing pages. No attempt has been made to include all detached or scattered manuscript items, especially when locations of such are cited in the notes.

Federal Records

The National Archives, General Services Administration, Washington, D.C. (See *Your Government's Records in the National Archives*, rev. ed., for detailed listings of subsidiary series of records contained in the following record groups [RG]. See also *List of National Archives Microfilm Publications* for the various series available on microfilm.)

RG 75, Records of the Bureau of Indian Affairs, Department of the Interior. Particularly useful were the documents found in the following series:
Letters received by the Office of the Secretary of War relating to Indian affairs, 1800–23 (microfilm designation M-271).
Letters sent by the secretary of war relating to Indian affairs, 1800–24 (M-15).
Records of the Cherokee Indian Agency in Tennessee, 1801–35 (M-208).
Documents relating to the negotiation of ratified and unratified treaties with various Indian tribes, 1801–69 (T-494).
Special files of the Office of Indian Affairs (M-574) relating to the Cherokees. In particular File No. 31 (Roll No. 4), "Nathaniel Smith . . ."; File No. 53 (Roll No. 6), "Elias Boudinot, John Ridge, and Major Ridge, Cherokees, claims of heirs, 1839–46"; and File No. 249 (Roll No. 69), "George E. Mountcastle and George M.

381

Lavender, claims against the Cherokees under the Treaty of 1835–36."

Letters sent by the Office of Indian Affairs, 1824–81 (M-21).

Letters received by the Office of Indian Affairs, 1824–80 (M-234).

Census Roll, 1835, of the Cherokee Indians east of the Mississippi (T-496).

Cherokee Removal Records, in particular the records of the Commissary General of Subsistence and of the First Board, the Second and Third Boards, and the Fourth Board of Cherokee Commissioners. Field Papers, Cherokees, Boxes 1–4.

RG 94, Records of the Adjutant General's Office, War Department. Volunteer Organizations and State Militia, War of 1812. Compiled Military Service Records.

RG 107, Records of the Office of the Secretary of War, War Department. Letters received by the Office of the Secretary of War: unregistered series, 1789–1861 (M-222); registered or main series, 1801–70 (M-221). Letters sent by the Office of the Secretary of War relating to military affairs (M-6).

The National Anthropological Archives (formerly the Bureau of American Ethnology), Smithsonian Institution, Washington, D.C.

Various materials relative to the Cherokee and Creek Indians, including the notes and notebooks of James Mooney, John R. Swanton, and A. S. Gatschet as well as several items attributed to John Howard Payne; also fragmentary records of a Board of Cherokee Commissioners.

Other Manuscript Collections

American Board of Commissioners for Foreign Missions (ABC). Archives, Houghton Library, Harvard University.

American Philosophical Society Archives, Philadelphia. Miscellaneous Manuscripts Collection (in particular papers concerning Cherokees and papers concerning Moravian missions).

Barde, Fred S., Collection. Oklahoma Historical Society, Oklahoma City.

Cass, Lewis, Collection. Western History Collections, University of Oklahoma Library, Norman.

Chamberlain, A. N. "History of the Presbyterian Church in the Cherokee Nation." Library, Oklahoma Historical Society.

"Cherokee Indian Letters, Talks and Treaties." Transcripts compiled by Louise Frederick Hays, WPA Project No. 4341. 3 vols. Georgia Department of Archives and History, Atlanta.

Cherokee Nation Papers. Western History Collections, University of Oklahoma Library.

"Cherokee Papers, 1815–1874." Transcripts compiled by Gaston Litton, Indian Archives Division of the Oklahoma Historical Society.

"Creek Indian Letters, Talks and Treaties, 1705–1839." Transcripts compiled by Louise Frederick Hays. 3 vols. Georgia Department of Archives and History.

Currey, Benjamin F., File. Georgia Department of Archives and History.

Dale, E. E., Papers (including Boudinot-Gold transcripts). Western History Collections, University of Oklahoma Library.

Dinsmoor, Silas, Papers. Ayer Collection, Newberry Library, Chicago.

Draper, Lyman, Papers. Wisconsin Historical Society, Madison. (Microfilm and typescripts of documents pertaining to southern Indians were consulted at the Western History Collections, University of Oklahoma Library; also miscellaneous transcripts were checked in the Grant Foreman Collection, *quod vide.*)

Ellsworth, J. C., and Frederic Ellsworth. "Extracts from a diary kept by J. C. [and Frederic] Ellsworth at Haweis Cherokee Mission in Georgia on the Coosa river." Indian Archives Division, Oklahoma Historical Society.

Foreign Mission School materials. Cornwall (Conn.) Free Library.

Foreman, Grant, Collection of notes, transcripts, and photostats. Gilcrease Institute of American History and Art, Tulsa. Oklahoma Historical Society.

Foreman, Stephen. "Journal and Letters of Stephan Foreman." Typescript, Western History Collections, University of Oklahoma Library.

Gallatin, Albert, Papers. New-York Historical Society, New York City.

Georgia. Governors' Letter Books. Georgia Department of Archives and History.

———. Records of the State Surveyor General (in particular the field notes of the survey of Cherokee lands, 1832). Georgia Department of Archives and History.

Gratz, Simon, Autograph Collections. Pennsylvania Historical Society.

Hargett, J. Lester, Collection. Western History Collections, University of Oklahoma Library (microfilm).

Hawkins, Benjamin. "Letters of Benjamin Hawkins, 1797–1815." Transcripts comp. Louise Frederick Hays, WPA Project No. 5993, Georgia Department of Archives and History.

———. "Sketch of Creek Country in the Year 1798 and 1799." Houghton Library, Harvard.

Indian Pioneer History Project for Oklahoma.
  Western History Collections, University of Oklahoma Library.
  Oklahoma Historical Society.

Jackson, Andrew, Papers.
  Library of Congress (microfilm consulted at Columbia University).
  Gilcrease Institute of American History and Art (one folder).
  Henry E. Huntington Library.

Lavender, George M., Account Book and Lavender genealogical papers. Georgia Department of Natural Resources, Atlanta.

McCoy, Isaac, Papers (including Journal), 1784–1846. Kansas State Historical Society.

Meigs, Return J. "Memorandum Book of Occurrences in the Cherokee
... Country, 1796–1807." Item No. 20, Indian Collection, Manuscripts
Division, Library of Congress.
Meigs, Return J., Papers.
Georgia Department of Archives and History (one folder).
Henry E. Huntington Library (Miscellaneous Letters).
Meigs, Return J., the younger, Journal kept while serving as secretary of
John F. Schermerhorn, U.S. Commissioner. Southern Historical Collec-
tions, University of North Carolina Library (microfilm M2972).
Miscellaneous Cherokee manuscripts.
Georgia Department of Archives and History.
Manuscripts Division, Library of Congress.
Special Collections, Princeton University Library.
Gilcrease Institute of American History and Art.
Western History Collections, University of Oklahoma Library.
Manuscripts Division, University of Tulsa Library.
Miscellaneous Indian File (Box 2). Henry E. Huntington Library.
Moravian Brotherhood records and manuscripts.
Moravian Archives, Bethlehem, Pa.
Moravian Archives, Winston-Salem, N.C.
Georgia Department of Natural Resources (excerpts from Spring Place
Diary, tr. Carl Mauelshagen).
Writer's files (letters and excerpts from Spring Place Diary, tr. Sophie
Wilkins).
New Echota and Vann Mansion reconstruction data. Georgia Department
of Natural Resources.
Paschal, George W., Letter Books. Eno Collection, Arkansas Historical
Commission, Little Rock.
Payne, John Howard, Papers.
Ayer Collection, Newberry Library, Chicago.
Luquer-Payne Collection, Special Collections, Columbia University
Library.
Gilcrease Institute of American History and Art.
Long Island Collection, East Hampton Free Library.
Manuscripts Division, Library of Congress.
Pennsylvania Historical Society.
Piburn, Anne Ross, Collection. Western History Collections, University
of Oklahoma Library.
Poinsett, Joel, Papers. Pennsylvania Historical Society.
Private Collections.
Clemens de Baillou, Athens, Ga.
Dr. T. L. Ballenger, Tahlequah, Okla.
Maj. Gen. Lee B. Washbourne, Jay, Okla.
Dr. Muriel Wright, Oklahoma City.
Ridge, Boudinot, and Watie Papers.

Western History Collections, University of Oklahoma Library.
Kansas State Historical Society (Stand Watie's Regimental Book).
Georgia Department of Archives and History (John Ridge folder).
Manuscripts Division, University of Texas (Ridge and Watie letters, photostats of which are available at University of Oklahoma).
Henry E. Huntington Library (Ridge accounts).
Ross, John, Papers.
Ayer Collection, Newberry Library.
Gilcrease Institute of American History and Art.
Western History Collections, University of Oklahoma Library.
Georgia Department of Archives and History (one folder).
Speck, Frank, Papers. American Philosophical Society.
Springer, William Greene, File. Georgia Department of Archives and History.
Starr, Emmet, Collections. Oklahoma Historical Society.
Tarvin, William J., Folder. Georgia Department of Archives and History.
Vaill Collection. Historical Manuscripts, Stirling Library, Yale.
Van Buren, Martin, Papers. Library of Congress (microfilm consulted at Columbia University).
Vaux, Robert, Papers. Pennsylvania Historical Society.
White, Willie Stewart, Collection. Southern Historical Collections, University of North Carolina Library.
Wirt, William, Papers. Maryland Historical Society, Baltimore.
Worcester-Robertson Family Papers. Manuscripts Division, University of Tulsa Library.

Theses and Dissertations

Hicks, J. C. "The Rhetoric of John Ross." Ph.D. diss., University of Oklahoma, 1971.
Holland, Cullen Joe. "Cherokee Indian Newspapers, 1828–1906." Ph.D. diss., University of Minnesota, 1956.
Reed, Gerard A. "The Ross-Watie Conflict: Factionalism in the Cherokee Nation, 1839–1865." Ph.D. diss., University of Oklahoma, 1967.
Van Hoeven, James William. "Salvation and Indian Removal: The Career Biography of John Freeman Schermerhorn, Indian Commissioner." Ph.D. diss., Vanderbilt University, 1972.
Vipperman, Carl Jackson. "Wilson Lumpkin and the Cherokee Removal." Master's thesis, University of Georgia, 1961.
Willis, William S. "Colonial Conflict and the Cherokee Indians, 1710–1760." Ph.D. diss., Columbia University, 1955.
Wilms, Douglas C. "Cherokee Indian Land Use in Georgia, 1800–1838." Ph.D. diss., University of Georgia, 1973.

Published Materials

Congressional Documents

American State Papers, Class II, *Indian Affairs*, Vols. I–II; Class V, *Military Affairs*, Vols. I–VII.
18th Cong., 1st sess., House Doc. 133 (Serial 102). "Memorial of John Ross, Geo. Lowrey, Major Ridge, and Elijah Hicks, Delegates from the Cherokee Nation of Indians, April 16, 1824."
20th Congress, 1st sess., House Doc. 106 (Serial 171). "Negotiation for Cherokee Lands."
20th Cong., 1st sess., House Doc. 219 (Serial 173). "Creek Indian [i.e., John Ridge] Broke, &c."
20th Cong., 1st sess., House Exec. Doc. 238 (Serial 174). "Creek Treaty — November 15, 1827."
20th Cong., 1st sess., House Exec. Doc. 248 (Serial 174). "Charges Against the Creek Agent since January 1, 1826."
23rd Cong., 1st sess., S. Doc. 512 (Serials 245–49). "Correspondence on the Subject of the Emigration of the Indians. . . ." Vols. I–V.
24th Cong., 1st sess., House Doc. 286 (Serial 292). "Memorial and Protest of the Cherokee Nation [against ratification and execution of the Treaty of New Echota]."
25th Cong., 1st sess., House Doc. 46 (Serial 311). "Brigadier General Wool [Court of Enquiry]."
25th Cong., 2d sess., S. Doc. 120 (Serial 315). "Report from the Secretary of War . . . in relation to the Cherokee Treaty of 1835."
25th Cong., 2d sess., S. Doc. 121 (Serial 315). "Documents in relation to the Validity of the Cherokee Treaty of 1835 [compiled by Elias Boudinot]."
25th Cong., 2d sess., House Exec. Doc. 453 (Serial 331). "Removal of the Cherokees [correspondence between the War Department and General Scott]."
25th Cong., 3rd sess., S. Doc. 199 (Serial 340). "Report of the Secretary of War, Transmitting . . . a statement of expenses incurred in negotiating and concluding the Cherokee Treaty of December 29, 1835."
25th Cong., 3rd sess., S. Doc. 277 (Serial 342). "Report from the Secretary of War, Transmitting . . . statements showing the persons employed, the funds furnished, and the improvements valued, under the Cherokee Treaty of December 1835."
26th Cong., 1st sess., S. Doc. 347 (Serial 359). "Report from the Secretary of War, exhibiting . . . the present state of difficulties which have existed, and the arrangements made, or attempted to be made, between the Government and the Cherokee people, April 1, 1840."
26th Cong., 1st sess., House Exec. Doc. 2 (Serial 363), pp. 354–427. Documents concerning Cherokee disturbances accompanying the Report of the Commissioner of Indian Affairs for 1839.
26th Cong., 1st sess., House Exec. Doc. 129 (Serial 365). "Memorial of the

Delegation of the Cherokee Nation, March 9, 1840."
26th Cong., 1st sess., House Exec. Doc. 222 (Serial 368). "Indians—Chero-
    kees, May 26, 1840."
27th Cong., 2d sess., House Rep. 1098 (Serial 411). "Removal of the Chero-
    kees West of the Mississippi."
27th Cong., 3rd sess., House Rep. 288 (Serial 429). "Removal of the Cher-
    okees, &c."
28th Cong., 1st sess., House Exec. Doc. 234 (Serial 443). "Memorial of
    the 'Treaty Party' of the Cherokee Indians . . . April 13, 1844."
29th Cong., 1st sess., S. Doc. 331 (Serial 476). "Memorial of John Ross and
    others . . . May 4, 1846."
29th Cong., 1st sess., House Doc. 185 (Serial 485). "Cherokee Disturbances:
    Message of the President . . . Relative to the Cherokee Difficulties."
29th Cong., 1st sess., House Rep. 683 (Serial 490). "Cherokee Indians [to
    accompany H. R. Bill No. 456]."

Congressional Proceedings

The Debates and Proceedings in the Congress of the United States, 1789-1824.
Register of Debates in Congress, 1824-37.
Congressional Globe, 1834-46.

Books and Articles

Abel, Annie Heloise. *The American Indian as Slaveholder and Secessionist.*
    Cleveland, 1915.
———. "The Cherokee Negotiations of 1822-1823." *Smith College Studies
    in History*, I (July, 1916).
Adair, James. *Adair's History of the American Indians.* Reprint ed. Samuel
    C. Williams. Johnson City, Tenn., 1930.
Adams, Henry. *History of the United States of America during the Adminis-
    trations of Thomas Jefferson and James Madison.* 9 volumes. New York, 1921.
———. *Life of Albert Gallatin.* Philadelphia and London, 1879.
Alden, John R. *John Stuart and the Southern Colonial Frontier.* Ann Ar-
    bor, 1944.
American Board of Commissioners for Foreign Missions. Annual Reports,
    1810-40.
Anderson, Mabel Washbourne. *Life of General Stand Watie.* Pryor, Okla.,
    1915; rev. ed., Pryor, 1931.
Anderson, Rufus, ed. *Memoir of Catherine Brown.* 3rd ed. Boston, 1828.
Armstrong, Zella. *History of Hamilton County, and Chattanooga, Tennessee.*
    Chattanooga, 1931-40.
Arnow, Harriette L. *Seedtime on the Cumberland.* New York, 1960.
[Arrington, A. W.] *The Desperadoes of the Southwest.* New York, 1847.
[Awtrey, Hugh R.] *New Echota: Birth Place of the American Indian Press.*

National Park Service Popular Study Series, No. 6 (pamphlet).

Baillou, Clemens de. "The Chief Vann House, the Vanns, Tavern and Ferry." *Early Georgia*, II, No. 2 (Spring, 1957): 3-11.

———. "A Contribution to the Mythology and Conceptual World of the Cherokee Indians." *Ethnohistory*, VIII, No. 1 (Winter, 1961): 93-102.

———. "Excavations at New Echota in 1954." *Early Georgia*, I (Spring, 1955): 18-29.

Ballenger, T. L., "Death and Burial of Major Ridge." *Chronicles of Oklahoma*, LI, No. 1 (Spring, 1973): 100-105.

Bartram, John, and William Bartram. *John and William Bartram's America.* ed. Helen G. Cruickshank. New York, 1957.

Bartram, William. "Observations on the Creek and Cherokee Indians, 1789." *Transactions of the American Ethnological Society*, III (New York, 1853), Part I, pp. 1-18.

———. *Travels of William Bartram.* Reprint ed. Mark Van Doren. New York, 1928.

Bass, Althea. *Cherokee Messenger: A Life of Samuel Austin Worcester.* Norman, 1936.

———. "Talking Stones." *The Colophon*, Part IX (1932): no pagination.

———. "Tsali of the Cherokees." *Sewanee Review*, L (Jan., 1942): 5-14.

Bassett, John Spencer. *Life of Andrew Jackson.* Garden City, 1911.

Battey, George M., Jr. *A History of Rome and Floyd Country.* Atlanta, 1922. Only Vol. I was published.

Beeson, Leona Selman. "Homes of Distinguished Cherokee Indians." *Chronicles of Oklahoma*, XI, No. 3 (Sept., 1933): 927-41.

Benton, Thomas Hart. *Thirty Years' View.* New York, 1854.

Berkofer, Robert F. *Salvation and the Savage: An Analysis of Protestant Missions and American Indian Response.* Lexington, Ky., 1965.

Beveridge, Albert J. *Life of John Marshall.* 4 vols. New York, 1916-19.

Bloom, Leonard. "The Acculturation of the Eastern Cherokee." *North Carolina Historical Review*, XIX, No. 4 (Oct., 1942): 323-58.

Boudinot, Elias. *An Address to the Whites, Delivered in the First Presbyterian Church on the 26th of May, 1826.* Philadelphia, 1826.

———. *Letters and Other Papers Relating to Cherokee Affairs.* Athens, Ga., 1837.

Bowden, Henry W. *American Indians and Christian Missions.* Chicago, 1981.

Brown, David. "Views of a Native Indian as to the Present Condition of His People." *Missionary Herald*, XXI (1825): 354-55.

Brown, John P. "Cherokee Removal, an Unnecessary Tragedy." *East Tennessee Historical Society's Publications*, No. 11 (1939): 11-19.

———. "Eastern Cherokee Chiefs." *Chronicles of Oklahoma*, XVI, No. 1 (Mar., 1938): 3-35.

———. *Old Frontiers: The Story of the Cherokee Indians from Earliest Times to . . . 1838.* Kingsport, Tenn., 1938.

Burke, Joseph C. "The Cherokee Cases: A Study in Law, Politics, and Morality." *Stanford Law Review*, XXI, No. 3 (Feb., 1969): 500-31.

Burt, Jesse, and Robert B. Ferguson. *Indians of the Southeast, Then and Now.* Nashville, Tenn., 1973.
——. *The Removal of the Cherokee Indians from Georgia.* Nashville, 1973.
Butrick, Daniel. *Cherokee Antiquities.* Vinita, Indian Territory, 1884.
Carter, Clarence E., ed. *The Territory South of the River Ohio, 1790–1796.* (Vol. IV of the *Territorial Papers of the United States*). Washington, 1936.
Carter, Samuel, III. *Cherokee Sunset: A Nation Betrayed.* Garden City, N.Y., 1976.
Caruso, John Anthony. *The Appalachian Frontier: America's First Surge Westward.* Indianapolis, 1959.
[Cass, Lewis.] "Documents and Proceedings Relating to the Formation and Progress of a Board in the City of New York for the Emigration, Preservation, and Improvement of the Aborigines of America, New York, 1829." *North American Review,* XXX (Jan., 1830): 63–121. (Short running title: "Removal of the Indians.")
Chamberlain, Paul H., Jr. *The Foreign Mission School.* Cornwall, 1968.
Cherokee Nation. *Laws of the Cherokee Nation.* (Laws, rulings and decisions of the Cherokee government from 1808 to 1830.) Tahlequah, Cherokee Nation, 1852.
Church, Mary B. "Elias Boudinot." *The Magazine of History,* XVII, No. 6 (Dec., 1913): 209–19.
Claiborne, J. F. H. *Life and Times of General Sam. Dale, the Mississippi Partisan.* New York, 1860.
Clewell, J. H. *History of Wachovia.* New York, 1902.
Collins, Linton M. "The Activities of the Missionaries among the Cherokees." *Georgia Historical Quarterly,* VI (Dec., 1922): 284–322.
Colton, Calvin. *Tour of the American Lakes, and Among the Indians of the North-west Territory, in 1830.* London, 1833.
Commissioner of Indian Affairs. *Annual Reports,* 1829–67.
Conser, Walter H., Jr. "John Ross and the Cherokee Resistance Campaign, 1833–1838." *Journal of Southern History,* XLIV (May, 1978): 191–212.
Corkran, David H. *The Cherokee Frontier: Conflict and Survival, 1740–62.* Norman, 1962.
——. "A Cherokee Migration Fragment." *Southern Indian Studies,* IV (1952).
——. "Cherokee Pre-History." *The North Carolina Historical Review,* XXXIV, No. 4 (Oct., 1957): 455–66.
Corn, James F. *Red Clay and Rattlesnake Springs.* Cleveland, Tenn., 1959.
——. "Removal of the Cherokees from the East." *Filson Club Quarterly,* XXVII (1953): 36–51.
Cotter, William J. *My Autobiography.* Nashville, 1917.
Cotterill, Robert S. "Federal Indian Management in the South, 1789–1825." *Mississippi Valley Historical Review,* XX (1933): 333–52.
——. *The Southern Indians: The Story of the Civilized Tribes before Removal.* Norman, 1954.
Couch, Nevada. *Pages from Cherokee Indian History.* Saint Louis, 1884.

Coulter, Ellis Merton. *Auraria: The Story of a Georgia Gold Mining Town.* Athens, Ga., 1956.

Covington, James W., ed. "Letters from the Georgia Gold Regions," *Georgia Historical Quarterly* [Collections of the Georgia Historical Society], XXXIX (1955): 401–409.

Crockett, David. *Davy Crockett's Own Story.* New York, 1955.

Cunningham, Frank. *General Stand Watie's Confederate Indians.* San Antonio, 1959.

Cunyas, Lucy Josephine. *The History of Bartow County, Formerly Cass.* [Cartersville, Ga.], 1933.

Dale, Edward E. "Arkansas and the Cherokee Indians." *Arkansas Historical Quarterly,* XIII, No. 2 (Summer, 1949): 95–114.

———. "Two Mississippi Valley Frontiers." *Chronicles of Oklahoma,* XXVI, No. 4 (Winter, 1948–49): 366–84.

Dale, Edward E., and Gaston L. Litton, eds. *Cherokee Cavaliers: Forty Years of Cherokee History as Told in the Correspondence of the Ridge-Watie-Boudinot Family.* Norman, 1939.

Davidson, Donald. *The Tennessee.* 2 vols. New York and Toronto, 1946–48.

Davis, Kenneth Penn. "The Cherokee Removal, 1835–1838." *Tennessee Historical Quarterly,* XXXII (Winter, 1973): 311–31.

Debo, Angie. *And Still the Waters Run.* Princeton, 1940.

———. *The Rise and Fall of the Choctaw Republic.* Norman, 1934.

———. *The Road to Disappearance.* Norman, 1941.

Delly, Lillian. "Episode at Cornwall." *Chronicles of Oklahoma,* LI, No. 4 (Winter, 1973–74): 444–50.

Dick, Everett. *The Dixie Frontier.* New York, 1948.

Downs, Randolph D. "Cherokee-American Relations in the Upper Tennessee Valley, 1776–1791." *East Tennessee Historical Society's Publications,* No. 8 (1936): 35–53.

Drake, Benjamin. *Life of Tecumseh.* Cincinnati, 1850.

Drake, Samuel G. *The Book of the Indians: Biography and History of the Indians of North America from Its First Discovery to the Year 1841.* Boston, 1841; reprint, 1851.

———. *Indians of North America.* New York, 1882.

Dwight, Edwin Welles. *Memoirs of Henry Obookiah.* Elizabethtown, N.J., 1819.

Eaton, John Henry. *The Life of Andrew Jackson.* Philadelphia, 1824.

———. *Memoirs of Andrew Jackson.* Boston, 1828.

Eaton, John Henry, and John Reid. *The Life of Andrew Jackson, Major General in the Service of the United States.* Philadelphia, 1817.

Eaton, Rachel Caroline. *John Ross and the Cherokee Indians.* Menasha, Wis., 1914; reissued, Muskogee, Okla., 1921.

Edwards, Bela B. *Memoirs of the Rev. Elias Cornelius.* Boston, 1833; New York, 1842.

Eggleston, George Cary. *Red Eagle, William Weatherford, and the Wars of the Creek Indians.* New York, 1878.

SELECTED BIBLIOGRAPHY391

Elliott, Charles Winslow. *Winfield Scott: The Soldier and the Man.* New York, 1937.

Eno, Clara B. *History of Crawford County, Arkansas.* Van Buren, Ark., n.d.

Evarts, Jeremiah. *Cherokee Removal: The "William Penn" Essays and Other Writings by Jeremiah Evarts.* Ed. Francis Paul Prucha. Knoxville, Tenn., 1981.

———. *Essays on the Present Crisis in the Condition of the American Indians.* Boston, 1829. (These essays first appeared in the *National Intelligencer;* they were reprinted in the *Cherokee Phoenix.*)

———. *Through the South and the West with Jeremiah Evarts in 1826.* Ed. J. Orin Oliphant. Lewisburg, Pa., 1956.

———. *Speeches on the Passage of the Bill, for the Removal of the Indians, Delivered in the Congress of the United States, April and May, 1830.* Boston and New York, 1830.

Ewers, John C. "Charles Bird King, Painter of Indian Visitors of the Nation's Capital." *Smithsonian Institution Annual Report for 1953* (Washington, 1954): 463–73.

Fairbanks, Charles H., and John H. Goff. *Cherokee and Creek Indians.* New York, 1974.

Featherstonhaugh, George W. *A Canoe Voyage up the Minnay Sotor, with an Account of . . . the Gold Region in the Cherokee Nation.* 2 vols. London, 1847.

Fenton, William N., and John Gulick, eds. *Symposium on Cherokee and Iroquois Culture.* Bureau of American Ethnology Bulletin No. 180. Washington, 1961.

Filler, Louis, and Allen Guttman, eds. *Removal of the Cherokee Nation: Manifest Destiny or National Dishonor?* Boston, 1962.

Fleischmann, Glen. *The Cherokee Removal, 1838.* New York, 1971.

Fletcher, John Gould. *Arkansas.* Chapel Hill, N.C., 1947.

Fogelson, Raymond D. *The Cherokees: A Critical Bibliography.* Bloomington, Ind., 1978.

Foreman, Carolyn Thomas. "An Early Account of the Cherokees." *Chronicles of Oklahoma,* XXXIV, No. 2 (Summer, 1956): 142–58.

———. "The Foreign Mission School at Cornwall, Connecticut." *Chronicles of Oklahoma,* VII, No. 3 (Sept., 1929): 242–59.

———. *Indians Abroad.* Norman, 1936.

———. "John Rollin Ridge." *Chronicles of Oklahoma,* XIV (Sept., 1936): 295–311.

———. "Miss Sophia Sawyer and Her School." *Chronicles of Oklahoma,* XXXII, No. 4 (Winter, 1954): 395–413.

———. *Park Hill.* Muskogee, Okla., 1948.

Foreman, Grant. *Advancing the Frontier, 1830–1860.* Norman, 1933.

———. *The Five Civilized Tribes.* Norman, 1934.

———. *Indian Removal: The Emigration of the Five Civilized Tribes of Indians.* Norman, 1932.

———. *Indians and Pioneers.* New Haven, 1930.

———. "John Howard Payne and the Cherokee Indians." *American Historical Review*, XXXVII (July, 1932): 723–30.

———. *Sequoyah.* Norman, 1938.

———, ed. "Journey of a Party of Cherokee Emigrants." *Mississippi Valley Historical Review*, XVII (Sept., 1931): 232–45.

———, ed. "The Murder of Elias Boudinot." *Chronicles of Oklahoma*, XII (March, 1934): 19–24.

Foster, George E. "Journalism among the Cherokee Indians." *Magazine of American History*, XVIII (July, 1887): 65–70.

———. *Reminiscences of Travel in Cherokee Lands.* Ithaca, 1898.

———. *Sequoyah, the American Cadmus and Modern Moses.* Philadelphia, 1885.

———. *Story of the Cherokee Bible.* Ithaca, 1899.

Franks, Kenny A. *Stand Watie and the Agony of the Cherokee Nation.* Memphis, 1979.

Freel, Margaret Walker. *Our Heritage: The People of Cherokee County, North Carolina, 1540–1955.* Asheville, N.C., 1956.

Fries, Adelaide L., ed. *Records of the Moravians in North Carolina.* 8 vols. Raleigh, 1943–55.

Fundaburk, Emma Lila. *Southeastern Indians: Life Portraits.* Luverne, Ala., 1958.

Gabriel, Ralph Henry. *Elias Boudinot, Cherokee, and His America.* Norman, 1941.

Gallatin, Albert. "Synopsis of the Indian Tribes." In *American Antiquarian Society Transactions*, II (1836).

Garrett, Franklin M. "De Kalb County during the Cherokee Troubles." *Atlanta Historical Bulletin*, II, No. 9 (1956): 24–29.

Garrett, William. *Reminiscences of Public Men in Alabama.* Atlanta, 1872.

Garrett, William R., and Albert V. Goodpasture. *History of Tennessee.* Nashville, 1900.

Gearing, Fred. *Priests and Warriors: Social Structures of Cherokee Politics in the 18th Century.* American Anthropological Association Memoir No. 93. Menasha, Wis., 1962.

Gilbert, William Harlen, Jr. *The Eastern Cherokees.* Bureau of American Ethnology Bulletin 133, Anthropological Paper No. 23 (1943), pp. 169–413.

Gilmer, George R. *Sketches of Some of the First Settlers of Upper Georgia.* New York, 1855; reprint, Americus, Ga., 1926.

Goff, John H. "Some Major Indian Trading Paths Across Georgia." *Mineral News Letter*, VI, No. 4 (Winter, 1953).

Gold, Theodore S. *Historical Records of the Town of Cornwall, Litchfield, County, Connecticut.* Hartford, 1877; revised and expanded, Hartford, 1904.

Goodpasture, Albert V. "Indian Wars and Warriors in the Old Southwest." *Tennessee Historical Magazine*, IV (Mar.-Sept., 1918): 3–49, 106–45, 161–210.

Goodwin, Gary C. *Cherokees in Transition.* Chicago, 1977.

Goodwin, Philo. *Biography of Andrew Jackson.* Hartford, Conn., 1832.

Goulding, Francis R. *Sal-o-quah.* Philadelphia and Macon, 1870.
————. *Sapelo.* Philadelphia and Macon, 1870.
Govan, Gilbert E., and James W. Livingood. *The Chattanooga Country, 1540–1951.* New York, 1951; reissued, Chapel Hill, 1963.
Green, Fletcher. "Georgia's Forgotten Industry: Gold Mining." *Georgia Historical Quarterly,* XIX, No. 2 (June, 1935): 93–111.
Gulick, John. *Cherokees at the Crossroads.* Chapel Hill, 1960.
Guttman, Allen. *States' Rights and Indian Removal: The Cherokee Nation vs. the State of Georgia.* Boston, 1965.
[Haight, Nicholas.] *Cherokee Land on Walden Ridge, East Tennessee.* New York, 1848.
Halbert, Henry S., and T. H. Ball. *The Creek War of 1813 and 1814.* Chicago and Montgomery, 1895.
Hall, Arthur H. "The Red Stick War." *Chronicles of Oklahoma,* XII, No. 3 (Sept., 1934): 264–93.
Hamilton, Charles. *The White Man's Road.* New York, 1951.
Harmon, George D. "Benjamin Hawkins and the Federal Factory System." *North Carolina Historical Review,* IX (1932): 138–52.
————. "The North Carolina Cherokees and the Treaty of New Echota." *North Carolina Historical Review,* VI (July 1929): 237–53.
————. *Sixty Years of Indian Affairs: Political, Economic and Diplomatic, 1789–1850.* Chapel Hill, 1941.
Hawkins, Benjamin. "Letters of Benjamin Hawkins, 1796–1806." In *Collections of the Georgia Historical Society,* Vol. IX. Savannah, 1916.
————. "A Sketch of the Creek Country in the Years 1798 and 1799." In *Publications of the Georgia Historical Society,* Vol. III. Americus, Ga., 1938.
Haywood, John. *Civil and Political History of Tennessee.* Nashville, 1821; republished, Nashville, 1891.
————. *The Natural and Aboriginal History of Tennessee, up to the First Settlements Therein by the White People, in the Year 1768.* Reprint ed. Nashville, 1959.
Heiskell, S. G. *Andrew Jackson and Early Tennessee History.* Nashville, 1918.
Henderson, Archibald. *Conquest of the Old Southwest.* New York, 1920.
Hitchcock, Ethan Allen. *A Traveler in Indian Territory: The Journal of Ethan Allen Hitchcock, Late Major General in the United States Army.* Ed. Grant Foreman. Cedar Rapids, 1930.
Hodge, Frederick W., ed. *Handbook of American Indians North of Mexico.* Bureau of American Ethnology Bulletin No. 30. 2 vols. Washington, 1905–12; republished, New York, 1959.
Hodgson, Adam. *Letters from North America.* 2 vols. London, 1824.
————. *Remarks During a Journey Through North America in the Years 1819, 1820, and 1821, in a Series of Letters.* New York, 1823.
Holland, James W. *Andrew Jackson and the Creek War: Victory at the Horseshoe.* Pamphlet. University, Ala., 1968.
Horan, James D. *The McKenney-Hall Portrait Gallery of American Indians.* New York, 1972.

Houston, Sam. *Writings of Sam Houston.* Ed. Amelia W. Williams and Eugene C. Barker. 8 vols. Austin, 1938–43.
Hutchins, John. "The Trial of Samuel Austin Worcester." *Journal of Cherokee Studies,* II (1977): 356–79.
In Memoriam — Hon. Geo. W. Paschal. Pamphlet. N.p., n.d.
Irving, Washington. *A Tour of the Prairies.* Ed. John Francis McDermott. Norman, 1956.
———. *The Western Journals of Washington Irving.* Ed. John Francis McDermott. Norman, 1944.
Jackson, Andrew. *Correspondence of Andrew Jackson.* Ed. John Spencer Bassett. 6 vols. Washington, 1926–33.
Jahoda, Gloria. *The Trail of Tears.* New York, 1975.
James, Marquis. *Andrew Jackson: The Border Captain.* Indianapolis, 1933.
———. *Andrew Jackson: Portrait of a President.* Indianapolis, 1937.
———. *The Raven: A Biography of Sam Houston.* Indianapolis, 1929.
Jefferson, Thomas. *Correspondence of Thomas Jefferson and Francis Walker Gilmer, 1814–1826.* Ed. Richard B. Davis. New York, 1946.
———. *Papers of Thomas Jefferson.* Ed. Julian P. Boyd. Princeton, 1950.
Johnson, Walter C. "The Cherokee Phoenix," *Southern Newspaper Association Bulletin No. 173,* Sept. 4, 1854, pp. 502–503.
Jones, Peter. *History of the Ojebway Indians.* London, 1861.
Kappler, Charles J., ed. *Indian Affairs, Laws and Treaties.* 2 vols. Washington, 1904.
Kendall, Amos. *Life of Andrew Jackson.* 7 parts. New York, 1843–44.
Kennedy, John Pendleton. *Memoirs of the Life of William Wirt.* 2 vols. Philadelphia, 1850. (Especially Chapters XV, XVII, and XIX of Vol. II.)
Kilpatrick, Jack F. *Sequoyah of Earth and Intellect.* Austin, 1965.
Kilpatrick, Jack F., and Anna G. Kilpatrick. *New Echota Letters: Contributions of Samuel A. Worcester to the Cherokee Phoenix.* Dallas, 1968.
———. *The Shadow of Sequoyah.* Norman, 1965.
King, Duane H., ed. *The Cherokee Indian Nation: A Troubled History.* Knoxville, 1979.
King, Duane, and E. Raymond Evans. "The Death of John Walker Jr.: Political Assassination or Personal Vengeance?" *Journal of Cherokee Studies,* I (1976): 4–16.
Knepler, Abraham Eleazer. "Education in the Cherokee Nation." *Chronicles of Oklahoma,* XXI, No. 4 (Dec., 1943): 378–401.
Knight, Oliver. "Cherokee Society under the Stress of Removal." *Chronicles of Oklahoma,* XXXII, No. 4 (Winter, 1954): 414–28.
———. "History of the Cherokees, 1830–1846." *Chronicles of Oklahoma,* XXXIV, No. 2 (Summer, 1956): 159–82.
Knowles, David E. "Some Account of a Journey to the Cherokees, 1839–40." *Friends Historical Bulletin,* VI (Nov., 1915): 70–78; (May, 1916): 15–21; (Nov., 1916): 42–50.
Kutsche, Paul. "The Tsali Legend: Culture Heroes and Historiography." *Ethnohistory,* X (1963): 329–57.

Lanman, Charles. *Letters from the Allegheny Mountains.* New York, 1849.
Lea, John M. "Indian Treaties of Tennessee." *American Historical Magazine,* VI (Oct., 1901): 367–80.
Leary, Lewis. "John Howard Payne's Southern Adventure, 1835." *Library Notes,* No. 1 (Feb., 1949): 2–11.
Leitner, Leander, ed. *The Walum Olum.* Brooklyn, 1952.
Lewis, Thomas M., and Madeline Kneberg. *Tribes That Slumber.* Knoxville, Tenn., 1958.
Litton, Gaston L. *History of Oklahoma.* 4 vols. New York, 1957.
Lossing, Benson J. *Pictorial Field-Book of the War of 1812.* New York, 1868.
Lumpkin, Wilson. *The Removal of the Cherokee Indians from Georgia.* 2 vols. Wormsloe, Ga., and New York, 1907.
McAffee, Robert B. *History of the Late War in the Western Country.* Bowling Green, Ohio, 1819.
McCall, George A. *Letters from the Frontiers.* Philadelphia, 1868.
McCoy, Isaac. *History of Baptist Missions.* Washington and New York, 1840.
McGinty, J. Roy. "Symbols of a Civilization That Perished in Its Infancy." *Early Georgia,* I, No. 4 (Spring, 1955): 14–17.
[McKenney, Thomas L.] *Catalogue of One Hundred and Fifteen Indian Portraits.* Philadelphia, 1836.
———. *Memoirs, Official and Personal, with Sketches of Travels among the Northern and Southern Indians.* 2 vols. in 1. New York, 1846.
———, and James Hall. *History of the Indian Tribes of North America with Biographical Sketches and Anecdotes of the Principal Chiefs.* 3 folio vols. Philadelphia, 1836, 1838, and 1848; republished in reduced format, ed. F. W. Hodge, Edinburgh, Scotland, 1933.
McLoughlin, William G. "Thomas Jefferson and the Beginning of Cherokee Nationalism, 1806–1809." *William and Mary Quarterly,* 3rd Series, XXXII (1975): 547–80.
———. *Cherokees and Missionaries.* New Haven, 1984.
———. *Cherokee Ghost Dance.* Macon, Ga., 1984.
———. "New Angles of Vision on the Cherokee Ghost Dance Movement of 1811–1812. *American Indian Quarterly,* V, No. 4 (Nov., 1979): 317–45.
———, and Walter H. Conser, Jr. "The Cherokees in Transition: A Statistical Analysis of the Federal Cherokee Census of 1835." *Journal of American History,* LXIV (1977): 678–703.
McLendon, S. G. *History of the Public Domain of Georgia.* Atlanta, 1924.
Malone, Henry T. *"The Cherokee Phoenix:* Supreme Expression of Cherokee Nationalism." *Georgia Historical Quarterly,* XXXIV (Sept., 1950): 163–88.
———. "The Cherokees Become a Civilized Tribe." *Early Georgia,* II, No. 2 (Spring, 1957): 12–15.
———. *Cherokees of the Old South: A People in Transition.* Athens, Ga., 1956.
———. "New Echota—Capital of the Cherokee Nation, 1825–1830." *Early Georgia,* I, No. 4 (Spring, 1955): 6–13.

396 CHEROKEE TRAGEDY

——. Return J. Meigs: Indian Agent Extraordinary." *East Tennessee Historical Society's Publications*, No. 28 (1956): 3-22.
Mansfield, R. E. *Life of General Winfield Scott.* New York, 1846.
Martin, Robert G., Jr. "*Cherokee Phoenix:* Pioneer of Indian Journalism." *Chronicles of Oklahoma*, XXV, No. 2 (Summer, 1947): 102-18.
Masterson, William H. *William Blount.* Baton Rouge, 1954.
Miles, Edwin A. "After John Marshall's Decision: *Worcester* v. *Georgia* and the Nullification Crisis." *Journal of Southern History*, XXXIX, No. 4 (Nov., 1973): 519-44.
Milling, Chapman J. *Red Carolinians.* Chapel Hill, 1940.
Moffitt, James W. "Early Baptist Missionary Work among the Cherokees." *East Tennessee Historical Society's Publications*, No. 12 (1940): 16-27.
Mooney, James. "The Cherokee Ball Play." *American Anthropologist*, III, No. 2 (April, 1890): 105-32.
——. "The Cherokee River Cult." *Journal of American Folklore*, XIII (Jan.-March, 1900): 1-10.
——. *The Ghost Dance Religion.* Bureau of American Ethnology 14th Annual Report, Part 2. Washington, D.C., 1896.
——. *Myths of the Cherokee.* Bureau of American Ethnology 19th Annual Report, Part I. Washington, D.C., 1900.
——. "Sacred Formulas of the Cherokees." In *Bureau of American Ethnology* 7th Annual Report. Washington, D.C., 1888, pp. 334-71.
——, and Frans Olbrechts. *The Swimmer Manuscript.* Bureau of American Ethnology Bulletin No. 99. Washington, D.C., 1932.
Moravian Brotherhood. *The History of the Moravian Mission Among the Indians in North America.* London, 1838.
Morse, Jedidiah. *Report to the Secretary of War on Indian Affairs.* New Haven, 1822.
Moulton, Gary E. "Chief John Ross and Cherokee Removal Finances." *Chronicles of Oklahoma*, LII, No. 3 (Fall, 1974): 342-59.
——. *John Ross, Cherokee Chief.* Athens, Ga., 1978.
Myer, William E. *Indian Trails in the South-East.* Bureau of American Ethnology 42nd Annual Report. Washington, D.C., 1925.
North Carolina Colonial and State Records. 26 vol. Raleigh, 1886-90, 1909-14.
O'Connor, Mrs. T. P. [Elizabeth Paschal O'Connor]. *My Beloved South.* New York and London, 1913.
Old Salem, Inc. *Old Salem, North Carolina.* Pamphlet. Winston-Salem, n.d.
Overmyer, Grace. *America's First Hamlet.* (A biography of John Howard Payne.) New York, 1957.
Owen, Narcissa. *Memoirs of Narcissa Owen.* Washington, D.C., 1907.
Parker, Thomas V. *The Cherokee Indians.* New York, 1907.
Parkerson, Medora Field. *White Columns in Georgia.* New York, 1952.
Parris, John. *The Cherokee Story.* Asheville, N.C., 1950.
Parton, James. *General Jackson.* New York, 1893.
——. *A Life of Andrew Jackson.* New York, 1859-60.
Paschal, George W. *Ninety-Four Years: Agnes Paschal.* Washington, 1871.

———. "The Trial of Stand Watie [To the Public]." Ed. Grant Foreman. *Chronicles of Oklahoma*, XII, No. 3 (Sept., 1934): 305–39.

Payne, John Howard. "The Captivity of John Howard Payne." *North American Quarterly Magazine*, VII, No. 33 (Jan., 1836): 107–24.

———. *Indian Justice: A Cherokee Murder Trial at Tahlequah in 1840 as Reported by John Howard Payne.* Ed. Grant Foreman. Oklahoma City, 1934.

———. *John Howard Payne to His Countrymen.* Ed. Clemens de Baillou. Pamphlet. Athens, Ga., 1961.

Peake, Ora Brooks. *A History of the United States Indian Factory System, 1795–1822.* Denver, 1954.

Pearce, Roy Harvey. *The Savages of America: A Study of the Indian and the Idea of Civilization.* Baltimore, 1953.

Perdue, Theda, ed. *Cherokee Editor: The Writings of Elias Boudinot.* Knoxville, Tenn., 1983.

———. *Slavery and the Evolution of Cherokee Society, 1540–1866.* Knoxville, Tenn., 1979.

Peters, Richard. *The Case of the Cherokee Nation Against the State of Georgia.* Philadelphia, 1831.

Phillips, Ulric B. "Georgia and State Rights: A Study of the Political History of Georgia from the Revolution to the Civil War, with Particular Regard to Federal Relations." *Annual Report of the American Historical Association for the Year 1901*, II, pp. 3–224.

Pickett, Albert James. *History of Alabama.* Birmingham, 1896.

Pierce, Earl Boyd, and Rennard Strickland. *The Cherokee People.* Phoenix, 1973.

Pilling, J. C. *Bibliography of the Iroquoian Languages.* Bureau of American Ethnology Bulletin VI. Washington, D.C., 1888.

———. *Proof-Sheets of a Bibliography of the Languages of the North American Indians.* Washington, D.C., 1885.

Pinkney, Edward Coote. *The Life and Works of Edward Coote Pinkney.* Ed. Thomas O. Mabbott and F. L. Pleadwell. New York, 1926.

Pitts, Lulie. *History of Gordon County, Georgia.* Calhoun, Ga., 1933.

Pound, Merritt B. *Benjamin Hawkins, Indian Agent.* Athens, Ga., 1951.

Prather, Susan (Verdery). *Tahlonika, the Cherokee.* Atlanta, n.d.

Prucha, Francis P. *American Indian Policy in the Formative Years.* Cambridge, Mass., 1962.

———. "Andrew Jackson's Indian Policy: A Reassessment." *Journal of American History*, LVI, No. 3 (Dec., 1969): 527–39.

Ramage, B. J. "Georgia and the Cherokees." *American Historical Magazine*, VII (1902): 199–208.

Ramsey, J. G. M. *Annals of Tennessee.* Charleston, 1853; Kingsport, Tenn., 1926.

Reid, John Phillip. *A Better Kind of Hatchet: Law, Trade and Diplomacy in the Cherokee Nation During the Early Years of European Contact.* Philadelphia, 1975.

———. *A Law of Blood: The Primitive Law of the Cherokee Nation.* New York, 1970.

Reply of the Southern Cherokees to the Memorial of Certain Delegates from the Cherokee Nation, Together with the Message of John Ross, Ex-Chief of the Cherokees. . . . Washington, D.C., 1866.

Richardson, James D., comp. *A Compilation of the Messages and Papers of the Presidents.* 10 vols. Washington, D.C., 1896-99.

Ridge, John. "The Cherokee War Path." Ed. with annotations by Carolyn T. Foreman. *Chronicles of Oklahoma,* IX, No. 3 (Sept., 1931): 233-63. (A narrative of Chief John Smith's exploits against the Osages, as told to John Ridge, followed by notes of expenses incurred by the Ridges at Honey Creek, commencing Dec. 1, 1837.)

———. "John Ridge on Cherokee Civilization in 1826." Ed. William C. Sturtevant. *Journal of Cherokee Studies,* VI (Fall, 1981): 79-91.

———. "Sequoyah and the Cherokee Alphabet." In Charles Hamilton, *The White Man's Road.* New York, 1951.

[Ridge, John Rollin.] *The Age of Terror in California.* (Reprint of "3rd ed." of Ridge's *Murieta,* along with a life of Tiburcio Vasquez by another hand.) Gilroy, Calif., 1927.

———. *The Life and Adventures of Joaquin Murieta,* by Yellow Bird. (Reprint of 1st ed.) Norman, Okla., 1955.

———. "The North American Indians." *The Hesperian,* VIII (March, 1862): 1-18; (April, 1862): 51-60; (May, 1862): 99-109.

———. *Poems.* San Francisco, 1868.

Rights, Douglas L. *The American Indian in North Carolina.* Durham, 1947.

Rockwell, E. F. "Parallel and Combined Expeditions against the Cherokee Indians . . . in 1776." *Historical Magazine,* XII, No. 4 (Oct., 1867): 212-20.

Rogin, Michael Paul. *Fathers and Children: Andrew Jackson and the Subjugation of the American Indians.* New York, 1975.

Ronda, James P., and James Axtell. *Indian Missions: A Critical Bibliography.* Bloomington, Ind., 1978.

Roosevelt, Theodore. *The Winning of the West.* 4 vols. New York, 1889-96.

Ross, John. *Letter from John Ross, Principal Chief of the Cherokee Nation of Indians, in Answer to Inquiries from a Friend Regarding the Cherokee Affairs with the United States.* N.p., 1836.

———. *Letter from John Ross, the Principal Chief of the Cherokee Nation, to a Gentleman of Philadelphia.* N.p., 1837.

———. *The Papers of Chief John Ross.* Ed. Gary E. Moulton. 2 vols. Norman, Okla., 1985.

Ross, Mrs. William P. *The Life and Times of Hon. Wm. P. Ross, of the Cherokee Nation.* Fort Smith, 1893.

Routh, Eugene Coke. "Early Missionaries to the Cherokees." *Chronicles of Oklahoma,* XV, No. 4 (Dec., 1937): 449-65.

Royall, Anne. *Letters from Alabama.* Washington, D.C., 1830.

Royce, Charles C. *The Cherokee Nation of Indians.* Bureau of American Ethnology 5th Annual Report. Washington, D.C., 1887.

————. *Indian Land Cessions in the United States.* Bureau of American Ethnology 18th Annual Report. Washington, D.C., 1899.

Rutland, Robert A. "Political Background of the Cherokee Treaty of New Echota." *Chronicles of Oklahoma,* XXVII, No. 4 (Dec., 1949): 389–406.

Sargent, Nathan. *Public Men and Events.* 2 vols. Philadelphia, 1875.

Sass, Herbert R. *Hear Me, My Chiefs!* New York, 1940.

Satz, Ronald N. *American Indian Policy in the Jacksonian Era.* Lincoln, 1975.

————. *Tennessee's Indian Peoples: From White Contact to Indian Removal, 1540–1840.* Knoxville, Tenn., 1979.

Schmeckebier, Laurence F. *The Office of Indian Affairs: Its History, Activities, and Organization.* Baltimore, 1927.

Schoolcraft, Henry Rowe. *Notes on the Iroquois.* New York, 1846; Albany, 1847.

————. *Personal Memoirs of a Residence of Thirty Years with the Indian Tribes on the American Frontiers.* Philadelphia, 1856.

Schwarze, Edmund. *History of the Moravian Missions among Southern Indian Tribes of the United States.* Bethlehem, Pa., 1923.

Self, R. D. "Chronology of New Echota." *Early Georgia,* I, No. 4 (Spring, 1955): 3–5.

Sevier, John. "The Executive Journals of Gov. John Sevier." Ed. S. C. Williams. *East Tennessee Historical Society's Publications,* No. 4 (Jan., 1932): 138–67.

Shackford, James Atkins. *David Crockett: The Man and the Legend.* Chapel Hill, 1956.

Sheehan, Bernard W. *Seeds of Extinction: Jeffersonian Philanthropy and the American Indian.* Chapel Hill, 1973.

Smith, James F. *The Cherokee Land Lottery.* New York, 1838.

Smith, Rev. W. R. L. *The Story of the Cherokees.* Cleveland, Tenn., 1928.

Stambaugh, Samuel C., et al. *A Faithful History of the Cherokee Tribe of Indians, from the Period of Our First Intercourse with Them down to the Present Time.* Washington, D.C., 1846.

Starkey, Marion L. *The Cherokee Nation.* New York, 1946.

Starr, Edward C. *History of Cornwall, Connecticut.* Cornwall, 1926.

Starr, Emmet. *Cherokees "West," 1749 to 1839.* Claremore, Okla., 1910.

————. *Early History of the Cherokees, Embracing the Aboriginal Customs, Religion, Laws, Folklore, and Civilization.* N.p., 1917.

————. *History of the Cherokee Indians and Their Legends.* Oklahoma City, 1921.

————. *Old Cherokee Families.* Norman, Okla., 1968.

Strange, Robert. *Eoneguski, or the Cherokee Chief.* Washington, D.C., 1839; facsimile edition, Charlotte, N.C., 1960.

Strickland, Rennard. *Fire and the Spirits: Cherokee Law from Clan to Court.* Norman, Okla., 1975.

Strong, William E. *The Story of the American Board.* Boston and New York, 1910.

Stuart, John A. *A Sketch of the Cherokee and Choctaw Indians.* Little Rock,

1837.
Swanton, John R. *Early History of the Creek Indians and Their Neighbors.* Bureau of American Ethnology Bulletin No. 73. Washington, D.C., 1922.
———. *The Indians of the Southeastern United States.* Bureau of American Ethnology Bulletin No. 137. Washington, D.C., 1946.
———. *Myths and Tales of the Southeastern Indians.* Bureau of American Ethnology Bulletin 88. Washington, D.C., 1929.
———. *Social Organization and Social Usages of the Creek Confederacy.* Bureau of American Ethnology 42ndAnnual Report. Washington, D.C., 1928.
Temple, Sarah Blackwell A. *The First One Hundred Years: A Short History of Cobb County, in Georgia.* Atlanta, 1935.
Thatcher, Benjamin. *Indian Biography.* New York, 1832.
Thoburn, Joseph, ed. "The Cherokee Question." *Chronicles of Oklahoma,* II, No. 2 (June, 1924): 141–242.
———. *A Standard History of Oklahoma.* 5 vols. Chicago and New York, 1916.
Traveller Bird. *Tell Them They Lie: The Sequoyah Myth.* Los Angeles, 1971.
Trollope, Frances M. *Domestic Manners of the Americans.* London and New York, 1832; reissued by Vintage Books.
Tucker, Glenn. *Tecumseh: Vision of Glory.* Indianapolis, 1956.
Turner, Francis. *Life of John Sevier.* Washington, D.C., 1910.
[Tuttle, Sarah.] *Letters and Conversations of the Cherokee Mission.* Boston, 1830.
Van Every, Dale. *Disinherited: The Lost Birthright of the American Indian.* New York, 1966.
Viola, Herman J. *Thomas L. McKenney, Architect of America's Early Indian Policy: 1816–1830.* Chicago, 1974.
Vipperman, Carl J. " 'Forcibly if We Must': The Georgia Case for Cherokee Removal, 1802–1832." *Journal of Cherokee Studies,* III (1978): 103–10.
Virginia. *Calendar of Virginia State Papers, 1652–1869.* 11 vols. Richmond, 1875–93.
Walker, Franklin. *San Francisco's Literary Frontier.* New York, 1939.
Walker, Robert Sparks. *Torchlights to the Cherokees: The Brainerd Mission.* New York, 1931.
Wardell, Morris J. *A Political History of the Cherokee Nation, 1838–1907.* Norman, Okla., 1938.
Washburn, Cephas. *Reminiscences of the Indians.* Richmond, 1869; reprint, ed. Hugh Park, Van Buren, Ark., 1935.
Whitaker, A. P. *Spanish American Frontier.* Boston and New York, 1927.
White, George. *Historical Collections of Georgia.* 3rd ed. New York, 1855.
White, Robert C. *Cherokee Indian Removal from the Lower Hiwassee Valley.* Cleveland, 1973.
White, Robert H., comp. *Messages of the Governors of Tennessee, 1796–1821.* 4 vols. Nashville, 1952–57.
Williams, Samuel C. "An Account of the Presbyterian Mission to the Cherokees." *Tennessee Historical Magazine,* 2nd ser., Vol. I, No. 2 (Jan., 1931): 125–38.
———. *Dawn of Tennessee Valley and Tennessee History.* Johnson City,

Tenn., 1937.
————. *History of the Lost State of Franklin.* Johnson City, Tenn., 1926.
————. "Nathaniel Gist, Father of Sequoyah." *East Tennessee Historical Society's Publications,* No. 5 (1933): 39–54.
————, ed. *Early Travels in the Tennessee Country.* Nashville, 1928; Johnson City, Tenn., 1930.
Wilms, Douglas C. "Georgia Land Lottery of 1832." *Chronicles of Oklahoma,* LII (1974): 52–60.
————. Cherokee Settlement Patterns in Nineteenth Century Georgia." *Southeastern Geographer,* XIV (1974): 46–53.
Wilson, Rufus Rockwell. *Washington: The Capital City.* 2 vols. Philadelphia and London, 1902.
Woodward, Grace Steele. *The Cherokees.* Norman, Okla., 1963.
Woodward, Thomas S. *Woodward's Reminiscences of the Creek or Muscogee Indians.* Tuscaloosa and Birmingham, 1939.
Wooten, John Morgan. *A History of Bradley County.* Nashville, 1949.
Wright, Muriel H. *A Guide to the Indian Tribes of Oklahoma.* Norman, Okla., 1951.
————. *Springplace Moravian Mission and the Ward Family of the Cherokee Nation.* Guthrie, Okla., 1940.
Wyeth, Walter N. *Poor Lo! Early Indian Missions.* Philadelphia, 1896.
Yellow Bird. See John Rollin Ridge.

Newspapers and Religious Journals

Arkansas Gazette (Little Rock)
Arkansian (Fayetteville)
Athenian (Athens, Ga.)
Atlanta Constitution
Augusta Chronicle and Georgia Advertizer
Augusta Constitutionalist (Georgia Constitutionalist)
Baptist Missionary Magazine
Boston Courier
Boston Recorder
Cartersville (Ga.) *Courant*
Cherokee Advocate (Tahlequah, Cherokee Nation)
Cherokee Phoenix and Indian Advocate (New Echota)
Christian Spectator (New Haven, Conn.)

Federal Union (Milledgeville, Ga.)
Fort Smith (Ark.) *Herald*
Georgia Journal (Milledgeville)
Macon (Ga.) *Telegraph*
Missionary Herald at Home and Abroad (The Panoplist)
National Intelligencer (Washington, D.C.)
New York Herald
New York Journal of Commerce
New York Observer
New York Post
New York Tribune
New York Weekly Commercial Advertiser
Niles' [*Weekly*] [*National*] *Register*
Raleigh Register and North Carolina Gazette

Red Bluff (Calif.) *Beacon* [ed. John
   Rollin Ridge]
Religious Intelligencer (New Haven,
   Conn.)
Savannah Georgian
Savannah Republican

Sunday Oklahoman (Oklahoma City)
*United Brethren's Missionary
   Intelligencer and Religious Miscellany*
Vinita (Okla.) *Chieftain*
Western Herald (Auraria, Ga.)

INDEX

Acadians, exile of: 328
Act of Union: 341–42; failure of Takatoka
    council to effect, 333
Adair, Black Wat: 33
Adair, George W.: 334, 342
Adair, Red Wat: 33
Adams, John: 220
Adams, John Quincy: 154–57, 157n, 158,
    160, 167, 172, 202–203, 206; and New
    Echota Treaty, 292
Adams, Mrs. John Quincy: 157
Adawehis: 8; *see also* conjurors
Address to the Whites (Boudinot): 196
Alabama, state of: 62, 82, 143, 161, 165, 254,
    278, 284, 295, 309
Alabama Indians: 57
American Board of Commissioners for
    Foreign Missions: 97, 110–12, 115, 121,
    133, 153, 170, 193, 196, 226, 235, 240,
    253, 261
American Eagle (newspaper): 149–50
Americans: 37, 52–55, 62, 66, 68, 75, 79,
    190, 232
Amnesty for Ridge-Boudinot assassins: 341
Ancient One, The: 7; *see* Watie, David
Ancient Red: 14
Andover Theological Seminary: 127, 134
Andrew Ross Treaty: 261
Anet'sa (ball-play): 35n
Ani-Yunwiyah: 8–9; *see also* Cherokee
    Indians
Appalachian Mountains: 7, 21, 82, 304
Arbuckle, Gen. Matthew: 340, 342
Arguelles' Boarding House: 285, 291
Arkansas, state of: 3, 94, 95, 110, 126, 129,
    239, 300, 304, 306, 311, 324, 328, 342
Arkansas River: 47, 50, 305
Arsee: 178; *see also* black drink, ceremony of
Athens, Ga.: 231, 296
Athens, Tenn.: 284, 319

Attakullakulla: 8
Augusta, Ga.: 136, 188, 231

Baldridge, John F.: 249
Ball-play: 35 & n, 39–40, 192, 256, 275;
    Cherokee name of, 35n; evolution into
    lacrosse, 35n,
Baltimore, Md.: 92, 116, 157, 160–61, 215
Baptists: 191; defend Cherokee progress, 225
Barbour, James: 171, 173–74
Barnett, Col. William: 86, 92–93
Bascom, Rev. Reynolds: 134, 136
Basel, Thomas: 134
Beanstalk, Joseph: 338
Beard, Capt. John: 24
Beecher, Dr. Lyman: 128, 131, 150, 151, 235
Bell, John (white), suppressed report of: 334
Bell, John A. (Cherokee): 102 & n, 289n,
    334; open letter of, 341; Treaty Party
    delegate, 342
Bell, Samuel: 265
Benton, Thomas Hart, on ratification of
    New Echota Treaty: 292
Bethlehem, Pa.: 101, 120
Big Warrior, Chief: 54–55, 63, 82–83, 86;
    death of, 164
Bishop, Col. W. M.: 271–72, 284
Blackburn, Gideon: 40–41, 97, 100
Black drink, ceremony of: 178, 180
Black Fox, Chief: 42, 61; removal promotions
    of, 45–46
Blair, Col. James: 42
Blood Law: 29–30, 341n; abolition of clan
    revenge, 41; reenactment of, 208; wording
    of, 209; invoked against Treaty leaders, 334
Bloody Fellow, Chief: 20
Blount, Gov. Willie: 57, 72
Bogan, Shadrach, fraud of: 249–50
Bone Polisher (Cherokee): 40
Boston, Mass.: 130, 133–34, 153, 193, 195,

403

INDEX

407

Downing, Louis: 344
Dragging Canoe, Chief: 8, 11, 16-17, 20, 23, 37
Duck (Cherokee): 277
Duck, Chief: 51n
Duck-wa (Cherokee): 338
Dunlap, Gen. R. G.: 257
Dutsi (father of The Ridge): 7, 8; takes family to Sequatchie, 11; trains son as hunter, 14-15
Dwight, Rev. Edwin: 126-28
Dwight, Theodore: 234-35
Dwight, Rev. Timothy: 127-28
Dwight Mission (new): 313

Earle, Col. Elias: 43-44
Eastern Cherokee Nation: 333
Eaton, Maj. John: 206, 211, 217-18, 232, 261
E-kan-nah-sil-kee (tract of land): 183
Ellsworth, Frederic: 160-61, 201
Emuckfau, battle of: 73
Enitachopco, battle of: 73
Etome Tustunuggee (Creek): 165
Etowah (Hightower), Ga.: 26n, 72; battle of, 26
Etowah (Hightower) River: 20, 26 & n, 82, 161
Evarts, Jeremiah: 115, 134, 170, 214-15
Everett, Edward: 221; qouted, 210; speech on Cherokee affairs, 220; on Treaty Party memorial, 265-66

Fain, Capt. John: 18-19
Featherstonhaugh, George William: on Cherokees at council, 242-43
Female Academy (Salem, N.C.): 120, 160, 201
Fields, James (Jim): 122, 134; description of, 123
Fields, John: 254, 256
Flint River: 53, 87
Florida, state of: 35n, 114-15, 147n, 163
Floyd, Gen. John: 66, 71
Folsom (Choctaw): 115
Foreign Mission School (Cornwall, Conn.): 112, 114-16, 121, 128, 134, 149, 150; students of, 122; daily routine at, 125; founding and anniversary exercises of, 126; closing of, 153
Foreman, Grant: on John Ross, 205n; exonerates Treaty leaders, 251n
Foreman, James: 264, 342
Foreman, Tom: 263, 287; abuse of Major Ridge, 262
Forsyth, Gov. John: 204
Fort Armstrong, Ala.: 71-73
Fort Gibson, Indian Terr.: 312, 340-41

Fort Jackson, Ala.: 79-82
Fort Mims, Ala., massacre at: 62-63
Fort Smith, Ark.: 306, 311
Fort Strother, Ala.: 69, 71-73, 81, 92
Fort Williams, Ala.: 75, 79
Francis the Prophet: 115
Frelinghuysen, Theodore: 220, 253

Gadsby Hotel (Washington, D.C.): 163, 221
Gaines, Gen. Edmund P.: 87, 92, 167, 171, 314
Gallatin, Albert: 34, 100, 177-78, 241n
Gallegina (Buck): see Boudinot, Elias (Cherokee)
Gambold, Anna: 97-98, 100-102, 105-107, 109, 117, 119-20, 123-24, 130; botanical garden of, 103-104; death of, 137
Gambold, Rev. John: 56, 97-98, 100-103, 105-107, 109, 117, 119-20, 123-24, 130, 137; death of, 246
Garrett, John H.: 295, 308
General Council: see Cherokee council
Georgetown, D.C.: 89, 175
Georgia, state of: 6, 10, 20, 37, 71, 96, 100, 105, 143-44, 155-56, 158, 160, 164-65, 167, 168, 170, 172, 174, 196, 202-203, 208, 211, 214, 216, 218-19, 221-25, 232-33, 253-54, 259-60, 278, 281, 312, 319-20; reaction to Cherokee constitution, 204; and gold rush, 209; laws extended over Cherokee lands, 210; Cherokee code of, 210, 216, 224, 227, 235; survey of Cherokee lands, 217, 225, 245; and U.S. Supreme Court, 221, 235-36; lottery of Cherokee lands, 225, 247, 249-50, 251; and the missionaries, 225-26
Georgia guard: 226-28, 234, 242, 251, 273, 278; confiscation of Cherokee press, 281 & n; arrests Ross and Payne, 283-84
Georgia Journal (newspaper): 202, 210
Georgia Road: 46, 120
Gibbs, Adin C.: 134-36
Gilbreath, Polly: 309
Gillespie, Capt. John: 20
Gilmer, Gov. George: 211-12, 224n, 226-27; on Major Ridge, 260
Gilpin, John: 251
Gist, George: see Sequoyah
Glass, Chief: 20, 45-46
Going Snake, Chief: 142, 216, 325
Gold, Col. Benjamin: 128, 150-51, 153
Gold, Harriet Ruggles: 192-93, 195; love for Boudinot, 150-51; public reaction to engagement of, 151-52; wedding of, 153; and J. H. Payne, 281-82
Gold, Dr. Samuel: 130-32, 151, 186, 219
Goshen, Conn.: 151, 153